Art in the
Primary School

Art in the Primary School

BY KAY MELZI

Formerly Principal Lecturer in Art
Homerton College Cambridge

with 136 photographs by

WILLIAM PALMER

Head of Department of Biological Sciences
Homerton College Cambridge

OXFORD · BASIL BLACKWELL

To Pamela and Susan

Printed in Great Britain by Alden & Mowbray Ltd
at the Alden Press, Oxford
and bound at the Kemp Hall Bindery

Contents

Plates

 95. Shield of thin card decorated with candle drawing and ebony stain wash
 96. Tonal-colour exercise
 97. Painting in powder colour, part of project on 'Flight'
 98. Model of VC 10 made of balsa-wood
 99. Balsa-wood models of land-yacht and catamaran
100. Models of post mill and Chinese wheelbarrow
101. Painting in powder colour, part of project on 'Flight'
102. Models of hot air balloon and hydrogen balloon
103, 104. Collective work in which mosaic squares were built from peas, beans etc.
105, 106, 107, 108. Pages from 'The Old Elm Tree', made by children in a village school
109. Panel, made by using potato cuts with candle and ebony stain rubbings
110. Potato print panel, based on observations of fish
111. Bird panel, made by using potato prints and leaf rubbings
112. Potato printing on fabric
113. Fish mobiles painted in coloured inks on thin paper
114. Collage made of paper and wool
115. 'Kippers', a wax-crayon engraving
116. Torn-paper composition using candle and ebony stain rubbings
117, 118. Lino-cuts made following a visit to the Zoo
119, 120, 121, 122. Three-dimensional work in various media
123, 124. Weaving by 10 year old boys
125, 126. Fabric collages, made by using feathers and scraps of fabric
127, 128, 129, 130. Shadow puppets
131. Glove puppets with papier-mâché heads
132. Paper-bag masks
133. Clay models decorated with patterns scratched into coloured slip
134. Glazed clay models
135. Decorated papier-mâché and wire masks
136. Carving in chalk

Acknowledgements

I would like to express my gratitude to Dr. Dorothy Sarjeant, who first suggested the writing of this book.

The publisher and I wish to thank Messrs. Jonathan Cape Limited and Holt, Rinehart and Winston for permission to quote from *Stopping By Woods on a Snowy Evening* by Robert Frost, the University of London Press for a passage from *Art and the Child* by Marion Richardson, Chatto & Windus for the poem from *The Excitement of Writing*, Ed. A. B. Clegg, and the Literary Trustees of Walter de la Mare and the Society of Authors as their representative for the use of 24 lines from *The Scarecrow* and 8 from *The Fly*.

I would like to express my indebtedness to the many children and students, whose work has made so rich a contribution.

I am also most grateful to all my colleagues in the Art Department of Homerton College for the stimulus of their ideas, many of which are incorporated in this book. In particular I would like to thank Mrs. Marion Trim, with whom I have worked closely, Miss Christine Carpenter and Mrs. Christine Mitchell for their personal contributions and Miss Gillian Cresswell, a third year student, who designed the dust cover.

I think with particular gratitude of the late Betty Rea, for the support of her understanding in the early stages, for telling me so much about her own work with children and for letting us include photographs of their modelling and carving. Nan Youngman's interest, too, has been a constant encouragement.

I would like to express my gratitude to Mr. G. D. Edwards, Chief Education Officer for Cambridgeshire and the Isle of Ely and to Mr. M. M. Scarr, City Education Officer, for allowing us to use and photograph examples of work in the schools, and take part in actual teaching projects. I am also most indebted to the Heads and Staffs of these schools and have greatly appreciated their co-operation and help.

The Principal of the Bath Academy of Art, Mr. Clifford Ellis, kindly allowed us to photograph and describe some work of children taught by a Bath Academy student, and the Headmaster of Bedales Junior School (Dunhurst) also gave permission for us to reproduce and describe some of the work in his school.

On the literary side I am deeply indebted to Mrs. Christopher Morris for her invaluable help and criticism and for giving so generously of her time, and to Mrs. Taylor for her greatly appreciated assistance and personal interest in reading the manuscript. I would also like to thank Miss Mary Lauterbach, Mr. Anthony Crowe and Miss Norah Bartlett for their advice and interest.

Finally I would like to express my thanks to the Principal of Homerton College, Miss B. Paston Brown, for making it possible to use the work of students and of children connected with the College.

CHAPTER I

Some Characteristics of Children's Art

'Whatever are these daubs meant to be?'
'Why do they let children mess about like this?'
'A waste of paper—still, it keeps them quiet and they certainly like doing it.'

Comments of this kind made by grown-ups, parents perhaps, as they look at the paintings of young children, indicate the lack of understanding that may be encountered and that should be counteracted by the teacher through his own attitude towards the child's creative efforts. For we have only to watch the intense concentration with which the child works to realize how immensely significant these early creative experiences are for him—meaningless though the results may appear to us.

Whatever the extent of our teaching experience may be, most of us will have a general impression of the qualities that are found in children's work. We should, however, look at these characteristics more closely, if our teaching is to be really sensitive to the needs of children.

If we imagine a collection of children's paintings displayed in a classroom or school hall, what will be the qualities that speak most strongly? Our eye first may catch a storm picture, in which the colour and movement exhilarate us. Next to it is a group of paintings by younger children, each expressive in an individual way. Look at that picture of a magic tower, with its rich invention of shapes and colours. Here is a landscape, a patchwork of flat fields and ribbons of roads as if seen from the air—reminiscent of a Van Gogh painting in its fullness of pattern and texture. Here is another, where the houses seem to lie flat on the paper around the village green. In many of the paintings the children are using a non-representational, but yet visual language, expressive of their own personal logic. If we are unfamiliar with children's art, we may find these particular forms of expression difficult to understand; especially if we ourselves happen to have been brought up on standards based on photographic representation, by which criteria we may, without realizing it, be misjudging children's work (as well as other forms of art). Even so, the spontaneity and character in these paintings can hardly fail to hold us. But perhaps the aspects that come through most strongly are the colour and vitality of the whole exhibition.

These, then, are some of the qualities we find and value in children's work; qualities that, in our teaching and contact with children, we hope to safeguard and foster.

Certain teachers during the last sixty years have been quick to perceive these characteristics, and their findings have helped us to understand and appreciate children's art. We could call these gifted teachers the pioneers in art education. Largely due to the research of these artists and educators from many countries, we have now come to accept certain characteristics as part of a universal 'visual' language used by young children in various parts of the world.

At the beginning of this century Professor Cizek in Vienna provided abundant proof that children who were left free to 'grow, develop and mature' would reveal innate powers of creative expression. While still an art student, he took every opportunity of studying children's spontaneous work, in which their impulses, unhampered by adult instruction or interference, were expressed naturally, as in their crude chalk drawings on pavements and walls. Often, too, the children in his own lodgings liked to paint with him while he worked. It was not long before Cizek realized how different were the drawings produced in this intuitive way from those being done concurrently by the same children when they were taught in schools—differences that displayed an astonishing disparity of styles. He became deeply interested in children's art and it was to a great extent through his insight and understanding of children that teachers were inspired to think afresh about the purpose of teaching art.

His *Children's Art Class*, covering an age-range of four to fourteen, was formed in Vienna in 1895 when, possibly for the first time, children were encouraged to express visual ideas in ways natural to them, without being prematurely forced into moulds of naturalistic representation. And the paintings that emerged provided the breakthrough: they were unsophisticated, child-like and personal in colour.

In this country we probably owe most to Marion Richardson who, first as a teacher, and then through her work as Art Inspector for the London County Council, had so profound an influence on art teaching, as we have come to know it. Her inspiration continues to be implicit in much of the enlightened art education to-day and she, perhaps more than any other one person, has helped to bring about a truer understanding of the nature of children's art. Not that children's art, with its indefinable power to enchant, can ever be *understood*. As Picasso put it, it is like trying to understand the song of a bird. Nevertheless, just as we are beginning to understand more about birds' song, we also know more than we did about the development of children's art. Some knowledge of the natural phases of this development is essential for the teacher.

All educators who have made a concentrated study of children's work and of the significance of their results, underline the same fundamental principle: that the child has an inherent impulse to create and that the recurring forms of creative expression follow certain directions of natural growth. As a result of the research that has been carried out on children's art, we are now more easily able to recognize the various characteristics in creative expression as we follow its development through from the earliest phases to those of adolescence.

Various interpretations are to be found in some of the books mentioned on page 278. Although the emphasis in these accounts varies as much as the terms used for definition, basically the same sequences of development are traced, sequences that we recognize when we directly study children's work.

Viktor Lowenfeld and W. Lambert Brittain in *Creative and Mental Growth*,[1] and Herbert Read in *Education Through Art*,[2] make particularly extensive surveys of these developmental stages, throwing a light on their relation to other aspects—whether mental, emotional or physical—of the child's personality. For our purpose we can select four main stages of visual and creative development that children generally pass through in the Nursery and Junior schools from the age of two to eleven.

[1] *Creative and Mental Growth*, by Viktor Lowenfeld and W. Lambert Brittain (Macmillan Company, New York, fourth edition, 1964).
[2] *Education Through Art*, by Herbert Read (Faber & Faber, paperback edition, 1961).

1 Scribbling   —age 2–5
2 Symbolism   —age 5–7
3 Schematic   —age 7–9
4 Visual realism—age 9–11

This tabulated sequence will help the teacher to know approximately what to expect from the children at different ages. Naturally there can be no hard and fast rules. There are transitional periods when the stages overlap, and every child may not necessarily pass through all the phases. Thus while we may generalize about the relationship of visual expression to chronological age, it would be unwise to expect every child to conform to the characteristics attributed to his particular age group. Perhaps there is no 'average' child—only the individual child whose particular personality determines his modes of expression and speed of development.

In my own experience I have known children as young as eight draw representationally, as well as young people in the Secondary school who have worked in a flat, two-dimensional way. An overemphasis on an accepted pattern of development can only be a disservice to the child. Our concern must always be directed towards the needs of each individual within a group, so that in all art activities he is allowed to develop in his own way and time. There is no advantage in attempting to accelerate his progress from one stage to the next. Far from wanting to turn him into a miniature grown-up, we want him to experience as complete an enjoyment as possible within each stage of his natural growth.

SCRIBBLING

It has been said that 'scribbling is to drawing much what babbling is to speech', and certainly it is through these first explorations that the child discovers the elements of a visual language.

By the time he is two he enjoys moving a crayon or thick pencil over paper, making random scribbles that are in essence an extension of his own physical movements. The marks are meaningless in themselves and are put together without any sense of ordered arrangement. The child is fully absorbed in the feel of making the strokes and is at first hardly aware of the visual appearance of the marks he makes.

Gradually he gains greater muscular control and a significant stage in his visual development is reached when he begins to relate the visual results to his physical actions, watching the effects produced as he moves the crayon up and down, to and fro horizontally, or in sweeping curves and circles.

Most of us, at one time or another, must have watched a small child drawing with a stick on an inviting patch of smooth, unbroken, moist sand. Perhaps we were astonished at the certainty with which he made the big shapes, using large arm movements from the shoulder. At school the understanding teacher encourages these natural movements, by providing blackboard space for drawing, thick chalks, soft pencils, paint and supplies of inexpensive, white paper of various shapes and sizes. (Further reference to these materials is made in Chapter 8.) The scribbles should glide easily on to the paper; it is therefore important to provide crayons that are soft and smooth and to see that the consistency of the paint will allow the child to make large, uninterrupted strokes with the brush.

Soon he finds he can repeat the different types of scribble lines, and before long he begins to name his scribbles, 'This is my Mummy', 'This is me'. To adult eyes the scribbles may have as little meaning as they had before, but the child has in fact begun to relate the visual shapes to imaginative thinking and to the communication of ideas. This is another important step in the development of his creative expression.

The young child who is at the scribbling stage may want to spend only a short period at one time in drawing and painting, but during this period he will work with an intense concentration and sense of purpose. He must work in an atmosphere of encouragement and enthusiasm, created by the supervising adult. A teacher's—or parent's —lack of understanding at this stage may seriously undermine his confidence.

These spontaneous beginnings are gradually developed by means of more consciously controlled movements. No. 19, 'My Blue Picture', painted by Christine at the age of three, shows a number of scrubbed on brush strokes and patches of colour placed together in a rhythmical arrangement. The large oval form near the lower right-hand corner is of pure ultramarine, and is surprisingly dominant, in spite of being surrounded by strong variations of reds—colours one might expect to come forward. In No. 20, a painting by a six-year-old boy, the large forms and lines have been enriched by a scallop-rhythm, and by smaller, separate yet related strokes, placed at right angles to the larger shape. Such precisely controlled forms emerge naturally from the child's earlier experience in drawing and painting. In this way he acquires the essentials of a visual vocabulary which he uses with increasing deliberation as his need grows to express more specific ideas.

The sheer pleasure of finding out about materials and how they are used, the enjoyment of the purely physical sensation of painting, of making colours and shapes in paint, are all important experiences to the child. His sense of fulfilment and confidence provides a sound basis for the creative activities which will follow at later stages. This preliminary phase varies in length of time with individuals and is, of course, also dependent on the opportunities each child has for this kind of spontaneous outlet, whether at home or at school.

SYMBOLISM

Soon after the stage of abstract scribbling in crayon or paint, or often concurrently with it, the first symbols appear. The child begins to use smaller wrist movements and to make more consciously controlled shapes—or symbols—through which he expresses his ideas visually. A drawing of a human being may at first consist of little more than an isolated scribbled circle to which two lines, suggestive of legs or body, are attached. Crude and rudimentary as these symbols are, they effectively express the essentials of the child's visual ideas.

In Christine's drawing, No. 22, done soon after her 'Blue Picture' her own feelings about people are vividly conveyed. I knew Christine and her family well: for some time she had been producing sheets of scribbling and abstract drawings. Although she often gave names to her completed paintings, there had not yet been any indication of recognizable things in her work. However, on this particular day I asked if she would like to make a picture of her mother; she agreed without hesitation, and the whole drawing was finished within a short time. After completing 'Mummy', Christine included herself, and then added her father, brother and other people of personal interest to her (I was included, too). She spoke aloud while working, first naming each person, then as she drew each head she said, 'Two eyes, a nose, two lips'. Her drawing, forcible in its economy of statement, tells us a great deal. To Christine, human figures were like high towering columns, each with an all-important face. Things of significance to her, such as the features, were included, while other parts, like the arms, feet and details of clothing, were left out entirely, as irrelevant to the main concept. She did not consciously plan these omissions or distortions—she simply drew in the only way right for her at that moment. A few days later her symbols might again have changed. The child, in his intuitive symbolism, has something in common with the caricaturist who, in order to put his ideas across with the maximum effect, also selects, exaggerates and omits, though he does it with a conscious purpose.

Children make symbols to depict the many familiar things of their environment: people, houses, animals, birds, aeroplanes, trains, machines, boats, trees and flowers, as well as the countless images of their fantasy.

In these early stages the child invents fresh symbols from day to day, and as his range of experiences deepens so he develops his symbols in greater detail. No. 21 shows two adults known intimately by the child. The symbols have been adapted to express the essence of these particular people, and succeed in catching the difference between them.

THE SCHEMATIC STAGE

Children continue to use symbols—now much elaborated—combining them in a logical rather than a visual way. The child draws what he knows, not what he sees. Eagerly he expresses his feelings about all that interests him, relating his many ideas in flat, diagrammatic settings, in which perspective, foreshortening and volume play no part.

He has his own concepts of space and these differ greatly from those held by the majority of adults, at any rate in this country, who are concerned with a representational concept of space. This of course is not true of all cultures and in the art of many countries—as in Ancient Egypt—we find a total disregard for perspective in the representation of space. Nor is it true of all adult artists in our own western society; one can think of many recent painters who arrange their subject matter two-dimensionally on the flat surface of the picture.

The child at first thinks of himself as the centre of space and in his drawings places the various symbols relatively to himself. We see this in No. 33, where the separate parts of the pram are placed to one side of the girl, who dominates the little group as the figure of importance—'I am taking my baby sister out in the pram'. We see the baby inside the plan-like view of the body of the pram, the open hood with the rain both above and below it, wheels that are near but not actually attached to the pram, and the girl herself who has been drawn with particular emphasis on the face, hands and feet. The baby's role is a relatively minor, passive one and it has been drawn with the minimum of detail, without either hands or feet. Everything in the drawing has been placed in the space around the girl, everything considered from her point of view.

In the next stage, however, the child begins to draw himself—together with all the objects of his imagination—as standing on the ground, which in symbol form is depicted as a thin strip, or single 'base-line'. The introduction of the base-line marks an important step in the child's development as through it he relates himself and all the things in a picture to an environment or setting. The base-line may represent a floor, a street, or any surface of ground. Nos. 20 and 21 have a strip along the base and in Nos. 31, 32 and 34 we can sense the strip of ground along which the children wheel their prams. Nos. 23, 24, 51, 52 and 106 also have an implied base-line.

In each of Nos. 27 to 30 the figures are grouped around the pond, which provides the focal interest. No. 27 is particularly interesting in that the feet of the children are all placed against the pond; the base-line—on which they stand—has been bent round to form a circle. (Before the children drew their pictures they saw and played with visual material, discussed in Chapter 3.) These pictures are also interesting as examples of schematic drawings. A child produces his own 'schema' for people and objects by evolving a series of symbols, some of which he uses repeatedly. We see how this has been done in the generalized drawings of the people in each of Nos. 27 to 30. The greater divergency of symbol seen in the boats may have been the result of the children having played with a variety of boats immediately before drawing.

There is no overlapping of shapes in these four drawings. Each picture reveals aspects that were of particular significance to the child who drew it. In No. 27 the feet, for example, were of special importance to Rebecca. In No. 28 we see Vincent's interest in the children holding hands, whereas in No. 29 Amanda was much more interested in the differences of clothes and hair-styles. The child who drew No. 30 included five dogs in her scene; in each case she drew under the body a row of the four legs she knew to be there. In No. 58 Anne drew the legs of the horse in a similar way, again prompted by what she knew rather than by what she saw. No. 32 also shows the power of this logic. The baby was drawn in detail in the pram; then the coverlet was scribbled, logically, over the baby, almost obliterating it.

No. 34 shows an amazingly sophisticated treatment of a figure, for a five-year-old, with its detail of the hair, high-heeled shoes, patterned dress and sense of fashion. But this child had an adolescent sister who took a great interest in clothes and obviously influenced the drawing. Nevertheless the sky above is shown as a plain strip, very typical of a five-year-old's way of seeing.

Nos. 35 and 36 show the same subject treated in very different ways. In No. 35 Stephanie started with an outline drawing—we can see the four legs in a row under the body—which she then covered almost completely as she drew, very expressively, her impression of the dog's long, soft, curly hair. Vicky has also made a very complete logical statement about her dog. Her treatment of its hair brings to mind a story told of a boy in Professor Cizek's class. The boy had drawn a sheep and had scribbled a spiral, looping line all round its shape. A visitor looking at the drawing said: 'Aren't you going to draw the wool all over?' to which the boy replied: 'But the wool is only on the outside.'

Young children are concerned primarily with the expression of ideas. They do not 'copy' directly, but their store of memory-pictures grows through actual observation and children notice the smallest details if these are of significance to them.

In her painting of 'Chestnut Trees', No. 23, Anthea, five years old, has expressed what she knew and felt, making a full, well-ordered composition. The conkers, large and prickly, obviously of particular importance to her, have been emphasized in size and are painted with the utmost care, arranged in a beautiful pattern, abundantly filling the spaces between the trees. The trees are solidly painted in browns and then, surrounding each tree, is an outer layer of brilliant yellow —the autumn leaves that she knew to be on the outside. There is no over-lapping; each form is complete as a statement and is shown in its most characteristic aspect. Again, in painting the sky as a thin band across the top of her picture, Anthea has shown what she knows—

that is, the sky above—not what she actually sees. Sometimes it seems to me that this strip across the top, so familiar to us, causes more perplexity than any other symbol; I have known classes where the children's persistence in painting the sky this way has been a source of constant worry for their teachers who, with corresponding persistence, have vainly tried to persuade the children that sky and ground should meet.

If it is accepted that young children's graphic expression has its own characteristics, and that these usually have little in common with realistic conventions of depth, perspective, scale and proportion, then a child's failure to conform to such standards cannot be regarded as a 'mistake'. By attempting to impose on a child types of expression foreign to his stage of development, teachers may only succeed in destroying the liveliness and sincerity of his work.

Two Autumn Themes, Nos. 23 and 24

It is interesting to compare No. 23, Anthea's 'Chestnut Trees', with No. 24, John's 'Avenue', both autumn themes. While Anthea's painting, which is at the schematic stage, is purely two-dimensional, John's is more realistic, with some foreshortening along the tops of the trees. On the other hand, the trees, houses and car are all approximately on one base-line. In fact his painting is at a transitional stage, combining aspects of symbolism and realism. There is a considerable feeling of depth which is suggested by the front view of the car, the bird and the downward direction of the falling leaves. John has recognized the individual differences of the large houses behind the trees, but the trees themselves are treated as flat symbols. By showing the relative scale of the trees, houses and car he has further emphasized the realistic sense of depth. He has then enjoyed painting each leaf with a large brush dab and, by stressing the size of the strokes, has suggested the heavy density of falling autumn leaves. Each painting is, in quite different ways, a genuine expression of the child's feeling.

Transparent and Covered Drawings

The child's preoccupation with what is known is sometimes expressed in 'transparent' drawings in which, as for instance in No. 26, the outside of the basket and the flowers inside are shown simultaneously in one drawing. Similar deviations from reality are found in some forms of primitive art, such as the 'X-ray' drawings of the Kwakiutl

Indians, British Columbia. In one painting the artist may show what he knows exists—for instance, the exterior form of a wolf, together with the vertebrae, ribs and the human figure that has been swallowed.[1] Similarly, a child may first draw the outside of a house, with chimney, windows and door: and then on the same drawing add the staircase, tables, chairs and perhaps the people inside.

These details may be left in linear form, or what is inside may be entirely covered by being scribbled or painted over on top, that is, on the 'outside'. A child often obliterates a detailed drawing by layers of scribbling or paint, as in No. 32, the pram drawing already mentioned.

I recall one small girl, in an Infant school, making a splendid person in fabric-collage. She had been excited at finding some scraps of gorgeous silver brocade, which she used with obvious pleasure for the dress. When these had been pasted in position, she thought her lady needed a coat and, after some searching, selected several bits of fur, which she then pasted in a layer on top of the dress, covering it completely. It was a triangular-shaped fur coat, and the dress was where it belonged, underneath the coat. The child was highly satisfied, indeed delighted, with each stage of the work and with the final result. Perhaps she was talking to herself, rather than trying to communicate.

Scale and Proportions

In young children's drawings scale—that is, relative size—is frequently used to emphasize what is, to them, of the greatest importance. Colin's collage figure, No. 16, in which the head is disproportionately large in relation to the body, is a characteristic example.

The human face is of special significance in the child's earliest memories and impressions. He associates it with a vital coming-towards-him feeling, at first perhaps apprehended only as a form looming into vision over the side of his cot or perambulator. Then, as he comes to perceive the face more fully, his own emotional response towards it deepens. What could be more natural than that, in his early drawings he should make the face huge? It is also understandable that his first representation of a human being may take the form of the head alone.

[1] *Primitive Art*, by Leonard Adam (Penguin Books, revised edition).

I have just been looking at a reproduction of an expressive picture by a girl of thirteen, one of Marion Richardson's pupils at Dudley High School. The title is 'Head Mistress Interviewing Parents'. The head mistress is seen on the right-hand side of the picture, a great, formal, seated figure, so vast that she nearly fills one half of the painting. With calm dignity she looks towards a group of about thirty parents, all infinitesimally small in comparison. They stand, crowded and huddled together, forming a narrow band that stretches from the top left-hand corner across to the bottom right-hand edge of the picture. The head mistress (her face in profile, the eye front-view, her body front-view and the feet side-view) is surrounded by space and looks tremendously impressive in her detached isolation. The painting, in no sense accurate representationally, is intensely vivid in its communication of idea. Perhaps those of us who are parents may feel in sympathy with these parents; for me the painting recalls memories of school-meetings in which our children's work and progress were discussed with the head mistress and staff—when the atmosphere seemed laden with the parents' collective uncertainties and hopes. The girl was not representing the actual appearance of things, but was expressing an emotional experience of a particular situation. Let me add at once that in the schools I personally have in mind, the Heads and staff could not have been more approachable or helpful, as doubtless was the austere head mistress in the painting!

It is interesting that the picture I have just described was painted by a girl who, though well past the Primary school stage, was nevertheless expressing her ideas largely through an emphasis on the symbolic significance of relative size. But, viewed in the wider context of world art, perhaps it is not so strange. We find parallels in some Egyptian work, several thousand years B.C., where for instance the king is distinguished from his subjects by being depicted as much larger.

In the fine carving in the Romanesque and early Gothic churches of Europe, similar departures from reality are found; as, for instance, in the strange beauty of the elongated stone figures on the portals of Chartres Cathedral. Or we can imagine how unearthly and awe-inspiring the immense, disproportionately tall, mosaic figures of the Emperor Justinian, Theodora and their attendants, in the church of San Vitale, Ravenna, must have seemed in Byzantine times. And in our own time, many painters and sculptors have, in their search for fresh values, found inspiration in the art of primitive peoples and in African negro sculpture in which the features most significant to the artist are often exaggerated.

Many painters of the twentieth century have, through their rediscovery and exploration of such visual idioms, brought into fresh focus this relationship between children's art and art in its widest sense. Countless examples can be found in different periods, where, as with children, the expression of a subjective vision of reality has produced non-realistic art.

Composite Drawings

Children may combine several different viewpoints in one drawing or painting, selecting the most telling aspect of each part (No. 37). A typical instance is that of the front-view eye shown in a side-view face (Nos. 17 and 18), or the case where both eyes are shown on the same side of a face. In fact, all that is *known* about the person or object may be incorporated in one drawing. Picasso and his contemporaries, in their Cubist paintings, explored some of the possibilities of a visual synthesis of view-points. Such forms of expression are sometimes deprecatingly described as 'non-realistic'. Perhaps the terms 'realistic' or 'realism' used in this connection are somewhat ambiguous; the combination of several expressive characteristics may surely bring us as near, if not nearer, to a many-sided reality than the representation of one view-point at a time. Such personal interpretations provide other facets of reality—different, certainly, but possibly equally true.

In any case, whatever our personal reactions may be, we should be prepared to accept that a value judgement such as 'good', in relation to children's art (or any other art form) may not necessarily be synonymous with 'naturalistic representation'.

In such remarks as 'That's a good drawing for a child of six' or 'The perspective in John's drawing is very good' or 'The proportions in this figure are less good', 'good' could usually be substituted by 'representationally correct'; yet all types of visual expression should be regarded as potentially 'good', provided that, whatever the differences in style and emphasis, the work has sprung from genuinely creative impulses.

Pattern and the Child's Way of Seeing

We are constantly reminded, as we watch children playing and working (in art the two are interwoven), of their natural enjoyment of pattern.

Notice with what delight the small child plays with collections of buttons, beads, shells and pebbles, selecting and arranging them in colours, sizes or shapes; or again, how greatly children love the repetition of rhymes and jingles in skipping, hopping and stepping games. Iona and Peter Opie in *The Lore and Language of Schoolchildren*[1] have made a comprehensive collection of such rhymes, handed on from generation to generation and kept alive through the rhythm of constant repetition.

In children's early scribbling, drawing and painting, this sense of repetition plays an important part. No. 25, 'The Tractor', was painted by a six-year-old boy. He liked the clear robust pattern of the corn stooks and this he has shown with direct simplicity. The forthright characteristics of his painting call to mind similar qualities in some medieval illuminated manuscripts. There could be little doubt that this was painted by a country child, thoroughly familiar with his subject. How well he has found ways of expressing the different attributes: the rough irregularity of the stubble, the firmness of the tractor and the weight of corn in the waggon—corn into which he could sink. Incidentally, this picture, though painted fairly recently by a Fenland child, is already of some historic interest; for with changing farming methods such stooks have now largely been replaced by mechanically constructed, rectangular bales.

We have seen how, in portraying everything as he knows it to be, the child often uses flat, diagrammatic forms, with little overlapping or awareness of perspective. This leads to spread-out arrangements, often very decorative in their two-dimensional pattern. In such drawings a predominance of right-angled shapes contributes to the sense of pattern. We notice in No. 39 how the trees are logically placed at right-angles to the road. If we folded the paper up, along the edge at either side of the road, the trees would in fact appear to be growing perpendicularly to it and we should see them forming an avenue. The child may well have turned the paper around as she drew, so that she was directly experiencing the relationship of trees to road. In No. 27, Rebecca, drawing the figures at right-angles to the pond, may also have moved her paper round as she drew.

[1] *The Lore and Language of Schoolchildren*, by Iona and Peter Opie (Clarendon Press, Oxford).

Many children of eight and nine years become natural decorators, and an abundance of pattern is a characteristic of all their work, whether as decoration on a clay model (No. 133), in printed designs (No. 112), in imaginative painting (No. 48) or as an enrichment of the written page (No. 107). Such children may particularly enjoy the somewhat similar qualities found in the pattern and colour of the popular folk art of most countries.

Colour

By the turn of the century extreme reactions against outworn forms of academic art led to changing aesthetic values. Countless 'movements' each with a particular 'ism' emerged, but common to this diversity and flux of creative expression was the realization that art is an outcome of the artist's (and the child's) personal vision. This individual quality is particularly evident in the tremendous richness and variety seen in the way artists use colour. Matisse, Chagall, Rouault—a few names to which we each might add further personal preferences—regarded colour as a means of re-creating, rather than reproducing. Matisse's descriptions of how he used colour explain this well and could also be relevant to children's work.

If upon a white canvas I jot down some sensations of blue, of green, of red—every new brush stroke diminishes the importance of the preceding ones. Suppose I set out to paint an interior: I have before me a cupboard; it gives me a sensation of bright red—and I put down a red which satisfies me; immediately a relation is established between this red and the white of the canvas. If I put a green near the red, if I paint in a yellow floor, there must still be between this green, this yellow, and the white of the canvas a relation that will be satisfactory to me. But these several tones mutually weaken one another. It is necessary, therefore, that the various elements that I use be so balanced that they do not destroy one another. . . .

I am forced to transpose until finally my picture may seem completely changed when, after successive modifications, the red has succeeded the green as the dominant colour. *I cannot copy nature in a servile way, I must interpret nature and submit it to the spirit of the picture*—when I have found the relationship of all the tones the result must be a living harmony of tones, a harmony not unlike that of a musical composition. For me all is in the conception.[1]

[1] From *Artists on Art*, compiled and edited by Robert Goldwater and Marco Trevis (Pantheon Books, New York).

Matisse continues:

To paint an autumn landscape I will not try to remember what colours suit this season, I will only be inspired by the *sensation* that the colour gives me; the icy clearness of the sour blue sky will express the season just as well as the tonalities of the leaves. My sensation itself may vary, the autumn may be soft and warm like a protracted summer or quite cool with a cold sky and lemon yellow trees that give a chilly impression and announce winter.

My choice of colours does not rest on any scientific theory, it is based on observation, on feeling, on the very nature of each experience.

Monet, Seurat, Matisse and the rest may now be regarded as 'old masters', but we can imagine what an impact this explosion of expressive colour must have had on a Europe that had for centuries 'bathed its pictures in brown gravy'. Some eighteenth-century painters finished off their paintings with a heavy coat of dark varnish, to imitate 'old masters'—paintings once bright, which had darkened with dirt, varnishing and time. The excitement about this new treatment of colour must have contributed to the growing appreciation of the colour in children's paintings.

Often it is through the colour that the emotional intensity of a painting is most strongly conveyed. In No. 37, 'My Mother', the whole picture was painted in brilliantly strong reds and pinks (Matisse's sensation of bright red). Red may have been the colour that appealed most strongly to the boy, a colour therefore through which he could best express his feeling for his mother.

On the other hand, in No. 38, another painting of the same subject, also by a six-year-old boy, great interest in local colour was shown. His mother's brown coat and black hat were painted with a degree of representational accuracy consistent with the general realistic concept.

We cannot separate colour from qualities of tone, texture, balance and arrangement in a painting. Thus in No. 37 the whole conception is symbolic, whereas No. 38 is a more naturalistic representation throughout. The position of the figure (the head still rather large) suggests movement in space, in marked contrast to No. 37, in which the flat composite figure is quite static. Interestingly enough, the non-realistic 'red' painting, No. 37, with its crude, vivid clarity, makes the more powerful impact. It is a painting not easily forgotten.

It is often asked, 'Can colour be taught?' Personally, I believe that if colour is to have meaning for the child, this must come through his own instinctive response, and that each child in a class will respond in a different way to the infinite possibilities in the enjoyment of colour.

However, there are schools in which instruction in the use of colour, based on systems and colour theories, is given. Admittedly this more frequently happens at the secondary stage, but I have seen specific 'methods' in the teaching of colour introduced even in the Primary school. While these theories, based on scientific research into the natural laws of light and colour, are in themselves of great interest, I feel that for children this approach is over-intellectual in emphasis and that work resulting from such teaching can easily become impersonal and stereotyped. How lifeless a whole set of 'correctly' coloured patterns may seem, each with a carefully controlled balance of harmonies, contrasts and discords—all theoretically sound, yet lacking any spark of individual inspiration and adventure. On the other hand, I do think that with the right kind of encouragement, with opportunities for experiment and an abundance of visual stimulus, much can be done to bring out and develop children's innate feeling for colour. Practical suggestions are discussed in Chapter 8.

VISUAL REALISM

When he is about ten years old the child begins to look more consciously at the visual appearance of the world around him and gradually his own drawing becomes more representational in character. Nos. 47, 60, 66 and 68 are some examples that show this growing feeling for greater representational accuracy.

Drawings that are in the transitional stage—from a diagrammatic form of expression to a more visual realism—become increasingly rich in detail. 'My Village' (No. 9) shows this merging of the two ways of seeing. Many of the details, such as the car, the cows and the patterns made by the crops, are treated in a schematic way (that is, the same form is used repeatedly); but instead of the strip of sky at the top, the sky now appears to come down as far as the line of the distant hills. We see a cloud near the horizon, and the rays of the low-lying sun relate the sun to the hills.

One result of the child's greater awareness of actual appearances is the realization that people and objects often appear to overlap—they may partially or entirely cover one another—according to their relative positions to each other and to the observer.

In No. 47—a representational painting—parts of the branches and nest are covered by the large leaves that surround and often overlap it. We are as it were brought close to the nest and therefore see only limited areas of the space surrounding it, rather as if we were looking at it through field-glasses, or had chosen this close-up through the viewer of a camera. In this painting Keith has shown only part of the bird that flies downwards towards the nest. Its head appears in the top left-hand corner, its body is not seen because it comes outside our immediate range of vision. We cannot think of Anne, aged five, who painted No. 67, showing only part of a bird in this way. Consistently she has used her symbols—in exactly the same way each time—to show the head, the body and both the wings; one bird it is true is flying in the opposite direction to the others, but it has nevertheless been thought of as an identical symbol.

Keith and Anne were of very different ages, but these basically different ways of seeing may be found even in the work of children of the same age. No. 48, for example, is another painting of a bird and nest theme by a ten-year-old boy. Here we are struck by the symmetrical patterns made by the decoratively veined leaves that are repeated rhythmically on either side of the flat branches. Roger has expressed space as a two-dimensional area, whereas Keith has introduced depth by means of recession and foreshortening. In no sense is one painting 'better' than the other: each is a genuine expression of experience. In Nos. 4, 10, 18 and 66, 'Goldfish', 'The Seagull', 'The Milkman' and the drawing of a boat, we note how some parts are covered by others that appear to pass in front.

On the whole we find that children in the lower Junior school draw chiefly in outline (No. 64). Larger areas are usually treated as plain colour or as flat patterned-textures, as we see in Nos. 85 and 86, and in Nos. 89 to 92.

The use of light and shade as a means of expressing solidity of form may be seen in the work of a few children in the upper Primary school, but is more commonly found in the drawings and paintings of children in the Secondary school, when the representation of realistic appearance has become more emphasized.

The romance and mystery of light has a particular appeal for the adolescent. Nevertheless, older children in the Primary school may also experience great pleasure in experimenting with the effects on colour and shape of different forms of lighting (see Chapter 5, page 76), Night scenes or subjects depicting smugglers, pirates, road-workers and miners may become dramatized by new conceptions of light.

Older children in the Junior school are ready to place increasing reliance on observation. Chapter 5 suggests ways in which this can be encouraged. In all work based on observation the stress should be on interpretation—on using observation of people, animals or natural objects as a means of nourishing the imagination. Observation at this stage may therefore relate closely to many aspects of picture making, some of which are described in Chapter 3. It is important that children should experience intense looking, but this should never be allowed to lead to meaningless copying, either of objects or of pictures. How far removed the making of superficial copies can be from the child's real powers of visual expression is shown by the following experience. Week after week a class of ten-year-olds copied postcards or other small pictures. The selection of cards they could use included many portraits and the children were quite skilled in reproducing an accurate copy. A student who began to work with them decided to introduce drawing based on actual observation from life. She had noticed their copies of sketches of people—they used small sketchbooks—and she thought therefore that for them to draw directly from life would be an appropriate development.

The lesson was spent in drawing one or two of the children, who in turn sat for the whole class. The results were astonishing. The children, far from being able to draw with any real understanding, were in fact at a much earlier stage of visual development than is usual at their age, and were using symbols generally associated with the work of much younger children. It seemed as if their weekly copying, superficially able though it had been, far from building up their understanding of form, had actually retarded their powers of visual expression.

During the stage of visual realism the differences between the interests of boys and girls tend to become more marked. Girls show considerable feeling for decoration, especially in relation to dress, and their pictures—particularly of people—include a frequent use of pattern. Activities and media which naturally encourage decorative treatments, such as paper and fabric collage, candle rubbings used either pictorially or for patterns, and printing and dyeing techniques, have an especially strong appeal to them.

Boys frequently show a preference for mechanical forms and like to make detailed drawings of implements and machinery. Scenes in which a wealth of detail can be included, such as harbours, airports and railways, provide suitable subject-matter; pen and ink, or charcoal are appropriate media, and this is a stage when drawing is much enjoyed.

The aspects of a subject that are most interesting to the child are often treated with great detail, whereas at an earlier stage the important parts were shown by an exaggeration of size in relation to the rest.

We must allow boys and girls to develop the interests that are most meaningful to them, but we should also take care not to assume too arbitrary a division of interests. We have found that when boys have a free choice of subject, they by no means limit themselves to tough themes. Nos. 10, 47 and 48 were subjects chosen by boys and could hardly have been treated more sensitively. The atmosphere should be such that a boy can feel free to paint the most tender subject without fear of being thought sissy. On the other hand at this stage he will often want an outlet for full-blooded, dramatic subjects, with which he can feel closely identified.

In this chapter I have traced the stages usually met with as children develop. Yet it must be emphasized that not everyone develops in this, or in the same, way. Some people remain 'natural' painters all their days.

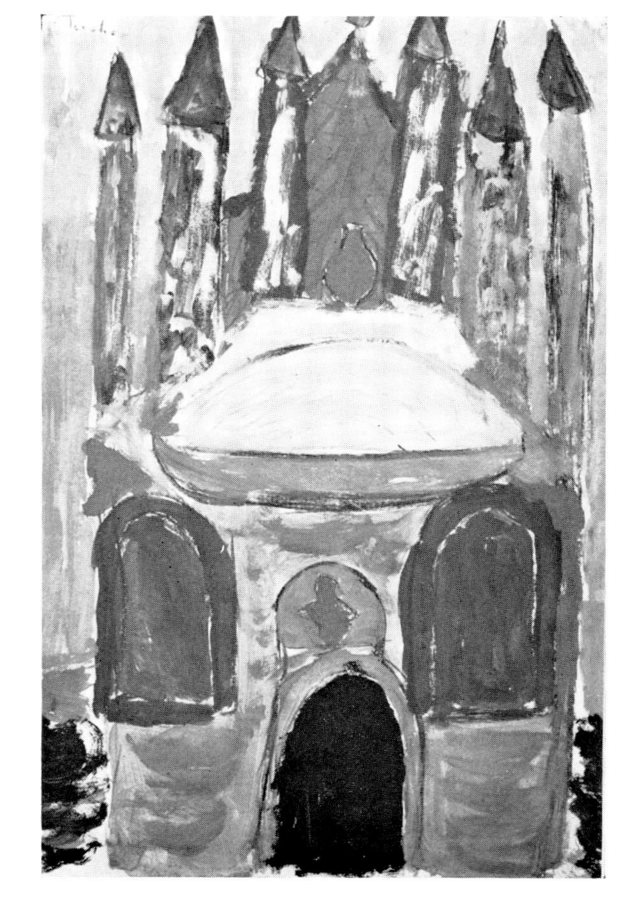 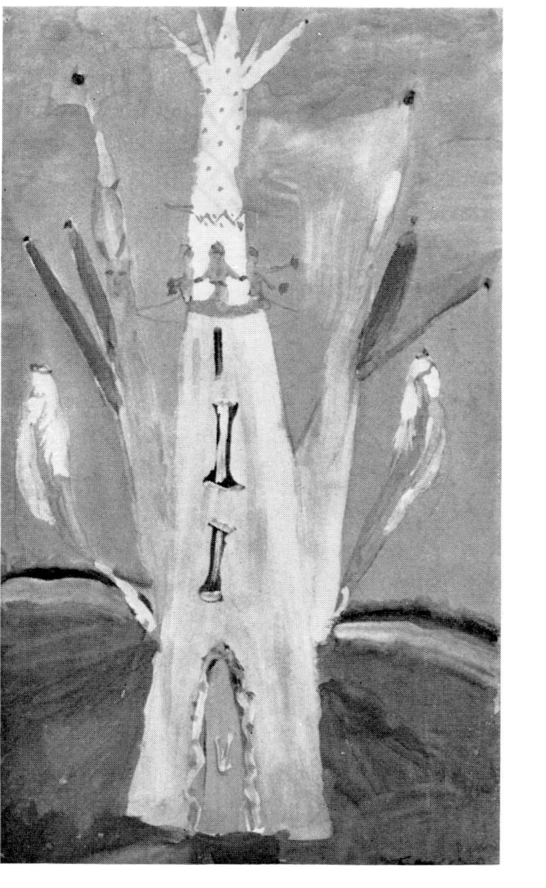

1   'The Tower', paintings in powder colour, about 23" × 14", by Francesca, aged 10, and Anna, aged 9,   2
see page 262.

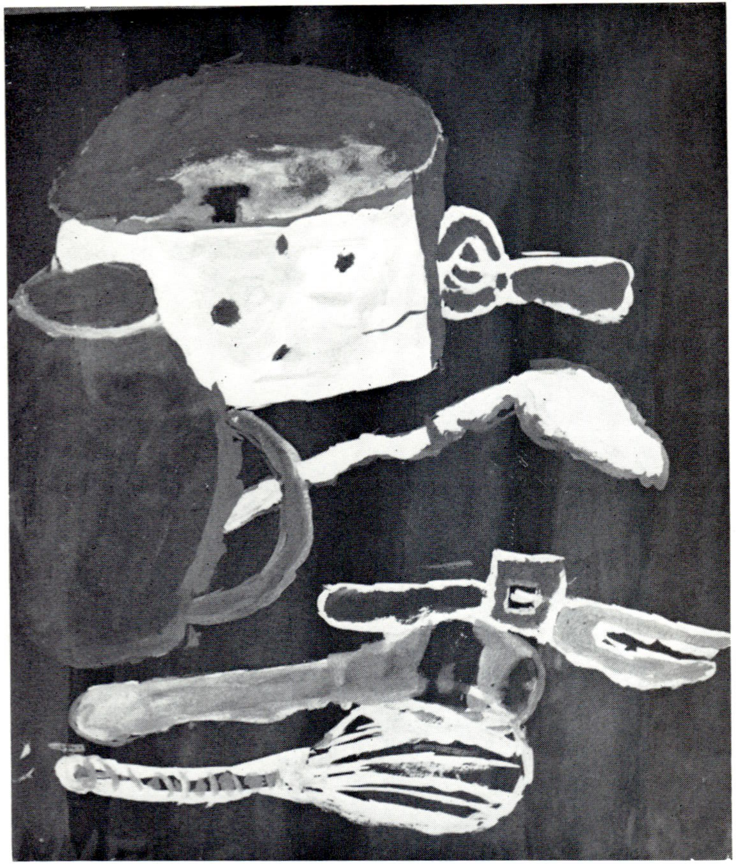

3 'Kitchen Still-life', a painting in powder colour, 24″ × 19″, by an 11 year old girl, see pages 36, 152.

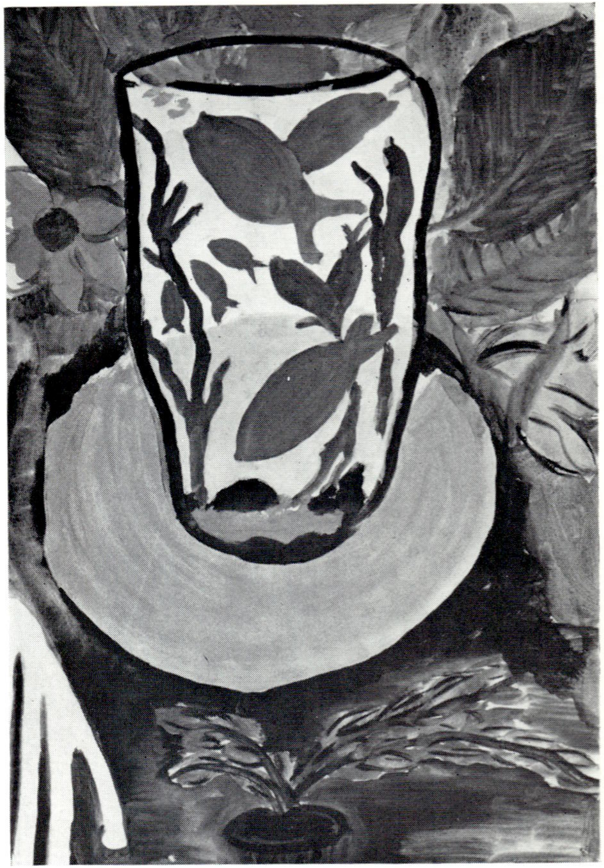

4 'Goldfish', a painting in powder colour, 22″ × 15″, by Gabrielle, aged 10, see pages 18, 152, 262.

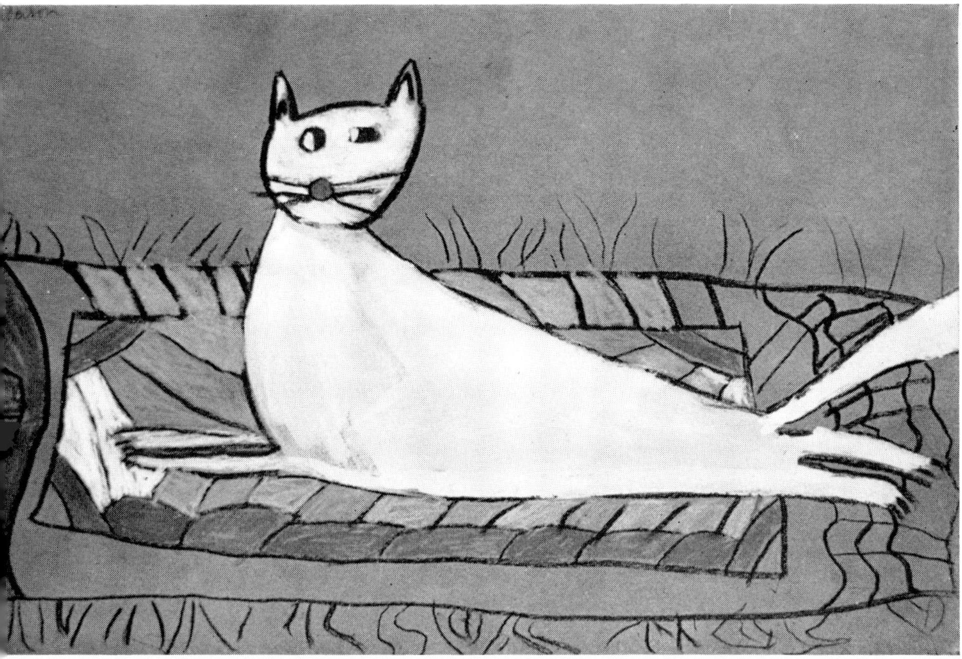

'My Cat', a painting in powder colour, 23″ × 16″, by Paul, aged 7, see page 262.

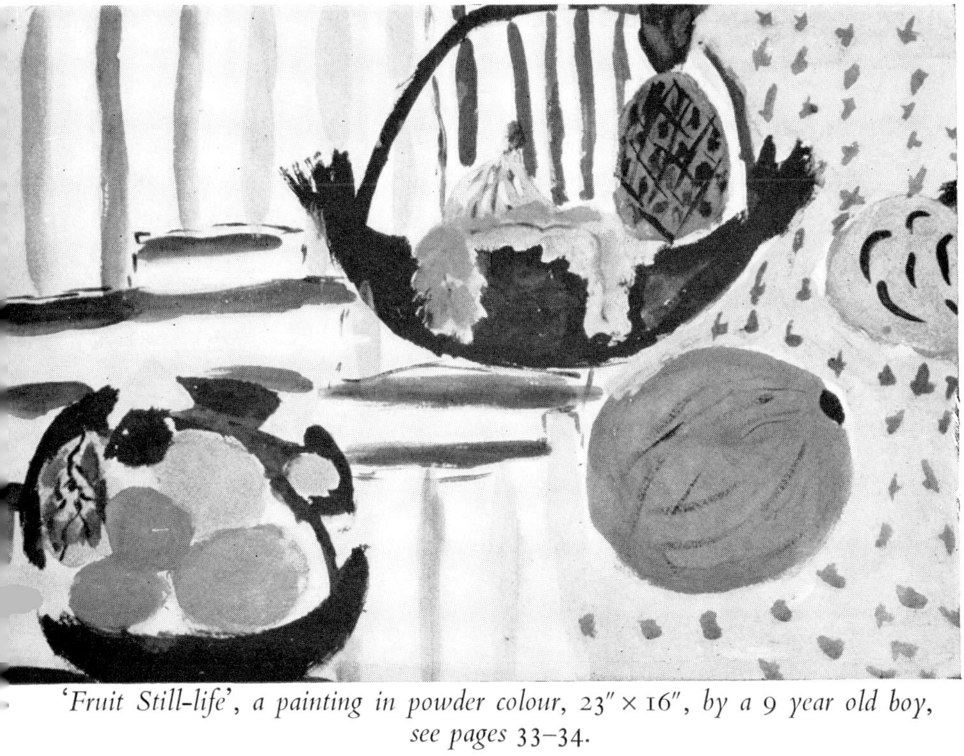

*'Fruit Still-life', a painting in powder colour, 23″ × 16″, by a 9 year old boy,
see pages 33–34.*

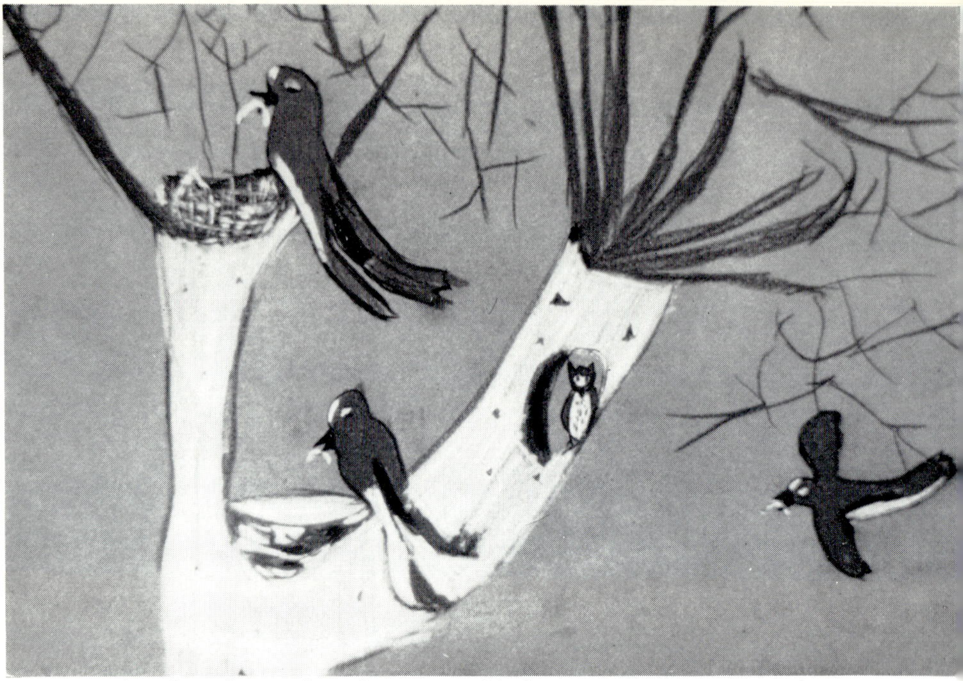

7   *'Birds and Nests', a drawing in black, terra cotta, and white conté, 25" × 18", by Nicholas, aged 7, see page 50.*

8   *'Squirrels', a drawing in charcoal and pastel, 23" × 16", by Diana, aged 9, see pages 50–51, 73.*

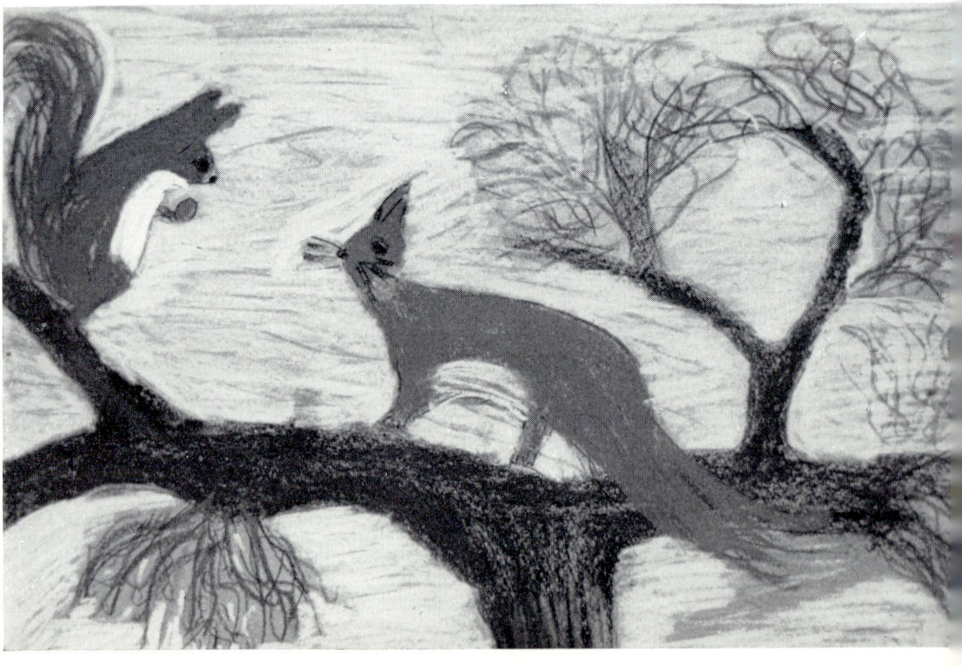

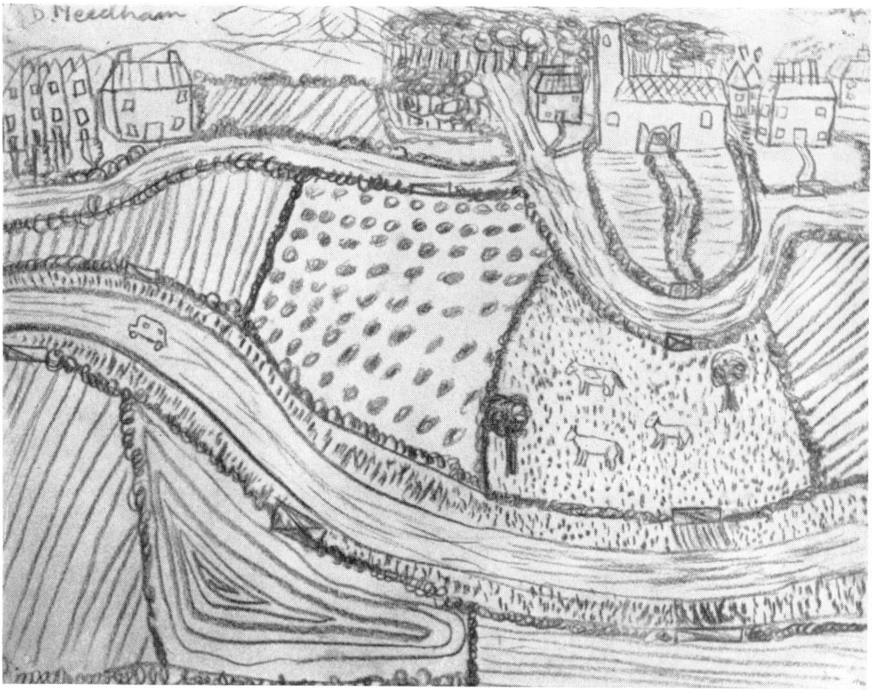

9   'My Village', a drawing in charcoal, 20″ × 16″, by Barbara, aged 10,
see pages 17, 41.

10   'The Seagull', a painting in powder colour, 25″ × 18″, by James, aged 11,
see pages 18, 20, 260.

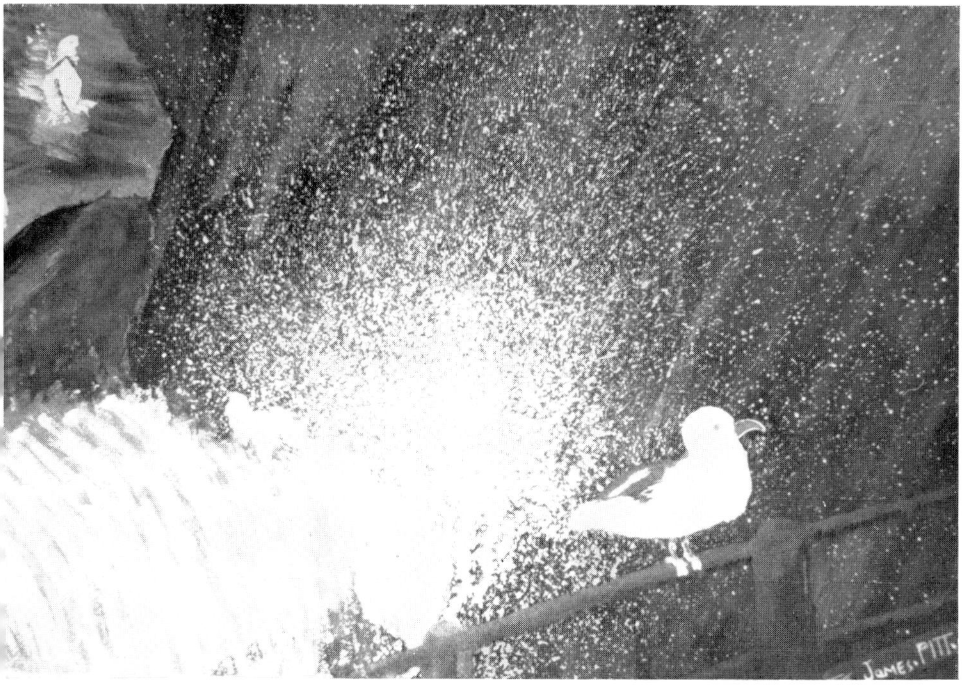

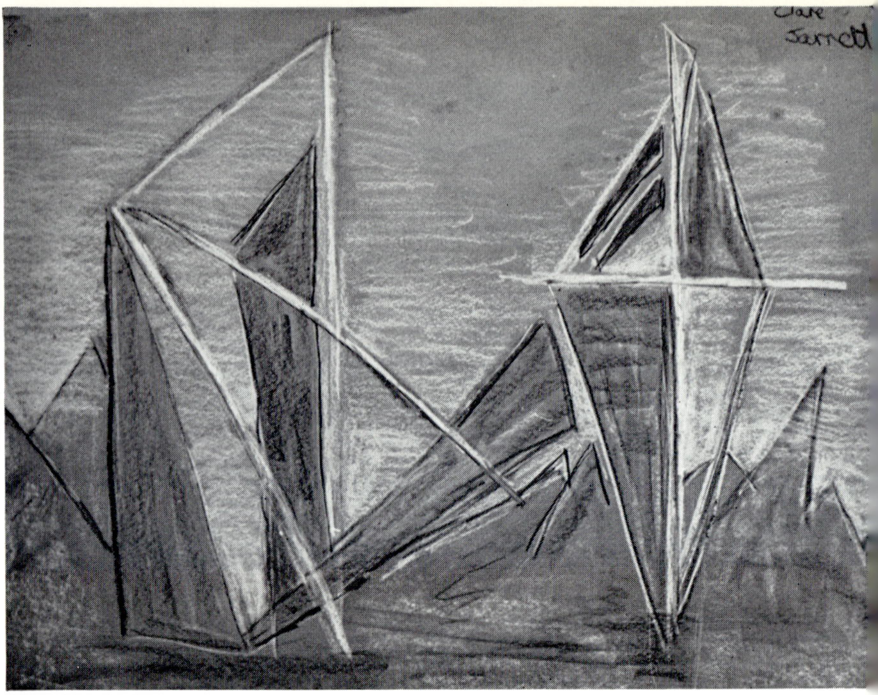

11 *A drawing in black and white conté, 25″ × 20″, inspired by balsa-wood models, by Clare, aged 11, see page 63.*

12 *Composition in paper collage, 23″ × 15″, by Francesca, aged 9, see page 169.*

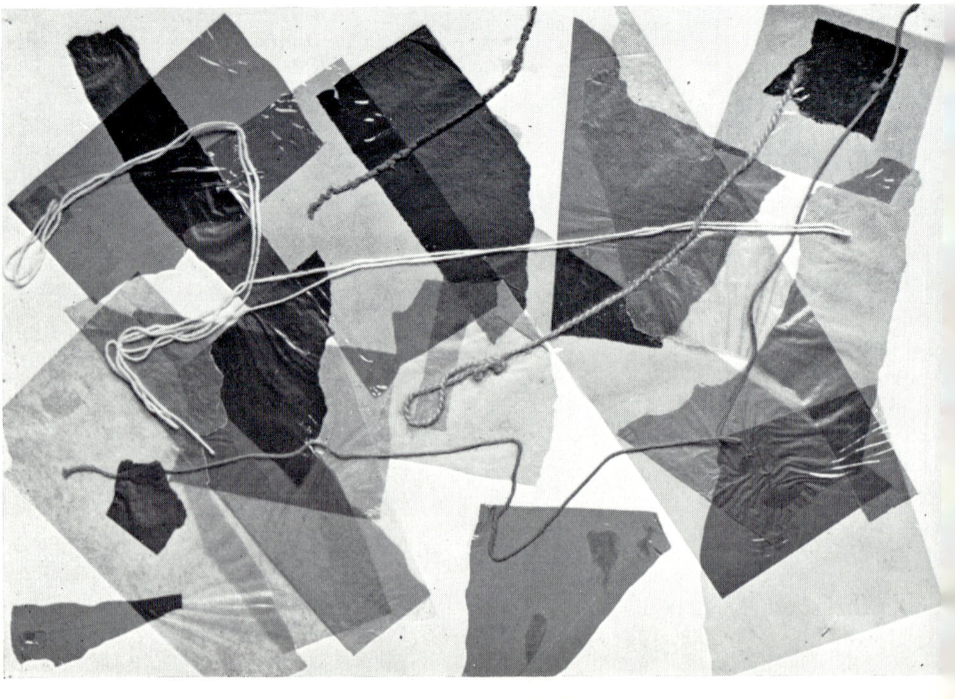

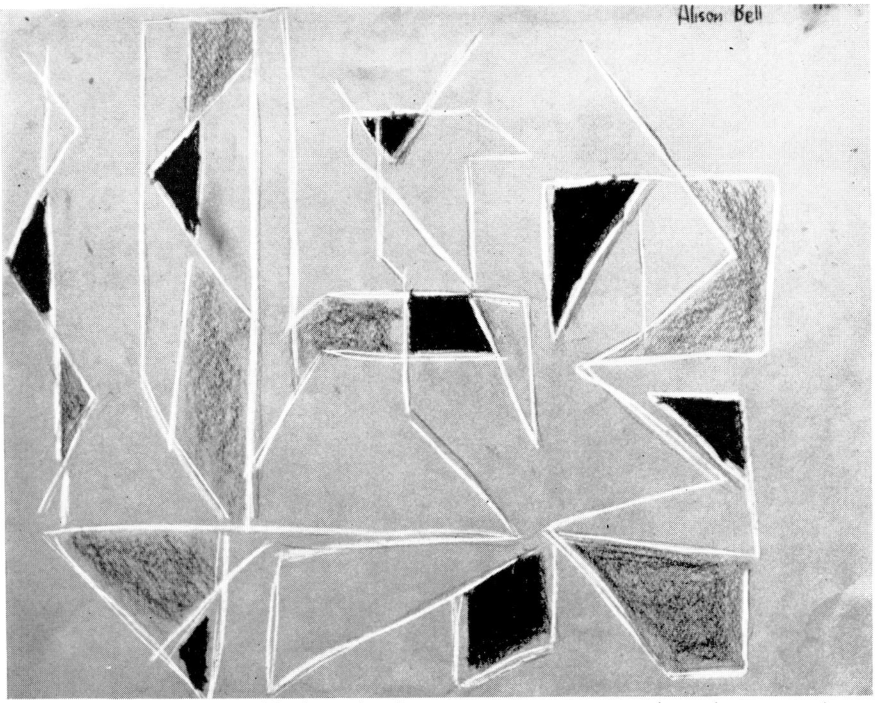

13   *Composition in black and white crayon, 25″ × 20″, by Alison, aged 11,
interpreting a balsa-wood construction, see page 63.*

14   *Free constructions in balsa wood by 10 and 11 year old boys; height of tallest model
16 inches, see page 73.*

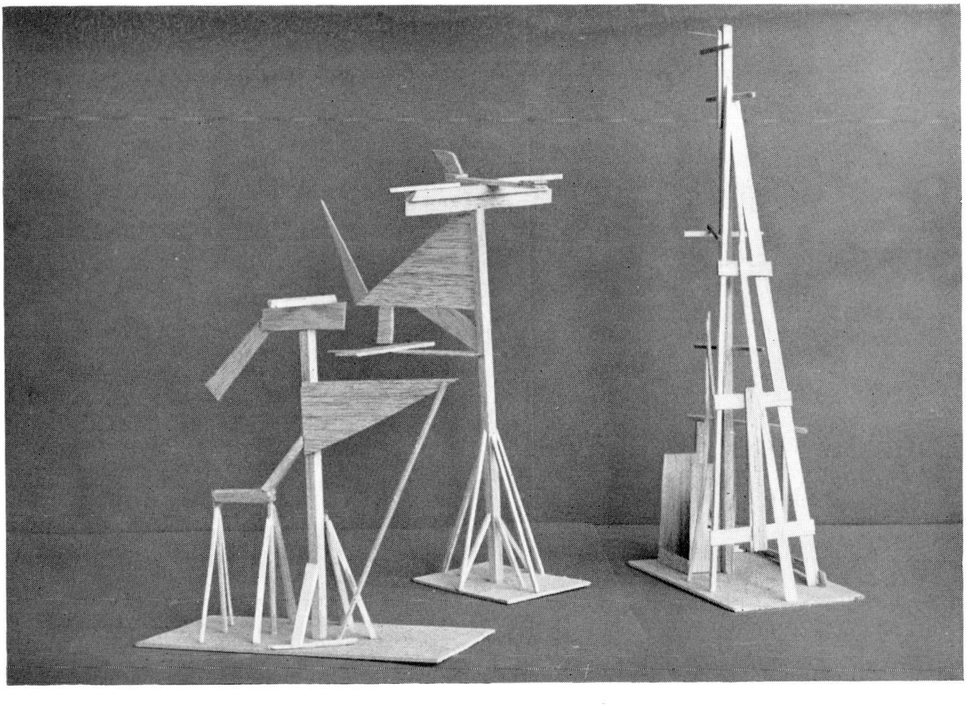

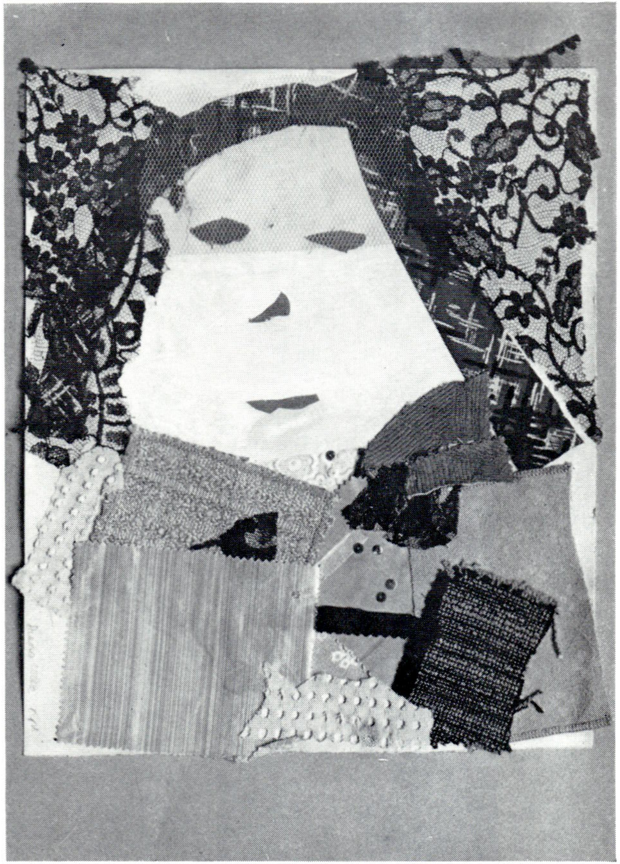

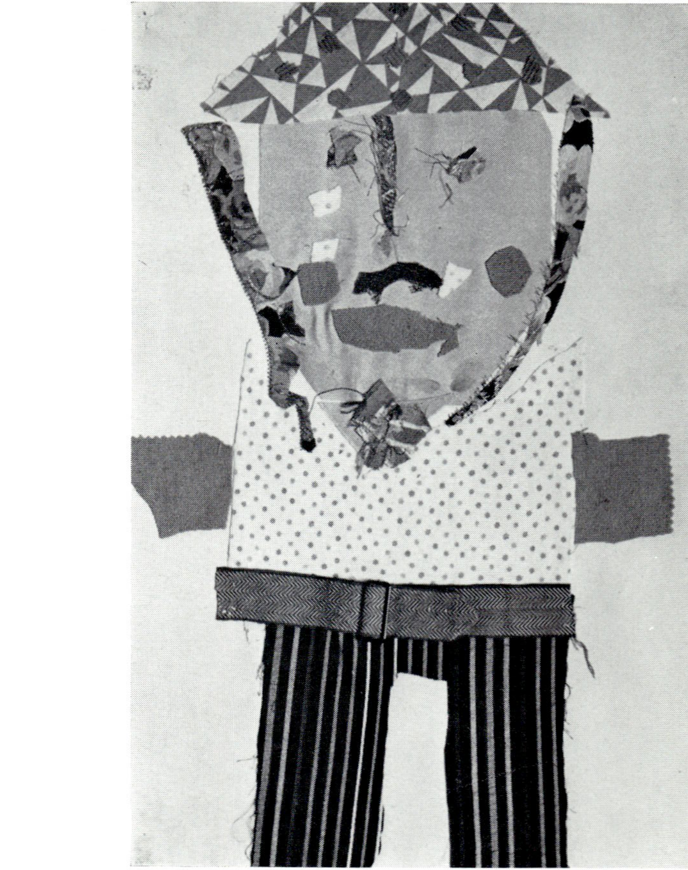

15   *Fabric collage portrait, 18″ × 15″, by Diana, aged 8,*
see pages 78, 169.

16   *Fabric collage figure, 18″ × 12″, by Colin, aged*
5, see pages 11, 78, 169, 171, 257.

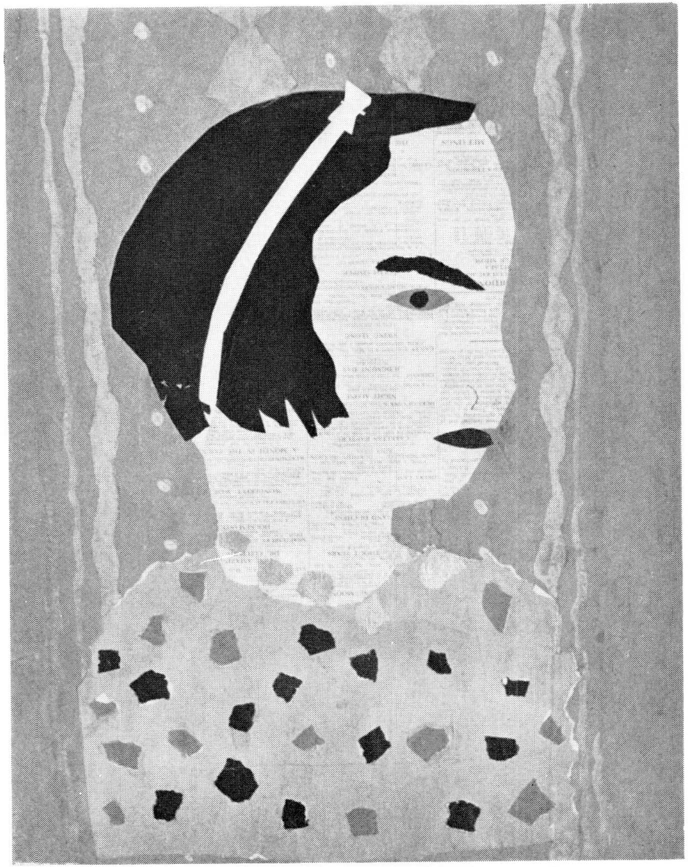

17   *Portrait in cut paper with painted background, 19″ × 11″,
by a girl of 9 years, see page 13.*

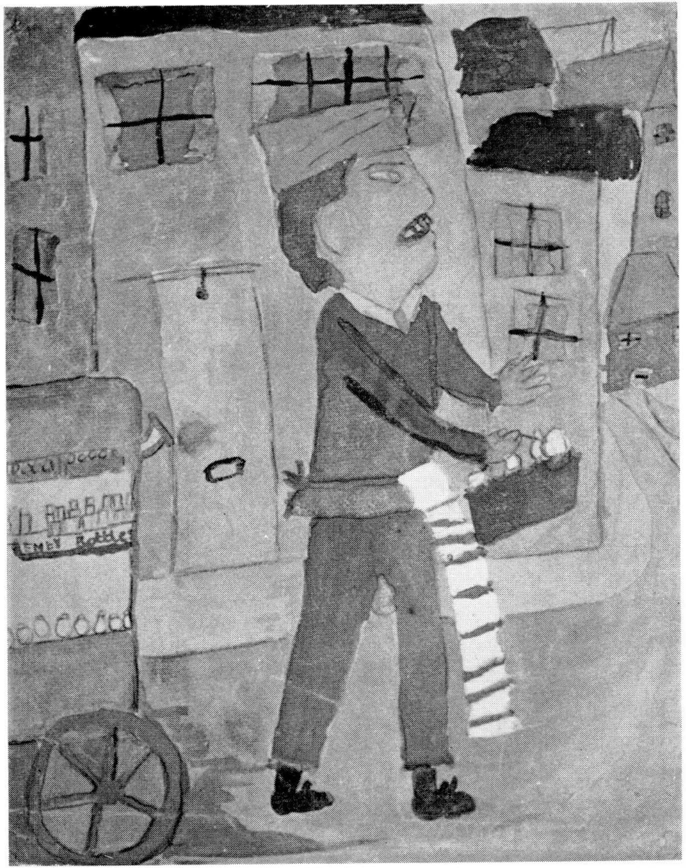

18   *'The Milkman', a painting in powder colour, 25″ × 20″,
by a girl of 8 years, see pages 13, 18.*

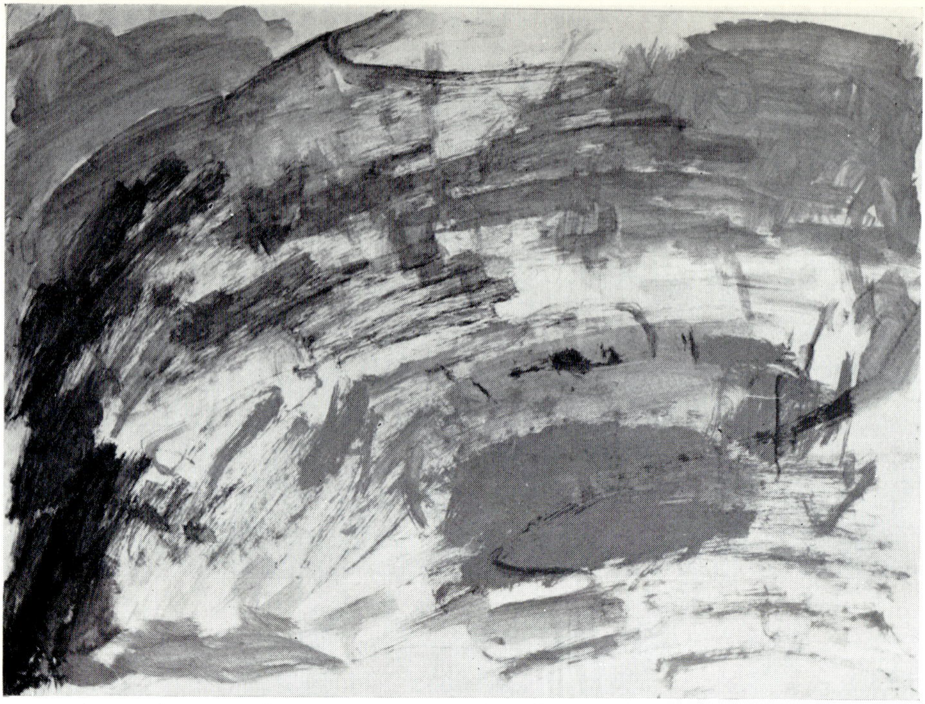

19   *'My Blue Picture', a painting in powder colour, 20″ × 15″, by Christine, aged 3, see pages 5, 150.*

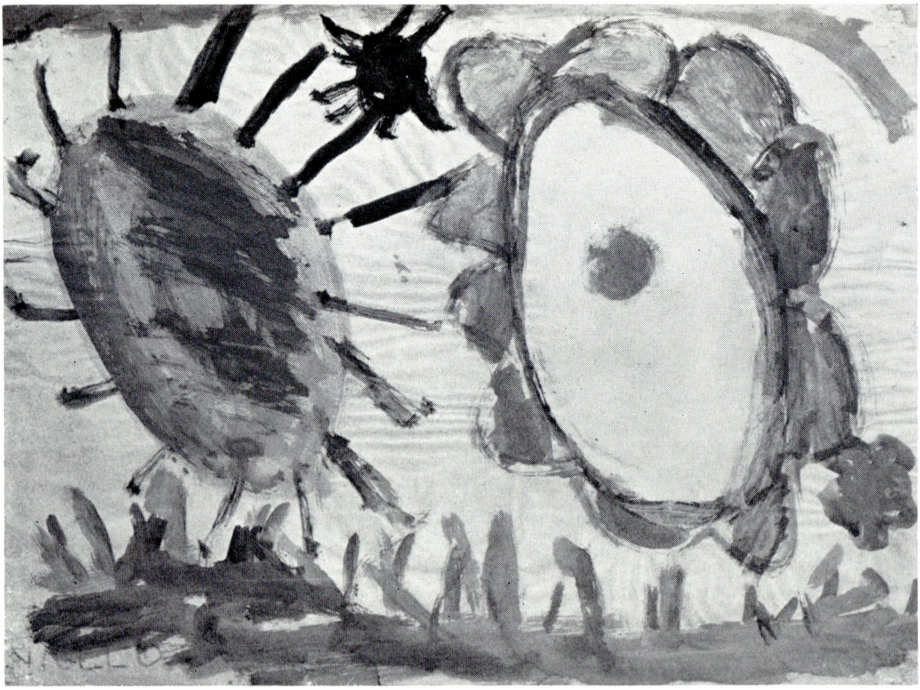

20   *'Magic Flowers', a painting mainly in yellows and violet, 20″ × 15″, by a 5 year old boy, see pages 5, 8, 150.*

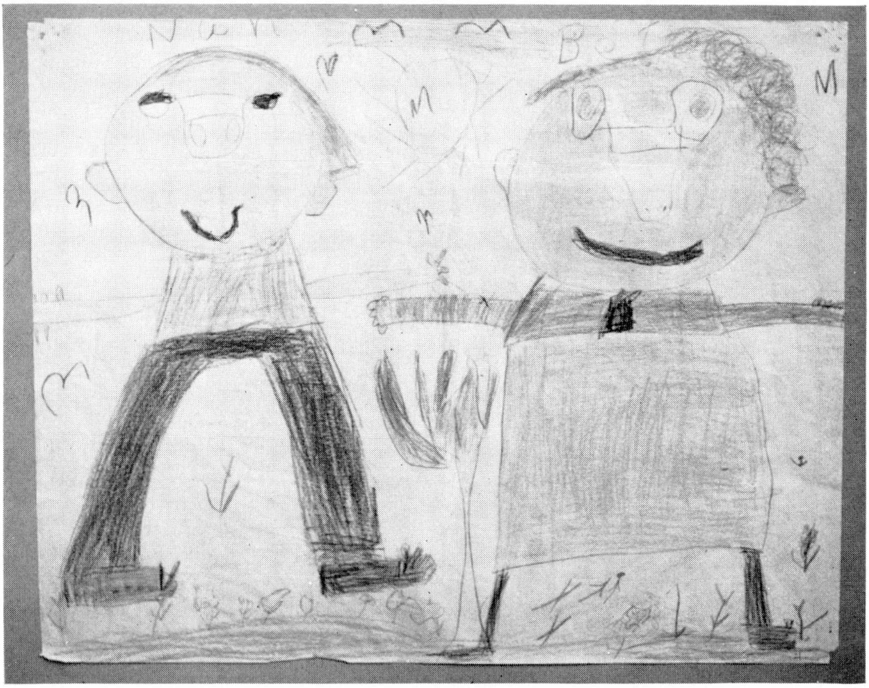

21   'Nan and Betty', a crayon drawing, 22" × 17", by Judy, aged 5, see pages 7, 8.

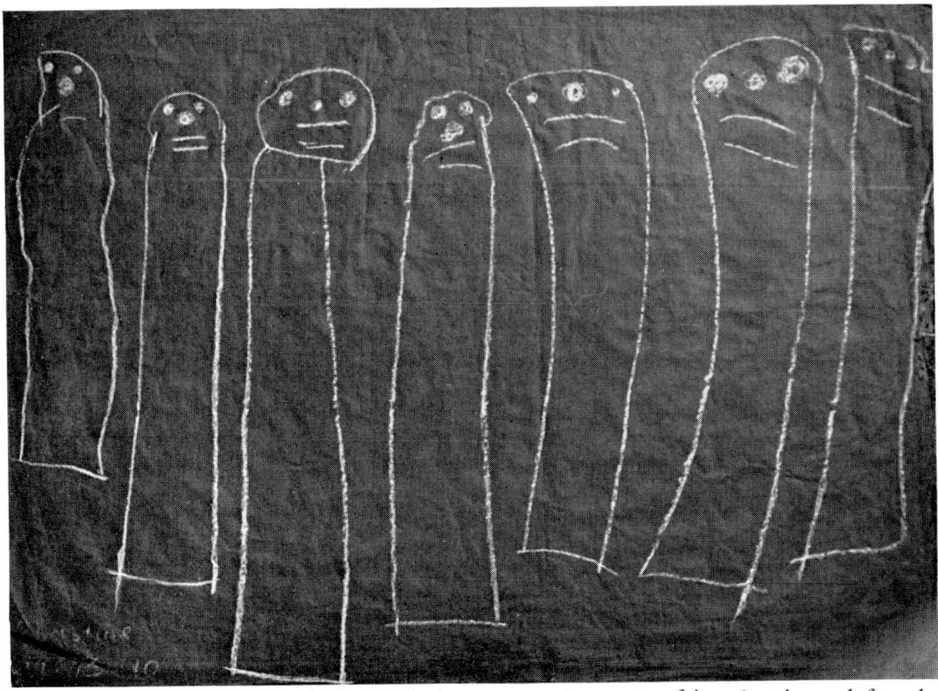

22   A drawing in white chalk on dark paper, 30" × 22", of her family and friends, by Christine, aged 3, see page 6.

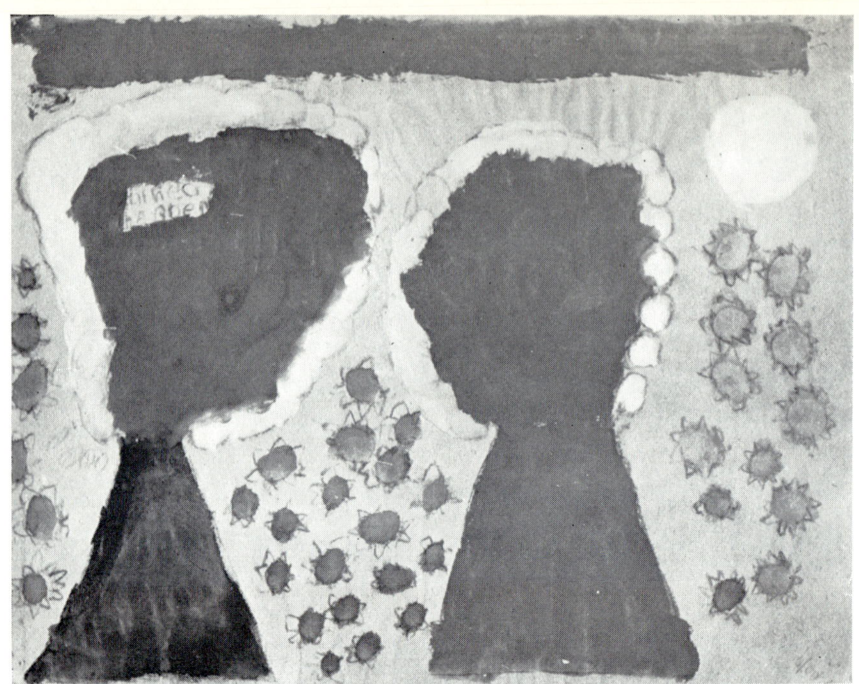

23   'Chestnut Trees', a painting in powder colour, 20″ × 16″, by Anthea, aged 6, see page 9.

24   'Brooklands Avenue', 20″ × 16″, by John, aged 7, see page 10.

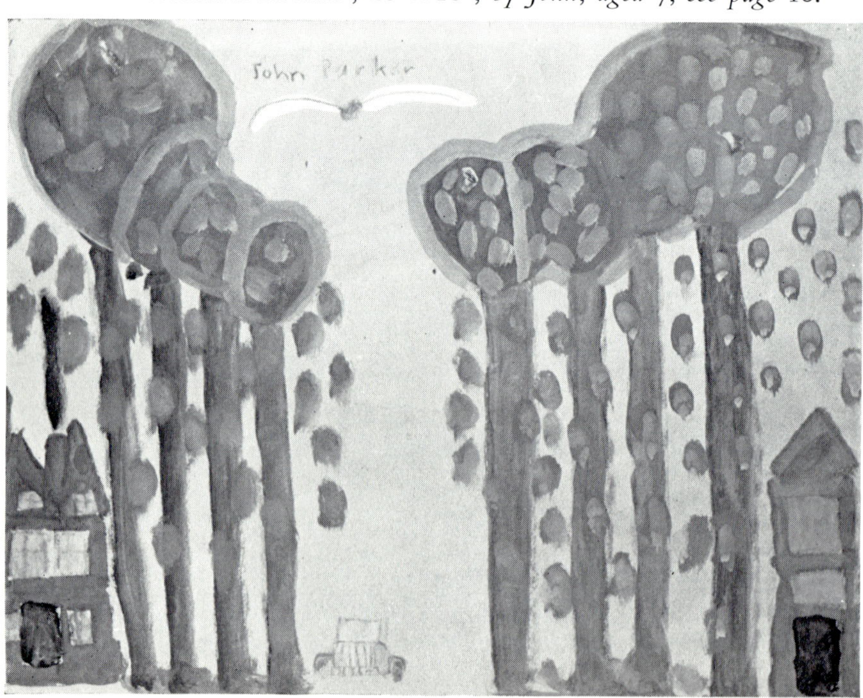

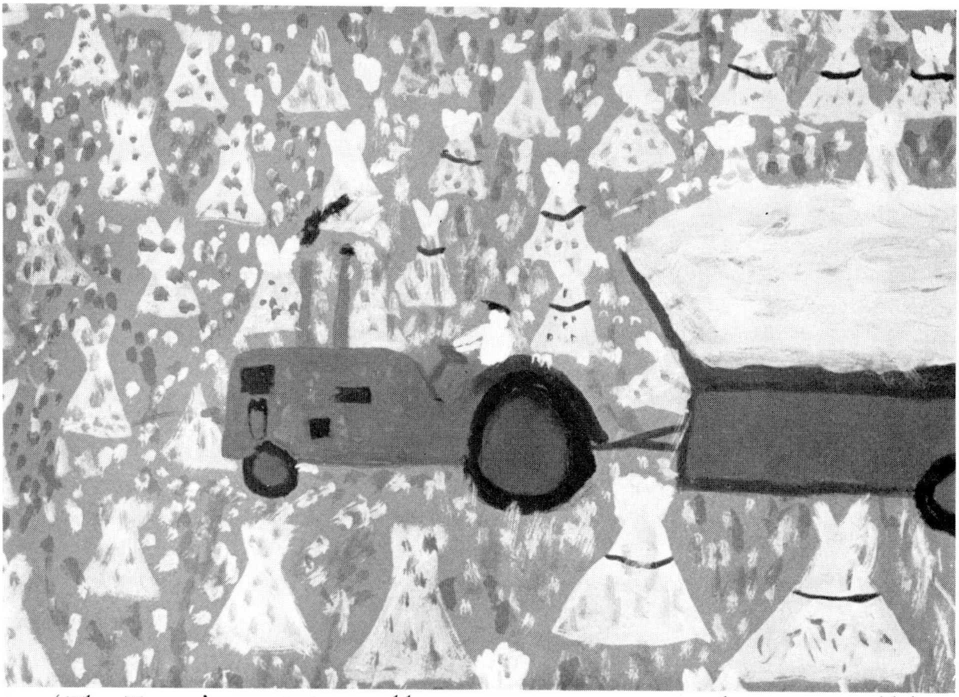

25   'The Tractor', a painting on blue sugar paper, 25″ × 29″, by a 6 year old boy,
see page 14.

26   A 'transparent' drawing in white chalk on dark paper, 21″ × 15″, by Anne, aged 5,
see page 10.

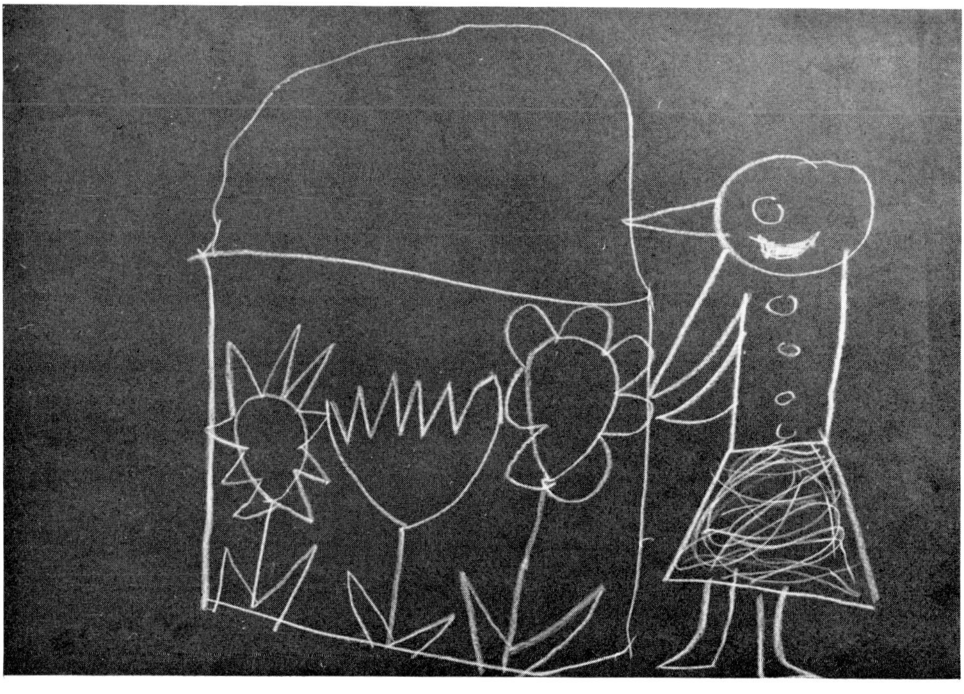

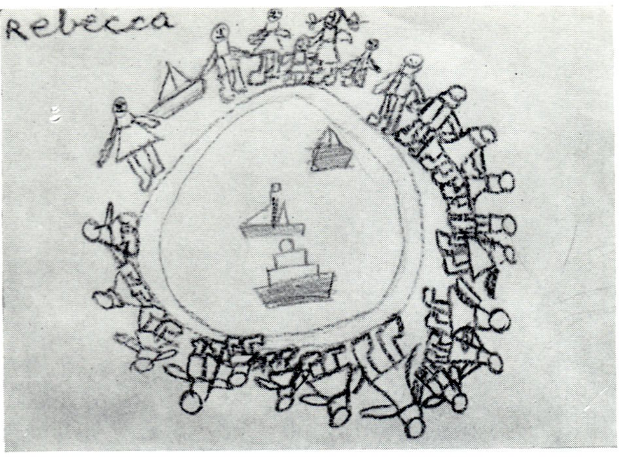

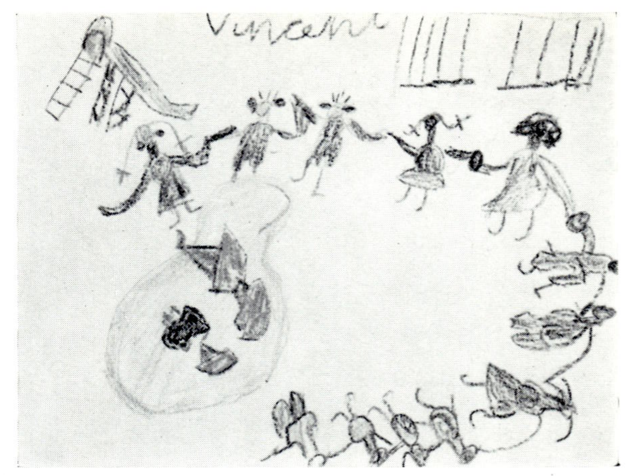

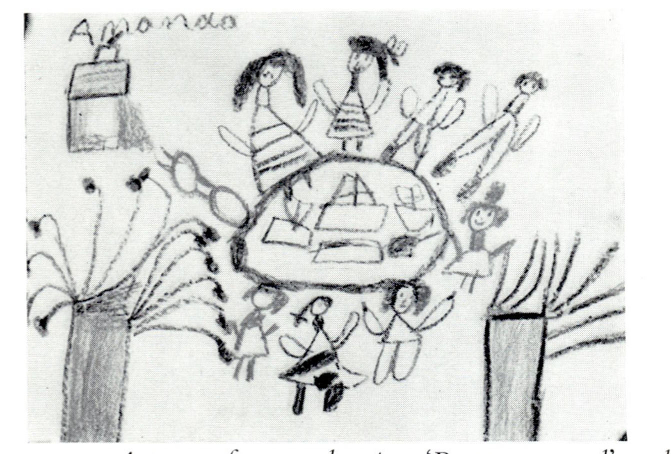

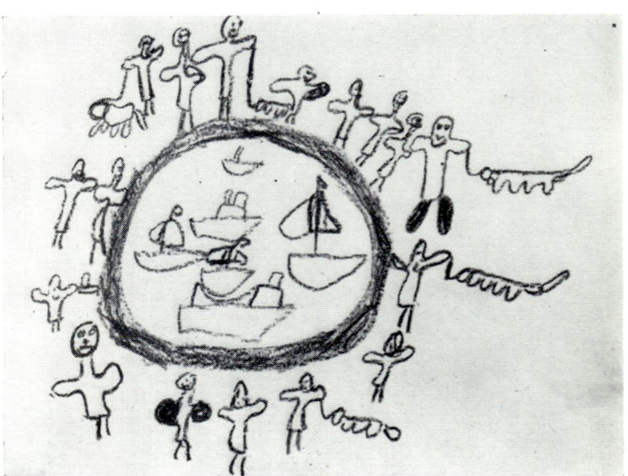

A group of crayon drawings 'Boats on a pond', each 12″ × 9″, by children of 6 to 7 years, see pages 8, 14, 31.

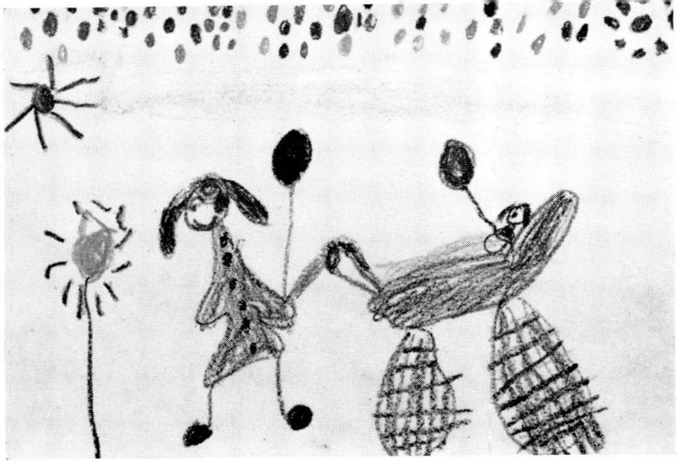

31

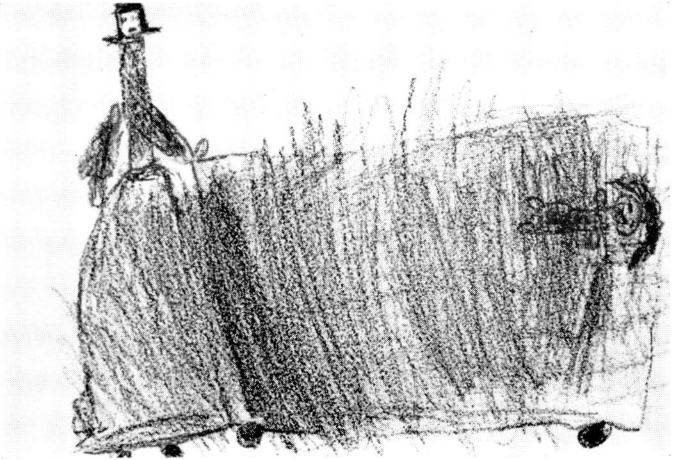

32

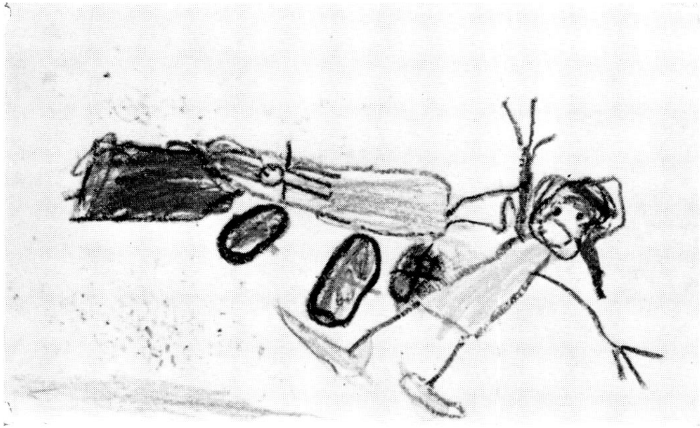

33

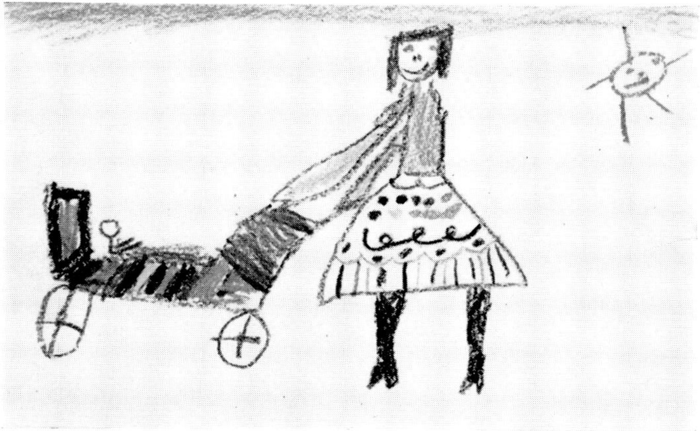

34

A group of crayon drawings 'A Walk with a Pram', each about 11″ × 7″, by 5 year old girls, see pages 8, 9, 11.

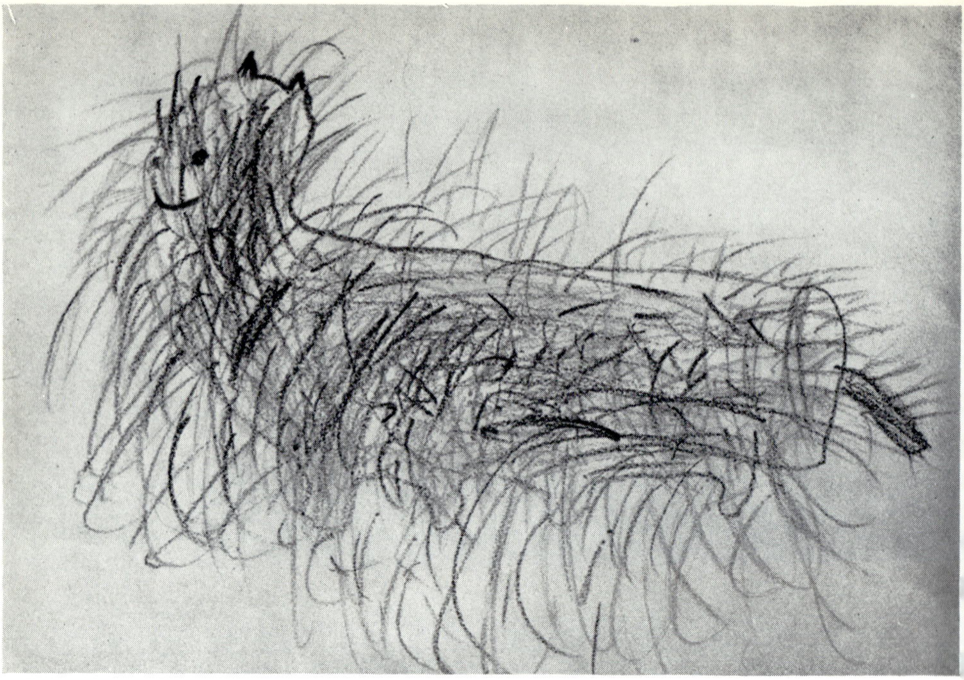

35

Crayon drawings of 'My Dog', each 10″ × 7″, by Stephanie and Vicky, both aged 6, see page 9.

36

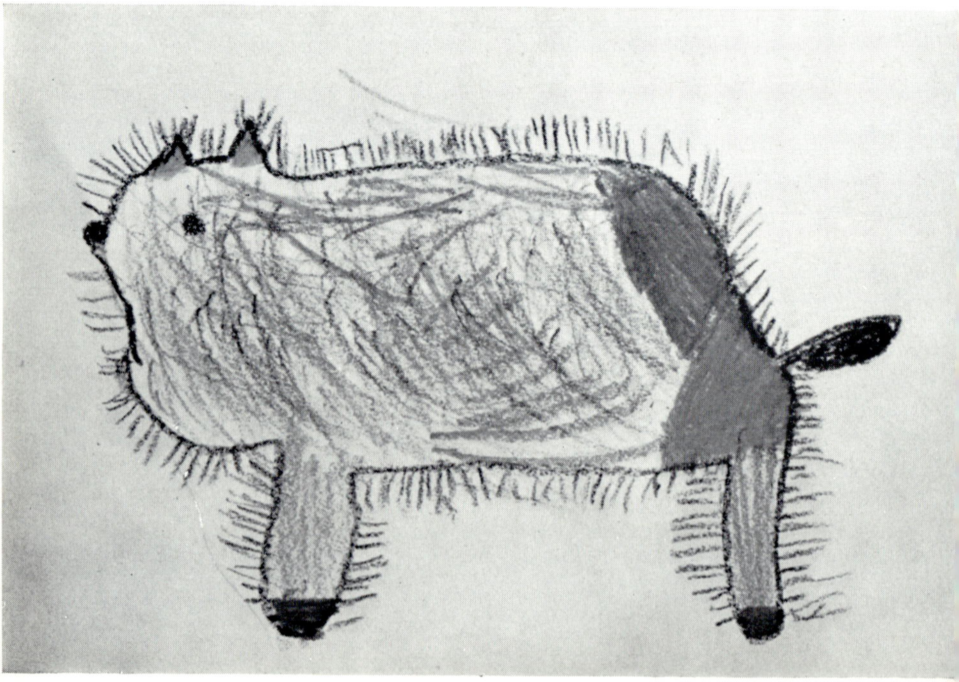

CHAPTER 2

Stages of Visual Development and Evaluation

The range of visual expression to be found in a class of children of the same age was effectively brought home to me in my first teaching post. My head mistress, interested in the work we were doing and anxious that it should go forward well, one day inquired when were the Lower Thirds going to 'do' perspective.[1] Apparently it had been my predecessor's custom to teach perspective at this stage and so far there had been no indication of this kind of lesson in our rather free and easy painting. Being inexperienced and very uncertain of the children's needs I did in fact attempt to introduce a course of lessons on linear-perspective to these ten-year-old girls. My own ideas of perspective were, in any case, rather nebulous, but I set to conscientiously and prepared the work as thoroughly as I was able. We started off, I remember, with some tentative blackboard diagrams of cubes, ellipses and eye-levels, which could only have served to accentuate the general feeling of surprise and confusion. This introduction was to provide the working basis for our next stage: the drawing of a street-scene in perspective. Soon the Lower Thirds and I were inextricably caught up in a tangle of misunderstood principles; with pencil, rubber and ruler we struggled, and I can still see the results in my mind's eye. A few children it is true had some real grasp of the problem, displaying a remarkable control of converging lines and an enviable skill in dealing with all the detail that had to be adjusted, precisely and correctly, within the foreshortened structure. But most of the drawings were meaningless. Tortured lines enclosed awkward shapes, curiously unrelated to hypothetical eye-levels and to the receding lines of roof-tops and street edges, which together we had so laboriously constructed, step by step. My own inept teaching and the children's lack of interest inevitably led to chaos. As a result the children lost much of the confidence and enjoyment they had been

---

[1] 'Perspective' is not of course the only method of conveying an illusion on a flat surface of distance or of three-dimensional form. Colour, tone and texture have also to be considered here.

experiencing, and I had to work hard to regain the kind of relationship that seemed essential for 'successful' art lessons.

But however little the children may have learned from this unfortunate experience, at least it led to some rethinking on my part. I realized that art teaching must above all be planned to suit individual needs and that it could not be wholly a matter of class instruction. In this instance a handful of children had already discovered perspective naturally, and were therefore using it consistently; whereas for many of them it cut right across the two-dimensional expression natural to them.

Looking at it another way, it would have been equally frustrating to withhold guidance from those children who were themselves wanting to use a more representational approach, and whose work would have benefited by a certain amount of directed observation.

Variations of this kind are seen in No. 44, a photograph of two horse groups modelled by thirteen-year-old girls, using clay for the first time. One has a strong sculptural sense, its heavy masses related three-dimensionally in depth. It could equally satisfactorily have been photographed from any other direction, since it 'works' as a solid composition from whatever point it is seen. Movement is conveyed by the interplay of the different planes and thrusts, while the finer textures also add to the rhythm of the form. The model on the right-hand side of the photograph is more two-dimensional in feeling, and has a poetic quality of its own, expressed with directness and innocence of vision. How satisfyingly is the horse related to the formalized branches of the tree and with what love and care has the detail of the leaves been described. We can see the group as a whole only from the front-view position in which it was mainly modelled; seen end-on, the horse has far less significance. The detail scratched on the leaves (which are exaggerated in size) and on the horse's mane adds to the whole decorative quality, which can be compared in spirit with English Staffordshire figures. These two models stand for basically different, but equally genuine, forms of creative outlet, in each case revealing a particular kind of vision.

Nos. 45 and 46, the work of very much younger children, suggest a strong kinship. No. 45, modelled in plasticine by a six-year-old girl, has a sculptural quality in common with the left-hand figure in No. 44; while No. 46, 'A Dog looking at a Little Girl who has fallen down', also modelled by a six-year-old girl, is reminiscent of flat, 'ginger-bread' figures, with all the characteristics of two-dimensional symbolism.

We might usefully compare three further examples, Nos. 40, 41 and 42. The subject was 'The Forest' and these were pictures painted by eight-year-old girls, using similar materials, working in the same conditions and, I was going to say, with the same teaching. But this is not quite accurate for we see immediately that, with these children's differing visual ideas, any teaching, to have meaning, would have to be modified to meet their different modes of expression.

We started with some discussion of forests and various questions were asked by the teacher. 'How big are the trees? Are they very tall? Are they fatter than you are? Can you hide behind the trees? They are certainly larger than the ones near school. They are so dense near the top that you can hardly see the sky through the leaves. Can the sun pierce through the leaves? What does it look like in between the trees? Is it very dark? What are the colours you see? The branches and leaves make a roof high up over your heads. Are some of the trees very close to you? So close that you can touch them? Are there any paths through the forest? Where do they lead to? Is the forest strange? Mysterious? Quiet and very still? Who lives in the forest? Are you alone? What does it feel like to be in the forest?'

Questions such as these build up a sense of atmosphere and help the children to feel themselves identified with the subject. As they think out their answers and contribute their own ideas, a variety of individual images are formed in their minds. 'The trees are so tall we couldn't climb them. The trunks are too fat for us to reach round with our arms. Sometimes you can see the sky through the leaves. Your feet have to push through the piles of leaves on the ground. However quietly you try to walk they make a crackling noise. It's rough and bumpy on the ground, some of the roots stick out. I saw some toadstools growing in the woods. There are strange animals in the forest. They hide if they hear a noise. I've seen an owl up in a tree. It's dark right inside the forest. It's very quiet. The forest makes you feel very small. If you see some light through the trees you know how to find your way out of the forest.'

In the three pictures reproduced, individual differences are very apparent, but each painting in the class was an equally personal interpretation of the subject.

In No. 40, the forest has been seen as a flat pattern of evenly spaced tree trunks, with branches and roots treated in an almost identical way. The leaves are shown by means of quite regular brush blobs; in fact the whole pattern element is so strong that the painting still reads clearly as a pattern when seen upside-down.

No. 41, on the other hand, has been imagined representationally, with an emphasis on depth. Relative size is used realistically to express the illusion of recession—the width of the path, and the size of trees and flowers diminishing in the distance. We feel we can go into this painting, along the path and beyond the distant trees, whereas in No. 40 we follow the surface-pattern in a flat plane from one side to the other. No. 41 has a representational accuracy derived partly from remembered images of trees and foliage.

No. 42, the last of the three pictures, though painted in quite a crude way, with little of the technical skill seen in No. 41, nevertheless strongly conveys an atmosphere of the strangeness of the forest, and of its immensity, accentuated by the small figure in the front. Of the three this painting expresses its mood with the greatest intensity.

As the children worked I tried to gauge each individual's needs. I was therefore careful not to confuse the painter of No. 40 with suggestions as to how she might make her picture more representational; rather, through a readiness to consider the painting from her point of view, I tried to help her realize her own ideas as completely as possible.

On the other hand, the painter of No. 41 needed a different kind of stimulus. Together we looked at trees from the classroom windows, noticing characteristics of growth. We became interested in the different types of trees, what they were, how we recognized them, and whether each tree had a special shape. We asked ourselves whether the trunks grew differently and whether they differed much in size, or in the roughness or smoothness of bark. Through direct looking, the child was able to extend her own visual ideas which, as had been clear from the start, were tending towards realism.

As I expected, she used colour naturalistically, delighting in mixing subtly related greens and browns, based on those she actually saw in nature. The painter of No. 40 used colour decoratively, with strong blacks, browns, reds and blues vigorously intermingled as part of the whole pattern. In No. 42, the colour suggested the heavy depth of the forest; grey-blues, misty greens and deep greys predominate, with a few strokes of vermilion on the small hat.

Had I been asked to mark these paintings, how impossible, and indeed mistaken, this would have been. How could they be assessed? Each girl, as I knew, had worked with absorbed interest. To me all the paintings coming from such involvement needed to be regarded seriously.

On this occasion the children, as they finished their paintings, followed up their work by making small classroom exhibitions on the theme of Trees. There was all the excitement of a treasure-hunt as, working in small groups, they collected photographs and cards, or found reproductions in books and magazines, with fairly free access to my own collections. The range included Persian manuscripts, Chinese and Japanese paintings and prints, medieval paintings, Peter Breughel's landscapes, and some Giotto frescoes. The Impressionists, Expressionists and other more recent painters were especially appreciated, and paintings of Monet, Van Gogh, Gauguin, the Douanier Rousseau, Paul Klee, John and Paul Nash were shown in the little displays. One of the girls was delighted when she discovered a reproduction of a fruit-tree, heavily laden with blossom, in one of our books, *In a Shoreham Garden*, a watercolour and gouache by Samuel Palmer.

By this time we had travelled far from our original 'Forests', into new worlds, the children's own paintings providing the bridge. The emphasis was on the enjoyment of looking; the children were not required to explain their personal reactions and preferences as, at this stage, this could have spoiled their spontaneous response. There was, however, a good deal of discussion and together we tried to find answers to the many questions that arose. Through this introduction to some of the many ways of seeing, the children quite naturally came to respect the artist's right to select and express things in his own particular way.

The various examples of children's work described in this chapter show how the stages of visual expression (see Chapter 1, page 4), may not necessarily correspond with chronological ages.

The last three pictures discussed, all painted by girls of eight, range from the schematic stage (No. 40), to that of visual realism (No. 41). No. 42 is not easily placed in any one category; the trees and forest are painted as a generalized impression, whilst the figure (not very clearly seen in the photograph) is treated as a symbol. As I have said, this painting, despite its lack of technical control, tells us more of the child's feeling about the forest than shall we say No. 41 which, though painted with considerable mastery of technique, conveys less of the atmosphere. Without decrying naturalistic representation, we must remember that technique and photographic accuracy are not the only attributes that make a painting.

EVALUATION OF WORK

The question of whether children's work in art can, or indeed should be marked, may arise; for it is still possible to find Primary schools where some kind of grading is attempted. I say 'attempted' because to me marking seems almost impossible to do satisfactorily at the Primary stage.

We have seen how extreme can be the differences in the work of children of the same age; which then are the particular qualities that we should rate highest in our scale? How are we to establish such values? It is more than likely that were the same set of paintings to be marked by several people the results would be very different, each one being influenced by the subjective reaction of the marker. While one person might look for evidence of imagination, or for qualities of colour, another might set more store by purely imitative, representational expression. Some might regard neatness as important, others would show little concern for technical skill. Apart from these difficulties of achieving objective standards, is it appropriate or desirable to grade creative expression? We may need to remind ourselves of some of the chief aims in art-teaching—for if we think the natural development of the individual really matters, then we should discard competitive stimuli as likely to undermine this natural growth.

If marking is found to be an indispensable incentive to work, then surely the teaching itself is at fault, and there must be some failure to stimulate and hold the children's interest sufficiently. By introducing a balanced range of activities it should be possible to sustain the children's creative effort through the appeal and satisfaction of the work itself. We have only to watch a classful of children absorbed in work that has meaning for them, to realize that the real educational value of the activity lies in their involvement in it as much as or perhaps more than in the results produced. Such values cannot easily be represented by any system of marking.

Given the impetus of purposeful enjoyment in the work, there should then be no need for additional stimulus, for by the introduction of competitive factors the children's awareness of visual qualities can too easily be obscured. Even 'inter-house' competitions, while arousing interest, can overstress competitive aspects, the children becoming more concerned with the number of paintings produced by a house, or with the stars of commendation decorating their work, than with the ideas communicated by the pictures or with actual qualities of colour, paint and form.

There is nevertheless a very real need for attractively presented, non-competitive classroom displays of children's work. The reassurance and satisfaction of knowing their work is appreciated and cared for immediately establishes an attitude of confidence and purpose. In large classes it naturally is not always possible—nor necessary—to display each child's work every time. Sometimes it may be an advantage to select a few paintings that bring out some particular aspect. Each child's work should be included from time to time (every fortnight perhaps) in such displays and fairly frequently a determined effort should be made to have everyone's work on view at the same time. Various ways of exhibiting effectively are discussed more fully in Chapter 11.

But perhaps the most disturbing feature of assessment concerns the individual child, who may fall below whatever standards have been accepted. The cumulative sense of failure, experienced by children who, week after week, have been unable to measure up to a certain level, can hardly be overemphasized. To belittle or ridicule results which may have sprung from the child's personal feelings quickly destroys his will to work. Even to ignore work consistently, passing it by without comment while that of other children is praised, can contribute to a child's feelings of inadequacy and disappointment. To put it quite simply: every child needs to know that his efforts matter. When both teacher and child understand this, then the most unpromising products may be expanded and developed beyond all expectation, and the child will be willing to accept and act on constructive criticism and suggestions.

Recently I was reminded of how deep is this need for children to be certain of our underlying approval. A small four-year-old girl had just joined the art club. It was her first visit and she seemed to settle well, working very quietly and with much interest; she was absorbed in her painting, and I purposely left her undisturbed. However, she had heard my remarks to other children near her and, when we were together, fetching clean water, she looked up and said: 'And mine is a lovely painting, isn't it?'

But approval certainly does not mean indiscriminate praise; the children themselves would be the first to notice when this had become so automatic as to be meaningless. Though we would not match one child against another, we do expect each individual to be conscious of the qualities in his own work; to know what might usefully be worked at next; to recognize the improvement that may have occurred; in fact to be really involved in the interest and development of his work. In this way, though he will not be faced with evaluations that grade his results in relation to those of other children, a child will be aware of his own progress as, at frequent intervals, he and his teacher consider together what he has produced over a period of two or three weeks. Each child's results therefore need to be kept over a period of time, perhaps in separate paper-folders. Where some such system has been introduced it has proved to be a valuable means of helping children to feel a personal responsibility towards their own work.

The kind of development I have in mind is illustrated in Nos. 51 and 52. These two paintings were done by an eight-year-old boy, over a five-week interval. His first picture reveals his initial diffidence and uncertainty. Partly intimidated by the size of the paper and partly because of his own lack of experience, he placed all the little items of his painting along an imagined base-line, at the bottom edge of the paper—the house, the tree and the small man with his umbrella and hat being blown by the wind. The boy had certainly made an effort to fill the paper, but the thunder-clouds and lightning are not really related to the whole shape and there is little feeling for an integrated composition. Looking at this painting with him I would first have said how much I liked the little figure and the way it was being blown along by the wind. Then I might have suggested how he should draw just as well in his next picture but that everything could be much larger, making a fine picture that could be seen even from the other side of the room. Together we would have looked at some of the paintings on the walls, noticing what big shapes had been used; how well the larger patches of colour looked and how we could often see the actual brush strokes in a painting. In this way positive suggestions would have been made without undermining the little confidence he had. After this first painting he was encouraged to experiment freely with brush work; and imaginative subjects were introduced which depended more on a personal interpretation than on established ideas of 'right or wrong'. His later painting, No. 52, shows something of his growing assurance and pleasure in using paint. It will be seen that there has been little change in the actual forms themselves, but that he has found ways of using his particular visual concepts much more expressively. The shapes themselves are related with more assurance to the shape and size of the paper, enabling him to communicate his story with a greater visual coherence.

Such encouragement and guidance helps each individual to experience similar possibilities of development, within his own range of expression. This kind of personal achievement provides a real stimulus, based on values directly connected with art, and therefore rewarding in its own right.

CHAPTER 3

Visual Material as a Basis for Picture Making

In the next chapters I shall discuss actual approaches to picture making, considering them under four headings: visual material, imaginative expression, observation and memory, and collective activities. But it is important to stress the arbitrary nature of these divisions and to remind ourselves that in actual fact something of all these aspects will be found in most forms of creative expression. Good art teaching cannot easily be classified: the only generalization we can make is that it should embody certain fundamental principles, some of which are described in the following paragraphs.

Children need variety in the choice of subject and in the ways in which these are presented. They will soon lose interest if the approach becomes so predictable as to rob them of the excitement of the unexpected. They need the stimulus of a wide range of working materials, inviting in themselves and challenging in use. Most important is the teacher's role—his personal enthusiasm and his initiative in finding attractive things of many kinds to stimulate the children and to provide sources of visual nourishment.

In some quarters art teaching has swung from an overemphasis on formal instruction and technical skill to such extremes of freedom in self-expression that the children are simply left to flounder in a welter of 'free art' materials. If the children we teach are to experience the fullest satisfaction of working creatively, then we must find a balance that combines opportunities for freedom in experiment with the security of some guidance and clearly defined requirements.

Children left to 'do something out of their heads' are often handicapped by meagre visual resources, which lead to impoverished expression. But simply 'setting' a subject is not in itself enough, and vague titles like 'a day in the country', 'my summer holiday' or 'a visit to the zoo', with little initial introduction or follow-up in the teaching, are likely to produce thin work.

This vagueness and withdrawal on the part of the teacher stems from a fear of imposing adult standards, or from an uncertainty as to how and when to give appropriate guidance (or dare we say teaching?). Whatever the reason, the child is left high and dry, with nebulous images of partially remembered incidents associated with the subject or with memories of illustrations which he may have seen in books or on hoardings. He has little idea how to set about relating these fragmented impressions visually.

Visual experiences are vital to the development of the child's imaginative powers, and even in the Infant school some children will be able to re-create the excitement of things they have seen. We see this in Nos. 27, 28, 29 and 30, drawings by five-year-old children, done after they had themselves played with some small boats. Their teacher had collected a few attractively painted little sailing boats, dinghies and steamers, each one only a few inches long. The children loved them and spent some time watching them and playing with them in a trough of water. When the teacher suggested they might draw the boats on a pond, perhaps with themselves and their friends, several children began at once, each translating his vivid experience in a personal way. In this instance fairly small sheets of paper, 12 × 9 in., were provided so that the detail of their quick, intense drawings should not become too scattered. Because they really had something to say, the children expressed their ideas fully and with a particular urgency.

Generally speaking, however, younger children are less dependent on the 'planned' subject, and it is with the older groups in the Primary school that more specific themes may usefully be introduced; but whatever the age of the children, creative expression should be closely related to first-hand experience and interest.

Visual Material for Older Juniors

One approach to imaginative painting is through the use of evocative visual material. This can sometimes take the form of large, attractively presented groups of objects, displayed in such a way that everyone, even in a large class, is able to get a general view. Each child, selecting only certain parts, develops these in his own way.

Suppose for instance that we have a collection of differently shaped bottles placed on a table, the top of which is not far below the children's eye-level. Some of the bottles we may have filled with brilliantly coloured dyes. Together they provide an exciting interplay of contrasting sizes, forms, colours and tones. There are tall, slender bottles; shorter, sturdy ones; bottles with long necks and sloping shoulders; others more square in shape. Some are of very dark glass, deep green-blacks, others of the palest whitish-greens. Through the glass our coloured dyes glow vividly. To introduce a contrast to the general shininess of the group, some bottles—perhaps one-pint milk ones—have been painted with a matt, white emulsion paint. All these are placed on rectangular areas of coloured papers, so that the whole effect is visually attractive.

On another occasion, the bottles could be combined with grape-fruit, oranges or other circular shapes—coloured balls might be borrowed from the Physical Education stock—the theme becoming one of 'cylinders and spheres'. Thus we have introduced the children to two fundamental forms: the cylinder or column, depicting ideas of stability, support and upward growing forms; and the sphere, complementing the thrust of these verticals.

In this way we plan a subject carefully, presenting it in an attractive but not over-finalized arrangement. This approach is not, however, a return to formal object drawing, with its emphasis on skill of accurate representation; the aim is more to develop powers of perception and originality. How then can this be done?

First, gather the children as close as possible around the group, and spend a little time looking at and handling the objects. During this introductory stage, the children are invited to move the bottles about and, together with their teacher, they become interested in the effects of different arrangements. We may try putting some bottles in front of others, or to one side, or behind, perhaps over-lapping them. Then we may ask: 'How do they look, placed in these different ways?' Later, some children may be painting at desks quite far from the subject, but as they are not directly copying it, nor having to look at the bottles all the time, this need not be a disadvantage. Individual children, however, should be able to return to the group for a closer view, if they need to.

Someone draws our attention to the shape of the space between two of the bottles, and we now become aware of these 'in between' parts as well. 'Do we like this bottle in front of the tall dark one? What about a white one next to it? How do these three relate? Should we try a space and then another bottle? Here are four of the same height; do they look well together?' Some of the children find this a dull arrangement, so we try varying the heights.

Through direct experiment and an easy give and take of ideas, the children become interested in possibilities of selection and arrangement, that is, in 'composition'. Suitability of scale or relative size is also considered, and if a piece of paper measuring 15 × 22 in. is held behind the bottles, the children will see that they can be reproduced in their actual size on such paper.

The children, knowing they are choosing certain parts only (the whole group of bottles would certainly be too large and complex), begin to look selectively. Some are quick to see the elements of a composition and will settle to painting almost immediately. For others, ideas take shape only after they have experimented fully with different possibilities of placing. A spot-light with colour filters can intensify the visual experience. Rich and unexpected colour effects can be produced by holding a sheet of coloured cellophane over the bulb of a light. (Such possibilities are also discussed on page 77, Chapter 5.)

The children will be thinking about colours for the backgrounds and table tops (the in-between shapes). With this in mind I have found it helpful to provide a collection of differently coloured materials pinned lightly on to a piece of fibre board. Most scraps can be plain in colour, lime greens and clear yellows, different pinks, lilac and turquoise; with perhaps some striped or simply patterned materials interspersed. These can be placed with the stripes running sometimes vertically, sometimes horizontally, the stripes themselves varying in width and colour. The whole effect should stimulate ideas and, while none of the colours or patterns need be reproduced exactly, the child's interest in colour will be increased. The child who asks: 'What colour shall I put here?' is in particular need of opportunities for this kind of first-hand experiment, to enable him to make decisions that are the outcome of his own responses. Children painting self-portraits, with the use of mirrors, may also find this a pleasant way of trying out various background possibilities, moving about and seeing themselves reflected in front of the different colours.

Groups of many commonplace things could be introduced in this way, attractive in themselves, though not in an arty sense. In No. 6 the two baskets, borrowed from a greengrocer, were the largest shapes in our big fruit group. I had often noticed these baskets in a shop window and found the owner willing to lend them for a day or so. They provided a good basis; an inexpensive pineapple and a small melon, together with numerous other fruits (bought with an eye to their shape, size, texture and colour) added to the interest.

They were all put on a rather low table—the floor would also have been suitable—so that the fruit was seen almost in plan, unlike the bottles which had been placed on a higher level where their most characteristic shapes would be seen to best advantage.

In this fruit group, individuals again selected and adapted quite freely, not attempting an exact copy from any one view-point. Observation, nevertheless, played a real part in this freedom of inter-pretation. In No. 6, we see how the boy has looked for the charac-teristic shapes and has noticed the relative sizes of the fruit and baskets; he was not very gifted imaginatively, but the group caught his interest (the colour alone aroused his response) and in his picture he used the basic shapes well. Sometimes the unusual, in this case the pineapple and melon, can heighten interest. The children were es-pecially fascinated by the pineapple, coming up constantly to feel its knobbly surface and to compare its texture with that of the other fruit and of the baskets. Perhaps part of its appeal on this occasion lay in the fact that the children knew that at the end of the period they would be allowed to taste, as well as see and feel it.

Whatever the theme, and many possibilities come to mind, the groups need to be presented in such a way as to encourage personal expression. Sometimes the things chosen may, in themselves, be of a kind likely to be dealt with imaginatively. Nos. 62, 63 and 64 indi-cate the range and flexibility of interpretation we might hope to see coming from the same basic material.

The theme, illustrated in No. 61, was one of 'volume and space'. The objects in the group were all everyday things: boxes of different sizes and proportions, cardboard cylinders and drums, cubes and rectangular blocks. Many had been painted white. Combined with these solid forms were things in which the surfaces were broken up in various ways, such as interlocking, right-angled cardboard grids (from packing boxes), wire paint-pot holders (supplied with Infant school painting-easels), wire milk-bottle containers and cook-ing grids. In collecting the objects for this group consideration of visual qualities, similar to those discussed in relation to most other work, again provided the basis for selection:

1   A range in the scale or relative size of the objects.
2   A variety of form—straight, curved, rectangular, cylindrical, fat, thin.
3   A contrast of solid with perforated or partly 'open' surfaces.
4   The interrelation between solids and voids.

All these features were seen against variously coloured tissue-papers, pinned on to a screen which was placed behind the whole group. The papers were arranged in rectangular blocks, parallel to the verticals and horizontals of the objects. The colours ranged from black to palest blues, pinks and yellows, and were themselves suggestive of different moods or perhaps of certain times of day or night.

This subject led to some particularly interesting work in the children's art club (Nos. 62, 63 and 64). In an introductory discussion I aroused the children's curiosity by asking what the group suggested to them. If a city, then what aspect of a city? Were they interested in the strength of great blocks thrusting into space? Or were they thinking of intricate scaffolding contrasting with the solid masses and tower-like structures? Perhaps some would visualize evanescent forms emerging from the heavy mists of early morning. Or were they imagining the lights from innumerable windows at night?

Ideas were touched on lightly, the aim being to help towards a clarification of visual images. In all these approaches, however, we were careful to safeguard the personal qualities in children's work; for while a certain amount of suggestion is valuable in bringing their ideas to life, over-suggestion can easily stifle individual concepts. On this occasion, the greatest incentive may well have been provided by the evocative qualities of the group itself.

In Nos. 62, 63 and 64 we see that the choice of medium was also important to the children. Colin, aged six years, expressed what he had to say in a very direct charcoal drawing, No. 64. He had no wish to paint, and his detailed line-drawing certainly holds together as a completely conceived idea. In No. 62 Jacqueline enjoyed the areas of colour in the buildings and sky as much as their tall, thin shapes; whereas Paul, in No. 63, became immensely interested in the actual qualities of paint, putting his colour on with a palette knife and greatly enjoying the thick surface textures that he discovered could be produced in this way, He interpreted the theme in terms of a formal relationship of abstract shapes, using strong, primary colours for his very ordered composition. Through some of the characteristics of his own work he became interested in the later abstract painting of Mondrian, in which he could recognize similar qualities.

Once the practical work was launched, I found that photographs of scaffolding and industrial structures and paintings of skyscrapers in New York and other cities provided stimulating additional interest. It so happened that some of us had recently seen the film *West Side Story*, in which the photography, with its far-ranging shots and exciting angles, was also closely related to our interests.

On the whole I prefer to use ordinary, homely things, avoiding 'artistic' objects already too closely associated with conventional still-life painting.

Kitchen utensils have been used as the theme in No. 3. This is a vigorous painting, in which much of the aesthetic interest has again been provided by qualities of contrasting scale and shapes: the heavy solidity of the jug and dish are emphasized by the open detail of the fish-slice and the smaller cooking implements. Here, as in Nos. 69 and 70, the children were recording fairly closely the actual arrangements of groups prepared for them. Nos. 69 and 70 also show the children's response to these everyday things. I remember coming into the room shortly after the class had started working, and wondering, as my eyes caught sight of eggs that had just been broken into frying pans, whether I had mistakenly chanced upon a cookery lesson. A student was taking art with a large class in cramped conditions, in an old type of classroom where desks were clamped to the floor—making ease of movement or rearrangement of furniture almost impossible. But, as often seems to happen in schools where physical conditions are difficult, creative work really counted; the student had been given a free hand, and was fully encouraged in her experiments. In this instance she had prepared the two still-life groups during the lunch hour, placing them on small low tables, so that the children looked down on to the shapes. She introduced the work with half the class at a time, discussing the main points of interest, first about one group, then the other. In both cases there had been a little egg-breaking ceremony, and the children's excitement at these unexpected happenings was clearly revealed in their painting.

Many objects can be used as a basis for still-life painting, provided that the value of a wide range of form, colour, tone, scale and texture is kept in mind. Fish, such as kippers, herrings, mackerel, sprats and prawns, arranged quite simply on plates, pans or newspapers, offer good material for classroom groups. Sometimes it may be possible to arrange the room so that four variations of a theme—or else groups based on four quite separate subjects—can be placed in different corners, enabling about ten children to use each group.

Children may learn much about composition by working in small groups of six to ten, selecting their own still-life themes for painting. They will need to spend quite a lot of time experimenting with possible effects, discriminating between this or that form, size or colour, until, after a certain amount of trial, a final arrangement of objects is agreed upon. The children should be able to place their groups in various positions, for example on the floor, on a chair-seat, or perhaps on a window-sill, so that they become aware of the effects of different view-points. They may sometimes arrange their groups on pieces of hardboard, about 15 × 22 in., a convenient size for them to handle and move about. Children who have been partly responsible for the planning and preparation of their subject matter will be thoroughly interested in the essentials of their theme before starting on the actual practical work.

In all these approaches, the children's personal responsibility in making decisions in matters of selection and discrimination is as important a part of their experience as the actual results they may produce. They should therefore be encouraged to bring things for groups themselves; but, however eagerly they may do this, the teacher will often need to add to these in order to ensure a really stimulating collection. This is especially true if a class of forty, working in smaller units, is preparing groups for painting. A large number of objects will be essential for real selection to be possible.

Many sources of supply are available. Kitchen pots and pans have already been mentioned; other suggestions are: Physical Education equipment, bottles and simple apparatus from a laboratory, plants and gardening tools, games, chessboards and playing cards, musical instruments, mechanical accessories from a workshop, such as bolts, nuts, cog-wheels, springs and chains. In addition to the objects themselves, various pieces of coloured paper (light, dark, patterned, plain) should be available, together with pieces of material (about half a yard is enough). These pieces of material should also be of great variety (ginghams and striped or checked tea-towels are useful) so that the children are offered opportunities of real choice.

Collecting

I imagine that as teachers we must all become inveterate, or at any rate 'professional', hoarders, accumulating material of all kinds. It was probably through the response of the children themselves that I first realized the extent to which a small attractive toy or object, left lying around, could fascinate and arouse an immediate interest. Encouraged by the children's enthusiasm, I found myself acquiring all manner of things and, as together we looked at this or that one, we found doors opening on to countless imaginative ideas.

Although all this was exciting, it was not without certain practical difficulties, for as our stock of interesting objects grew, so too did the problem of storage. We have gradually eased this problem by evolving systems of labelled shoe-boxes, which, when stacked on top of one another, are quite economical in their use of space.

Sometimes just one object shown to the children will suggest a number of associated ideas. The barge-can, No. 54, has often led to a spontaneous interest in barges and canal tugs, in waterways, locks and weirs. Children whose imaginings have grown from this particular starting-point would not necessarily have included the can in their paintings: but, stimulated by it, they have pictured the unloading of boats in wharves, and barges, piled with tons of coal from the pit-heads, chugging along big canals like the Grand Union. In certain districts children recall horse-drawn boats, or remember a local lock or bridge. A few would possibly become more interested in the people of the waterways, seen in close-up groups in the cabin or by the tiller. For each child, as for each one of us, a different idea would be evoked. A similarly wide range of associations can be suggested by numberless other carefully chosen objects, such as the storm-lamp and owl in No. 53, or the small, wooden, Sicilian horse and cart, No. 57.

We emphasize the visual characteristics of all the evocative material we provide in order to excite the children's spontaneous enthusiasm. This means that as well as offering good pictorial possibilities, the objects should be of some intrinsic interest, likely, through their aesthetic qualities, to deepen the children's powers of perception. The objects need not necessarily be expensive, indeed many of our treasures are those that we have unexpectedly found in some small shop or junk-yard. The owl, which I was able to buy very cheaply, has proved to be a recurring source of interest. As its glass dome has long since been broken, children are able to stroke and feel the softness of the feathers. Direct experience of this kind contributes to the sensitivity of their painting.

Included in our collection are several old lamps of different types, a model of a French fishing smack, some small toy boats, floats, corks, nets, ropes and baskets. We also have toy cranes, small model aeroplanes, a model caravan and some Czechoslovakian and Polish painted toys such as roundabouts and dolls, painted wooden birds and carved pinewood fish from Russia. Small German wooden farm-wagons, Chinese paper lanterns and some Christmas tree decorations such as coloured glass birds and fish are much prized.

This looks like the beginning of some rather formidable inventory, but it may suggest the kind of things that can either directly stimulate the children's creative readiness or indirectly provide a general liveliness of visual interest. All children need abundant opportunities to enjoy and assimilate visual qualities that may, in turn, extend their own range of expression.

In Nos. 58, 59 and 60 we see how the 'horse and cart' subject has been interpreted by children of different ages. Anne, six years old, particularly liked the plumage of the harness and also the pattern on the horse's legs and on the cart. After a few moments of concentrated looking, she painted her picture without further reference to the objects, and we see how readily she has incorporated her preliminary observations with her own system of symbols. The horse's legs are as she knows them to be, though she has used the stripes that she saw on the actual hooves, painting these as a pattern over the whole of the legs. She has also expressed something of the feeling of the horse's arched neck and head. The tail, which she did not really see, has been included. In place of the complicated harness she has shown a much simplified saddle, which she saw in her mind's eye as an unfore-shortened, oblong shape; and the intricate decoration on the cart has been modified to the simpler zig-zag, familiar to her through her own previous experience in painting. The free handling of the sky, painted in strokes of various blues, suggests a sense of atmosphere and movement.

The subject also attracted Sarah (nine years old), who was beginning to need opportunities for more exact observation in her work. Her painting as a whole had become rather careless and formless; and often she lost interest before her work was completed. In this painting, No. 59, her concentration on the detailed ornament has perhaps led to a rather over-neat, tight treatment, but, regarded as one of her first experiences in more purposeful looking, we realize how important this stage must have been for her. Afterwards her painting developed well, and she began to express her growing interest in actual things with greater freedom and in more fully integrated compositions.

In Nos. 58 and 59 the main interest has been in the horse and cart; but in No. 60, painted by an eleven-year-old girl, her attention was focused on the human situation as well.

For older children ideas might have been introduced by such questions as: 'To whom might the cart belong? Which country did it come from? What would the climate be like? What kind of architecture? Where might it be going? What kind of clothes would the people wear?' (Books on national costume should be available for reference.)

In our art club a large number of successful paintings have been produced by older children using this subject; 'successful' in that each painting was an expression of a personal interpretation.

The horse and cart are quite small, less than three inches in length; this very diminutiveness of size can in itself be a means of arousing interest. The brilliantly coloured silk Chinese birds, No. 55 (sold inexpensively in many of the bigger shops during the Christmas weeks), are also very small, yet, when presented in certain ways, they can be impelling enough to excite the children's imagination, suggesting a great variety of shapes and colours (No. 56). The crests, heads, ruffs, wing feathers and tails are all distinctive in character and, by stimulating the child's awareness, will encourage him to use his own powers of invention.

In Nos. 55, 65 and 93 the groups have been placed partly on small mirrors that could suggest the idea of water. All these groups were small enough to be placed on table tops of about 14 × 20 in., and they may indicate ways in which certain aspects of imaginative painting can be introduced in crowded classrooms with the minimum of space. Similarly, a small tea trolley, easily wheeled about the room, can serve as a base for such little groups, as well as being useful for displays of books and small classroom exhibitions.

The small group shown in No. 65 is a further illustration of how we might try to set in motion the children's own ideas. In the drawing and paintings, Nos. 66, 67 and 68, we see some of the different levels of response to this material. Children sometimes prefer just to draw, and we notice in No. 66 how sensitively the charcoal has been used. Those whose drawings include a good deal of detail are often afraid of 'spoiling' their work when they paint, and they may well be encouraged to explore possibilities of various drawing techniques more fully. For example, the drawings shown in Nos. 9 and 66 are complete in themselves. Painting such drawings could easily lead to rather inhibited attempts to 'fill in' the shapes, without the directness of approach that should be associated with painting. Some children tend to be natural draughtsmen; others instinctive painters, thinking in terms of broad areas rather than in line. All should, of course, have opportunities of experimenting with both aspects; those with a strong interest in drawing may also be introduced to other media, such as pen and ink, drawing with the brush, pastels, conté, and wax engravings.

CHAPTER 4

Imaginative Expression

I. SUBJECTS STIMULATED BY DISCUSSION

Day to day activities, seasonal interests, and topical events offer promising material for imaginative painting, so long as they are introduced for a specific reason and at a time when the subject will have an immediate relevance. For example, only if the children have themselves just visited the fair are they likely to feel personally identified with its possibilities for a painting. Themes of this kind, should, therefore, be related to the children's first-hand experience.

Fairs, circuses, markets, airports, stations, harbours and seaside places known to the children, are subjects that suggest a range of varied yet related activities, from which the child may select whatever part especially appeals to him. If we imagine a fair is in the town, the children will in discussion quickly build up a general impression of the whole scene. Eagerly they recall the excitement and life, the music, the colour and movement. They describe the people and the many stalls, the gas-flares, the swings and the different kinds of roundabouts, the donkeys and ponies. Talking about it introduces a lively interest, and awakens innumerable ideas and memories.

The problem, then, is how to help in the selection of particular aspects from what could easily seem an overwhelming wealth of material. Without some guidance the children might produce drawings which could become little more than a series of small, unrelated shapes.[1] We try, therefore, through definite questioning and suggestion, to help the child expand and clarify his own ideas. We might say:

---

[1] Drawing of this kind is not the same as 'Enumerative' drawing, which, for some children, is a natural form of expression. In such work a great number of things are included, each rich in detail, but with little conscious correlation to the picture as a whole. The drawings (see Herbert Read's *Education Through Art* (Faber & Faber), plate 16b) may be extremely full and decorative, quite different in character from the rather sparse, disconnected effects that are the result of muddled or inadequate visual images.

'Which part are you choosing for your picture? Will it be one main thing, like the big slide, or a particular roundabout? Whatever you decide on, it will need to be very important; make it a fine, large shape that fills your paper—it may even go off your page. If there are several things, then these too will be so large that you can only just fit them in.

'Will you paint the fair as it is in the morning, before the people from the town have come to look round?

'Some of you were there on Saturday afternoon. Perhaps you will make just one big portrait of yourselves and your friends eating candyfloss or toffee apples.

'John told us about the fair at night, when the lights made beautiful patterns. Perhaps his picture will show the coloured lights of the big wheel making a great shape in the dark sky.

'If your picture is of one of the booths in the evening, the glow from the lights may show up the faces of the people close by, while the others will nearly disappear in the darkness.

'Would dark or light paper be best for your painting?

'Which way will your picture be on the paper?

'Close your eyes, and imagine what you see. Then, when you are ready, begin with the most important things.'

Materials will have been left absolutely ready for the children to start drawing or painting as soon as they see their mental picture. Having planned and organized everything before the lesson, the teacher is then free to be with the children as they settle to work. Some of them may need immediate encouragement in the early stages, after which they are able to continue with confidence:

'.What a fine, large roundabout! You'll be able to show some of the painted patterns on it.'

'I like your start, what lovely shapes you've made.'

'That's a good idea of yours, it should work out well.'

'Let me hold your picture away from you, so that you can see how it is going to look.'

Others will be so deeply absorbed that they need little more than a passing nod of approval; we can imagine how frustrating it is for children to have to break off in order to talk about the work they really want to get on with.

Some will need specific help, and a word at this stage may make the whole difference to the success of their work:

'You've got a good idea there, I do like your slide and people. But aren't they very small? Do they really show up well enough? How does your picture look when I hold it away from you? Are you going to be disappointed if it all looks so lost? Why not start again? We all have to sometimes. Keep the same scene, but make it much larger. Let me know when you've done this and we'll look at it again together.'

This kind of child may need constant encouragement, with many positive suggestions, so that he gains greater confidence in his whole approach. He needs to know that we are genuinely interested in each stage of his work, that his problems are also our problems; his achievements a matter of importance to us.

2. SUBJECTS STIMULATED BY POETRY AND PROSE

Subjects from time to time can be usefully suggested by poems, descriptive prose, or by carefully prepared verbal descriptions. In these the value lies largely in the atmosphere and in the scene suggested by the words; appropriateness of choice can, therefore, hardly be overestimated, and only examples of real worth should be considered.

How often are inferior pictures—of sentimentalized children and animals, for instance—put before a class! I have just come across such an illustration, intended for classroom use, in a teacher's journal. A simpering little girl, dressed in a party frock, balances on one leg as she waters tall hollyhocks (why always hollyhocks?) with a 'dainty' little watering-can. She is tripping along the crazy pavement, at the end of which several birds are perched on an elaborate bird bath. This enfeebled child has nothing in common with the crude vitality of real children—how much more telling an actual photograph would be—and the whole superficiality of conception is a travesty of direct experience. Meretricious values of this kind are only too prevalent, and perhaps one of the first essentials in our dealings with children is our responsibility to introduce and maintain standards.

A poem chosen as a starting point for picture making should have the power to suggest ideas that can be seen as relationships of shapes, movement, colour and texture.

In Robert Bridges's *London Snow*, for example, we find a number of visual suggestions:

> When men were all asleep the snow came flying,
> In large white flakes falling on the city brown, . . .
>
> Lazily and incessantly floating down and down;
>   Silently sifting and veiling road, roof and railing;
> Hiding difference, making unevenness even,
> Into angles and crevices softly drifting and sailing.

The opening lines suggest with economy a complete picture. We can imagine, too, how the next lines, describing the snowfall, could take on particular meaning for children, if snow had recently fallen and they had themselves seen the veiling of '*road, roof and railing*'. The language would help them to respond to the familiar environment with a fresh visual interest, noticing new shapes and colours.

For older children, Thomas Hardy's *Snow in the Suburbs* can offer an even more precise and delicate picture of a snowfall:

> Every branch big with it,
> Bent every twig with it;
> Every fork like a white web-foot;
> Every street and pavement mute:
> Some flakes have lost their way, and grope back upward, when
> Meeting those meandering down they turn and descend again.
> The palings are glued together like a wall,
> And there is no waft of wind with the fleecy fall.

A poem often helps children to enjoy an event—in this case the snowfall—with a greater perception, and teachers may find it helpful to build up their own stock of poetry, so that they have something in reserve for almost every occasion.

Older children may also enjoy John Keats's *Meg Merrilies*, particularly passages selected from the first stanzas:

> *Old Meg she was a gipsy,*
> *And lived upon the moors;*
> *Her bed it was the brown heath turf,*
> *And her house was out of doors.*
> Her apples were swart blackberries,
> Her currants pod o'broom;
> Her wine was dew of the wild white rose,
> Her book a churchyard tomb.
>
> *Her brothers were the craggy hills,*
> *Her sisters larchen trees;*
> *Alone with her great family*
> *She lived as she did please.*

> No breakfast had she many a morn,
> No dinner many a noon,
> *And 'stead of supper, she would stare*
> *Full hard against the moon.*

The lines in italics seem to offer the most promising pictorial possibilities, as they suggest a breadth and variety of shape; whereas the others, with their emphasis on detail, could easily detract from the unity of the whole picture. Thus, when sometimes a whole poem may be unsuitable, certain striking phrases and images can offer a stimulus for painting. One vivid sentence alone can be sufficient, for instance:

> And thou art long, and lank, and brown,
> As is the ribb'd sea-sand.

—from *The Rime of the Ancient Mariner* by SAMUEL TAYLOR COLERIDGE

or even a few words:

> 'The forest's afire'
> —from *October's Song* by ELEANOR FARJEON

For children who are inclined to dwell rather too much on separate parts, losing the feeling of the whole, it can be helpful to introduce a subject purposely simplified by the quality of lighting. Marion Richardson writes: 'My choice of dark, dimly-lighted subjects was deliberate. In full daylight it is difficult to see the unity and coherence of things; each separate object seems to detach itself and call, "Look at me, look at me, I am here". All things are one by twilight. Just occasionally we let a poem give us our picture.'[1] She then quotes Masefield's *Twilight*:

> Twilight it is, and the far woods are dim, and the rooks cry
> and call.
> Down in the valley the lamps, and the mist, and a star over all;
> There by the rick, where they thresh, is the drone, at an end,
> Twilight it is, and I travel the road with my friend.

Again in Walter de la Mare's *Nod*, separate parts could be unified by qualities of light:

> Softly along the road of evening,
> In a twilight dim with rose,
> Wrinkled with age, and drenched with dew,
> Old Nod, the shepherd goes.
>
> And all the birds that fly in heaven
> Flock singing home to sleep.

[1] *Art and the Child*, by Marion Richardson (University of London Press), p. 16.

For children familiar with a country environment, these lines could bring to mind personal memories of just such moments.

W. B. Rand's *Pedlar's Caravan* also provides some possibilities, though these would, I think, need to be developed much further through the child's own awareness. Parts of the poem may lack the clarity of simple visual ideas (for our purpose it is perhaps too anecdotal) but, combined with additional stimulus, it could provide a useful starting point. With visual images in mind, we may decide that the first two verses have most to offer.

> I wish I lived in a caravan
> With a horse to drive, like a pedlar-man!
> Where he comes from nobody knows,
> Nor where he goes to, but on he goes.
>
> His caravan has windows two,
> With a chimney of tin that the smoke comes through,
> He has a wife, and baby brown,
> And they go riding from town to town.

Each of these stanzas gives a clear image that could be expressed through shapes and colours in a painting.

The next lines, on the other hand, have such detailed descriptions that it would be easy for the child to focus too much attention on the many separate items and lose the visual clarity of a complete picture.

> Chairs to mend and delf to sell
> He clashes the basins like a bell.
> Tea-trays, baskets, ranged in order,
> Plates, with the alphabet round the border.

A more general discussion, drawing on the children's first-hand observations and memories of different types of caravans, would help them to form their visual ideas and, by asking questions, we could encourage them to give a 'local habitation and a name' to their imaginings.

A few bare twigs, fixed in some plasticine, could perhaps suggest a setting of a road-side copse where the caravan is drawn up for the night. Using a torch, the children might try out different kinds of lighting, so that for some the idea of a night-scene could come to life. In this way, imaginative expression, stimulated partly by a verbal idea and partly by visual experience, would be developed.

On the other hand, Walter de la Mare's poem *The Scarecrow* immediately conveys a series of complete pictures, vividly expressed:

> All winter through I bow my head
> Beneath the driving rain;
> The North wind powders me with snow
> And blows me black again;
> At midnight 'neath a maze of stars
> I flame with glittering rime,
> And stand, above the stubble, stiff
> As mail at morning prime.
> But when that child, called Spring, and all
> His host of children, come,
> Scattering their buds and dew upon
> These acres of my home,
> Some rapture in my rags awakes;
> I lift void eyes and scan
> The skies for crows, those ravening foes,
> Of my strange master, Man.
> I watch him striding lank behind
> His clashing team, and know
> Soon will the wheat swish body high
> Where once lay sterile snow;
> Soon shall I gaze across a sea
> Of sun begotten grain,
> Which my unflinching watch hath sealed
> For harvest once again.

Robert Frost's *Stopping by Woods on a Snowy Evening* is another poem that could be suggested for seven- to ten-year-old children. The visual picture is so much a part of the whole sense of atmosphere that it allows for many levels of interpretation.

> Whose woods these are I think I know.
> His house is in the village though;
> He will not see me stopping here
> To watch his woods fill up with snow.
>
> My little horse must think it queer
> To stop without a farmhouse near
> Between the wood and frozen lake
> The darkest evening of the year.
>
> He gives his harness bells a shake
> To ask if there is some mistake;
> The only other sound's the sweep
> Of easy wind and downy flake.

The woods are lovely, dark and deep.
But I have promises to keep,
And miles to go before I sleep,
And miles to go before I sleep.

Interest may sometimes be reawakened by visualizing a familiar scene from a new view-point, thus investing quite ordinary things with a fresh significance. Some poems may do this for us. Mrs. Sybil Marshall, in *An Experiment in Education*,[1] refers to Harold Munro's poem *Milk for the Cat*, describing how well it enabled her children to imagine the daily setting, as seen by the cat, providing them with a new sense of size. The following passages suggest similar possibilities:

Through the pale green forest of tall bracken-stalks,
Whose interwoven fronds, a jade-green sky,
Above me glimmer, infinitely high,
Towards my giant hand a beetle walks
In glistening emerald mail; and as I lie
Watching his progress through huge grassy blades
And over pebble boulders, my own world fades
And shrinks to the vision of a beetle's eye.

W. W. GIBSON

Clock-a-Clay[2]
In the cowslip pips I lie,
Hidden from the buzzing fly,
While green grass beneath me lies,
Pearled with dew like fishes' eyes,
Here I lie, a clock-a-clay,
Waiting for the time of day.

While grassy forest quakes surprise,
And the wild wind sobs and sighs,
My gold home rocks as like to fall,
On its pillar green and tall;
When the pattering rain drives by
Clock-a-clay keeps warm and dry.

—from JOHN CLARE

[1] *An Experiment in Education*, by Sybil Marshall (Cambridge University Press, 1963), pp. 98–9.

[2] Ladybird.

Thaw
Over the land freckled with snow half-thawed
The speculating rooks at their nests cawed
And saw from elm-tops, delicate as flowers of grass,
What we below could not see, Winter pass.

EDWARD THOMAS

The Fly
How large unto the tiny fly
  Must little things appear!—
A rosebud like a feather bed,
  Its prickle like a spear; . . .

A loaf of bread, a lofty hill;
  A wasp, a cruel leopard;
And specks of salt as bright to see
  As lambkins to a shepherd.

WALTER DE LA MARE

The whole question of relative scale and different view-points can be further illuminated by introducing children to the use of the microscope, showing greatly magnified grasses, mosses and other minute natural forms.

In Nos. 7 and 8 the children imagined they had climbed high up into the tree, where even the smallest twigs would appear important to them. Both these drawings were free interpretations of a visual stimulus. No. 8 was drawn after the child had looked closely at some squirrels in a case, adapting her observations to fit in with her own ideas. She visualized the tree as it might have seemed to the squirrel, jumping from branch to branch, balancing itself with its tail, moving lightly along the branches.

It is sometimes helpful to suggest that the children draw, rather than paint, perhaps supplying them with a restricted range of coloured crayons. A limitation of this kind can in itself be a means of encouraging the child to explore the expressive qualities of a medium more fully. Nicholas used only black, brown and white conté for his drawing (No. 7).

We had been given one or two beautiful nests, and these we fitted into some small hawthorn branches, placing them against a plain, light colour. The children enjoyed the delicacy of the small twigs and the various scraps woven into the nests, and compared these textures with the solid forms of the branches. They experimented with the conté, trying it on its side, on the edges and on the corners; and each child discovered the best ways to use it. In No. 8 we see a spontaneous, vigorous drawing, in which observation and symbolism are closely merged. Some of the older children, on the other hand, made much more of the nests, and recorded the intricate detail with a loving attention.

In order to avoid smudged drawings we have found it useful to fix the work from time to time, whilst it is actually in progress. Fixative can be bought in pressurized drums, so that the teacher can easily and quickly spray the drawings as he moves about the room (see Appendix B).

Many of the splendid Biblical stories can be a source of great inspiration. 'Jonah and the Whale', 'The Flood' and parts of the book of Revelation are just a few examples. The painter of 'The Flood' (No. 50), a ten-year-old girl, must have been stirred by the powerful description to have communicated her own feelings so expressively.

And the waters prevailed exceedingly upon the earth; and all the high hills, that were under the whole heaven, were covered. Fifteen cubits upward did the waters prevail; and the mountains were covered. And all flesh died that moved on the earth, both of fowl, and of cattle, and of beast, and of every creeping thing that creepeth upon the earth, and every man.

Genesis VII, 19–21

The very language suggests a broad visual conception, concerning issues of life, death and calamity, and it is this feeling, rather than an emphasis on narrative, that is brought out movingly in the painting. We too feel the vulnerability of the people and the sense of disaster.

Or to take another example, we see in No. 49 how vividly the violence of a storm may be conveyed through some of the descriptive passages in *King Lear*:

> . . . Where's the king?
> Contending with the fretful elements;
> Bids the wind blow the earth into the sea,
> Or swell the curled waters 'bove the main,
> That things might change or cease; . . .

> . . . Strives in his little world of man to out-scorn
> The to-and-fro conflicting wind and rain.

> Blow, winds, and crack your cheeks! rage! blow!
> You cataracts and hurricanoes, spout
> Till you have drench'd our steeples, drown'd the cocks!
> You sulphurous and thought-executing fires,
> Vaunt-couriers to oak-cleaving thunder-bolts,
> Singe my white head! . . .

King Lear, Act III, Scenes i and ii

Passages of this kind, read aloud and talked about with the children, can conjure up the force of the wind's movement as it sweeps broadly through the landscape, perhaps with the darkness of stark shapes seen against the queer light and colour of the sky. For some, the memory of a particular experience may come to mind. Individual images and recollections are again stimulated by means of a short period of discussion and questioning.

'How powerful was the wind? Was actual damage done? to houses? to trees? How would it feel? Have you scrambled and struggled over rough moorland? Have you been pushed along by the wind or have you struggled against it with your whole weight?'

We try to picture the desolation of remote places, hidden from man, perhaps comparing these with the neatness of cultivated gardens or recreation grounds.

'Can you imagine the hardness of great boulders pushing through coarse grasses and undergrowth? What trees would survive in this bleakness?—trees blasted by lightning? Perhaps their bare branches driven by the wind make dark patterns against the sky?

'Is it a day-time storm or is it thundering in the night? How will you show if it is day or night? Will the brush-strokes help to express the movement of the storm? The sky will be dramatic, and may reflect the fury of the storm.'

Further point can be given to these ideas by producing a number of large stones, flints, lumps of rock and a few angular, bare branches. Close observation of these will suggest a new range of exciting forms. Children should be able to handle these objects, so that they can appreciate tactile as well as visual qualities.

It should also be possible for them to experiment with different effects of lighting, using torches and lamps, directed on to the forms in various ways, dramatizing them through extreme contrasts of light and dark. (See page 77 for another such experiment.) Small groups of children could try out different arrangements of stones,

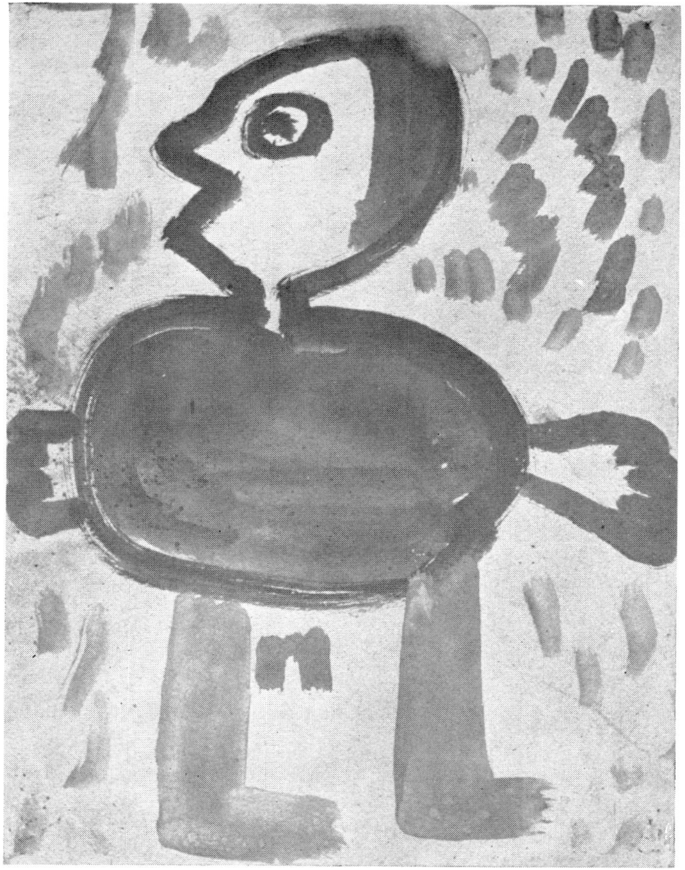

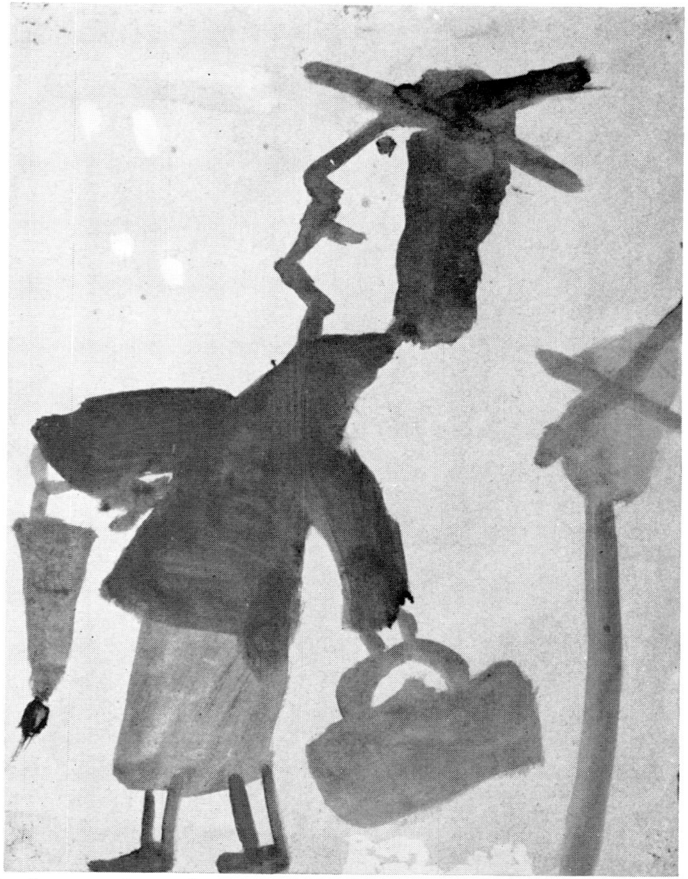

37　　'My Mother', paintings in powder colour, each 18″ × 14″, made in the same lesson by two 6 year old boys working from　38
the same introduction, see pages 13, 16, 78.

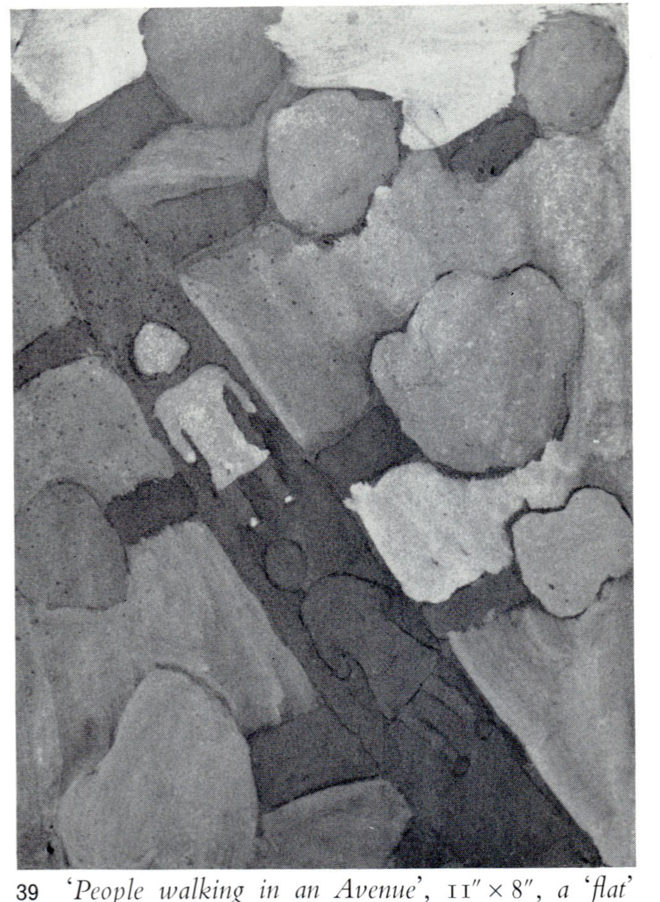

39 *'People walking in an Avenue'*, 11″ × 8″, a *'flat'* painting with a predominance of right angles, by an

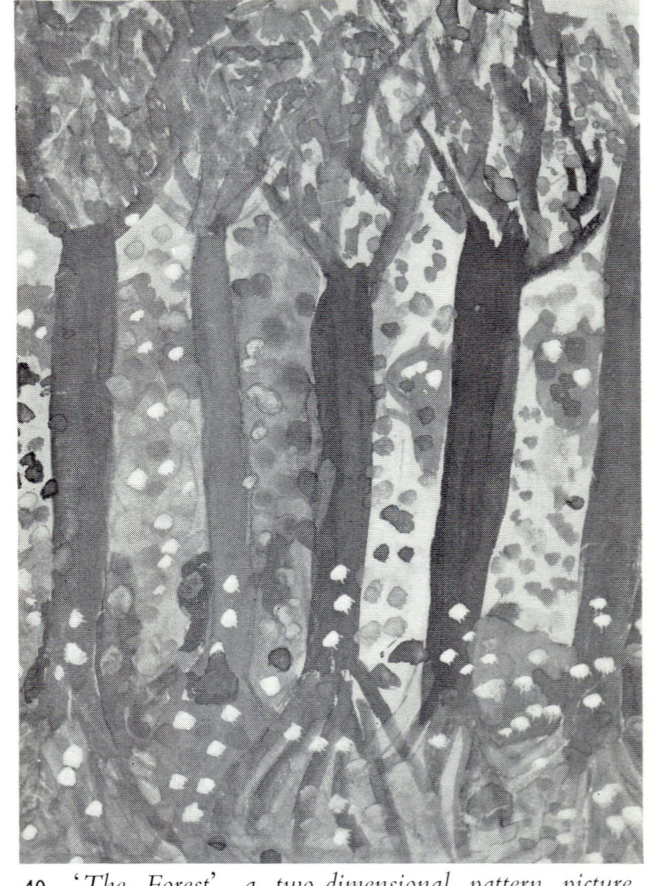

40 *'The Forest'*, a two-dimensional pattern picture, 24″ × 18″, painted in powder colour by an 8 year old girl. see page 23.

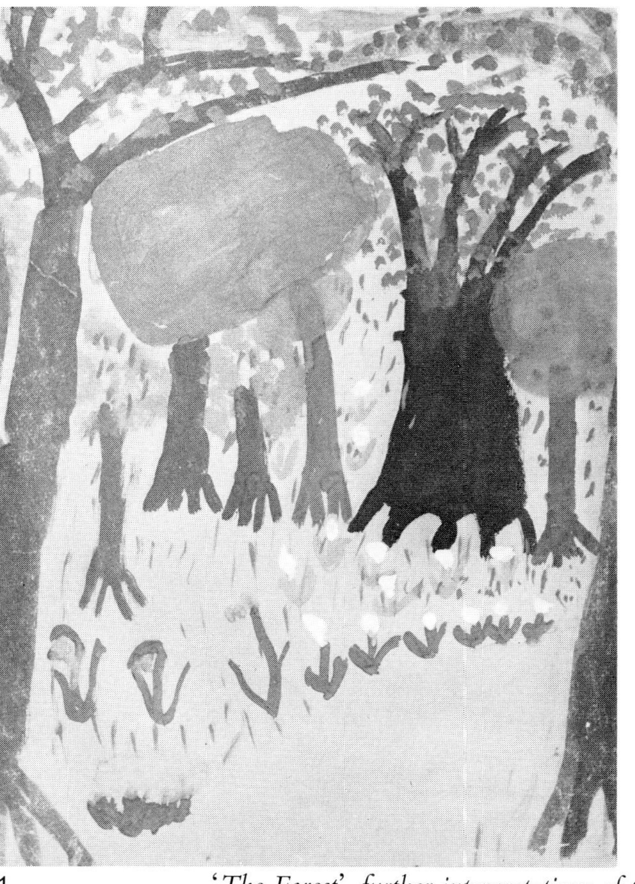

41

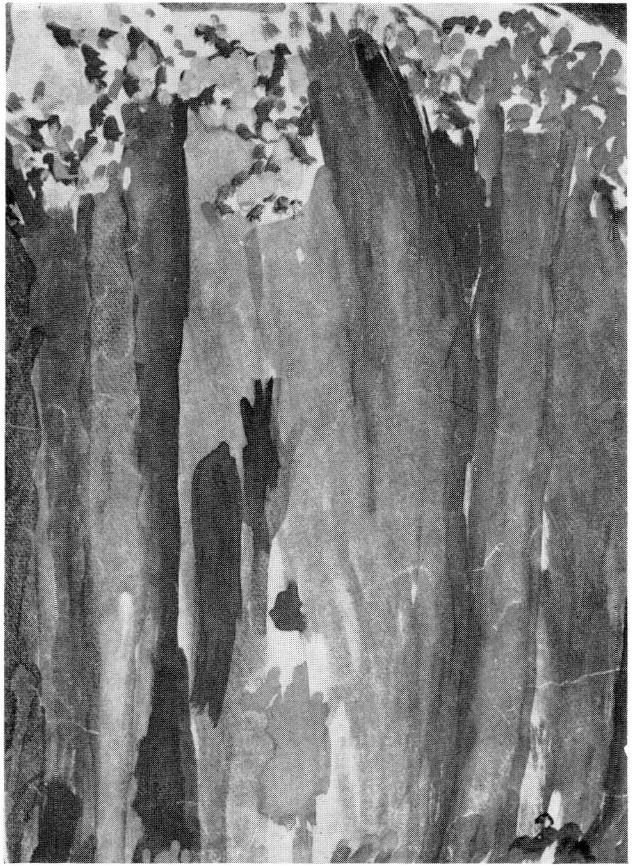

'The Forest', further interpretations of the same subject by 8 year old girls, see page 23.

see page 23

42

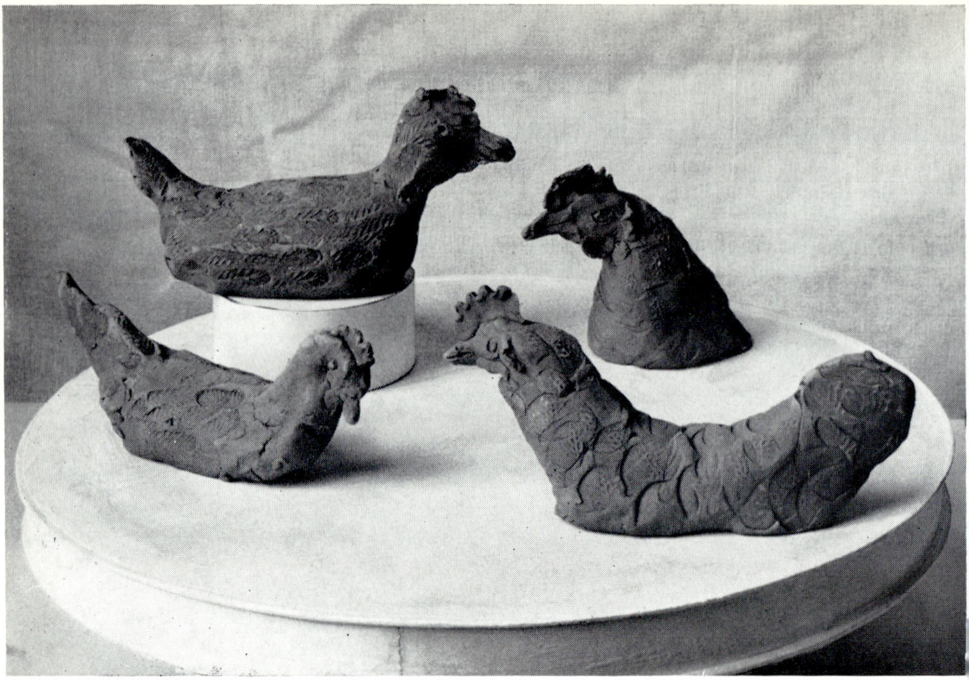

43   *Hens modelled in red clay by children of 11 and 12 years; length of largest model about 6 inches, see pages 85, 223.*

44   *Horses modelled in white clay by 11 year old girls; length of each model about 8 inches, see pages 22, 210, 223.*

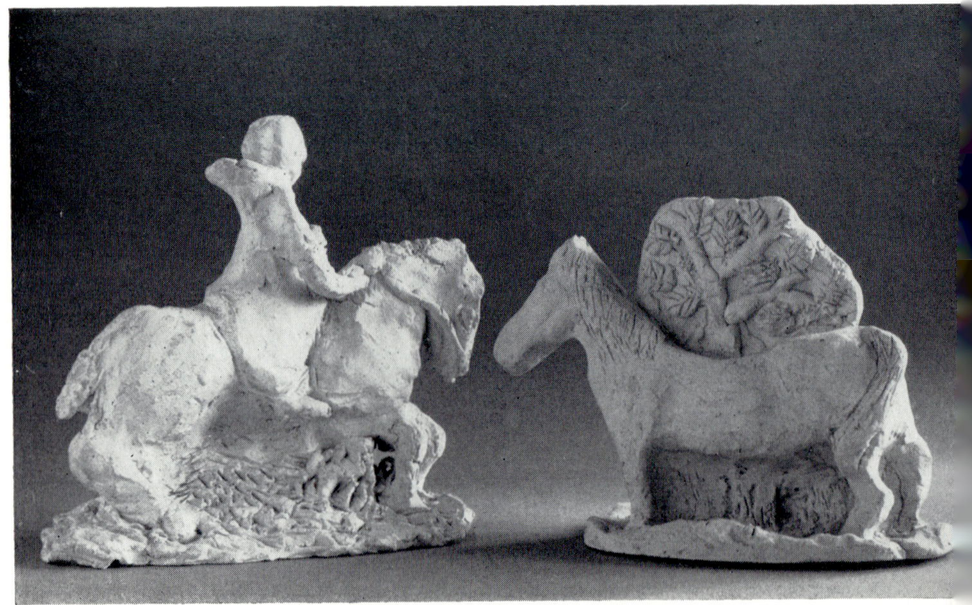

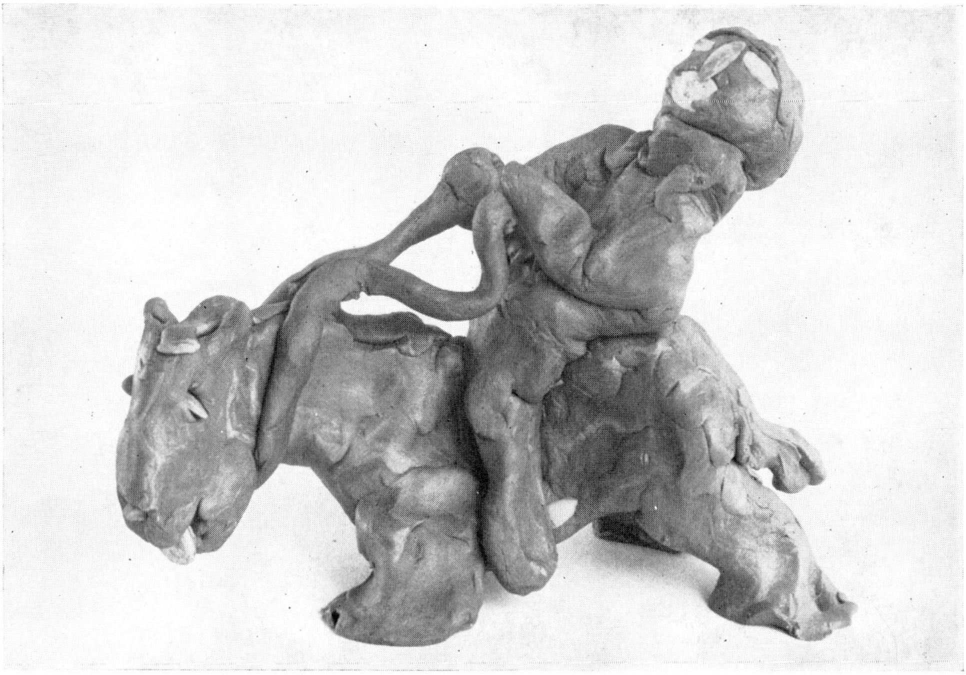

45   *'Horse and Rider', modelled in plasticine by Diana, aged 6; length of model about 6 inches, see pages 22, 210, 212.*

46   *'A Dog looking at a Little Girl who has fallen down', plasticine model by Joy, aged 6; length of figure about 6 inches, see pages 22, 210.*

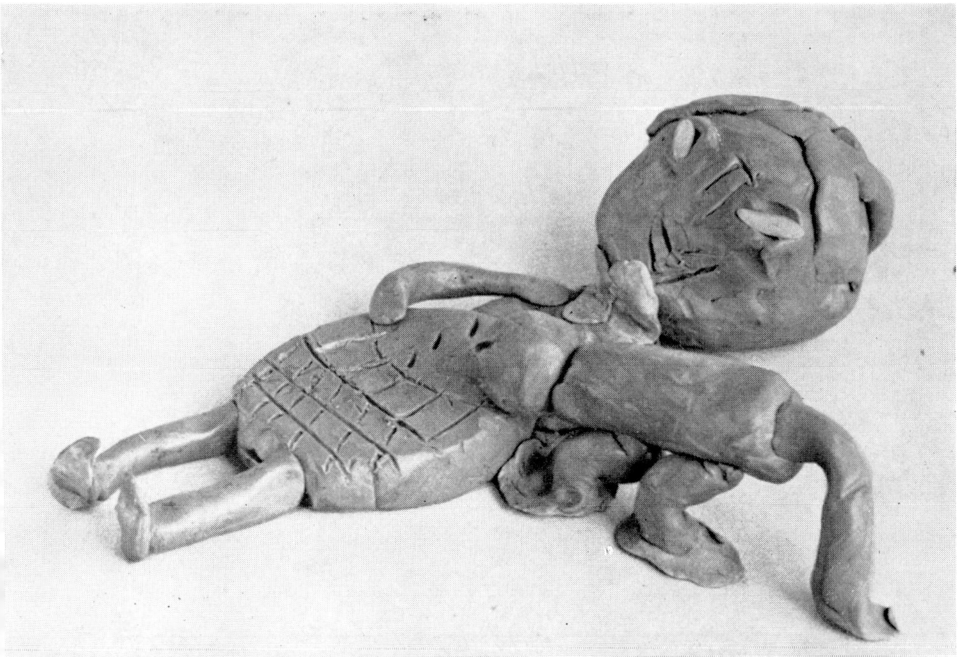

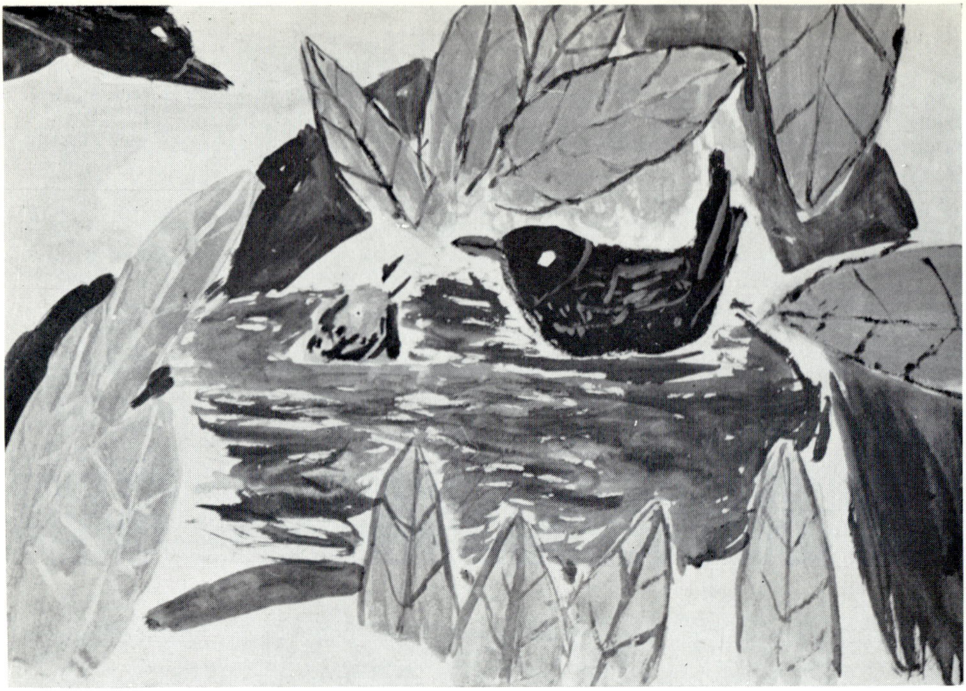

47

'Bird in Nest', *paintings in powder colour, 22″ × 15″, by Keith and Roger, both aged* 10, *see pages* 18, 20, 152, 163 *and* 15, 18, 20.

48

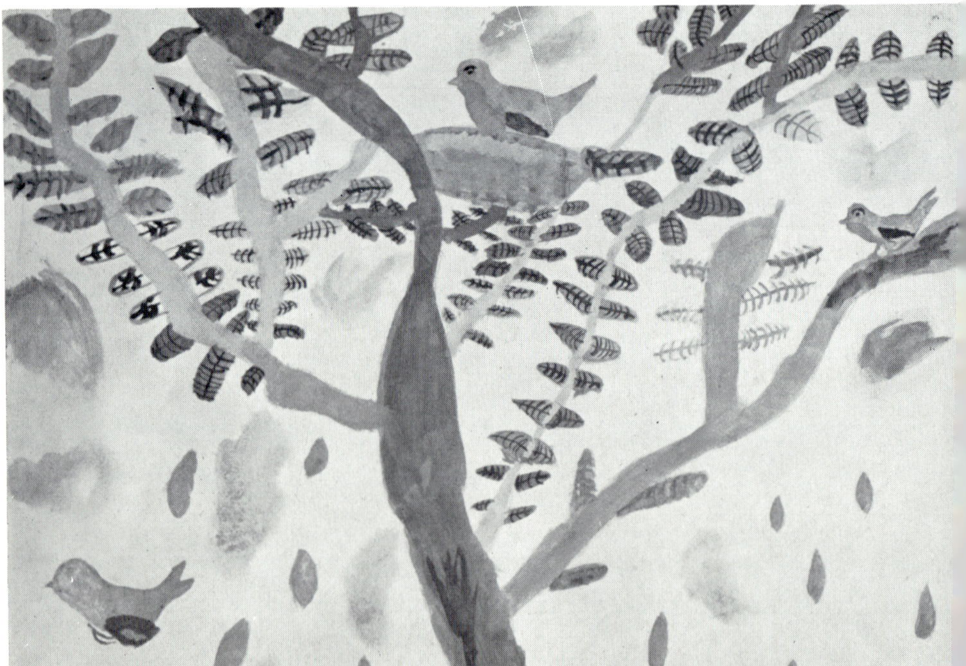

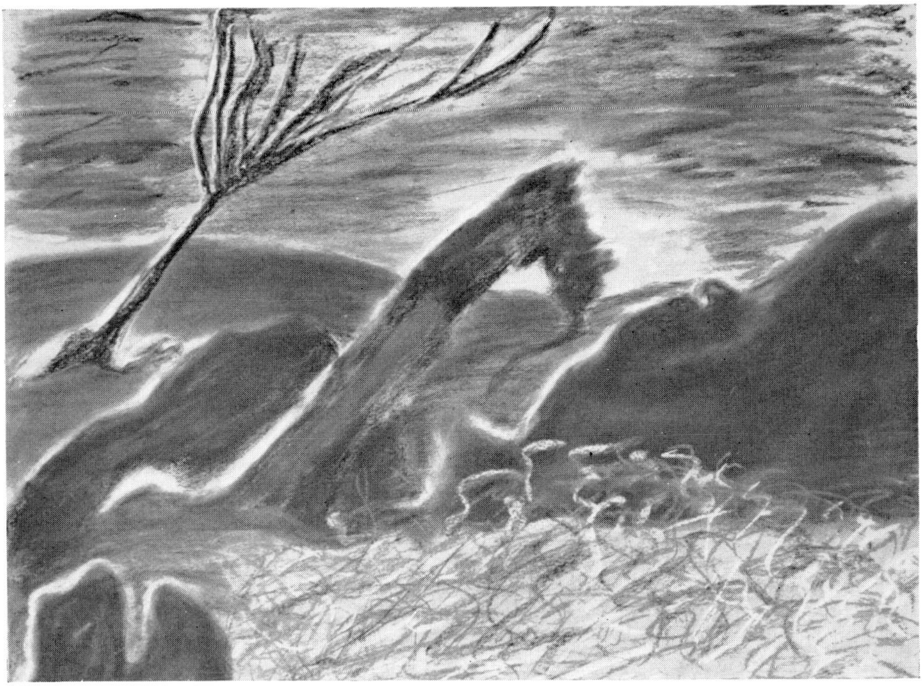

49

Imaginative pictures made after reading the well known dramatic descriptions in King Lear, Act III, scene 1, and Genesis VII, 19–21: 'The Storm', 23″ × 16″, by Philip, aged 11, and 'The Flood', 25″ × 20″, by a 10 year old girl, see pages 51, 63 and 51, 152.

50

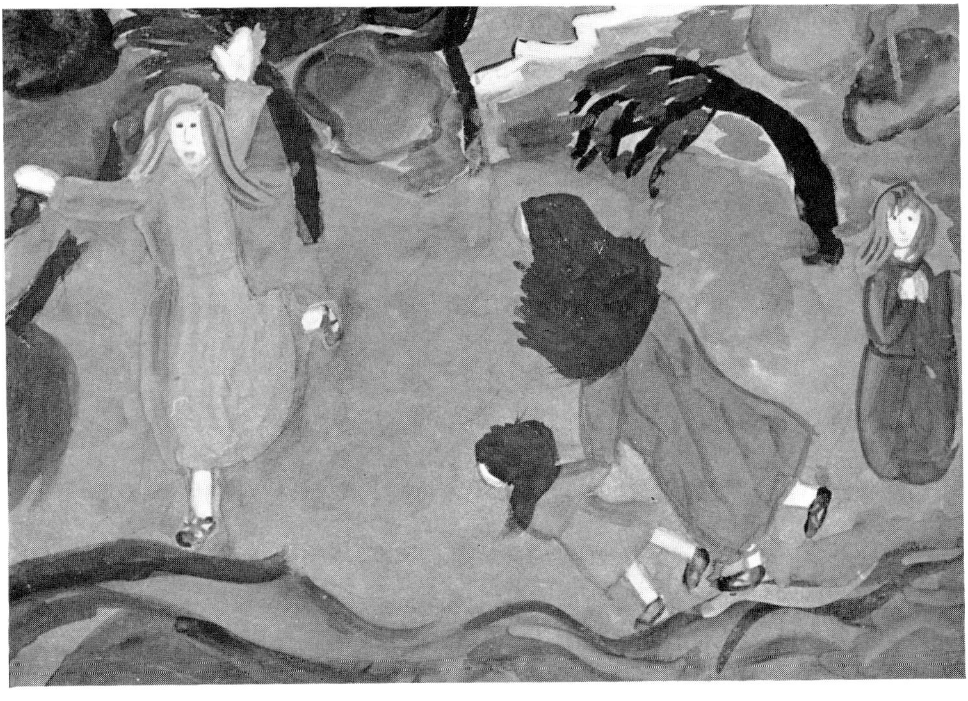

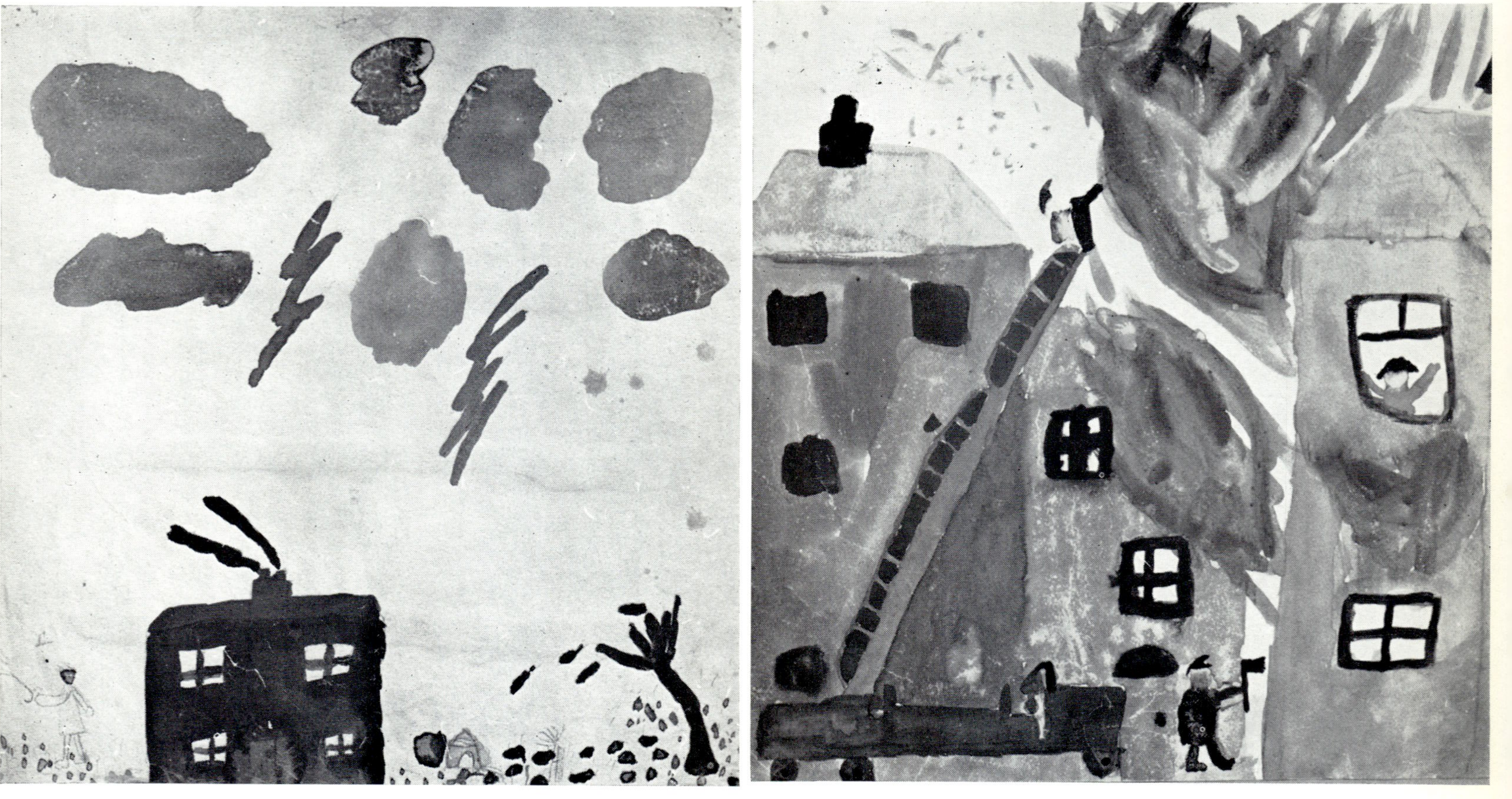

51 *Two paintings in powder colour, each 19″ × 18″, by an 8 year old boy, indicating the development of his work over a period of five weeks, see pages 8, 28.* 52

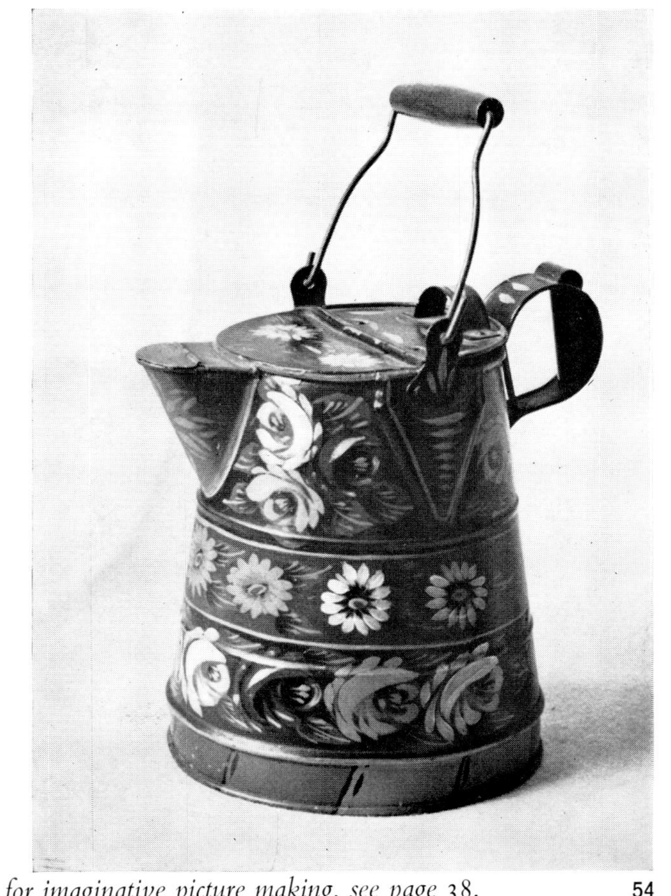

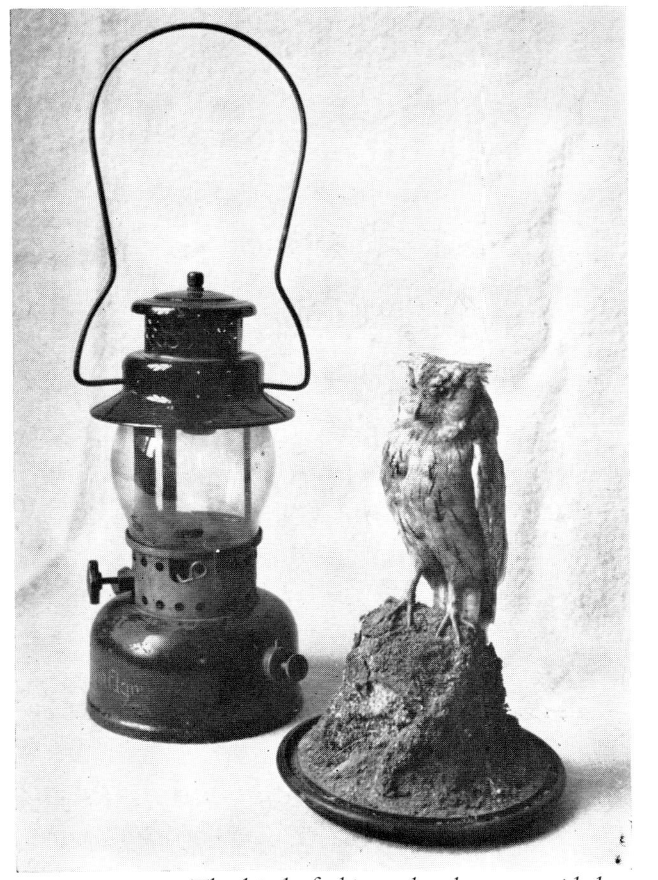

53   *The kind of objects that have provided many ideas for imaginative picture making, see page 38.*   54

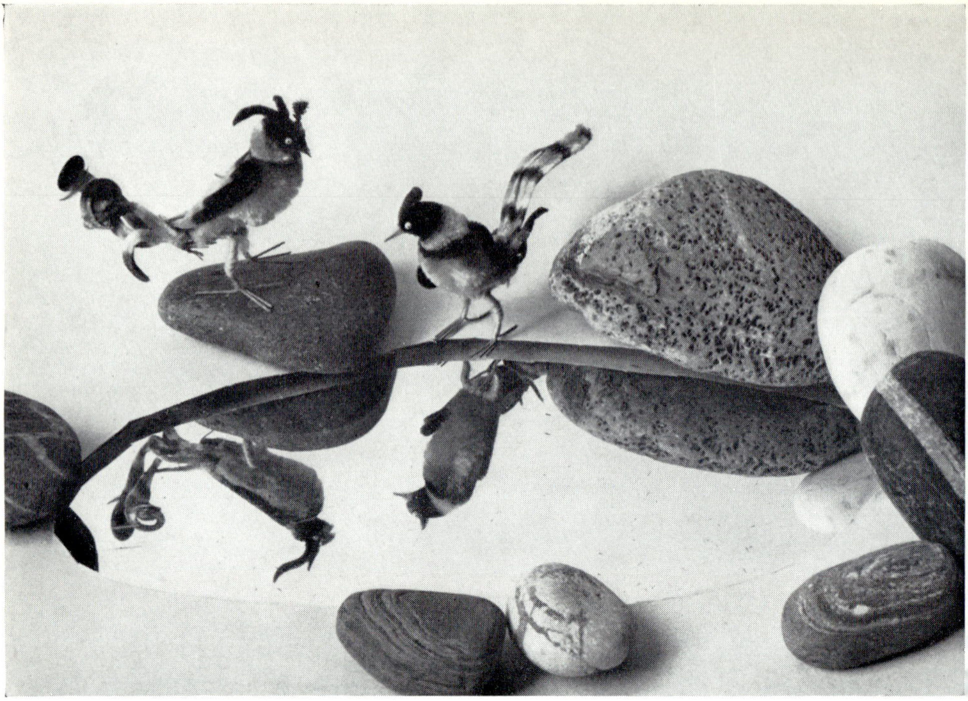

55 *Brilliantly coloured Chinese birds, pebbles, and a small mirror suggest a range of pictorial possibilities, see page 40.*

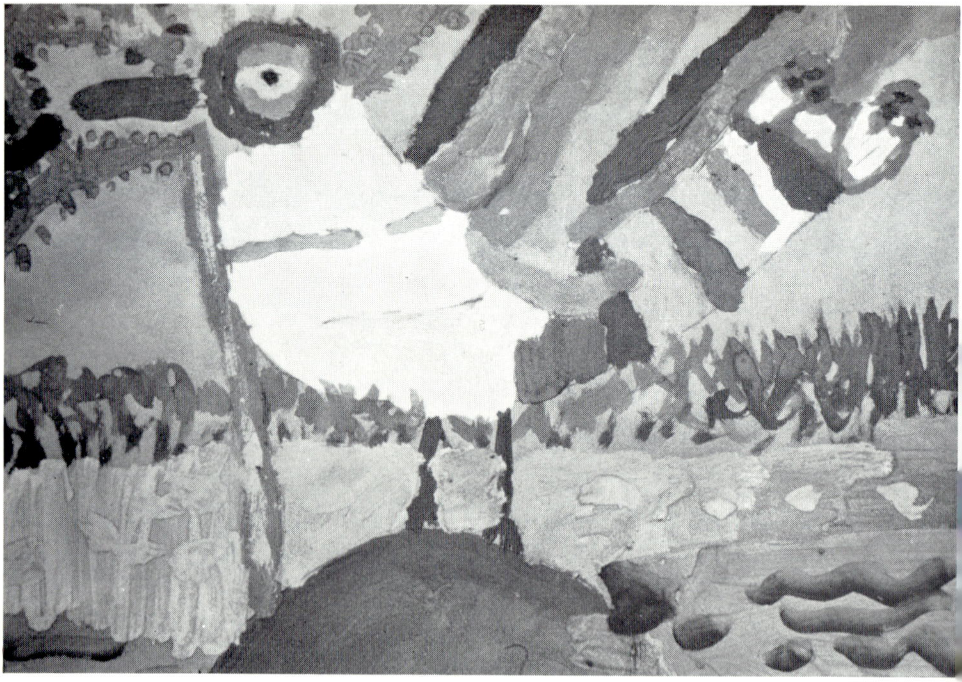

56 *A bird picture, 22″ × 15″, painted by Rosamund, aged 8, after seeing the group above, see pages 40, 163.*

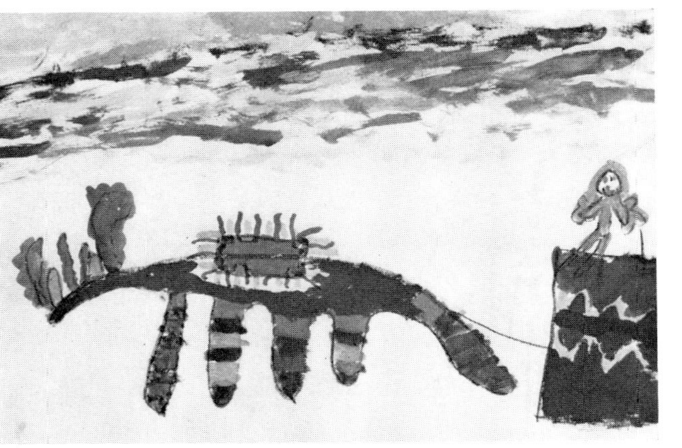

57

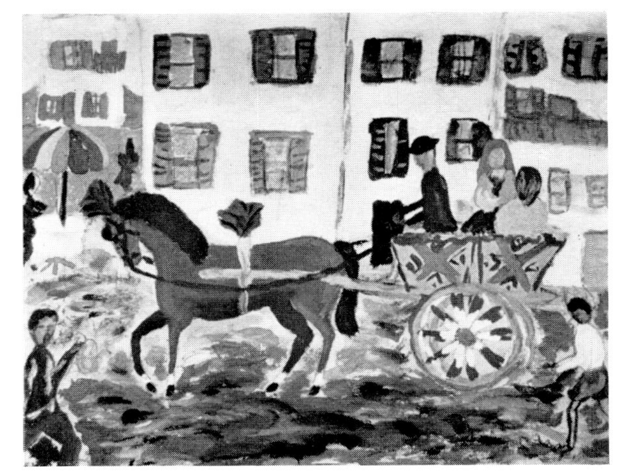

58

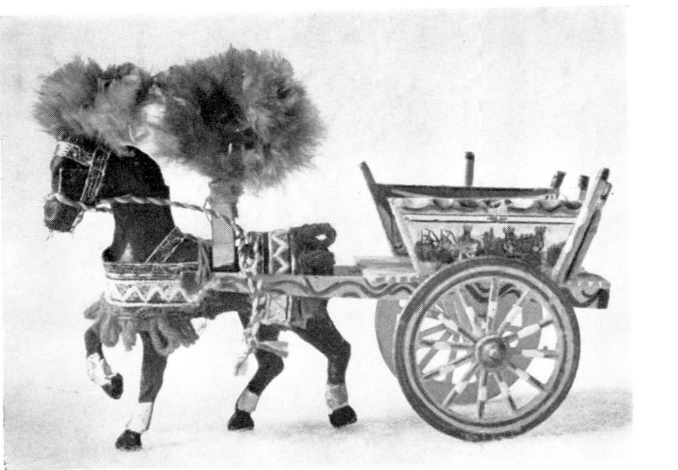

59

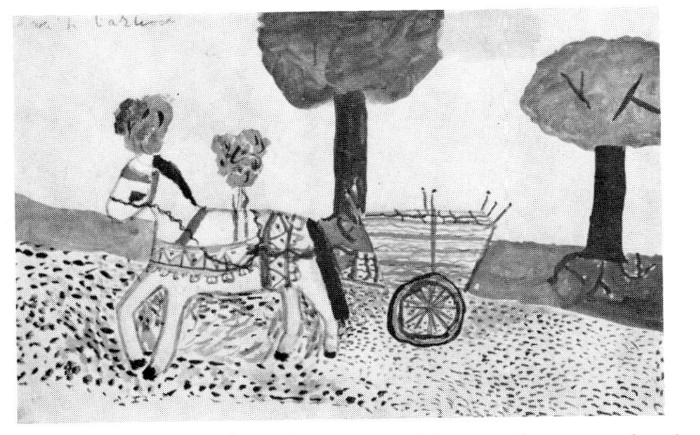

60

Model of a painted Sicilian cart and horse, about 5 inches long, with three interpretations of it painted in powder colour: No. 58 by Anne, aged 6; No. 59 by Sarah, aged 9; No. 60 by Celia, aged 11. All about 20″ × 15″, see page 39.

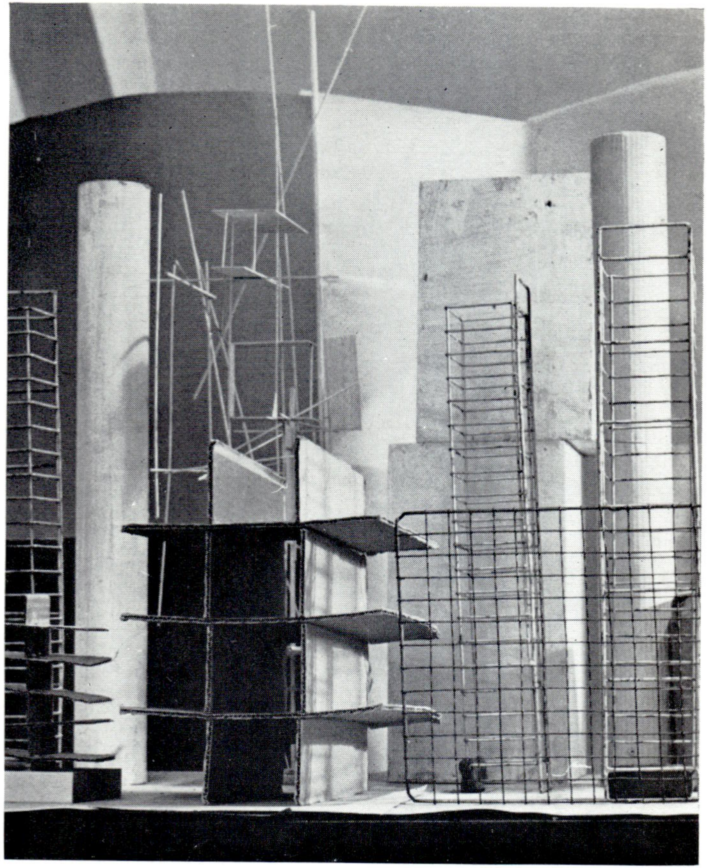

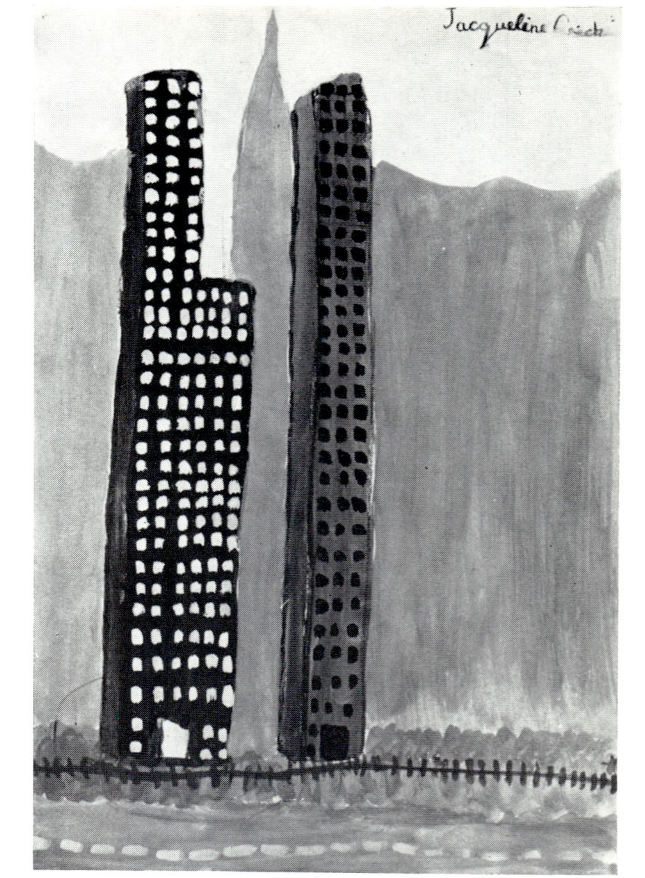

61   *A collection of cylinders, cardboard packings, and wire grids used as a visual stimulus. Height of cylinders about 24 inches, see page 34.*

62   *'City-scape' by Jacqueline, aged 9, a painting in powder colour, 20″ × 15″, suggested by No. 61, see page 34.*

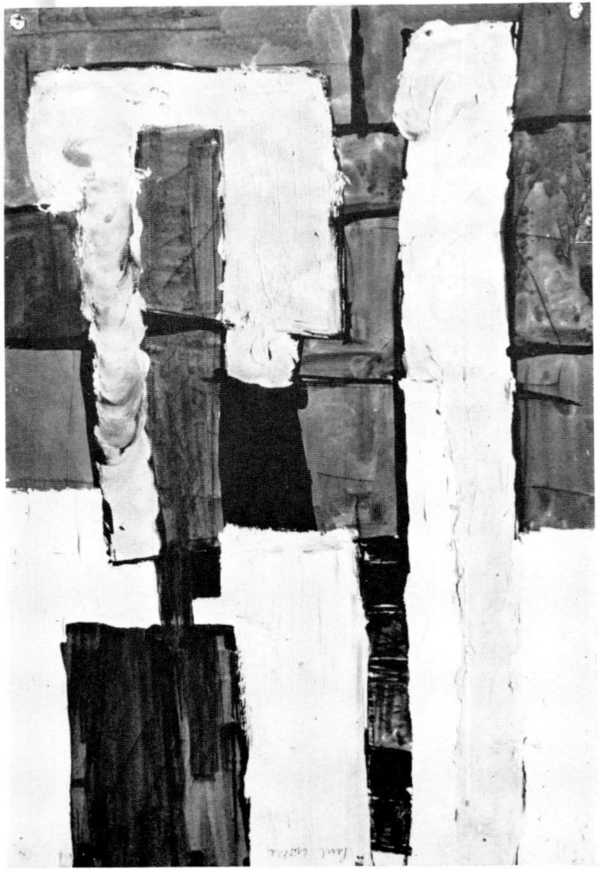

63 *Composition, 23" × 16", by Paul, aged 11, an interpretation of No. 61, developed as an abstract painting, see pages 34, 152.*

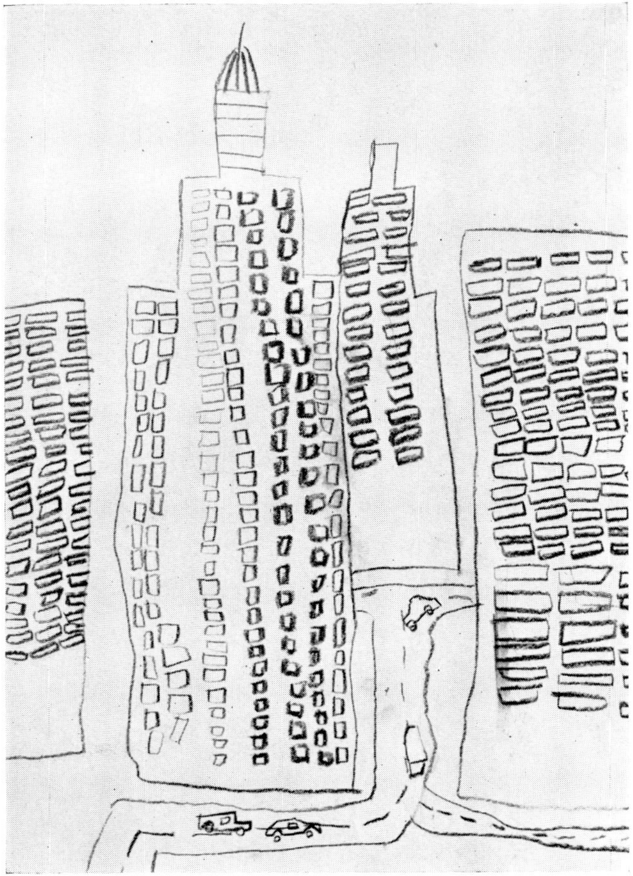

64 *'City-scape' by Colin, aged 5, a charcoal drawing, 20" × 15", also based on the material in No. 61, see pages 18, 34.*

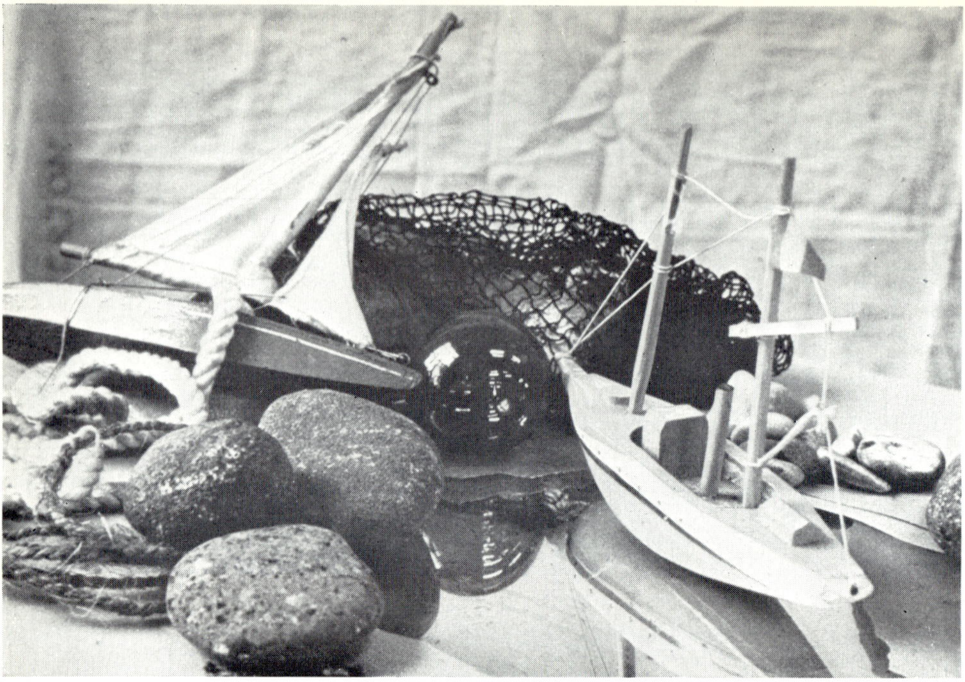

65 *A group of boats, stones, nets, rope and a small mirror, the whole fitting on to a table about 24″ × 18″, see page 40.*

66 *An imaginative drawing in charcoal, 20″ × 16″, by Michael, aged 12, for which he used the group above as a starting point, see pages 17, 18, 41.*

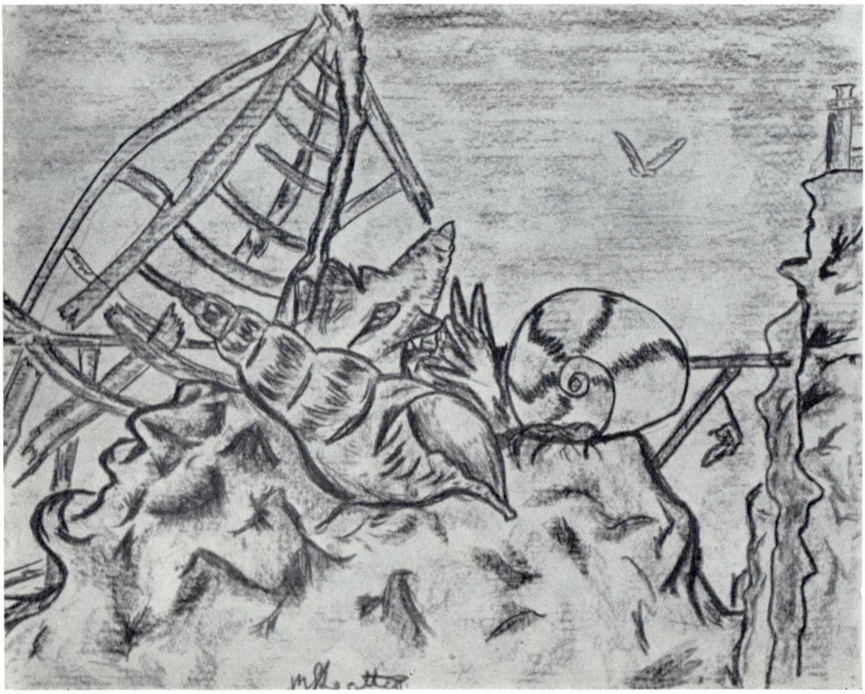

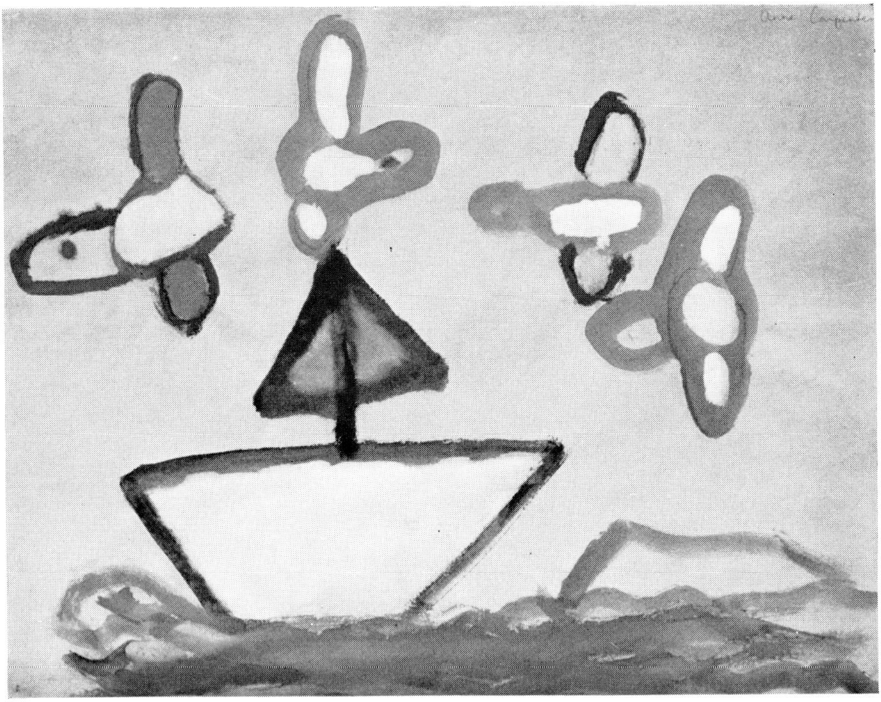

67

Paintings in powder colour, 25″ × 20″, for which No. 65 provided the initial interest, by Anne, aged 5, and Robert, aged 10, see pages 17, 41.

68

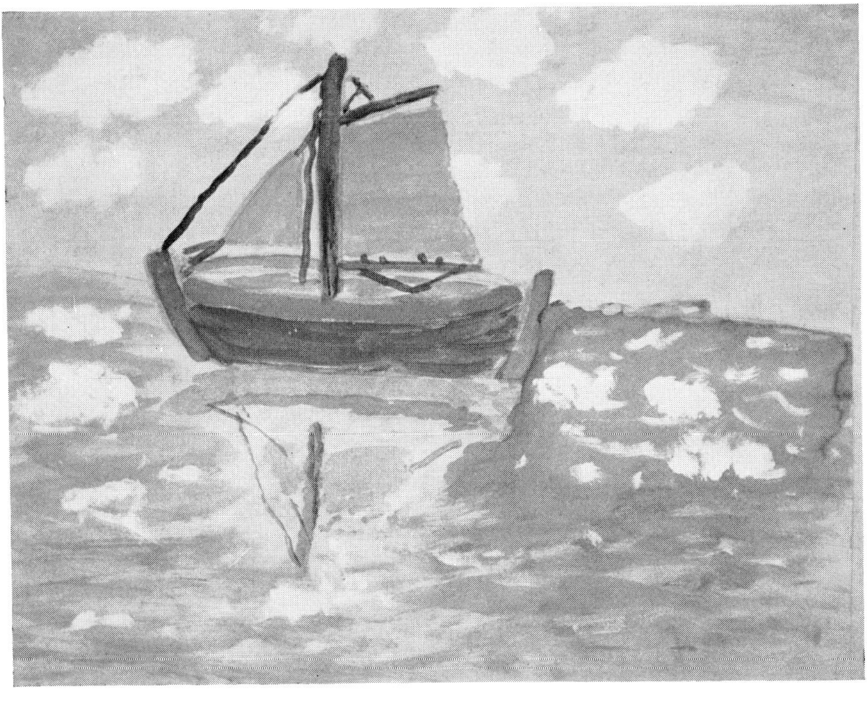

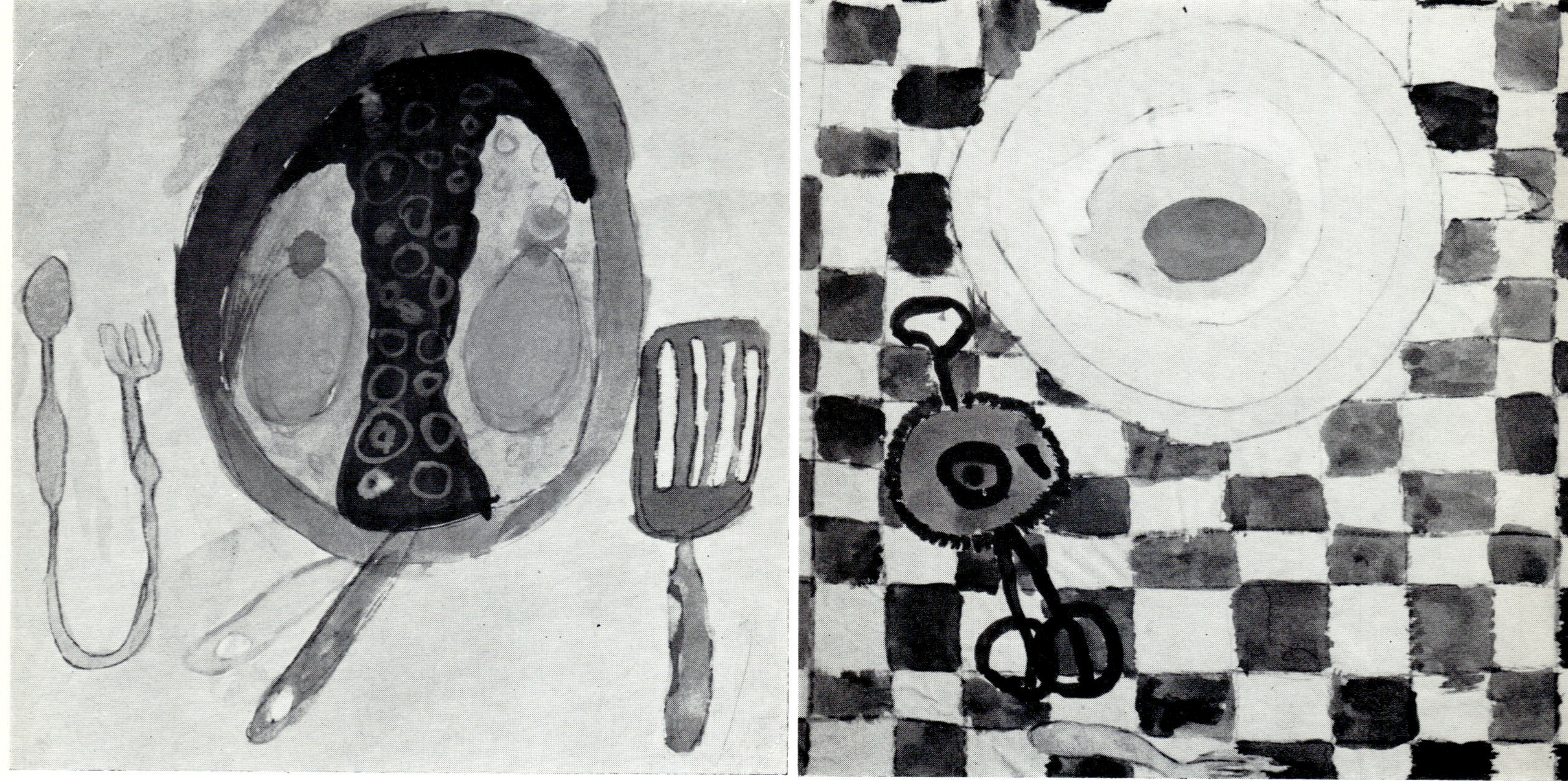

Pictures in powder colour, each 15″ × 15″, painted by 9 year old children from kitchen groups set up in the classroom, see page 36.

shifting them about, seeing the different effects of, say, first one placed in front of the other, then behind it. Different directions of light could be made to play on them from either side and from behind. It could be that even a small stone, perhaps with a hole through it, would suggest weathered forms from which deep hollows have been worn away. Such a stone, seen with a light shining through it, might convey effects of depth and mystery. Through lively, personal participation of this kind the children enjoy identifying themselves with the subject, making it intimately their own, before they even start to draw or paint.

We can usually expect some children to be quick in realizing their own original ideas, possibly with little, if any, reference to the visual material provided. They may prefer to come back to it later on, once their own work is well started. Others, before they can visualize something clearly enough, will benefit by the additional stimulus of this kind of directed looking.

Parts of *Macbeth* also offer good visual stimulus and I remember a set of particularly vigorous, imaginative paintings done by ten-year-old boys and girls, after hearing Banquo's description of the witches:

> *Macbeth:* So foul and fair a day I have not seen.
> *Banquo:* How far is't call'd to Forres?—What are these,
> So wither'd and so wild in their attire,
> That look not like the inhabitants o' the earth,
> And yet are on 't? Live you? or are you aught
> That man may question? You seem to understand me,
> By each at once her choppy finger laying
> Upon her skinny lips: you should be women,
> And yet your beards forbid me to interpret
> That you are so.
>
> *Macbeth*, Act I, scene iii

Creatures that could so startle Banquo must indeed have seemed wildly strange, and the children, imagining it all through Banquo's eyes, and perhaps sharing something of his fear of the supernatural, invented beings far removed from any human form of life. These moved in eerie settings of desolate heathland and were indeed unlike 'the inhabitants o' the earth'. Perhaps equally important, they were unlike the conventional witches of hackneyed illustrations. For with subjects of this kind there is the danger that, instead of reflecting the children's interpretation, the paintings could easily become little more than imitations of pictorial clichés. For this reason a fresh emphasis is needed, and I try to avoid references that, through repetition, have become outworn and superficial. The lines quoted above seem to me all the more likely to encourage original expression than, shall we say, the familiar—

> Double, double toil and trouble;
> Fire burn and cauldron bubble.

or

> And now about the cauldron sing,
> Like elves and fairies in a ring,
> Enchanting all that you put in.

Macbeth, Act IV, scene i

Hearing these familiar lines, the children, unable to break away from memories of stereotyped picture-book illustrations, would find it much more difficult to feel and say things freshly for themselves.

Literature and poetry, such as the Greek myths, the Norse sagas and Arthurian legends, can provide many more sources for painting. Children may also be excited visually by parts of poems such as Tennyson's *Morte D'Arthur*, Dryden's *Fire of London*, Edmund Gosse's *Charcoal Burner*; and, nearer their own time, by much of the imagery found in the writing of D. H. Lawrence, T. S. Eliot and Dylan Thomas. These are only suggestions, and teachers will want to make their own choices from modern poetry. Ultimately what matters is the teacher's personal response. It is hardly practical for him to offer children material for which he himself has no feeling, for unless the writing has meaning for the teacher, how can he convey its essence to the children?

3. VERBAL DESCRIPTIONS.

A verbal description of something we may see or imagine can also provide a basis for picture making.

The name of Marion Richardson is outstanding in this connection. With her particular sensitivity and understanding of visual qualities, she had the gift of investing entirely ordinary scenes with a sense of magic and significance. In her descriptions, each one of which is satisfying in its direct simplicity of language, she conveyed the atmosphere of a scene through a precise indication of visual relationships, with definite suggestions as to relative scale, view-point and composition. So vivid were these impressions in her own imagination, that she was able to communicate them with great intensity.

Although this form of introduction is especially appropriate for older children, it may from time to time be useful with older groups in the Primary school.

Here is one of her descriptions:

. . . As I stood waiting for a tram one evening I saw that the little greengrocer's shop on the far side of the road was lovely as a picture. It was getting dark and beginning to rain, and the shopkeeper had let down his awning to keep the pavement dry. This was important, because most of his goods were arranged on the outside of the shop in a neat and lovely display of boxes and bags. On the left was the door (at this moment the little owner himself standing at it) through which you went if you wanted to buy the more precious things, such as grapes, pineapples, peaches and flowers. In my eyeful (this was my way of describing the range of the picture) I saw right up to the roof of the house, and even a strip of the violet-blue sky above. I saw, too, a part of the shop on the right, next door, and the whole of the dark, mysterious archway on the left of the greengrocer's, which led to his yard at the back. Let us look now at the windows upstairs. These were all dark, except for one in which there burned a lovely little light. I felt sure that the greengrocer's wife was in that room, probably mending his socks. Now look to the right: the blinds here are drawn and the shop shut—all dark and quiet. The pavement is the moving and lively part of the picture. People hurry to and fro. Sometimes they stop, put down their umbrellas and make a purchase. You will not find a single colour for this picture ready-made in your paint-box. The colours are all deep and strange, and you will have to mix them.[1]

In Marion Richardson's book, *Art and the Child*, there is a reproduction of one of 'The Little Fruit Shop' pictures (plate 26), painted by a twelve-year-old girl after she had listened to this description.

I know that teachers have sometimes questioned the validity of this approach on the grounds that children might become too dependent on the teacher's influence, at the expense of their own ideas. I think part of the answer lies in the pictures themselves. If we compare 'The Little Fruit Shop' picture with the verbal passage, we shall find the painting is more of an interpretation than a reproduction, although the framework of the description is implicit in the arrangement of the main shapes and in the subtlety and mood of the colours. These expressive, personal qualities in children's painting were seen in

[1] *Art and the Child*, by Marion Richardson (University of London Press), pp. 15–16, plate 26.

Marion Richardson's big exhibitions held at the County Hall in London, in the pre-war years. Perhaps one of the most revealing features of these exhibitions was provided by the display of complete sets of work. In these sets, *all* the work, that is to say forty or more interpretations of the same subject from one class, were shown. The results were of high quality; they kept to the essentials of the initial description, yet the diversity and individual qualities in the paintings clearly ruled out any suggestion of undue influence.

But, however good the description may be, it is by no means the only basis for picture making, and to regard it in this way would almost certainly lead to an over-reliance on the teacher. If it is wisely used, it can help children (especially, perhaps, those with little inventive ability) by giving them a visual structure and vocabulary, through which their own imaginative ideas may grow. Children will gain an element of security in their work, and freedom of interpretation will be encouraged.

A similar approach to Marion Richardson's description can be seen in the following extract from a poem, *Our Street at Night*[1] written by a ten-year-old boy.

> Night time falls over our street.
> The lamps shine down on the red brick houses.
> One or two weary workers clomp home
> From a hard day's work.
> The blinds are down over the windows
> At the Co-op across the road.
> From the fish-shop a delicious smell
> Steals out into the night air.

In *The Excitement of Writing*, edited by A. B. Clegg, we find a fascinating collection of poems and word-pictures by children, in which they have expressed their ideas with a clarity and sharpness that could also lend vitality to their painting. The teachers' accounts of how these came to be written help us in our understanding of the principles involved and we appreciate how near to each other are the outlook and aims underlying creative expression in English and art.

The actual wording of a description has to be precisely considered, and here I am reminded of a story told by Nan Youngman: A teacher, who attended a refresher course, became interested in the

[1] From *The Excitement of Writing*, edited by A. B. Clegg, with a foreword by Denys Thompson (Chatto & Windus).

possibility of introducing pictorial work by means of descriptions. She prepared one carefully, describing an old lady, sitting by a window, knitting. The whole idea was of course expanded, and came over well; the children really 'saw' the picture. When the teacher said 'You can either draw the whole of the lady or you can do her just to the waist', one particularly literally-minded child in fact did just this and made the lady's body end abruptly in a straight line at the waist, the chair continuing below.

The main forms and their scale in relation to the paper need to be clearly suggested (Marion Richardson's 'eyeful'). But the description should also be of such a kind as to allow the child to develop his unique interpretation. Again, some suggestions regarding colour can be made, but we should be careful not to deprive the child of his own initiative in its use. It is more helpful to refer to the interplay of varying tone values than to actual colours. The final picture will be more likely to read well if there is some balance between paler and darker tones and we can suggest this without fear of destroying the personal character of a painting.

In describing an industrial scene I might put it this way: 'The blocks of warehouses, the tall factory chimneys and the open network of scaffolding and cranes were seen as dark shapes against the lighter colours of the sky', leaving the personal matter of the choice of colour to the individual.

We may try to bring out relationships of patterned areas to plain ones: 'Your beautiful cat, with the different markings on its soft fur, shows up well against the lighter (or darker) colour of the carpet', or, of one pattern related to another: 'The striped markings on your cat look fine against the pattern of the rug'.

While a description should therefore be worded so as to sharpen an imagined subject it should also allow each child full scope to develop his own slant on the theme. One child's industrial scene, for example, might be composed of strange, dreamlike chimneys and cranes that reared up unexpectedly light against an almost black sky. In another painting the chief elements of the description might be used to make a more realistic representation of a scene. In each case the word-picture would have served as a point of departure.

Perhaps the following description, which was made for the older children in the art club (see page 254) may illustrate these points.

You have come upon a high wall which you know surrounds a very old, neglected, but once beautiful garden. There is an opening low down in the wall and curiosity impels you to look through. From this low view you cannot see the sky, only the dense tangle of tall grasses and big leaves that make a deep framework for the garden beyond. This may be a magic garden, in which strange weeds and flowers, different from any you have seen before, are growing twined together by huge, trailing creepers. Undisturbed in this garden are big ferns, making spread-out, criss-cross patterns.

You can see all kinds of flowers and leaves, some heavy and large, some almost square, others long and narrow. Some have smooth edges, others are spiky or wavy. There are straight stalks and curved ones, and clusters of smaller leaves grow from some of the taller stems. Perhaps there are patterned markings on the leaves.

The garden is so overgrown that you can only see a small opening as you peer through the patterns made by these many close-up shapes. The leaves, stalks and flowers are all close together, sometimes touching, sometimes showing little patches of colour between them.

As you are crouching close to the wall, you do not see the stones round the opening. You look at the strange garden again, and what you see through the hole will just fit on to your piece of paper, filling it completely.

This is not intended as a 'model' description—each one would naturally need to be worked out by the individual teacher, with certain children in mind—but I have tried to show how some of the considerations essential to picture making might be brought in.

1. *The Subject*

The garden-theme was chosen because it could be treated freely and imaginatively, either representationally or as an abstract painting. It was a subject likely to convey a sense of atmosphere and to hold the children's interest.

2. *Visual Material*

A stimulating range of visual material could be linked to the theme —to be used by some, if not necessarily by all the children.

a.   Photographs of tropical plants and trees.

b.   A number of actual plants.

3. *View-point and Scale*

In this description the view-point is established by the spectator's— or the child's—position, as he thinks of himself crouching down to look through the low opening in the wall. This limits his range of vision to what he imagines he may see through the opening, thus providing him with the basis of a composition. The whole description directs his attention to this area. He does not see the stones surrounding the hole, only the garden within. Because it is suggested that the scene through the opening will just fill his paper he visualizes shapes that are large enough in scale to suit the size of his paper.

As he imagines himself peering through the hole, he sees the leaves, the trailing creepers and ferns at really close-quarters. From this low view-point the sky (thought of as space above and around objects) will not come into his picture.

The plants are described as 'close together', 'sometimes touching', leaving only 'little patches of colour' between their forms. This suggests their nearness and the closely knit arrangement of their compact shapes. These interrelated, large shapes are grouped around a focal area. 'You can only see a small opening as you peer through the patterns made by these many close-up shapes' thus giving a structure to the composition.

4. *Visual Forms*

The description suggests variations of shape and size, that could add interest to the children's paintings. The leaves are 'large and broad', 'long and narrow'; curved shapes are contrasted with straight ones, clusters of small shapes may be seen against bigger forms; the ferns make 'spread-out, criss-cross patterns'; always the visual qualities are stressed.

Much of the experience gained through pattern making will carry over to picture making of this kind. The child who has a wide visual vocabulary will be able to convey more fully the atmosphere of his scene.

Visual perception, with subjects such as the 'garden' theme, can be heightened by using the microscope. Once the children's own ideas are fairly well established, they can be shown various greenhouse plants with distinctively marked leaves, such as tradescantia, begonias and variegated ivy. With the help of a magnifying glass their own ideas about pattern and colour may be extended by looking into the very heart of flowers, or by studying the markings on leaves at really close quarters. Through their own painting children can also become receptive to the work of certain other painters. The 'garden' description could well lead to an appreciation of Henri Rousseau's Mexican tropical paintings.

Organization

The organization of a painting period, in which a poem or description will be used, has to be planned with special care, if the children are not to lose momentum.

1   If there is to be some choice of materials, such as the size or colour of paper, sheets could be left ready to be collected by the children as needed. Similar arrangements are useful where a choice in paints, inks, pastels, etc., is offered. The selection is probably best limited to one or two alternatives at a time. Other working materials and equipment should be given out before the introduction.

2   If possible, the children should crowd round the teacher, sitting close together, perhaps on the floor. With a subject that depends largely on an element of atmosphere it is usually easier to put ideas across quietly in this way than by talking to a class of children seated in formal rows.

3   The general approach is outlined so that the children know what to expect and also to some extent what may be expected of them.

4   Reminders about picture making are touched on: the wisdom of planning the larger areas first, the need to visualize the picture as a whole, and the suitability of their choice of medium for the ideas being expressed, etc.

5   The poem or description is then read clearly enough for all to hear. This may seem obvious yet one frequently meets children in a class who have in fact not heard the introduction and do not really know what they should be doing.

6   A short period follows in which ideas can be discussed, focusing attention on the clearest images.

7   The poem, or parts of it, are then re-read and the children, listening—perhaps with closed eyes—find their ideas taking shape. After this second reading, they choose their paper, return to their places (where the rest of the materials are in readiness) and start quietly, while the first impressions are still complete and unspoiled.

CHAPTER 5

Observation

The need to introduce satisfying visual interests that will delight the eye is an important consideration at every stage of the Primary school.

With Infants the invitation to look, and if possible to touch and to feel, should be implicit in the way all visual material is presented.

In the Junior school it is the teacher's responsibility to think out ways likely to encourage children, as they become older, to 'see' with a growing sense of awareness; with this aim in mind we need to provide them with constant opportunities for direct observation, and for recording what they see in a number of techniques and different materials.

The children's response to their own environment can provide a wide source of interest in their work; the many facets of their home and school setting, the surrounding streets and country are all of particular significance to them. Much of the work at this stage will grow from their interest in people and animals; they will also be ready to study all kinds of natural organic forms through direct observation. Children belonging to a machine age should have, as well, abundant opportunity to discover for themselves something of the beauty inherent in machine-forms and in relationships between man-made objects. A group of cog-wheels may, for instance, be as visually satisfying as the florets of a composite flower.

The following photographs show a range of subject matter introduced by means of direct observation. In Nos. 43 and 71, Nos. 77–82 and No. 115 birds, animals or fish have provided the subjects. Nos. 72, 75 and 76 are drawings and paintings of natural forms and Nos. 85 and 86 are observed from life. Nos. 73 and 74 are examples of studies of mechanical forms.

The teacher's imagination and initiative in planning this work will obviously play an immensely important part, since for the children the value of the work will directly depend on the quality and range of their experiences. Children who have acquired the habit of really searching observation will learn to see the visible world with greater understanding. Many of us tend to look at things superficially, registering only what we expect to see, and it may well be that we shall ourselves become alive to fresh truths as we explore ways of analytical looking with the children.

Any work based on direct observation should be introduced in ways likely to arouse and maintain the children's natural curiosity and sense of wonder. We should also remind ourselves that in all work of this kind our chief concern will be for the honesty of the children's expression rather than for an imposed naturalism.

DRAWING MATERIALS

Materials likely to encourage children to draw broadly and with freedom are recommended. Most children will be able to express the essentials of their subject more readily with tools and media that invite a spontaneous ease of handling and that enable them to make direct statements fairly quickly. An over-careful approach may well produce tight, niggling drawings in which the child is so caught up with unrelated details that he misses the conception of the whole; his drawing will lack coherence, and before long he may lose interest and become discouraged.

Materials most likely to give children confidence in their work may include: charcoal, conté, crayons, pastels and large, soft pencils; inks and stains (neat or diluted) used with pens or brushes (sometimes with the handle-end of a brush), with small twigs or sticks, or with the flat or sharpened ends of pieces of balsa wood of varying widths. Different kinds of pens should be available, coarse and fine steel pens, felt pens, magic-markers, reed and bamboo pens (see page 197). In fact any 'tools' with which marks can be made can be used experimentally.

Through such a range of experiences children become sensitive to the qualities of different materials and techniques. They begin to visualize a subject in terms of a medium and are soon themselves able to select the tools and materials most appropriate to their purpose.

Papers of every tone should be available so that sometimes charcoal, inks and darker colours will be used on a light ground, at other times light crayons or paint will be seen to be more telling on a dark paper, as in the paintings of children holding sparklers, described on page 77. In the drawings Nos. 22 and 26 we see the use of white chalk on dark paper, while the study of shells, No. 75, and the picture of the white rabbit, No. 82, show how suitable dark paper can sometimes be for paintings that are predominantly light in tone. Either powder colour or tempera-block colours may be used in such work, as both types of paint are opaque and cover the ground well.

Examples of charcoal as a drawing medium are seen in Nos. 9, 64, 66, 71, 73 and 74.

Nos. 7, 11, 13, 80 and 85 show the use of white, black and brown crayons or conté; Nos. 21, 27–36 and Nos. 105–108 are drawings made with soft pencils or crayons; while Nos. 8, 11, 49 and 77 suggest the effects that may be produced by using pastels alone. Unfortunately pastels of a good quality are expensive for general use, but it is worth stocking a small supply, gradually extending the range by the addition of a few new colours each term. The photographs bring out the velvet-like textures of the medium, though they cannot show the glowing quality of the colours, which is also a characteristic of pastels.

Further examples of drawing techniques and materials suitable for use in the Junior school are seen in No. 72, a drawing made with a bamboo pen; in Nos. 81 and 115, wax-crayon engravings; in No. 95, a candle drawing, and in Nos. 117 and 118, lino cuts. These techniques are described in Chapter 9.

The teacher must sustain a keenly experimental attitude in order to keep alive creative interest, and children's work should never be allowed to degenerate into a series of undemanding, repetitive exercises.

When presented with subjects that are in themselves challenging, children usually become so absorbed that they intuitively find their own drawing techniques. While we should encourage the use of those methods that come to them most naturally, we should also be ready to extend their understanding of media, by means of occasional demonstrations indicating the scope of different materials and ways of using the tools. This is especially necessary before we introduce a new technique, or when the children have not used a particular medium for some time and need to be reminded of its possibilities.

The preparation of an art lesson may therefore mean a certain amount of preliminary experimenting with materials by the teacher, and much of the success of the work will depend on his own understanding of the media being used. The non-specialist teacher who is willing to do some preparatory work himself, in order to discover the potentials of each fresh material or process, will establish an excellent basis for his art-teaching; on the other hand a lack of such an understanding will inevitably mean that the children's work becomes thin and limited.

WAYS OF DRAWING

Children should be encouraged to use as fully as possible the particular characteristics of each medium. For instance, it may be helpful to show a class of older children some of the ways in which conté, or square-shaped crayon, can be used. On its flat side the conté will produce areas of tone, intensified or modified by drawing with varying pressures. Lines of different thicknesses can be made by using the end of the conté in various ways—on its side for broad strokes, on one of its corners for fine lines. Solid or partially solid areas may be built up by placing lines nearer or farther apart; these can be crossed in a variety of ways with other lines or marks, producing textures of different tones and densities. Continuous lines of the same thickness may be contrasted with lines varying between the full width of the conté and the finest line that can be made by one of its corners, the flowing, unbroken rhythm changing gradually from the broad to the fine and back to the broad. After this, the effect of intermittent, broken lines can be compared with that of continuous lines.

These experiments may be followed by others: a series of textures produced by different kinds of flecks, dabs, specks, spots, dashes and scribble movements, related in endlessly varied ways, sometimes in close, dense concentrations, sometimes in sparse, open arrangements. We may note how the transition from one extreme to the other (that is from the compact to the scattered) can be treated either as a gradual or as a sudden change. This approach to the use of conté, or square-ended crayons, applies equally to the introduction of charcoal, pen, paint and ink, in fact to any medium that may be used (see page 270).

Nos. 7, 8, 9, 66, 71, 72, 73 and 74 are drawings that indicate the range of personal styles likely to be developed in experimenting in the use of drawing materials. Any demonstrations of the use of tools or media should naturally be very brief, merely hinting at some of the possibilities which the children will be able to explore more fully through their own work.

We should also encourage children to discover the different effects produced by drawing with ink or paint on dry, moist or fairly wet paper (again trying out various types of brushes, pens and sticks). They will be fascinated with the chance effects caused by ink running and spreading on damp or wet paper and will become interested in the contrast between softer, blurred effects and the more sharply defined images produced on a completely dry surface. Sometimes they will find that these accidental qualities add to the interest of the final result.

Conté, charcoal, wax-crayons, chalks and other drawing media can also be tried on various thicknesses and types of wet or damp paper. Paper can be moistened by preliminary sponging before the actual drawing is done, or water can be applied with a brush over the finished drawing, or the two processes may be used alternately (in which case it is essential to use fairly tough paper, such as cartridge paper, sugar paper or strong wrapping paper). Some of the softer drawing materials work well when used in this way, producing attractive textures and tones, whereas others may prove to be too hard and scratchy to be satisfactory. Through exploring some of these possibilities children will become thoroughly interested in different surface qualities.

After a brief period of work their experiments can be placed on a table or pinned on to a piece of insulating board, to be seen and discussed by the whole group.

At a surprisingly early age, sometimes nine years or so, children will be ready to look at these different ways of drawing with a keen interest, provided that the atmosphere of the class is one in which each child's contribution and sense of personal discovery are fully respected. But older children particularly—who are beginning to think more critically about their own work—will learn through opportunities of seeing each other's experiments. Their growing appreciation and understanding of techniques should be of real help in extending the range of their own visual vocabulary.

Fundamental to all these approaches is the children's enjoyment of the qualities inherent in materials; they should learn to use and accept the characteristics and limitations of different media and tools, avoiding over-contrived mannerisms.

Experimental work of this kind should be introduced only from time to time and for quite short periods (perhaps ten minutes) at the beginning of a lesson. These 'samplers' can usually be done on fairly small pieces of paper, the size depending on the medium being used. But we should be careful not to think of these first trials as sets of graded exercises that have to be done before the real subject can be tackled. The same elements of investigation and excitement should be implicit in every stage of the work. Although older children, who are about to work in a particular medium, may find a few preliminary loosening-up exercises helpful, they will continue to explore its possibilities in their main work.

A class of ten- or eleven-year-old children may plan to make drawings of plants in pen and ink. Having picked a good variety of flowering grasses, each child selects a small group as a basis for individual drawing. The children then experiment with pen and ink techniques for a few minutes, so that their approach becomes flexible and rhythmic. Soon they lose their fear of making mistakes and the carefree nature of this introduction will help them to experience the feeling of spontaneous drawing. Their attention will be directed to finding out what qualities they can most naturally produce with a pen (or with whatever tool is being used). Although they will not at this stage be directly concerned with the grasses, some of their experimental scribbly pen lines and textures may later suggest ways of expressing effectively their delicate detail. Very soon the children will feel at home with the medium, and then they can more easily translate the essential qualities of the grasses into qualities of a pen and ink drawing. For instance, in No. 72, a study of a Horsetail, we see how the girl's careful observation of the plant has been expressed in terms of a very free, direct use of the pen. Drawings of this kind may be done quite satisfactorily with school pens and ordinary classroom ink, though broader rather than finer pens are on the whole recommended.

Many children of ten and eleven years—and sometimes younger— like to draw in great detail and will appreciate an occasional chance to work on a smaller scale. It is worth noting that even quite small drawings may convey a sense of breadth if they have been approached freely. On the other hand some of us will know from experience how pen and ink work, unless aspects of rhythm and directness are stressed, can all too easily become lifeless, cramped and finicky; especially is this so if children have been encouraged to 'go over' pencil drawings with a pen, instead of developing their ideas through the direct use of the tool.

THE ENVIRONMENT

Sometimes a short outdoor walk, taken near the school during the first part of an art period, can be a stimulating way of seeing and discovering fresh subjects. Wherever the school is situated, in an industrial city or a suburban area, in the heart of the country or near the sea, there will be abundant visual interest in its environment. It may be possible to visit a builder's yard, brick and timber yards, a derelict site, or find a place near the outskirts of a station from which trains and signals and the network of lines may be watched.

I remember such a journey of discovery, with a class of ten-year-old boys and girls, that produced a set of very successful paintings, in which each one was an interesting personal interpretation of images that had been seen and remembered.

The school, situated in a rather poor district, was a heavy-looking old building, with a playground of bare asphalt. Yet in the small streets leading from it the children quickly found much richness of colour and many interesting shapes. Perhaps the grocer's shop at the street corner attracted them—or the pattern made by a line of roof-tops seen against the sky—or a small child being pushed along in a pram, seen as a big shape against a wall of different coloured bricks. They noticed a group of people talking by an open door, with the patterns of the bricks around it making a framework for the people. They saw strange cacti and plants with varieties of leaves and flowers, placed on window-sills, showing up well against the darkness inside the rooms. Patterned curtains, heavy hangings, shorter net or lace curtains all added to the range of interest. A cat seated on a window-ledge suggested a subject for a close-up picture.

When we reached the Botanic Gardens, less than ten minutes' walk from the school, most of the class were particularly attracted by the many birds on and around the lake. Later several children made close-up pictures of moorhens standing or walking delicately on big, floating leaves, the water looking light around their dark, flat shapes.

Some were fascinated by the heavy, powerful trunks of great cedar trees, with patches of paler colours between the branches making a pattern of pale, angular shapes. Back in the classroom the children settled confidently to work, feeling they had something to say, each able to select from his many memory-images something that had particularly interested him.

Before starting out we had had a preliminary talk in which the main objects of the walk were discussed, with an emphasis on what we should look for: shapes, relationships, colours, tones and textures. The children therefore knew they would work on individual pictures when they returned and that they would select one experience from all their impressions, something that they felt could in itself make a good, full picture. Some took small bits of paper and pencils to make quick notes on the spot but most were prepared just to look and to build up a store of ideas from which they could later select.

Stages of Work

The children spent two afternoon periods, each of one and a half hours, on their paintings; it may be useful to note how the timing of the various stages worked out:

a.   The room was prepared and the materials given out during the lunch hour.

b.   Ten minutes: Introductory discussion in the classroom, explaining the point of the walk—how through it the children would be finding their own subjects—what kind of things they would look for—the different ways to look (either up, or down on to things, or at eye-level)—the arrangement and relationship of shapes and colours (composition)—the patterns made by shapes and by the repetition of shapes—the interest of colour (warm, cool, subtle, strong)—variety in the proportion of colours— variety in the scale (relative size) of shapes—variety in tone, that is in the impact and pattern of light and dark—how much a picture might contain—the interest of a close-up—the interest of patterned areas relative to plain areas—the interest in texture generally. By starting with these reminders of pictorial qualities I helped the children to tune in to visual characteristics and to relate these directly to a visual language.

c. About half an hour was spent on the walk. Then the children came back to the classroom and settled to work.

d. A good half-hour was spent on the actual paintings. Some children quickly roughed out one or two alternative compositions on small pieces of paper, to decide with my guidance which idea would probably work out best; others made a direct start on their picture. Children were reminded to block in the biggest shapes first and to use the whole of their paper. Some children felt happier planning lightly in charcoal first, but many began to paint at once, quickly and freely indicating the chief structure of their compositions in a pale colour. In all cases the compositions were shown to me before the painting was developed, to ensure that each child had a sound basis to work on. During this half-hour I was moving about the classroom, aware of each child's work and giving individual encouragement, advice and suggestions. Teaching was going on all the time. Some were advised to paint whole background areas first, and to build on these later; others to start by painting the actual forms and afterwards to work on the background tones and colours in relation to these. The possibilities and problems found in each individual's work thus became our mutual concern, child and teacher together finding the best ways of working.

e. Five to ten minutes were allowed for clearing up and looking at their partly completed paintings, while I indicated how these could be carried further. At the end of this first period the children already looked forward to the next stages of their work.

f. In the second week the children concentrated fully on painting, but only after their interest had been re-established by looking at and discussing several reproductions of outdoor subjects, large enough to be easily seen by the whole class. The examples chosen were varied so as not to over-influence the children towards any one style but served to remind them of the nature of visual qualities before they returned to their own paintings.

g. Grey, blue and soft green sugar paper was available for mounting, and as the children completed their paintings each chose (after considerable thought) the colour that he felt suited his painting best. Each mounted his own picture (using dressmaking pins), after which the paintings were put up and discussed.

It should be perfectly possible for a teacher in these circumstances to give a brief, positive criticism of the work, finding something good in each painting; at the same time making constructive suggestions for improvement. Sometimes, when all the work is displayed, some general weakness becomes apparent which can best be tackled by offering constructive criticism to the class as a whole, with positive ideas that could be kept in mind for their next paintings. Children who know that their work is really appreciated will be very ready to look at their results thoughtfully, discuss the various qualities, and see how these may be developed.

The walk had awakened the children's interest and had made it possible for them to select ideas from a range of material seen primarily in terms of shape, colour and tone. Experiences of this kind will encourage in children the habit of looking, and will help them to appreciate the visual character of an environment.

DRAWING FROM LIFE

We have noted the assurance and certainty with which very young children draw, and how one of the most natural forms of expression is to make a picture of themselves, of 'Mummy' or of some imagined being. Nos. 21, 22, 27–34 and 37 are all pictures of people, and in these we see with what directness children express what they know, in terms of their own symbolism. This emphasis on what is known rather than on what is seen remains a characteristic of most children's work during their first years in the Junior school. In their drawings and paintings of people they continue to use their own forms of symbolism—sometimes in quite elaborate detail—with an unquestioning confidence.

It is therefore particularly sad if, by the time children reach the top classes of the school, this natural buoyancy has given way to uncertainties about their own ability to draw. 'I can't draw people' may become a lasting conviction, and the pathetic request: 'Must we put people in?', will be familiar to many of us. Yet I believe it should be possible to retain children's earlier confidence and build on it as their work develops and changes.

On the whole, children in the upper Junior school begin to see things in a fresh way, and the symbols they evolved earlier move towards a closer approximation with outward appearances; the 'known' is gradually replaced by the 'seen'. Nos. 85 and 86, pictures by nine-year-old girls, indicate this changing vision; each study was intently observed from life. Sketching people can be a satisfying way of meeting this growing interest in observation. We need to remember, however, that in drawing and painting from life—as in every other form of art work—full scope should be allowed for each child's individual treatment of a subject.

In the Junior school, older children are ready to tackle quite difficult, challenging themes if these are introduced in ways which are visually exciting. Too often we underestimate children's ability and range of interest, offering them experiences that provide little creative stimulus.

Drawing from life sometimes consists of little more than children drawing members of their own class (usually wearing school uniform), on paper that is generally of the same size, with a given medium (almost always pencil). After a few lessons offering so little fresh impetus, the work is bound to lose much of its initial appeal. Because of this there is a corresponding falling off in the general standard of achievement. With life-drawing, as with other forms of creative activity, variety in both theme and presentation is essential if the children are to remain involved and enthusiastic.

Variety of Themes and Approaches

Dressing-up, acting, bringing people of different ages and types into the classroom, drawing people doing different things and studying groups of people as well as single figures are some of the ways by which the interest of the work may be retained and added to.

Dressing-up provides an excellent means of encouraging children to see forms and colours with a fresh awareness. It is therefore invaluable to build up an attractive collection of head-dresses, hats, veils, shawls, scarves, cloaks, coloured fabrics, sashes, belts, necklaces and feathers. Such things as artificial flowers, fans, sunshades and balloons will also appeal to the imagination. Baskets are particularly useful accessories, and it is worth while discovering sources from which fairly large baskets of various shapes may be procured.

Children naturally enjoy spontaneous dressing-up (sometimes concurrent work in mime and drama can be linked with their art activities) and will show sensibility and originality in their choice of dressing-up clothes. This enjoyment in the combination of colours and textures will, in itself, help to develop their powers of discrimination and selection.

Quick Drawings

For older Juniors, drawing people or animals directly from life may be introduced by means of a series of quick sketches (each taking about ten minutes) using any of the more sympathetic, softer drawing materials (see page 270). With these the child may freely block in the essentials of a position.

The child who knows that he has only a limited time for each drawing will be more likely to look for the general character and movement, rather than dwell too long on details. As a result the children's drawings will have a vigour and directness often lacking in the more laboured drawings on which greater time has been spent. Through these quick, introductory experiments, children acquire sound habits of observation likely to be useful in their future work.

Plenty of inexpensive paper should be available so that there need be no worry about spoiling it. Carefully trimmed sheets of a good quality newspaper can be satisfactorily used for this work.

Children should soon be able to select for themselves the more successful of their efforts, and with guidance will learn to recognize the qualities that are most satisfying visually. At the end of a work-period the teacher might organize a brief exhibition in the classroom, perhaps inviting each child to contribute one sketch, in this way encouraging the children's personal interest and sense of responsibility towards their work. Light, moveable insulating board, about 4×3 ft., is ideal for such a purpose, enabling the teacher to pin up work easily and quickly.

We should not, however, overstress the importance of the results themselves, vigorous and expressive though these may be. Perhaps the chief value of the work lies in the child's experience in looking, in selecting from what he sees, and in learning to record his impressions confidently.

Subjects and Methods of Treatment

When children are sketching or painting from life the subject needs to have both a strong visual and human interest. Sometimes this interest may be introduced through elements of the unexpected or the less familiar. An Indian friend wearing a sari, or mothers with babies and small children, may be persuaded to visit the class. Someone with a cat, or one of the children with a favourite pet from home, can provide an interesting theme (No. 85). People engaged in everyday occupations, two children carrying a really heavy basket, the school caretaker, someone with a bicycle, or two boys talking together as they stand with their cycles, are other examples.

Further suggestions include a girl brushing her hair, someone eating a piece of melon, playing an instrument, or holding a handful of balloons—this could combine with dressing-up and if the balloons were not produced until the actual introduction of the lesson the sense of surprise and sudden delight could play a valuable part. The possibilities are never-ending and are best suggested by the teacher's and the children's own interests and by any opportunities that arise.

Related Figures

In drawings or paintings involving two or more figures the chief interest is provided by the interplay of the shapes. Children may need help in seeing how the separate parts are related to the whole subject. As they look at the solid forms they should also notice the areas of space enclosed within these: 'What kind of shapes do the people together make? What sort of shape is seen between them? Is it a large shape? Is it bigger or smaller than the people's bodies? Are the people so near together that only tiny spaces are left between them? Can you see the shape made by the bent back of the person who is close to the upright side of the door? Perhaps you will show some of the door in your picture? Or will your people be somewhere quite different?'

If the subject is going to be treated in colour we might ask: 'What colour are the people's clothes? What colours do you see all round them? And between them? Does it look lighter or darker between the people? Are you going to have the same colours in your picture? Or will you use others?'

Such questions will help children, as they look, to relate the different parts to each other and to the whole. An awareness of this interplay between the positive and negative will also have a direct bearing on other creative work the children do, whether it is composing a picture, making a pattern or the construction of a three-dimensional form (Nos. 8, 14 and 112).

Many interesting subjects involving two figures come to mind: children playing a card game, chess, draughts, snakes and ladders, or making cats' cradles. These ideas have an immediate appeal for a class and in each case the figures would establish an area of focal interest in the composition.

It is often useful to direct the children's attention to a specific part. In the subjects just suggested this might be a close-up, filling the paper, of the shoulders, arms, hands and heads of the players, with a chequered board or part of the top of a table forming the base of the picture.

Concentrating on a limited area is one way of introducing good compositions, in that the main shapes will be large ones. Guidance of this sort helps to avoid disappointing results in which small, scattered items are lost in large areas of blank space. This degree of teaching does not mean imposing adult standards. We are not asking the child to draw in a particular way but are helping him to develop his own imaginative expression fully and satisfactorily by establishing some structure of composition and scale of drawing.

When the view-point and scale have been established, the teacher guides the children in looking for the linking patterns and shapes made by the bodies and heads, and the arms and shoulders of the people. An old sheet placed over a screen, behind the players, will help the children to see their subject more clearly, and will prevent it becoming too confused or lost in background shapes and colours. They should be able to see the light and dark shapes easily, noting how these are sharpest where the strongest contrasts of light and dark come and how some of the forms become merged in more generalized areas of tone. Sometimes, however, it is more interesting to see the figures against the chance arrangement of furniture in the classroom. Settings of this kind have an honesty of character which tends to be lost in more deliberately contrived backgrounds.

Some children may be particularly interested in the actual colours, recording them fairly representationally; others may adapt and change them freely, inventing their own, perhaps quite different, colour scheme. Work of this kind can be done with pastel, powder colour or tempera-block colour.

The children will also notice and discuss the importance of the hands in such themes. They may look at their own, and by holding them up, open, against their faces, note how their faces are nearly hidden by their hands. Some such direct realization of relative sizes may again help them to see their subject in larger, rather than smaller shapes.

The children acting as models should actually play the games, even if only for short periods, so that the class can watch the characteristic movements of the dealing and shuffling of cards or of making the moves. The onlookers will catch something of the players' excitement and of the atmosphere of the game.

One way of using such a subject is to let the children watch the group for a short time only, discussing the general mood of the subject, with special reference to considerations of shape, movement, colour, tone, view-point and scale of work. After this brief period of observation they set to work without further reference to the group, developing their memory-images imaginatively. Before the two players start their drawings, they should also have the opportunity of watching other children playing; though the fact that they have themselves been occupied in this way should be a direct help to them in their own efforts.

Recently, when we were using similar themes in the art club, I was reminded of children's readiness to pass into a world of their own imagination by a ten-year-old girl. After watching some of our youngest children playing 'Snap', she suddenly said: 'Can I turn mine into old men drinking in a pub?' This she did extremely well, placing her two old characters, smoking and drinking, in a setting of her own invention.

An alternative way of using a figure-subject is for the children to spend a longer period of time actually sketching the group from observation, making drawings that are complete in themselves. Probably about twenty to thirty minutes will be an appropriate time for each drawing.

Time needed for Drawings

The length of time needed for drawings or paintings will vary with individuals and as far as possible children should be allowed to work at their own pace. Many children will find half an hour enough for a drawing, others will need an hour or longer, depending partly on the way they work and partly on the extent to which the subject interests them. For instance, Josephine in her drawing of a girl with a poodle (No. 85) was so fascinated by finding ways of showing the different textures that she spent a good hour on her work, doing each part with an absorbed care, at the same time preserving the freshness and vitality of the drawing as a whole. On the other hand, the drawing of 'Jason' (No. 71) was one of two studies produced during the same session, each taking less than half an hour. In this drawing a complete statement has been made and any further development of detail would detract from its main unity and direct treatment.

Choice of Materials

If the drawings or paintings from life are to be worked at fully, they will need to be done on a stout paper, such as sugar paper, cartridge paper, or strong wrapping-paper. At the outset the teacher will remind the class of the drawing materials available, several kinds of drawing media having been set out in readiness. The children are then free to choose one out of the three or four possibilities. Charcoal, conté, superchrome-crayons, brush and ink, or stick and ink combined with white paint are suitable drawing media; the possibility of working on damp paper may also be kept in mind.

If the children have already experimented with particular drawing techniques, it can be useful for them to look back at their earlier work, and to consider its qualities in relation to their present theme. This carry-over from one experience to another helps children to appreciate more fully the interrelation of different aspects of creative work.

Another way of interesting children in the materials they will use is to tell them at the beginning of the period that they will be expected to try charcoal for one drawing, conté or superchrome-crayon for another, and that a third should be done in ink, using a brush, stick, bamboo or felt pen; the choice of order should then be left to them.

Some such possibility of choice, within a quite limited field, will help children to become consciously interested in different qualities.

Lighting

Different sources and types of lighting bring out unexpected aspects of a subject, literally helping it to be seen 'in a fresh light'. Certain effects and directions of light may emphasize broader areas of tone. This simplification of form often makes it easier for children to see relationships. Much of the detail will become fused into the general effect so that smaller, separate parts will be less likely to detract from the realization of the whole. Other effects of lighting may reveal the subject in terms of strong, sharp shapes that make quite a different visual impact.

Older children, shortly to move on to Secondary schools, are likely to be especially responsive to different qualities of lighting—its mystery or drama—and will be able to try out various possibilities for themselves. In this way they discover and develop their own critical faculties.

The experimental use of a reading lamp can dramatize a subject (No. 131), or areas of light can be emphasized by the source of light from a window (No. 136). Thus the whole mood of a subject may be influenced by different kinds of lighting. The use of a lighted hurricane-lamp or a candle might have entirely changed the atmosphere of our card-playing models, charging the scene with a new intensity or mystery. Coloured cellophane papers, inserted in transparency holders and used in a projector, may add to the range of this experimental approach.

If it can be arranged, children will like to watch the effect of candlelight on groups of figures or objects, with the warmth of its glow and the strange movement of shadows. We have seen how little is needed to set children's imagination to work, and any trouble we take in presenting things attractively, perhaps by discovering a special slant of interest, immediately nourishes the children's work. Different kinds of light may be shown by comparing, for example, candlelight with the colder light of sparklers.

One autumn, some of the most lively work produced by the children's art club resulted from such an experiment. Groups of children were given sparklers, which they took into a small darkened room. Here they lit their own sparklers with a quiet intentness, closely watching the spraying, darting movements, the little bursts of stars and the tiny threads of light. They watched the effects of light on each other's faces, then, as soon as their sparklers had burnt out, they returned to the studio and started to work. Light chalks, pastels, and dark paper were ready. Much of the children's excitement and intense concentration in looking was expressed by the vitality and sense of light in their pictures, but perhaps particularly by the intricate detail with which they remembered the sparklers. We have also on occasions used sparklers in full daylight, when even without the contrasting darkness, they have provided real inspiration.

Stages in Life Drawing

It should be stressed that these various forms of life drawing and painting, working directly from models, are only suitable for those children who are ready to record—albeit quite freely—what they actually see (children at this stage may be about ten or eleven years old).

Children of eight and nine years will often be ready to look at a subject with interest for a short time only—after which they will use it, to a greater or lesser degree, as a starting point for purely imaginative paintings. At this age they may begin to be fascinated by the possibilities of drawing from life (Nos. 85 and 86).

The youngest children, as we have seen in Chapter 1, express their ideas in a vividly personal language that is far removed from life. Infants will enjoy the stimulus of seeing people dressed up, or of watching animals, but they must be left free to express their ideas of these (if they wish to) in terms of their own symbolism. The robust individuality of young children's imaginative expression is shown particularly well in Nos. 16 and 37.

The two aspects, imagination and observation, may overlap and be closely interrelated. Thus a drawing or painting that was based at first on observation may be developed imaginatively or, in the course of making an imaginative drawing of some character the child may feel a growing need for closer reference to actuality and may become involved in quite deliberate observation (Nos. 15 and 89–92).

Paintings may be at a transitional stage, so that different ways of seeing will be found in one picture. In Nos. 17 and 18, for example, some parts are depicted as they are known to be (the full view of the eye in the side-view face), while other parts are represented with a greater sense of realism.

In our teaching we need to respect these personal attitudes, at the same time offering guidance in matters of general approach and composition.

PORTRAITS AND SELF-PORTRAITS

Teachers are naturally anxious to avoid the dangers of over-teaching or pure instruction, with the result that children are sometimes offered little, if any, real teaching. It is particularly disappointing when, in an art lesson, potentially good ideas fail to reach the children with any degree of success, owing to this lack of teaching content.

With this in mind, it may be useful to outline some of the teaching points affecting a specific subject, such as the painting of self-portraits (No. 86). An equally wide range of teaching material can be discovered in relation to most themes, and should be incorporated in the work, if a subject is to have full meaning for the children, and the treatment of it to afford them an absorbing experience.

Portraits with their strong human interest offer admirable material for picture making; they are also likely to encourage an understanding of good composition, because the children's attention will be focused mainly on a few, big, related shapes.

Working in pairs and making portraits of each other or, with the use of small mirrors, making self-portraits, are both excellent ways of introducing children to the idea of working from observation. The following notes have a particular bearing on self-portraits, but many of the points also concern other kinds of portraits and picture making generally.

Self-Portraits: An Account of a Lesson on Self-Portraits with Top Juniors

EQUIPMENT AND MATERIALS

1 A small mirror, about 5½ × 4 in. for each child. These may be borrowed or can be bought quite cheaply (two mirrors were used in No. 86).
2 Cartridge paper, quarto imperial size (15 × 11 in.)—this allows head and shoulder portraits to be approximately life-size. For portraits including all the upper part of the body, half imperial paper (22 × 15 in.) is more appropriate.
3 Charcoal.
4 A few old, soft rags should be available for flicking excess charcoal off paper.
5 A drum of fixative.
6 Painting equipment—powder colour or tempera-block colours are suitable.
7 Several pieces of patterned and plain materials, or pieces of wallpaper, for trying out different ideas for the background.
8 Some reproductions of different kinds of portraits to introduce an interest in general aspects of portraiture.

9 Reproductions of self-portraits in particular, for the children to look at only when their own work is well started, or for them to enjoy when it is finished.

STAGES OF WORK

1 Discussion, illustrated by a few carefully chosen examples of various kinds of portraits.
The range might include:

a. Portraits and portrait groups commissioned by particular patrons and public bodies for different purposes and places, for example, the church, the court, guilds, the state, public buildings, hospitals, schools and domestic houses.

b. The non-commissioned portrait painted largely for the artist's own interest.

c. The photograph—portraiture to-day—wedding groups, team groups.

2 Discussion, illustrated by examples of the different ways in which portraits may be considered:
Group portraits
Single figures
The full-length figure
The head and shoulders
Front view
Side view

3 The time spent on this general introduction will naturally depend on the age and response of the children. Once an initial interest has been established, attention is directed especially to self-portraits.
The children look at themselves in their mirrors, trying them out both far away and near in order to decide how much to include in their pictures and how large their heads or faces should be in the mirror space. Through these experiments the children become interested in various pictorial possibilities.

4 The teacher then gives a brief demonstration showing a suitable size for the head and shoulders on the paper. Children can relate the mirror-image to their paper more easily if the mirrors and the paper, though different in size, have roughly the same proportions. The teacher may draw in charcoal one or two very simple diagrams of heads, on paper that is the same size as that

to be used by the children. In one drawing the head should be made to look obviously much too small on the paper, while in the other it will fit more comfortably on the sheet, without leaving too much surrounding space. Comparing these different possibilities will help children to see which size is best for their pictures to fit most satisfactorily on to the paper.

Any teaching points (as in this instance the size of the head on the paper) should be made as simply and diagrammatically as possible, without the introduction of detail. Features may be omitted or else merely indicated so as not to suggest that there is any one 'right way' of drawing them. There must be no question of imposing the teacher's personal style on the class. On the other hand, children may be shown the scale of drawing that is expected, so that they can make a confident start, using good-sized shapes.

5 The children then lightly draw the main forms. During this time the teacher moves about amongst the class watching their general progress, ready with suggestions to help individuals in their own purposeful looking, but leaving them free to work out their own problems. A series of questions help the children to look for visual qualities and characteristics:

'What shape is your head? Where is it most curved? Are there some straight parts? Where does your head look widest? How is your hair done? Is it loose? Or have you plaits? Is your hair brushed back? Have you a centre or a side parting? Which side? Have you a fringe? How much of your forehead do you see?'

Children whose work shows a growing interest in realistic representation should be encouraged to examine carefully the things they try to draw and paint so that they learn something of their structure and character. In portraits, for instance, when they study the eyes they will notice, possibly for the first time, how these are usually partly covered at the top by the upper eyelids; this they may compare with the startled appearance of their eyes when they are opened so wide as to reveal the complete circular shape of the eyeball.

The finished portraits may not provide exact likenesses, but if they are based on this kind of searching looking, they are likely to have character and honesty. Although many children will find it fascinating to examine things so closely, this does not rule out the possibility that some—even of the older children—may continue to express their conception of things through a more personal symbolism.

Any drawing which is to provide a basis for painting should be kept broad and light in treatment, without the inclusion of much detail; a general indication painted in a pale colour could be equally, if not more, satisfactory. There are usually, however, a few children in a class who tend to draw so carefully in charcoal that their results are expressive and complete as drawings. While as a rule they should be allowed to work in the way that comes most naturally to them, such children should also from time to time be encouraged to paint straight on to the paper without first drawing, so that their understanding of qualities of colour and paint is widened.

Charcoal, chalk and pastel drawings may need to be sprayed with fixative, so that they do not become rubbed and smudged. Pressurized drums of fixative make it possible for the teacher to fix the drawings as he tours the room while the children are at work.

6   When painting, although there are no hard and fast rules, it is generally best for children to start on the larger areas of the face and head. Rough paper should be provided for trying out different colours. The teacher shows the class how, when mixing a really pale colour, it is easiest to start with some white paint on the palette, adding only very small quantities of other colours to this. Lemon yellow, yellow ochre, vermilion, crimson, as well as a blue and black, should be available for portraits, and a fair amount of white may be needed.

Many children delight in mixing the subtle colours they see as they study themselves in the mirrors; others may use colour quite crudely, keeping chiefly to pure, unmixed ones. Some may tend to ignore the colours they see and invent their own.

Appropriate questions again help to direct the children's interest: 'What is the colour of your face? Is it all one colour? How will you mix the different colours? What colour is your hair? What kind of brown? Is it a very dark brown? Or a paler one? How many browns can you see in the room? Is everyone's hair the same colour or are there variations? If you stroke and feel your hair, is it soft? Is it smooth and straight, or curly? How can you show this in your painting? Are you going to keep to the colours of your present clothes? Or will you think of another colour you like wearing?

Perhaps the colour of a favourite shirt or pullover? Or of a special dress?'

7   When the first few children have finished the painting of the face and head the whole class should stop working in order to consider how the backgrounds can be treated. As well as making their own suggestions, the children can look at a small collection of carefully selected, well-mounted post-card reproductions of self-portraits which have been kept aside to rekindle interest at this stage of the work.

Further questions will again help to bring out the visual aspects of the subject. 'How would a plain colour look? What sort of a colour? Warm or cool? Darker or paler in tone? A contrasting colour, or something merging closely with the present colours of the painting? Would a plain or patterned background be best?'

A collection of pieces of material and wallpapers, covering a range of colour, tone, texture and pattern should be available for practical experiment. Incidental reference to various reproductions will help some children to come to decisions about the treatment of the background in their own paintings; others will intuitively sense what is right for their pictures.

They can use their mirrors also to study the reflection of the colours and shapes in different parts of the room. Could these shapes be used in their paintings? Some of the class may see part of a classroom window behind them, possibly with the shapes of trees or buildings showing through the glass. A few children may more easily imagine or remember a setting. Perhaps they recall a patterned wallpaper at home, or the colours in the wall of a backyard. Others who are less ready to invent will find their personal ideas taking shape as they consider the suggestions and reference material offered in the classroom. The important thing is for children to think of the background as an essential part of the whole picture.

8   In portraits, as in most subjects, it is advisable for children to work from the broader areas to the detail. Some children have a particular feeling for detail and will enjoy developing their painting in this way. Pen and ink work may provide a means of relating detail to a painted basis.

An assortment of smaller brushes should be available, as well as some variety in the bigger ones (flat-ended and round) so that children can select and change their brushes to suit their needs.

9   The interest the children have experienced in their own paintings, can be extended to a wider enjoyment of portraits and painting generally, by means of small classroom exhibitions. These can be selected and arranged by groups of children, either to run concurrently with their practical work or to provide a conclusion to it. Each group chooses a certain aspect as a main interest, collects references and examples, and presents these in an attractive arrangement to the class (or even to the school, if some display space is available).

SUGGESTIONS FOR THEMES INCLUDE
Pre-Christian and early Christian portraits
Portraits connected with the Church
Court and society portraits
Historical portraits
Family groups, guild groups
Smaller portraits for houses
Self-portraits
Portraits of children
Portraits of old people
Portraits of animals, or people with animals
Non-commissioned portraits

Older children in the Primary school enjoy seeing paintings and sculpture done by artists of different countries, working at any time from the prehistoric to the present, and many children will like to find out all they can about some particular aspect or phase of painting. But with children of this age the emphasis will be chiefly on the human and visual interests of painting and we should guard against the work becoming too theoretical in character.

A collection of art magazines, photographs and catalogues should be available, as well as a few carefully selected reference books on the history of art (see page 279). Postcard reproductions can often be bought locally and from most of the larger museums and galleries.

Children who are discovering how to 'see' for themselves will respond to satisfying visual qualities and authenticity in other pictures they see; their own aesthetic standards will be developed and they are less likely to be influenced by the facile mannerisms and superficiality of inferior commercial art.

ANIMALS

Children, with their liking for animals, enjoy drawing and painting them (Nos. 71, 77–80, 82, 85). In schools where pets are kept, such work is easily introduced. The children's first-hand knowledge of the animals will help them to recognize and express their characteristic features with a real understanding.

Drawings based on observation may be done out of doors as well as in the classroom, and the enterprising teacher will try to extend the children's visual experiences by introducing any animals that are available: ponies, donkeys, goats, dogs, rabbits, cats (especially with families of kittens), guinea-pigs, hamsters, hedgehogs, tortoises, hens, ducks and pigeons. Occasionally it may be possible to arrange visits to neighbouring farms, where horses, cattle or sows with piglets may be sketched on the spot, or recorded from memory when the children return to school.

Some children have a special feeling for small creatures and should be able to watch and study these too. Tropical fish, tadpoles, insects, caterpillars, moths and butterflies can provide a source of interest, and a study of these may also link up with some of the ideas on relative scale and view-points discussed in Chapter 4.

An improvised arrangement of wire netting will provide a convenient enclosure for animals in the classroom, allowing them freedom of movement and making it possible for quite a large class to see them easily. The guinea-pigs in Nos. 77 and 78 were observed in this way. Alison's picture, No. 78, shows an imagined family of guinea-pigs, whereas Francesca was interested in making a more detailed drawing of the animals (No. 77). She had held the guinea-pigs in her arms and had felt their compact heaviness, which she then expressed so well in her drawing; we notice too how carefully she has looked at the detail of the heads and feet.

The modelling in No. 43 was the work of eleven- and twelve-year-old children in a County Secondary school. They were academically retarded, and found sustained concentration very difficult. On this occasion the student teaching them had hired two hens which she put in the classroom during the art periods, so that the children's interest was fully aroused and held, as they modelled the birds directly from life. They thoroughly enjoyed feeling the texture of the clay and responded fully to the opportunity of working in three-dimensional form. The results suggest how intently they must have observed the forms of the birds, with the precise and detailed features of the heads, and we can imagine the children's excitement as they experimented with various imprints on the damp clay, looking for textures that would best suggest the pattern of the feathers.

Nos. 79 and 80 are further examples of the kind of work that may grow from the excitement of direct observation. A student introduced a tame rabbit into the classroom and on another occasion, her own sheep-dog. There were over forty children in the class, working in the crowded conditions of an old classroom with the desks fixed to the floor. The student, however, was able to have the animals in the front of the room where the children could just manage to crowd around closely enough to see them.

Both the dog and the rabbit happened to settle quietly, unlike the guinea-pigs which moved about all the time. The rabbit remained on some straw in a coarsely woven basket, while the dog lay in a relaxed, sleeping position. In an approach of this kind, however, it is unimportant whether the animals remain still or not, since each child selects in his own way from what he sees, emphasizing what for him is most significant. It is probably easier for children to express essentials after watching recurring characteristic movements than if they have observed just one frozen position over a longer period of time.

When animals or people are being directly studied, we encourage each child to make his own interpretation rather than to copy exactly. The student who brought the rabbit and dog for the children to study was not attempting to get naturalism in their work—although some children in the class of their own accord worked towards this end, as we see in No. 79. Others more intuitively combined what they knew with what they saw, as shown in No. 80. Once the class had settled to work, a few children at a time were allowed to come nearer for a closer inspection of details, if they felt the need for additional information.

Satisfactory composition in a picture depends to a great extent on a reasonably large scale being used for the main shapes of the subject.

In the pictures of both the dog and the rabbit (Nos. 79 and 80) the size of each animal was satisfactorily related to the size and proportion of the paper, 24 × 10 in. and 24 × 18 in. By using paper that corresponded fairly closely to the actual size of the animals, the children could draw them nearly life-size, ensuring compositions of generous forms.

The animals were seen from many different view-points, from front, side and back. There were also several plan-like pictures. In No. 80, for instance, we note how the rabbit has been drawn as if seen from above, with the edge of the basket making a good, enclosing shape.

Baskets can often be successfully incorporated in animal pictures. The oval or circular forms contribute to the rhythm and compactness of the compositions, and the woven textures add interest. Sometimes the teacher may with advantage give a quick demonstration in charcoal, on paper of the same size as that to be used by the class, showing how the basket can be drawn so as just to fit the paper, or even how parts of it may be allowed to run off the edges. If the animal itself just fits into the basket, a suitable scale for the main shapes is immediately established.

In a lesson in which animals are used, the teacher should help children to look first for the basic rhythms of the animals' different movements and for their most characteristic shapes and positions. The children then study details such as the pattern caused by the growth of the hair and by any distinctive markings. The form of the head is discussed and the children note the essential qualities of different parts, such as the ears and eyes and the whiskers. They should consider all these in relation to the natural habits and life of the animals. If possible the children should also stroke the animals so that they feel as well as see the textures, this tactile awareness bringing further meaning to their work.

Our aim is to help children extend the range of their personal expression. Work with animal subjects needs to be very carefully planned, so that the introduction leads on smoothly to an uninterrupted start, while the children's visual images are at their clearest.

NATURAL FORM

The children's interest in natural objects—flowers, seeds, leaves, shells, pebbles, feathers and insects—brings a continuous richness to their looking. They like to peer at and pore over the delicate transparency of a dried leaf or study minutely the pattern on a butterfly's wing. This leads the child to become increasingly sensitive to underlying qualities of form, colour, tone, pattern and textures; qualities that have already been frequently mentioned and that are basic to the rhythms and structures of life.

Children will enthusiastically make their own collections of natural forms and, however small or simple these collections may be, the children should be encouraged to take pleasure in well-ordered, attractively set out arrangements. This aspect is of importance in the presentation of any visual material in the classroom; displays must be changed frequently, and paper mounts or coverings on tables should be kept clean and fresh.

A few small hand lenses should be available in every classroom. These can be quite inexpensive (see page 276), and children should become accustomed to using them for looking at the finer detail of natural objects. Ideally every teacher should also have the use of a microscope, through which new worlds may be explored. The enjoyment of nature and art are so closely interrelated that both teacher and children will discover the two interests overlapping and fusing in creative work, each illuminating the other.

The appreciation of shape, pattern and colour by very young children is experienced largely through being able to look at and handle actual specimens. The teacher therefore should introduce them to as wide a range of material as possible, including both animate and inanimate nature.

As the children grow older they will become interested in making some record of what they see. Here, as with other recording from observation, the drawing and painting materials provided should be of a kind likely to encourage freedom and directness in the work—charcoal, crayons, bamboo, reed and felt pens, powder colour or, for the oldest children, water-colour. From the first, children should try to express something of the general spirit and essence of the things that interest them most, in as vital and sensitive a way as possible. Some of their work may well be crude or untidy but will nevertheless have a life about it that could easily be lost in an over-neat, inhibited drawing, in which representational accuracy had been stressed at the expense of personal interpretation and selection.

The study of shells (No. 75), for instance, is a freely treated painting in which some precise knowledge of the structures of growth has been the outcome of close observation. In her group Gillian selected different shapes that together make a pleasant composition. Larger and smaller forms provide a variety of scale and the finer details contrast with the broader areas.

This personal interest is also seen in Alison's painting of a shell, No. 76. She brought a very beautiful, tropical shell to the art club one day; it had just been given to her and she was obviously fascinated by it. I suggested that she might like to paint it and she quickly settled to a period of absorbed study, in which she searched out the distinctive characteristics of the shell. She had not previously shown any particular inclination for such direct recording, but in this instance the intensity of her own interest provided the impulse. We see how well she has selected the main rhythms of a complex form, translating these into an expressive painting, in which she has emphasized the elements of pattern.

Alison's individual recording from observation seems far removed from the memories some of us may have of 'lessons' in which each member of the class was given some natural specimen, perhaps an autumn leaf or a single flower, which had to be represented as accurately as possible. 'Accuracy' implied an adult's way of seeing and usually aimed at an exact representation. While this method might have been appropriate for a few children who were gifted with a particular skill in realistic representation, the majority, unable to achieve these standards, felt a sense of frustration likely to undermine their whole attitude towards creative work.

Quite young children may respond to opportunities of working from nature, if they are allowed to do this in a creative way. Alison, whose shell painting we have discussed, was eight years old. Michael, a nine-year-old member of the art club, was also interesting in his personal response to natural form, in this instance to a group of pebbles and flints that had been displayed, partly under water, as a starting point for picture making. He was so fascinated by the shape and the feel of the pebbles that he filled his paper (15 × 11 in.) with a charcoal drawing which included no less than twenty-two stones. There was a small area of sky with clouds at the top of his drawing, and the rest of the sheet was beautifully and completely filled with outline-drawings of stones of different forms and sizes. The way he talked about the drawing further revealed his sensibility. He said about his stones: 'They are grey and shaped by the sea and in places there are little round holes with salt in them. These flint stones are of good quality, blacker, sharper and stronger than some of the flints I've found. The stones are shaped in all sorts of ways—just like motor cars. They shine and look different when they are covered with water.'

There must be many children in the Primary school with this kind of perception, and it rests with the teacher to provide material that can nourish and extend these natural interests.

MACHINERY

The range of visual language can also be widened by the observation of man-made objects. Children are fascinated by the diversity and interest of machinery and by mechanical forms such as bicycles, wheels, old clocks and watches, bolts, cogs, springs, chains and wire nettings of different meshes.

The drawings of bicycles, Nos. 73 and 74, bring out the strength and beauty of such forms and show how well the challenge provided by such a subject can stimulate real purpose in looking. Each child has seen the complex form in terms of a personal vision which has determined the way in which the structure and spatial relationships have been interpreted. No. 73 is three-dimensional, No. 74 basically two-dimensional, and the different view-points of each drawing reflect these personal ways of seeing. We note, too, how differently each child has used the charcoal. Each individual in a class should be helped to draw or paint or model as well as possible in the ways that come to him most naturally.

CHAPTER 6

Collective Work

Various kinds of planned collective work may form part of a general scheme of art, and can well be introduced about two or three times in a school year. As a rule such activities develop freely for at least two or three weeks before they are completed. A balance between individual work and group activities should be kept in mind, so that each child's personal work may benefit by the confidence and understanding he has gained through working with others on larger projects.

Collective work in art, rightly used, has endless possibilities, but if it is to be of real educational value it must be the genuine outcome of children working together experimentally, each individual contributing something to the whole effort.

Teacher-imposed schemes may produce results that look impressive when displayed in the classroom but that may actually have done little for the personal development of each child. 'Come and look at our frieze—I did that bit.' Comments of this kind indicate how important it is for the child to see his contribution take its place in the completed work. In particular, the child with less creative gift will gain in self-respect, and this newly found confidence may well influence the development of the rest of his work. The total result of any piece of co-operative work will be more telling in its impact than any of the individual parts can be and each child will benefit immensely by being associated with the completed achievement.

Collective work may be solely concerned with an art activity that is complete in itself or may, through art, be linked with other aspects of the curriculum. This is particularly valuable where it leads to a real interrelation between different areas of work and to joining up separate subjects and lessons. Art has to do with far-reaching experiences and is not something that can be stored away in a cupboard from one week to the next. Yet frequently it is thought of in isolation. Children, too, are apt to regard their school-work as a number of disconnected subjects—as one of Nan Youngman's pupils once said: 'O Lord, I've left me art on the bus.'

Where a connection between art and other subjects occurs spontaneously as a result of the children's widening interest, it can offer exceptional opportunities for creative thought and expression. But without some genuine link, the results too easily become little more than somewhat fragmented collections of drawings or cut-out shapes—perfunctorily related to the topic—straggling haphazardly across friezes that, perhaps too automatically, appear with each fresh project. We cannot expect collective work of this kind either to encourage a fuller understanding of the topic, or to increase the children's feeling for aesthetic qualities. An arbitrary connection will lead to a superficial response and we feel for the child, who, at the beginning of an art period said: 'Must we do our centre of interest this afternoon?' In such instances it might be well to abandon the topic for a few periods and enjoy art purely for art's sake.

Some teachers are particularly concerned to establish a true integration of subjects, and in *An Experiment in Education*[1] by Sybil Marshall, we see how inspiring for children such a fusion of experiences can be. In this book she describes vividly the widely ranging, integrated interests of the creative work done by the children in her school. She shows, through many examples of their work, how fully they enjoyed both perceptive and intellectual experiences, and how through these their own creative faculties in art, English and drama —to touch on a few facets only—came to life. In this approach, which Mrs. Marshall called her 'symphonic method', the children first felt some aesthetic interest and from this they explored outwards in many unforeseen directions.

It is essential that each child should contribute something to the finished whole. Yet sometimes, when a whole class is working on a planned project, it happens that only the 'best' results for actual use are finally selected. The teacher may be impelled to make this choice by his concern to establish what he thinks are good standards. He may even have so little confidence in the children's powers of invention and expression that he prepares templates for their use, or draws or plans considerable portions of the work before the children begin to take part. The children then are really only carrying out the teacher's ideas.

[1] *An Experiment in Education*, by Sybil Marshall (Cambridge University Press).

An instance of such misdirected teaching occurred recently when a student, with little personal experience in art, had a class of enthusiastic eight-year-old children with whom she was about to start on a cut-paper frieze. 'Under the Sea' was the well-worn subject and she had planned to make templates of the fish and seaweed for the children, so that each would have drawing and cutting guides, as she doubted whether they could manage the shapes on their own. The whole work was very thoroughly prepared; she hoped to help the children over the 'difficult' part, and by providing them with good shapes, to ensure 'successful' results.

Fortunately she allowed herself to be persuaded to give the children a free rein, and once she had had the courage to hand over to them she was astonished by the assurance and good commonsense with which they tackled the work. She was already then a good teacher, closely in sympathy with the children, and she and the class worked well together, thoroughly enjoying each fresh stage as the theme developed. In the discussions that arose she took an unobtrusive but valuable part, and by means of apt suggestions and questions gently guided the children's quick give and take of ideas. Opinions were expressed vigorously and alternative possibilities weighed up with a real sense of purpose.

She borrowed an aquarium of fish and with this direct source of interest the children were able to look for the distinctive qualities of fish. Some produced quite realistic fish, for others the fish were born more of the imagination and in some instances they consisted of somewhat incomprehensible shapes made up of crude patches of colour. Yet, despite these individual differences—or was it because of them?—the whole frieze was an entity, providing a fascinating variety of shape and colour, richly distributed along the full length.

Unnoticed, the student had brought further materials into the classroom, and at an appropriate point, when the need for some linking of the shapes had become apparent, a bundle of bits of dried seaweed appeared, as if by magic intervention. The children quickly put these in water, and watched with delight the unfolding patterns of the different structures of growth. Some rug-wool and soft cords happened also to be discovered near by, and a use was quickly found for these. 'Here, how would this do for seaweed?' was soon heard, and pasted rug-wool was pushed and poked into a variety of shapes on the frieze, relating the many cut-out forms by means of linear rhythms.

The room became alive with excited interest and concentration. Some children worked on the frieze, others with urgency were still completing individual work, anxious to have it ready. Some were just watching the seaweed, others dreamily listening to shells which by now had also appeared on the teacher's table. A few children were looking through the pages of reference books on maritime and river life and on water-plants and insects. The student had provided some of the books and, with the help of the children, had selected others from the school library.

For this student, who had been so unsure at first, the experience was a revelation of what children can do, provided that the atmosphere is one of confidence and encouragement, that the teaching content is absorbing and that the working materials are suitable. For the children, there had been moments of heightened creative experience that some of them were likely to remember long after the details of the work had faded from their minds.

FRIEZES

In many schools friezes and panels are introduced as Christmas projects. They are often designed to fit certain positions in the classrooms or corridors, possibly with each class being responsible for the decoration of one part of the school.

Sometimes children in our art club, or groups of students, spend the last two or three weeks of an autumn term making something for a children's home or for a ward in a local hospital. Our last two Christmas friezes—made by students—were prepared for particular walls in a children's reception centre. We were told later that the children had been fascinated by them, enjoying the pattern and movement of colour, and identifying themselves closely with the children playing in the frieze.

Both friezes related to winter. One included several groups of children playing out-of-doors, the other consisted of roof-tops and chimneys seen against the sky at night. The first was made of pieces of paper, torn, assembled and pasted on to a long roll of paper: in the other frieze the shapes were cut out with scissors.

A Winter Games Frieze in Torn Paper

A band of trees, deciduous and coniferous, provided a setting for four main winter activities. The paper was 14 ft. long and 1 ft. 8 in. deep. On the extreme left a number of children were making a large snowman. From this one's eye travelled to a group of boys and girls who were sliding on a frozen pond. Next came an extensive snowball fight, the variously coloured clothes of the children and the large snowballs making all manner of shapes against the darker colours of the trees. From here one reached the base of a long slope down which yet more children were tobogganing, making an effective conclusion for the right-hand end of the frieze. The general impression was one of movement and colour; but although so much was happening, the composition was by no means disconnected. The four main areas of interest were spaced fairly evenly along the length of the frieze. This helped to establish a sense of balance, while the movement of the brighter colours was unified by the band of darker tree-shapes which made a continuous background link from one end to the other.

The students working on it were astonished to see how the many individual units finally came together, making an attractive collective result that, in its decorative quality, far outstripped their original conception.

How, then, should we set about introducing and carrying through work of this kind? Answers to this question must naturally be worked out by each teacher individually tackling the various possibilities and problems and, together with the children, finding suitable methods of working. In every case, however, certain essential principles are involved, which are illustrated in the making of this particular frieze.

1   The materials were laid out in readiness:

    a.   Several rolls of different coloured frieze-paper (the back of wallpaper rolls can be used).

    b.   Boxes of coloured papers (with adequate ranges of colour, tone and texture).

    c.   Polycell or a cold water paste.

    d.   Old brushes or strips of stiff cardboard for pasting.

    e.   Saucers or mixing palettes for the paste.

f.   Plenty of newspaper to work on so as to ensure clean pasting techniques.

2   The idea of making a frieze for a specific purpose was introduced by some general discussion—the theme was suggested by the students.

3   Main colour possibilities were considered, with constant reference to the papers themselves: for example, what range of colours would be used? Which paper would serve best as a background for these colours? A light tone? A mid-tone? Or something darker?

4   From the numerous suggestions about winter subjects put forward by the students, the four activities already mentioned were selected:

a.   Making a snowman.
b.   Sliding on a frozen pond.
c.   Snowballing.
d.   Tobogganing.

5   It was then decided to place these in a setting of winter trees.

6   The students divided into six groups, four working on the figures and two on the trees.

7   A leader was chosen for each group, to be responsible for the materials and working-methods and also to watch the development of the work in relation to the whole frieze.

8   Some discussion took place between all six groups, as to the appropriate size of the children and trees compared with each other, and with the depth of the frieze. Some consistency of size is generally advisable. In this instance the students decided to make the figures taller than the length of their own hands opened out. A reference to a gauge of this kind is helpful.
The size of the people was considered with regard to the function of the frieze. It was to be displayed in a large room where it should be easily seen by many children.

9   Papers were chosen and, with constant consideration of colour and tone, direct tearing of the main shapes was begun. Students concerned with trees chose mainly greys, browns, blacks and greenish-greys. Some useful colours and textures were found in old wallpaper books. Even so the students felt the need for a greater variety of subtle colours, particularly of greens, and so,

to augment the stock, they painted sheets of white paper with such colours, thus gaining the desired variety.

10   The frieze-paper was unrolled to its full length on the floor. The background shapes, trees, ponds and hills, were put experimentally in various positions, adjusted and—when satisfactory—pasted down. These general decisions were reached by means of discussion, the students considering the whole effect as they pooled their ideas and suggestions.

11   In the meantime other students were preparing numerous 'children' in different positions—boys and girls of varying sizes, shapes and colours. People are usually best built up of separate pieces rather than torn out as single shapes—so that the placing of the different pieces can easily be altered to suggest movement.

Once the biggest background shapes were firmly fixed, members of each group began to experiment with various arrangements of the 'children' in their particular sections and soon these, too, were pasted into position.

From time to time everyone stood back from the work, in order to consider such questions as the carry-through of colour and the relationship of the parts to the whole. Were cool and warm colours well distributed? Could one's eye travel easily from part to part? Were some bits too isolated? Or some passages too demanding? Was the frieze too crowded in certain areas or too sparsely filled in other parts?

Finally the students had to decide how the snow should be treated. Should it be painted? Or kept to cut or torn paper? Or to a mixture of both? Would the background-spaces be best filled in solid? Or would this confuse and detract from the main shapes? Would a lighter, more open treatment be more in keeping with the general character of the whole frieze? Different types of white and off-white papers were tried out to decide which were the most suitable. Cartridge paper, it was felt, looked too hard but might possibly be used in small quantities, interspersed with softer tissue, kitchen and greaseproof papers. Blobs of cotton-wool were also tried, but it was generally agreed that these were too heavy and uninteresting in character, and that they detracted too much from the trees and the children. In the end roughly torn shapes were used which, with their soft irregularities, seemed best to express the idea of drifting snow.

Tearing all the shapes had contributed to the success of the frieze; as this meant that the chief shapes were kept as simple blocks of colour, since intricate shapes are less suitable for tearing. The fact that the shapes were mostly rather large also added to the breadth of the work.

The second frieze for this Christmas project was on a different theme. It consisted of the top halves of houses; their roofs, chimneys and television aerials making a variety of solid and open shapes in an irregular band against a night sky. This frieze too caught something of the atmosphere of winter; the sky was specked with innumerable groups of stars, and in the houses many lighted windows shone out in different kinds of yellow. The predominant pattern of the frieze was built up of a combination of the rectangular shapes of the houses related to the triangular shapes of gables.

No. 83 is part of a frieze rather similar in character to the first one described. In it we see the pleasant, softer edges that are produced by tearing rather than cutting the paper, a quality that in this case contributes to the whole sense of freedom and breadth. Sometimes cut edges look too hard. But at other times their precision may be more appropriate, as, for example, in No. 84, where the hard edges emphasize the clarity of the shapes.

In both Nos. 83 and 84 we notice how clearly the shapes 'read', or show up, in the compositions, because of the variety of tones that have been used. In each picture the tonal range passes from the very light, through the middle tones, to the very dark, and these extremes of light and dark make their impacts effectively on the mid-tone of the grey backgrounds. No. 84 also shows how satisfactorily paper, material, textured oddments and paint may be combined to produce an interesting variety of surface.

Other Possibilities

Although particular mention has been made of friezes, there are all sorts of other possibilities for collective work. Perhaps an old screen can be re-covered, a panel is needed for the back of a piano, or curtains are wanted for a Wendy-house.

The painted panels shown in Nos. 89–92, together with four others, were made to cover a large, old, dilapidated screen. Sheets of strong wrapping-paper were pasted together and the children placed these flat on the floor while they worked. Groups of four, five or six co-operated on each separate panel and at frequent intervals all the work was pinned up on the screen for the whole effect to be considered. The children discussed various possibilities and together decided on the theme of people to do with farm life. They were London children, and their paintings may strike us as somewhat remote from the realities of farming—we can imagine how differently the same subject might have been treated by children in the country. But in this instance the imaginative interpretation of each character, the expressive use of colour and the liveliness of brushwork fully justified the choice of subject. The panels looked attractive on the screen and were enjoyed there for a term or so, after which they were replaced by the work of another class.

MODELLING

Collective work can be done in various materials and in No. 133 we see three beautiful little figures, belonging to a Christmas crib, modelled in clay by a class of ten-year-old children. All three represent Mary, and how splendid that everyone who wanted to model Mary should have been encouraged and allowed to do so. In every kind of group-work the needs of the individual and the general demands of the communal work must be carefully balanced. These particular models illustrate well the urge that is so strongly felt by most children to decorate. The delicate repeat patterns were scratched into a red slip-surface that had been brushed over the lighter coloured body of the clay.

In No. 134, the three farm figures, also modelled by ten-year-old children, were part of a large farm group consisting of well over forty models. These included people, horses, cows, sheep, lambs, pigs, dogs, cats and many ducks, geese, hens and chicks. The theme was of general interest, and each child was able to contribute to the work in a personal way.

In most art-teaching we try to ask rather than tell; and with collective work in mind I recall a very lively circus, modelled in clay, that came into being in response to a request. A student was working with a class of eight-year-old boys and girls in a London school. She had organized things well: the floor near the children and their desks were protected by newspaper, small boards were ready for the work, and the lumps of clay she had prepared were of just the right consistency for modelling. She drew a large chalk circle on the floor in an empty part of the room and, the children having grouped round it, she asked: 'Will you help me to make a circus?' As each ball of clay was approximately the same size, the models related quite well in scale and could be grouped together satisfactorily. The children wanted to see their models in the big circle and felt they were really working with their teacher, who was indirectly guiding all the time without seeming ever to dictate.

PUPPETRY

Admirable opportunities for group activities in art arise while making properties and costumes for dramatic work. The introduction of various kinds of puppets also provides a class with worthwhile experiences in co-operating. In some schools the production of simple puppet performances forms an essential part of the general work and is regarded as a valuable means of creatively connecting various fields of interest. Small shows are prepared by one class for other groups to watch. Even the simplest, rough-and-ready presentations have a liveliness of character which expresses the children's inventiveness and dramatic sense. Yet often we find children taking home their carefully made puppets without having had the satisfaction and fun of actually using them in a real situation. A domestic science class might as well bake cakes and be forbidden to eat them.

This, however, did not happen with the glove puppets shown in No. 131. The six-year-old children used them most imaginatively in their spontaneous dramatizations of fairy stories and in their own original plays. Small groups took turns at giving performances, while the rest of the class made an enthusiastic audience. For about two weeks the children used any spare time available—before school or during break—to give little shows or to play with their puppets. For them the puppets became real personalities, who talked and moved and sang, changing their characters as they found themselves in new situations. The puppets were so constantly and vigorously handled that before long their general appearance suffered, yet their tattered condition showed how much they had meant to the children.

The simplest methods of production and construction—see Chapter 10—are of the greatest value to children, because they leave scope for improvisation and invention. In fact, useful and desirable though a specially designed puppet-theatre and stage may be, some make-

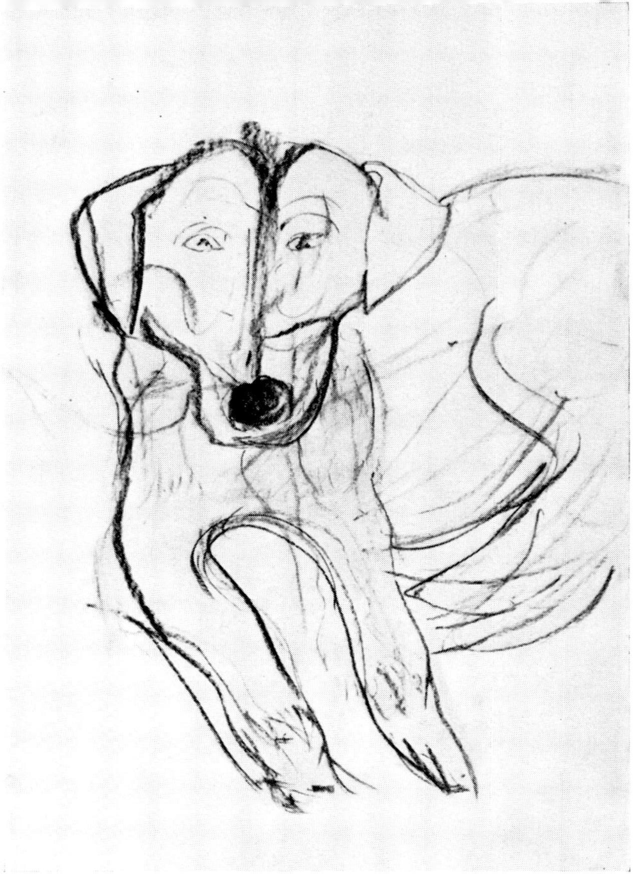

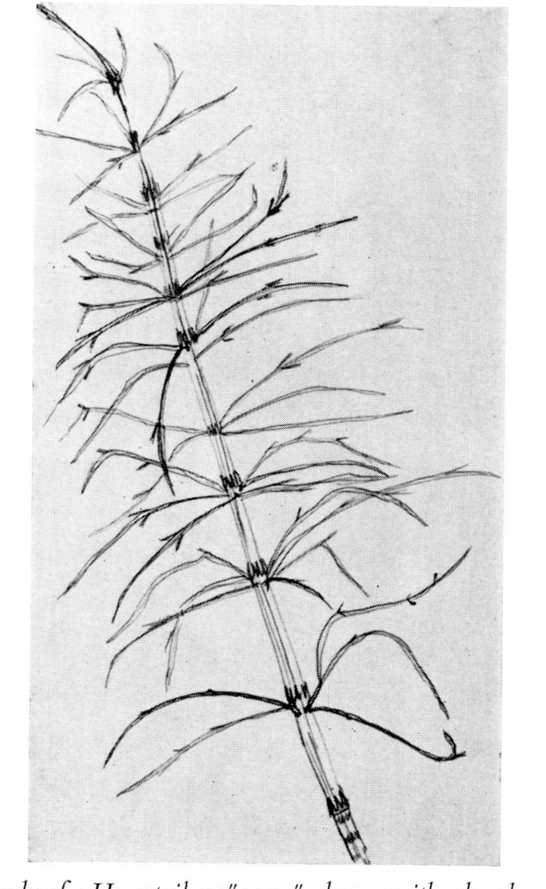

71   'Jason', a sketch in charcoal, 20" × 15", drawn from life by Vanessa, aged 11, see page 76.

72   Study of a Horsetail, 22" × 12", drawn with a bamboo pen and ink by a 12 year old girl, see page 66.

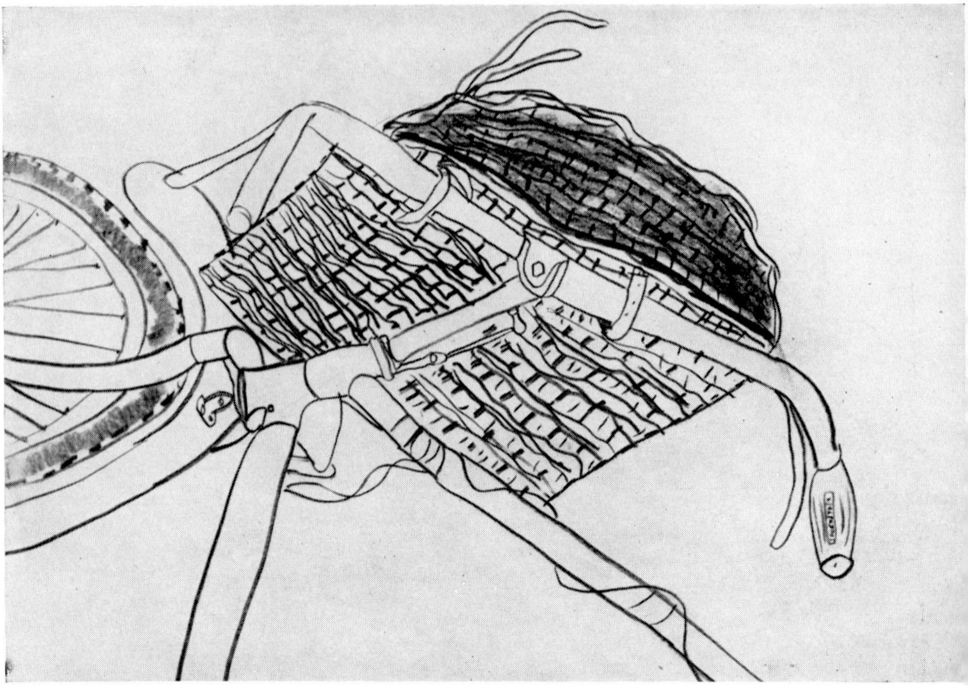

73

Studies in charcoal, 24″ × 18″, from direct observation of a bicycle, by John and Diana, both aged 10, see page 90.

74

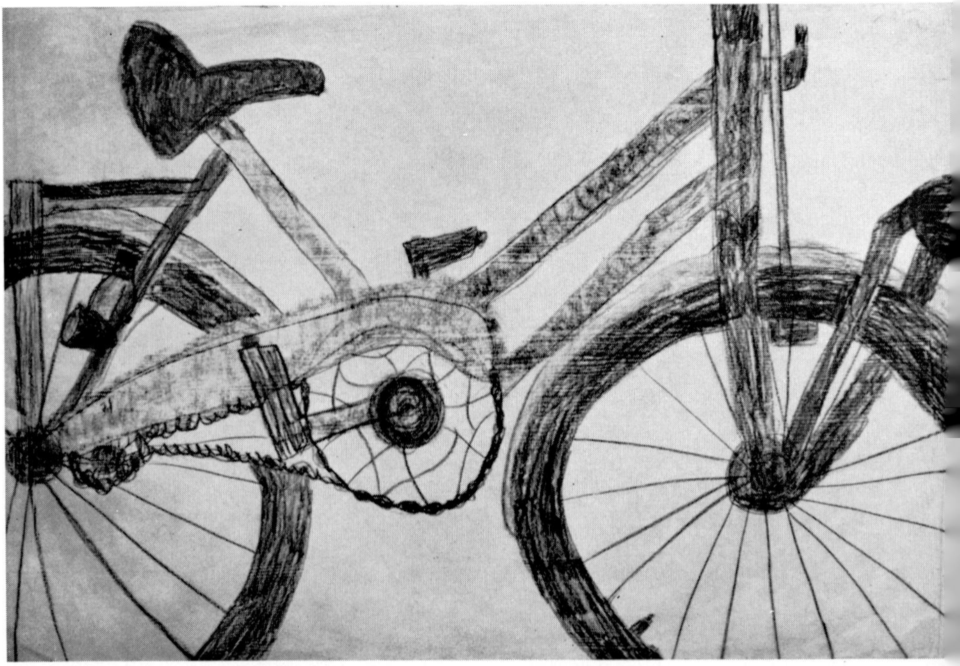

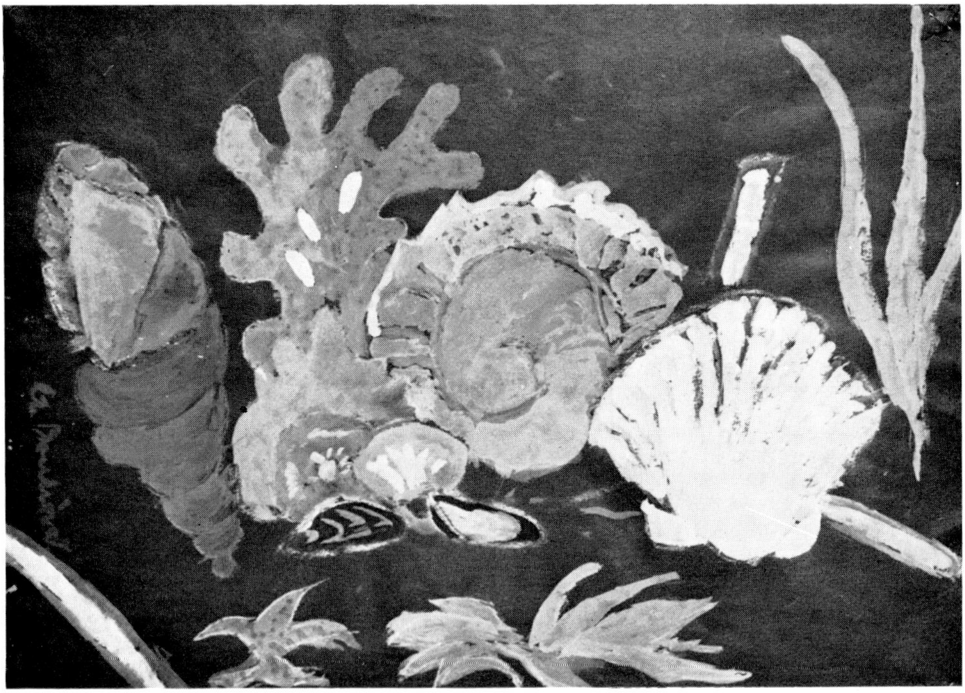

A study of shells, painted in powder colour on dark paper, 21″ × 15″, by Gillian, aged 11, and a pattern-painting, 9″ × 6″, made from one particular shell by Alison, aged 8, see page 89.

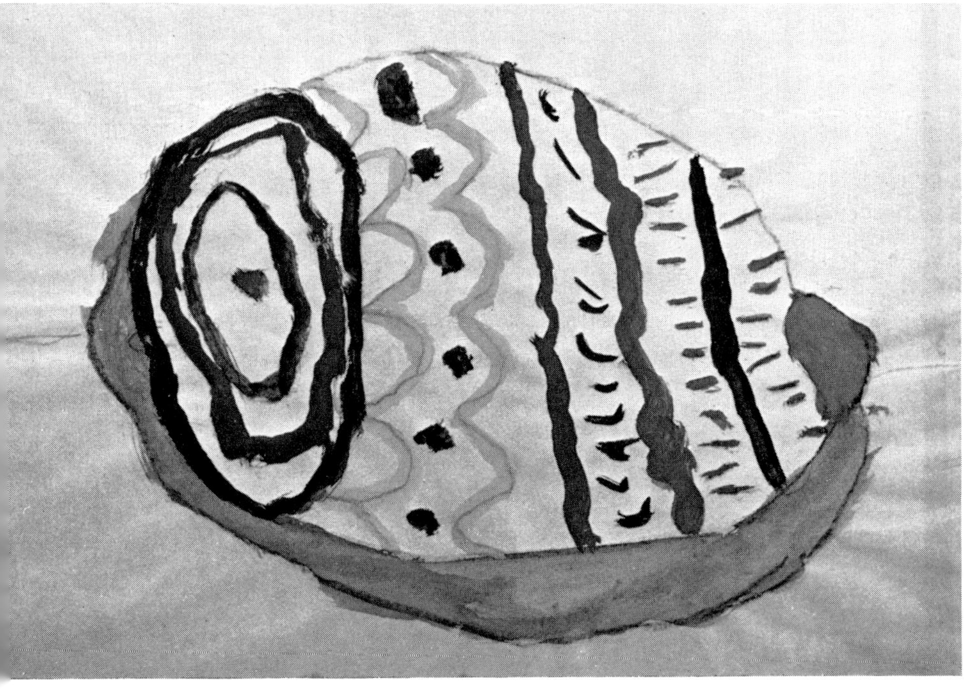

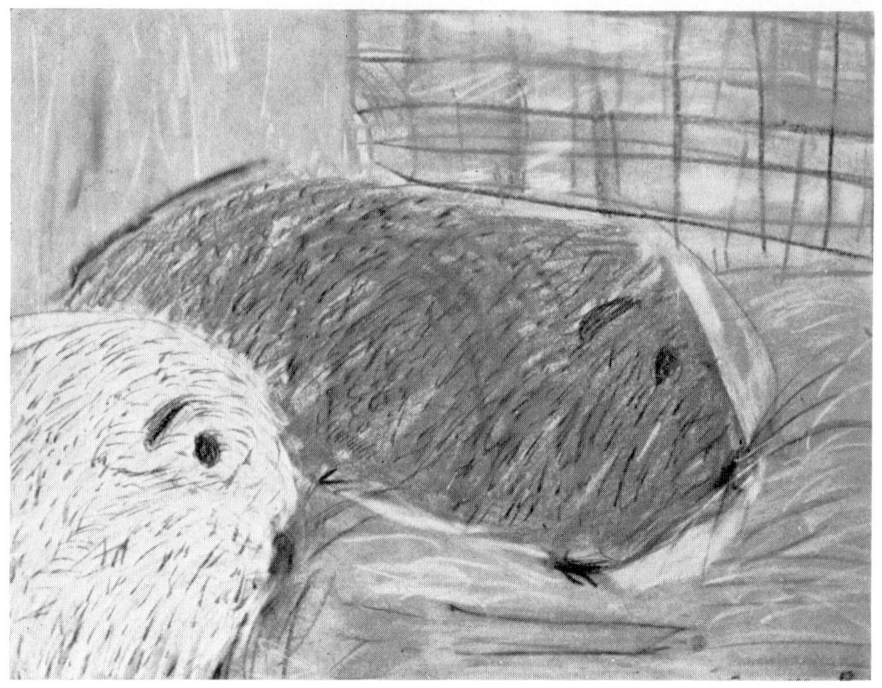

77

Pictures, 25″ × 20″, made by Francesca and Alison, both aged 10, after watching live guinea-pigs, see page 85.

78

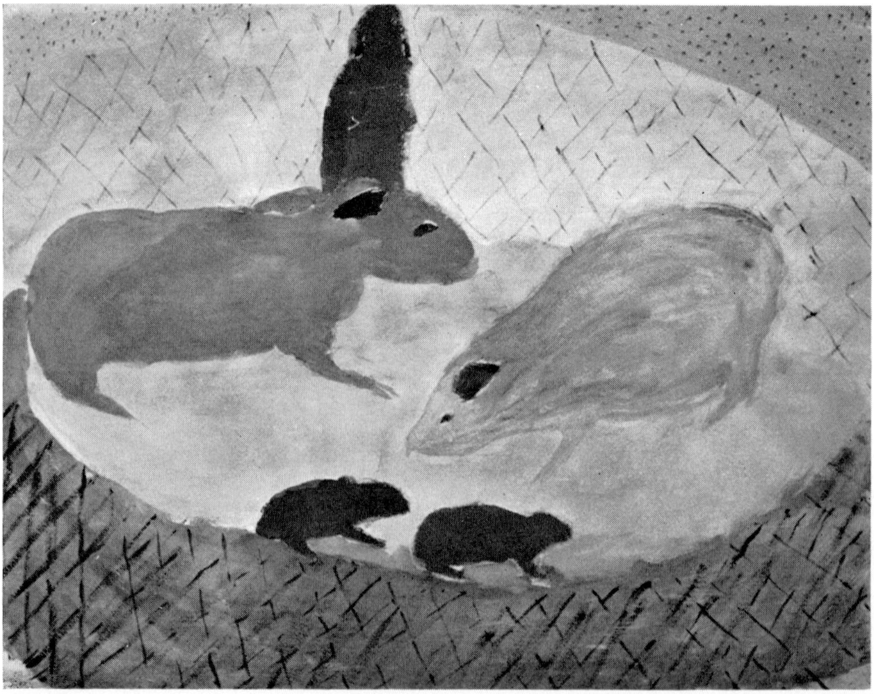

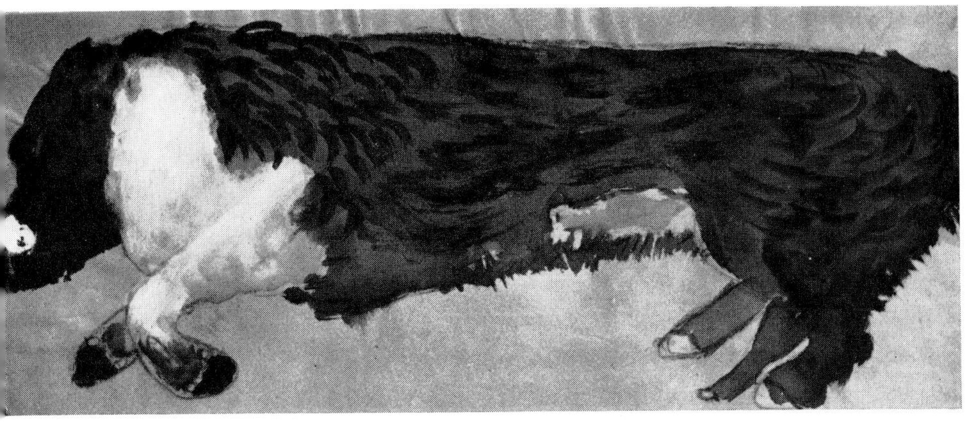

4 *sheepdog, 'Simm', and a rabbit in a basket used on different occasions as subjects for 9 year old children in a crowded classroom, see page 86.*

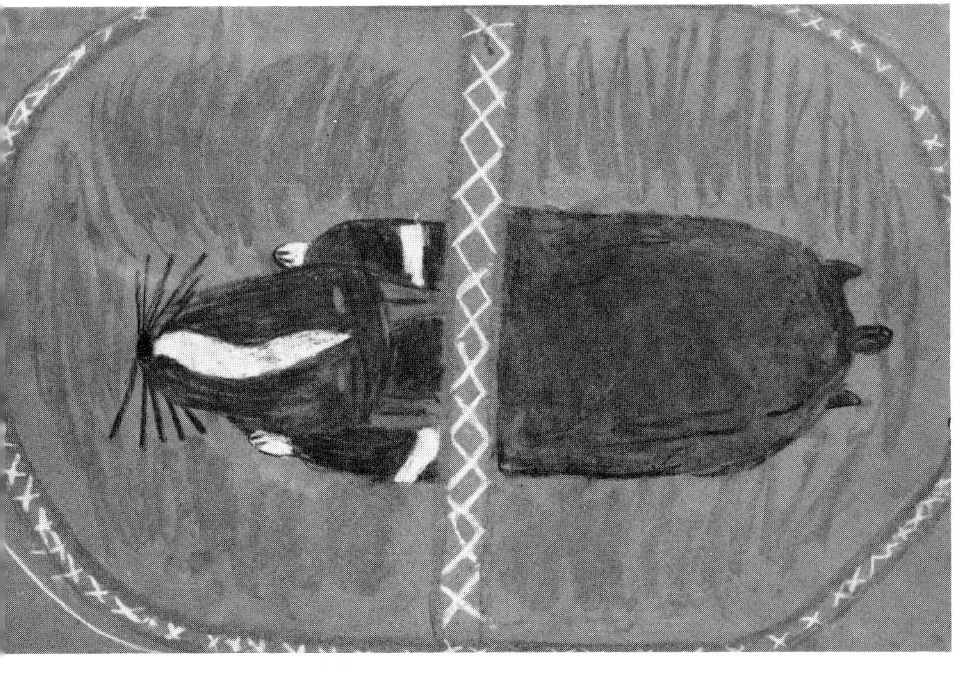

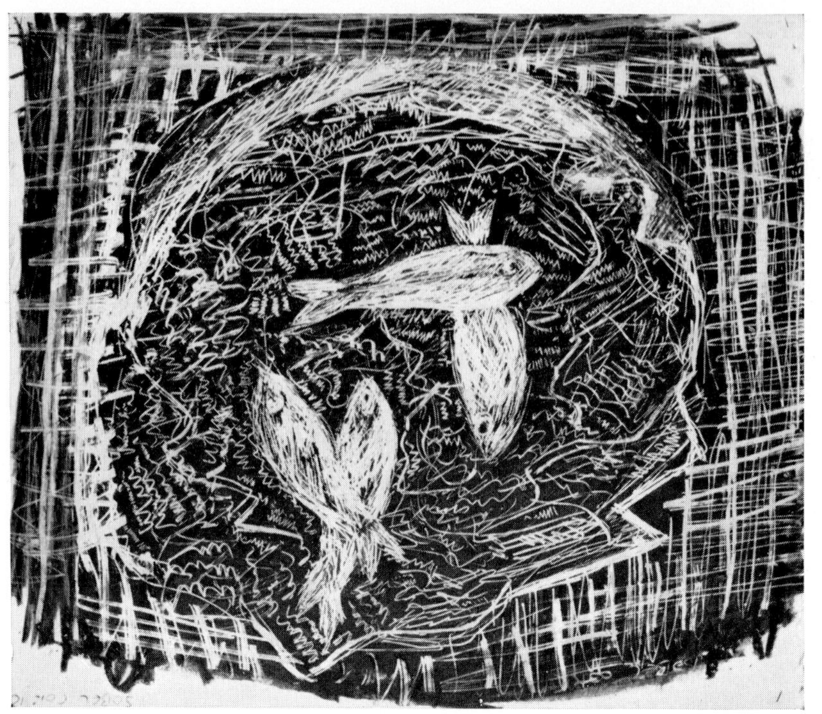

81   *'Sprats', a wax-crayon engraving, 14″ × 12″, by Isobel, aged 11.*
see pages 191, 258.

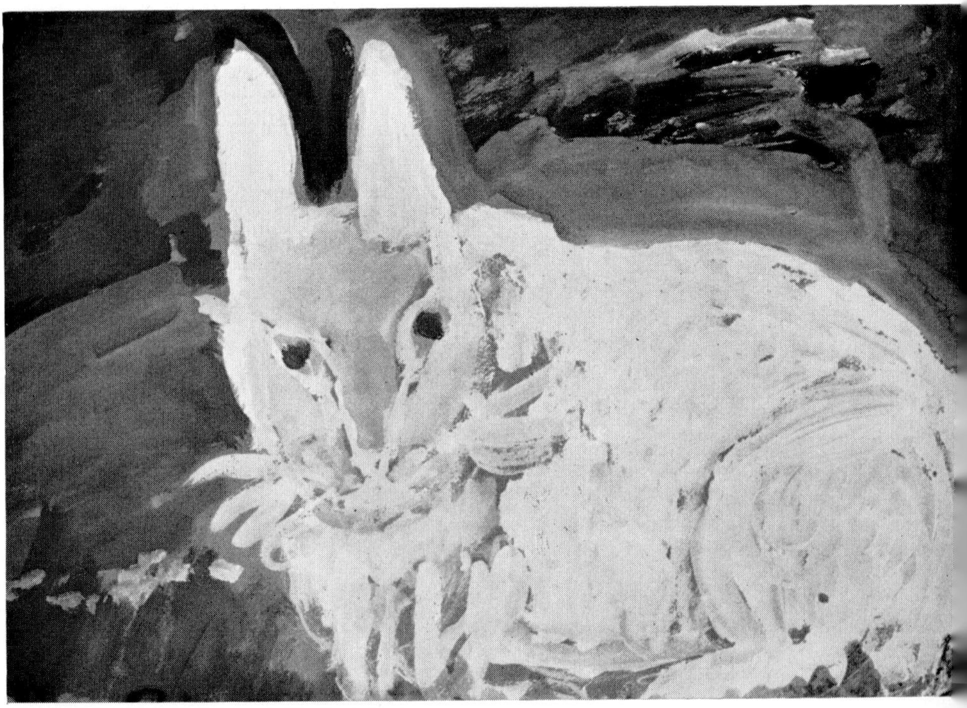

82   *A painting of a pet rabbit in powder colour on dark paper, 25″ × 18″, by Star, aged 12*
see pages 63, 262.

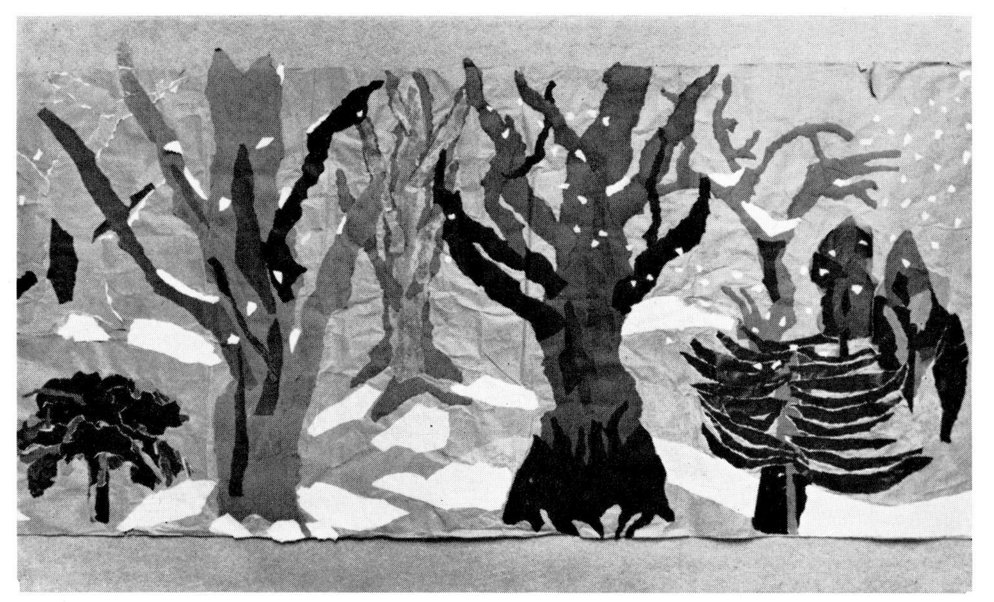

83   *Part of a 'winter' frieze in torn paper, 20 inches wide and 14 feet long, made by a group of students, see pages 98, 171.*

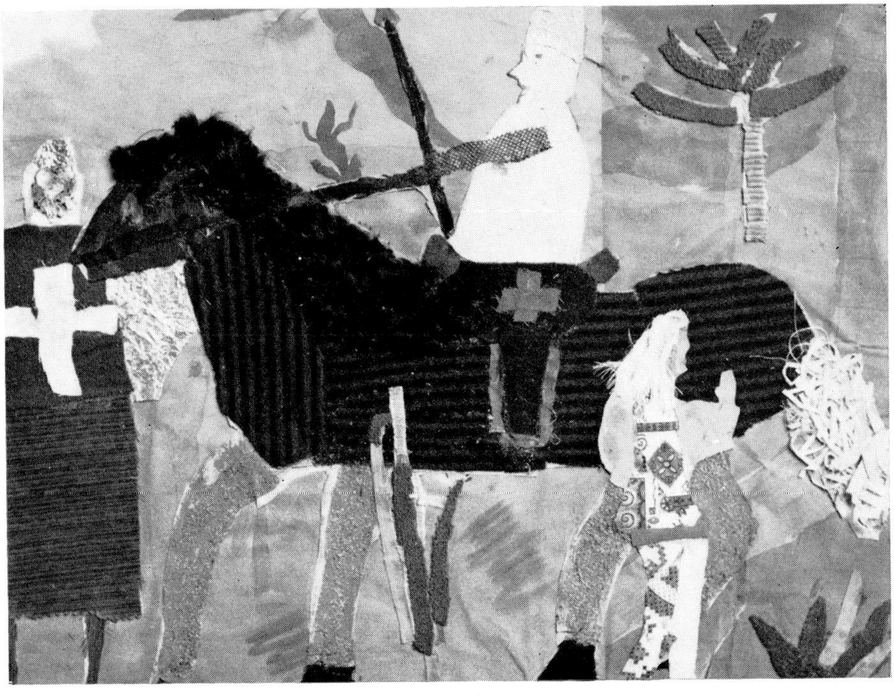

84   *'The Crusader', a paper and fabric collage, 20″ × 15″, by a 9 year old boy. This was one of forty panels forming part of a history project, see pages 98, 117.*

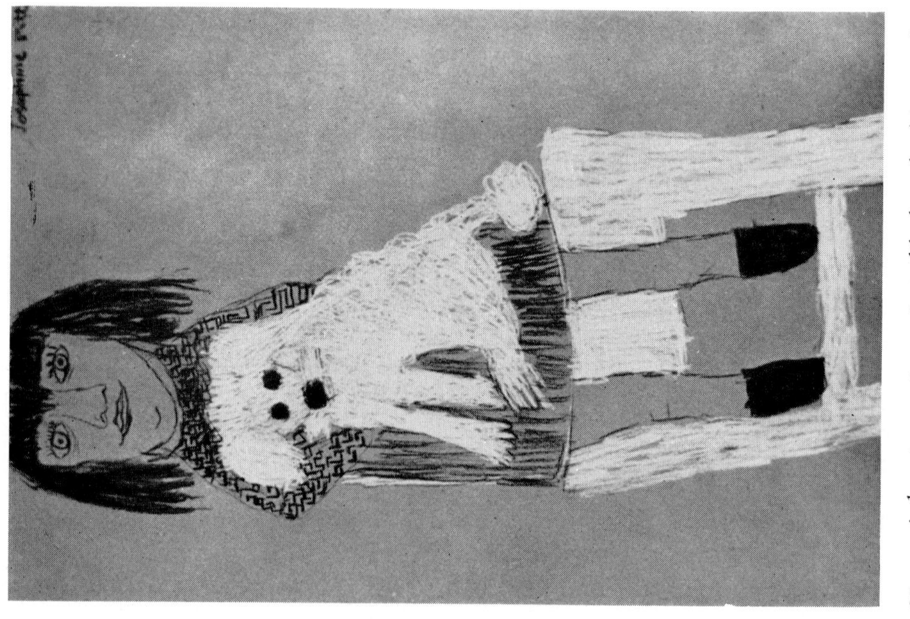

85   *A drawing, 22″ × 15″, in black and white conté on grey sugar paper by Josephine, aged 9, see pages*

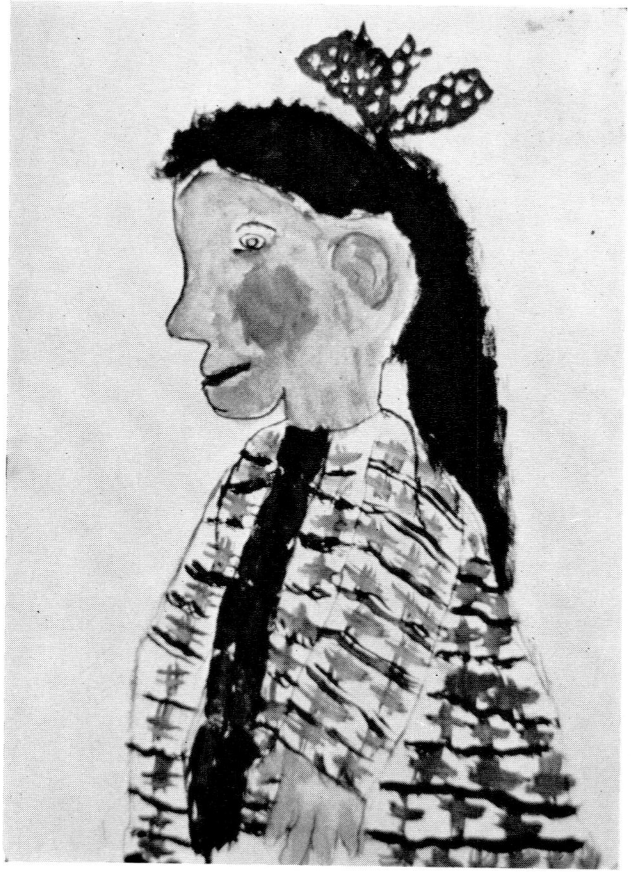

86   *A self-portrait, 22″ × 16″, painted in powder colour by a 9 year old girl, see pages 18, 78, 162*

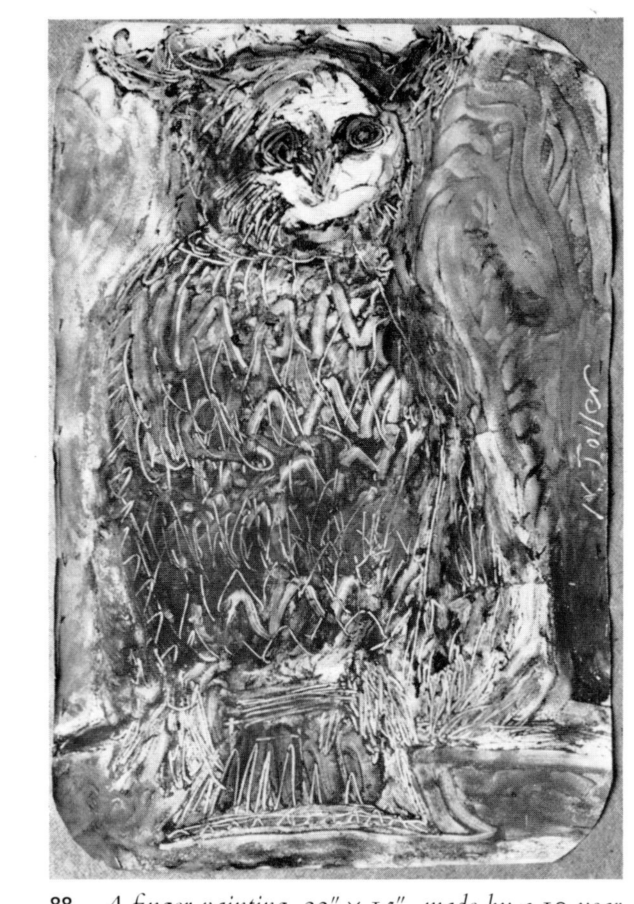

87 *This owl, 12 inches high, is a detail from a panel made by students, using potato cuts and candle rubbings, see pages 137, 192.*

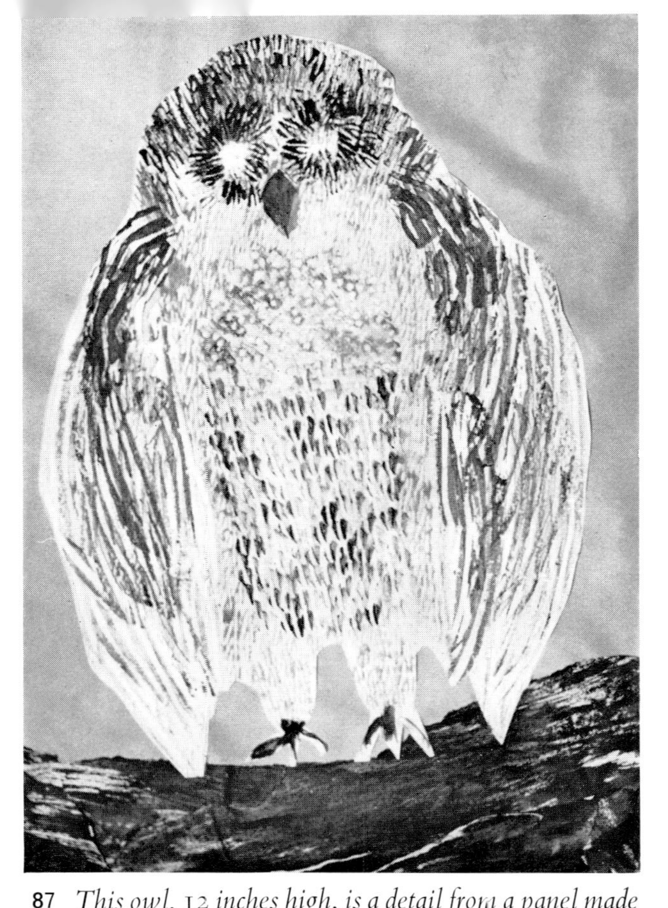

88 *A finger painting, 22" × 15", made by a 10 year old child after studying a stuffed owl, see page 166*

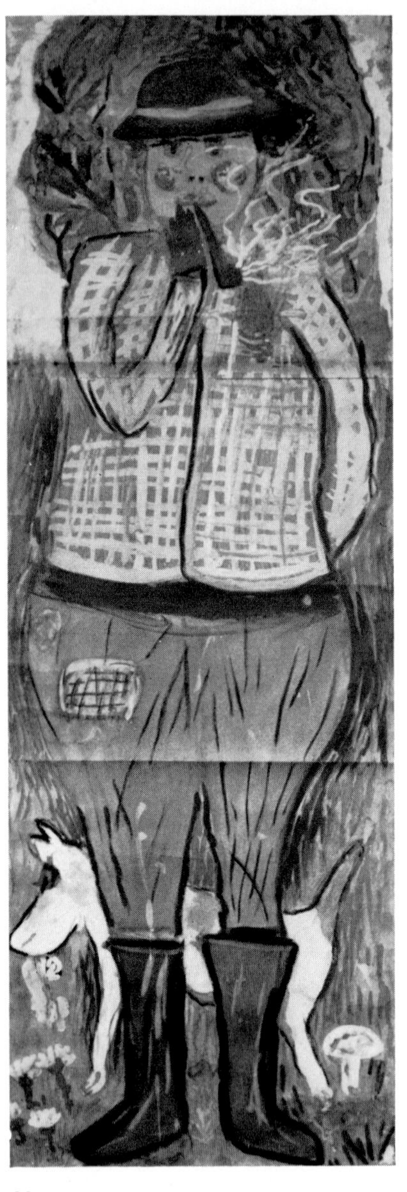

89

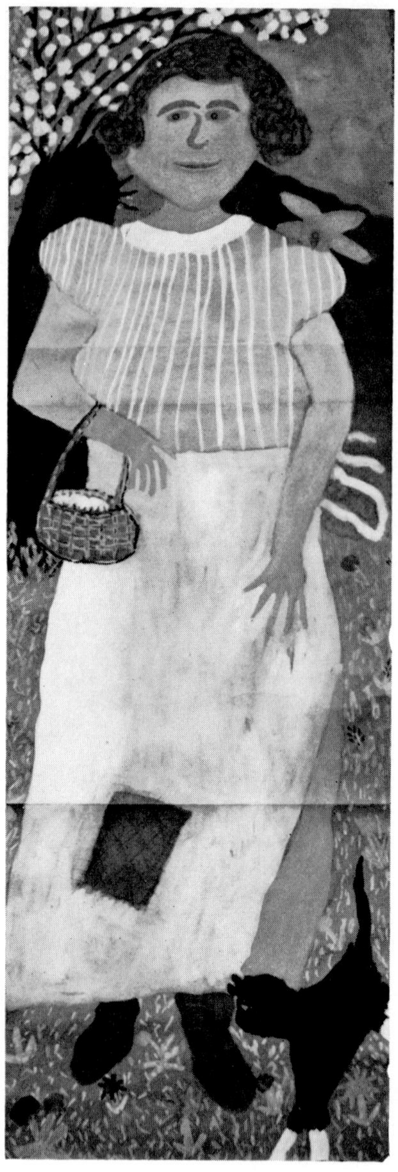

90

Four panels in powder colour painted to cover a screen. Each is 6 ft. × 2 ft. and

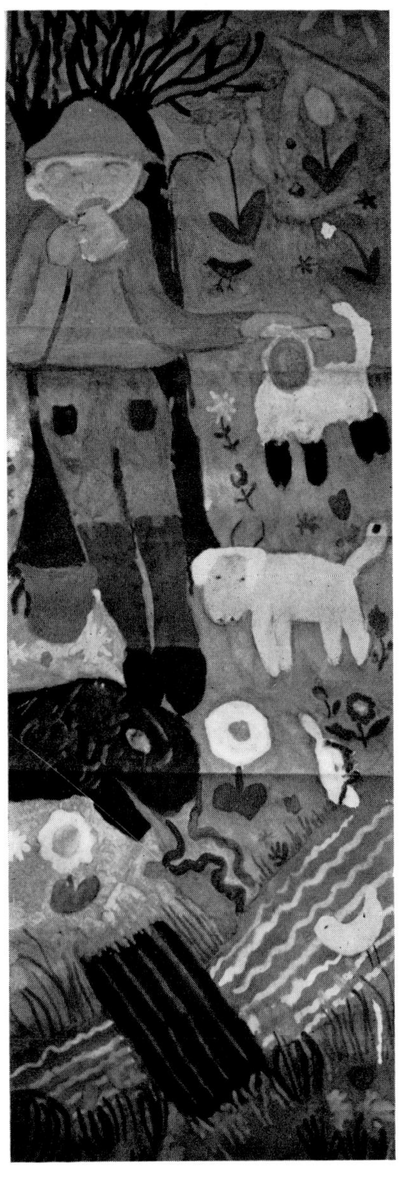

91

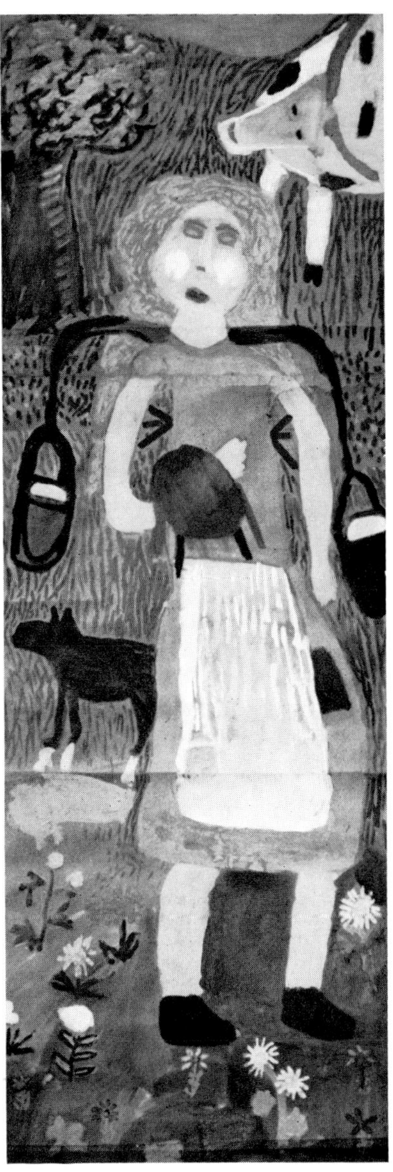

92

was made by a group of about six 10 year old children, see pages 18, 98.

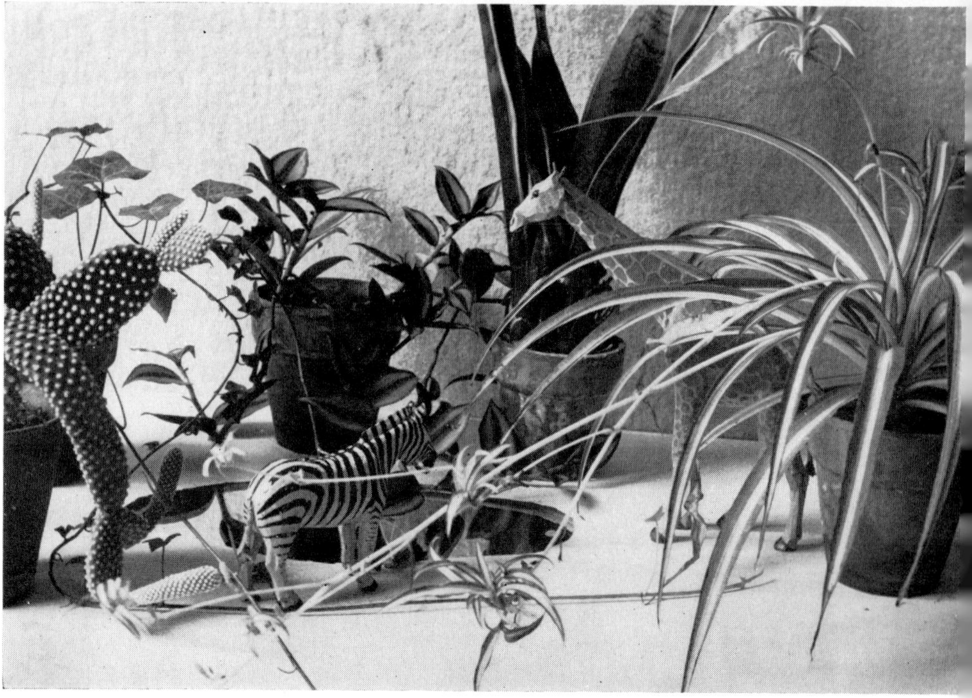

93 *A classroom group of plants, carved animals, and a small mirror, see page* 104.

94 *An imaginative picture of a jungle scene,* 22" × 15", *painted by a* 10 *year old girl after a discussion arising from the visual interest of the group above, see pages* 104, 163.

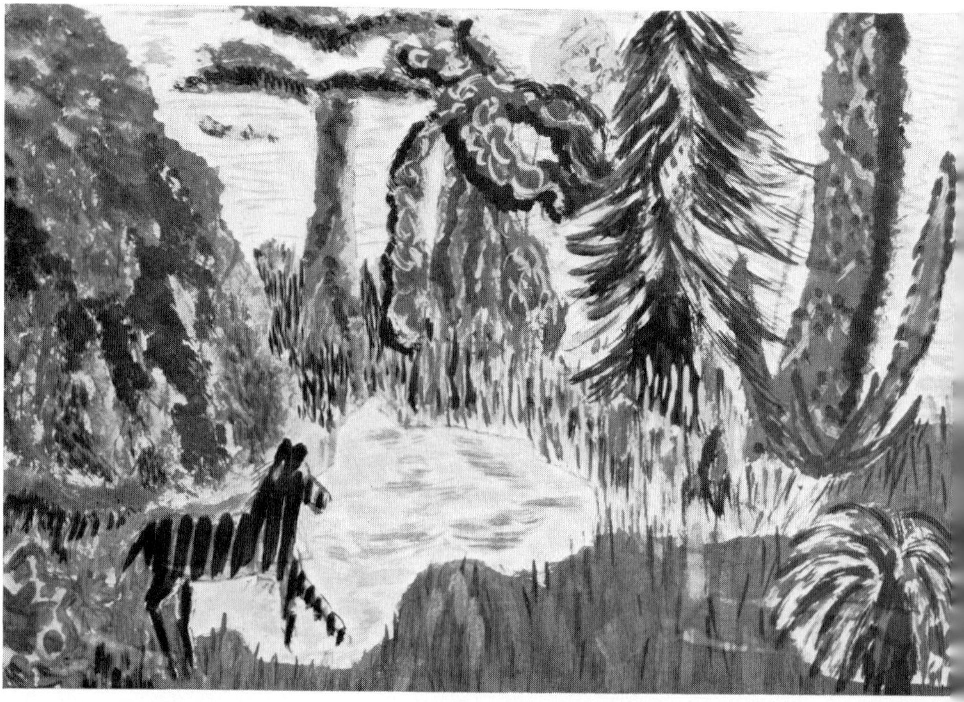

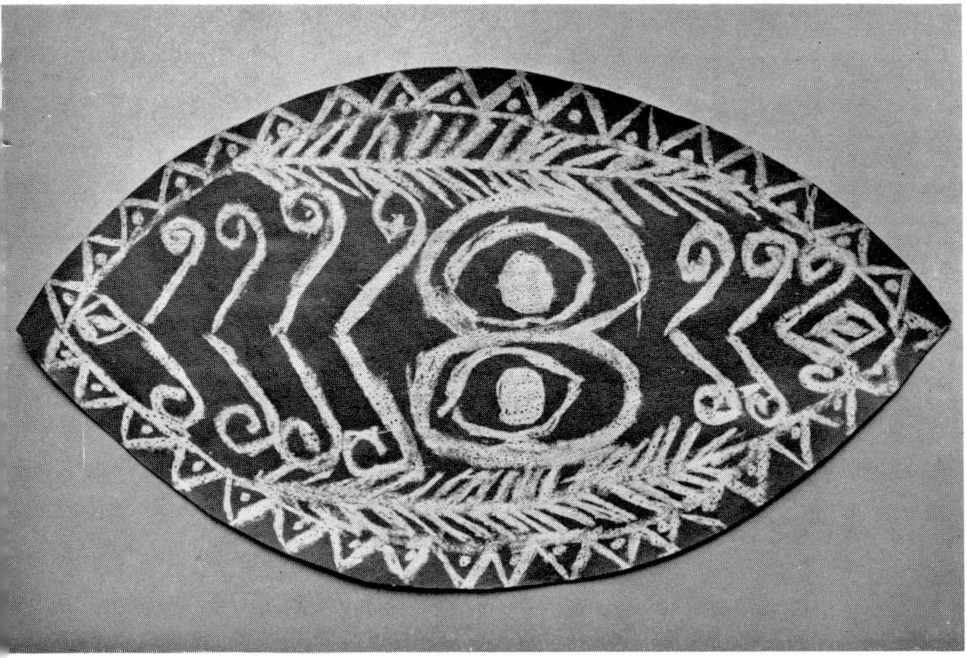

95   *A shield of thin card, length 22″, decorated with a candle drawing and ebony stain wash, by a 10 year old boy, see page 105.*

96   *Tonal-colour exercise, 23″ × 17″, by 10 year old children, see pages 103, 179.*

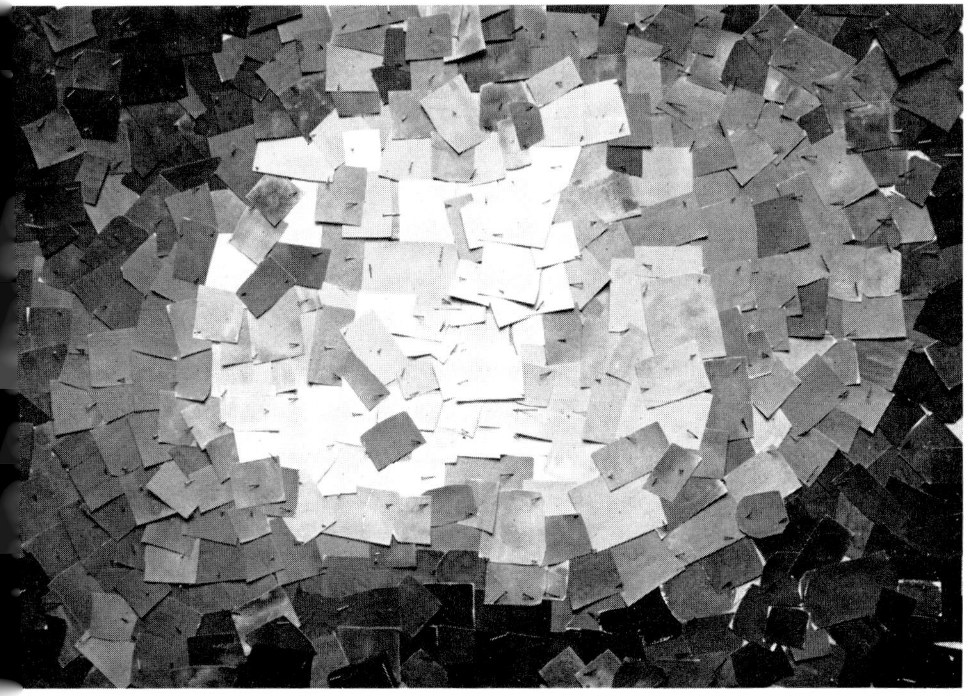

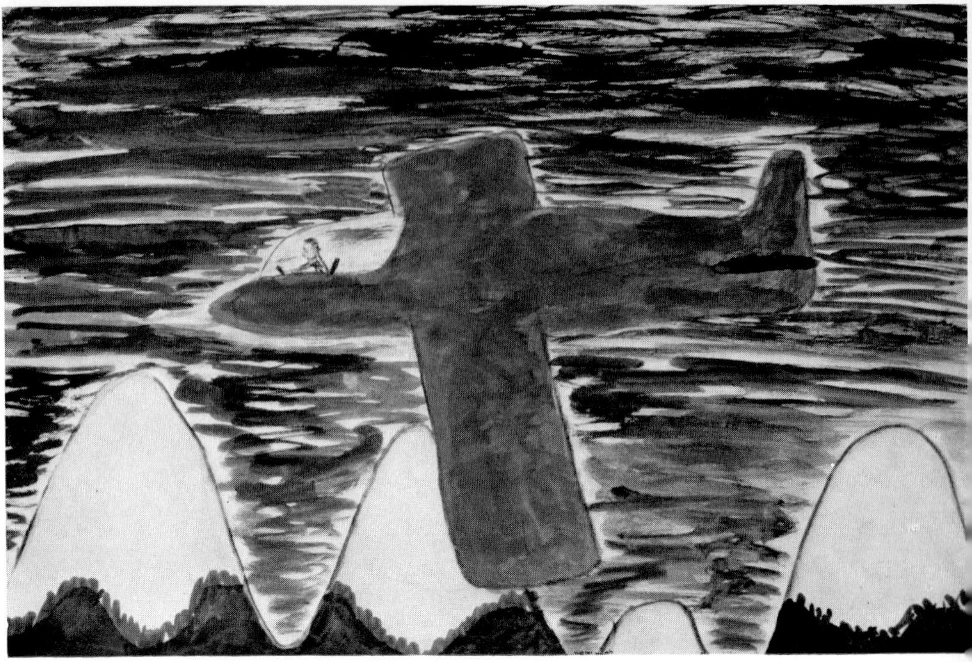

97 *A project on 'Flight' began with pictures of aeroplanes, such as this painting in powder colour, 22" × 15", by a 10 year old boy, see Chapter 6.*

98 *A model of a V.C.10, made out of balsa wood as part of the project on 'Flight'.*

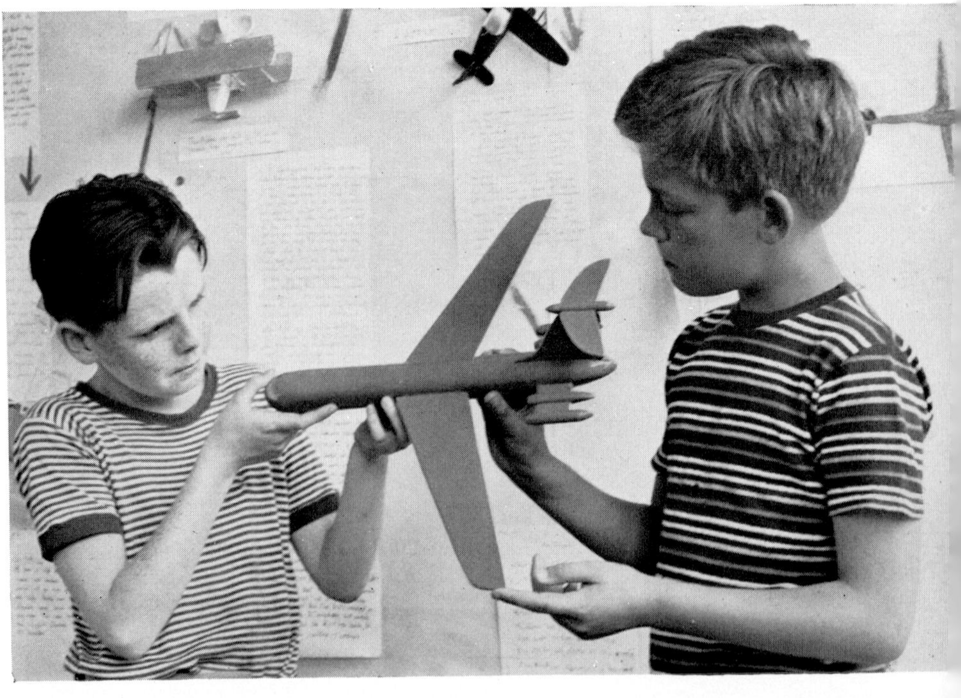

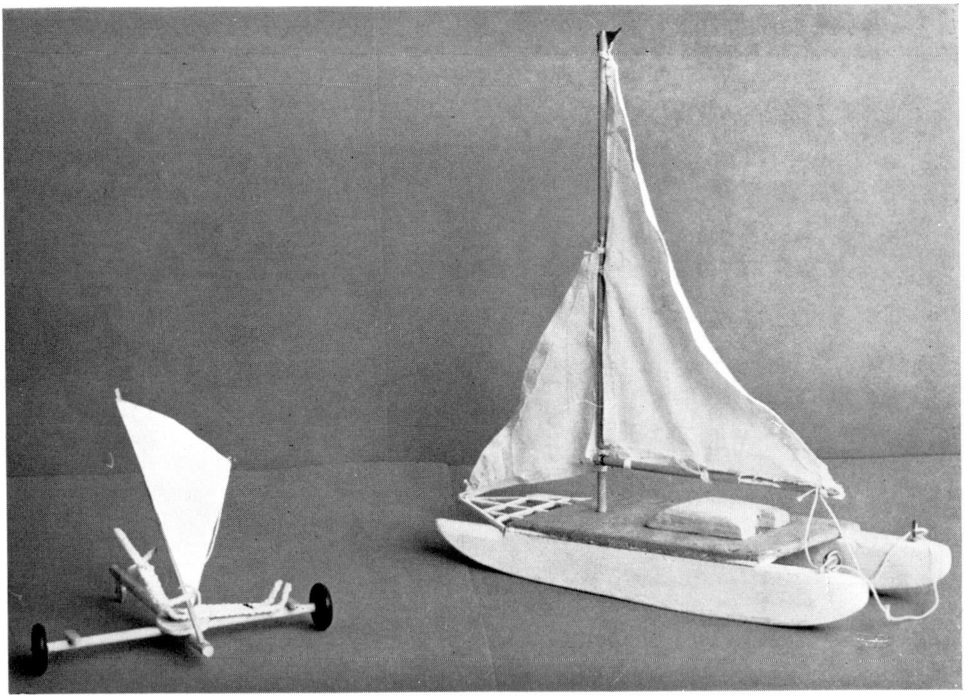

99   *These models of a land–yacht and a catamaran, made of balsa wood, arose from the children's interest in wind power, as described in Chapter 6.*

100   *Models of a post mill and a Chinese wheelbarrow, to illustrate the use of wind power.*

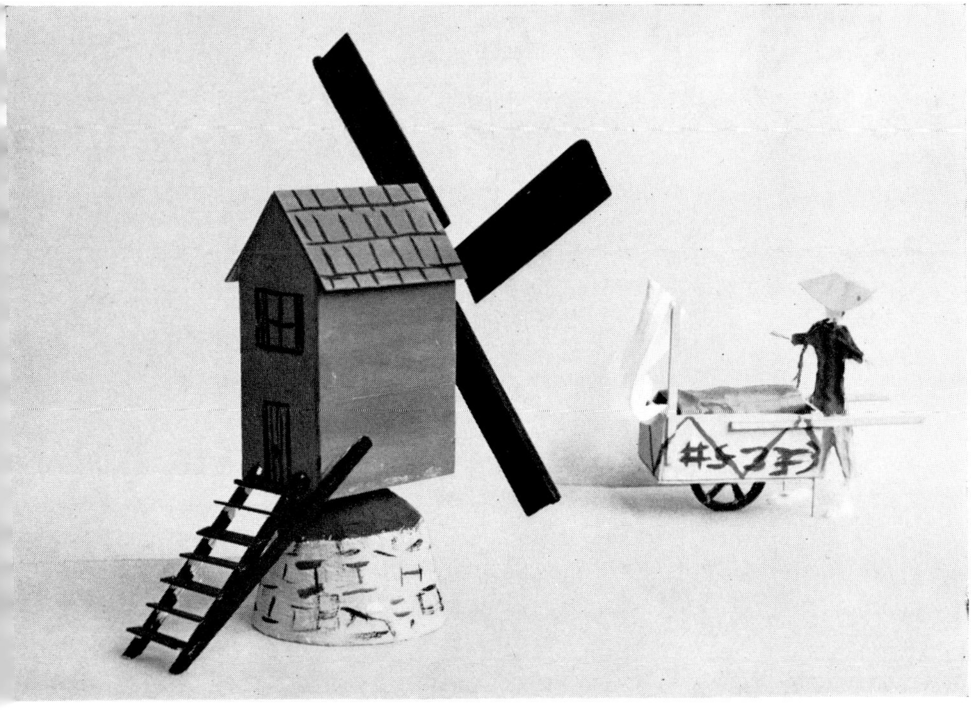

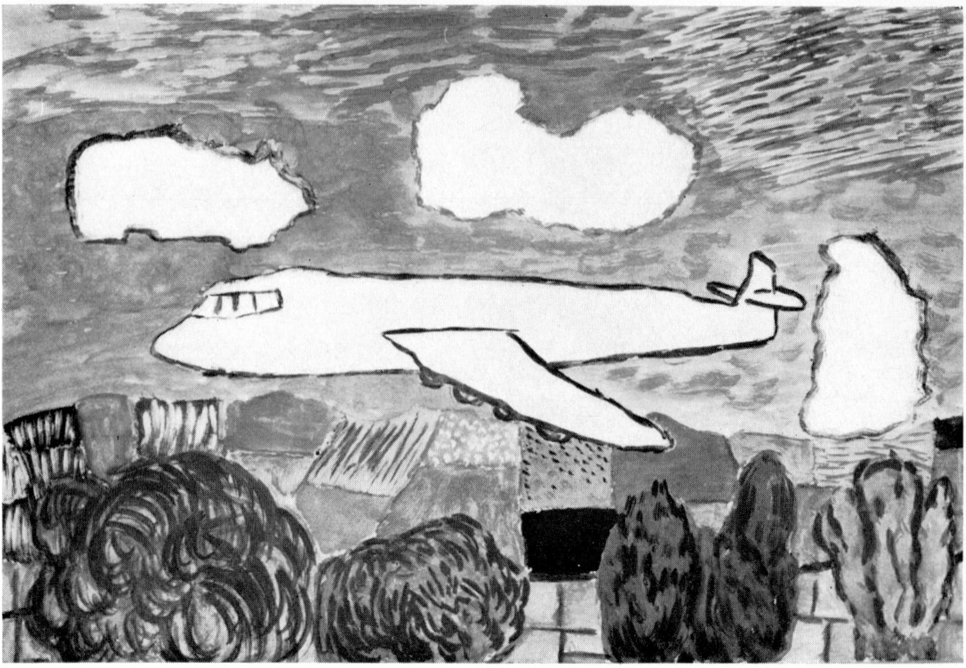

101 *A painting in powder colour, 22″ × 15″, by a 10 year old boy, one of many which provided the initial interest in 'Flight'.*

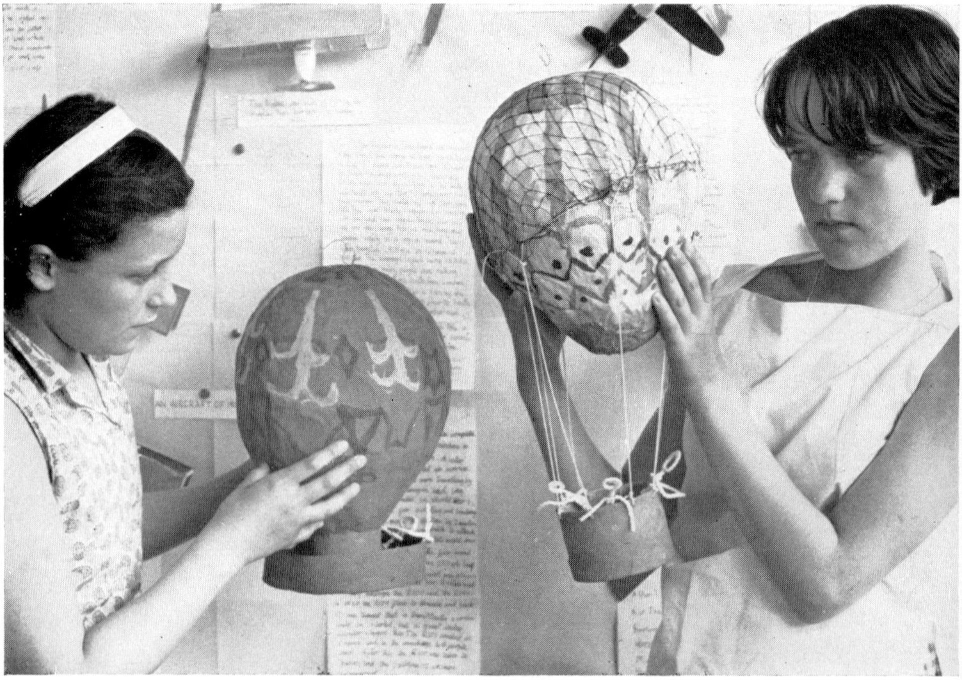

102 *Models of a hot air balloon and a hydrogen balloon made by 10 year old girls, see Chapter 6.*

shift arrangement, such as orange-boxes propped on desk tops or a clothes-horse standing on a table, may be equally if not more successful in stimulating children's imagination and in calling on their creative resources.

Several types of puppets may be introduced in the Primary school; glove puppets and shadow puppets can each provide the starting point for a number of varied, yet related activities. Creative writing, both dialogue and narrative, speech, drama, music, art and many aspects of stagecraft quite naturally merge in a production. With so wide a choice of interests it is possible for each member of a class to develop his own personal gifts and skills, or he may prefer to work at aspects with which he is less familiar.

Shadow-plays in particular create an atmosphere of enchantment and the shadow puppet can be enjoyed at many levels. In No. 127, Javanese puppets, we see extremes of sophistication and elaboration expressed through an elongated elegance of silhouette and movement. By way of contrast, No. 129 shows the telling simplicity of form that may be produced by quite young children. These puppets were made by six-year-old children who cut the shapes out of the thin cardboard sides of cornflake packets.

Some practical aspects of puppetry are described in Chapter 10.

AN EXPERIMENT IN INTEGRATION

Art is often included as a minor part of a general project, but in the work described in this section it was the interest aroused through some art lessons which provided the actual starting point for a term's topic with a class in a Primary school. Thanks to the kindness and co-operation of the Headmistress and her staff I was able to take some part in this activity.

The school stands within a few miles of an Air Force base, where most of the fathers worked. Many of the children were therefore accustomed to travel and had been to schools in foreign countries. Some had flown to and from places as far away as Aden and Singapore, and of the thirty-seven children certainly more than half had travelled by air.

Most of the children were ten years old and would be moving on to Secondary schools the following term. There was no streaming in the school and in this particular class the spread of ability was considerable. But the children worked well together, both as a class and in groups, and explored the many aspects of the theme with a sense of purpose and enthusiasm.

Bearing in mind their general background we decided on the theme of 'air' and planned to introduce this topic by means of imaginative paintings of aircraft. The class teacher, a drama teacher, and I worked closely together, and although we naturally discussed the range of work likely to be touched on, we were at the same time ready for quite unpredictable developments in the children's interests and were prepared to modify or extend our own ideas as the work unfolded.

Throughout the project small displays were arranged in the classroom. These were changed frequently, and included photographs, reproductions, maps, travel pamphlets and other related information, and we often noticed how the children's thoughts were given fresh direction through convenient access to this material. They were also able to choose books from their own school library and the class teacher always had a number of reference books available in the room. The flexibility of the time-table and general school organization made it possible to adjust a day's plans so that fresh interests could wholeheartedly be pursued as they arose.

It will not be possible to give a full account of all the work done by the children, but some record of the term's activities may indicate the range and the integration of work that grew quite spontaneously from their first paintings.

In the introductory art period the children, after about ten minutes of experimental brushwork, painted pictures of aeroplanes (Nos. 97 and 101). They had brought a number of model aircraft to school and these they studied and talked about in some detail. Skies too became interesting to them and the children enjoyed seeing a variety of reproductions of sky paintings. We looked at the subtle graduations of a Piero della Francesca sky, the glowing light and colour of the later Turners, and the dramatic quality of stormy skies painted by Vlaminck. Through such paintings the children became really interested in the ways in which skies may express the moods of different kinds of weather. They made their own small exhibitions of photographs and paintings, and frequently noticed the character and changing light of the skies which they would see through the large classroom windows.

But despite the general interest encouraged by these experiences, the children in their own paintings were rather unenterprising in their use of colour and needed more help in this direction. Therefore at the beginning of the second lesson, before they continued with their paintings, they had a 'mixing' session, exploring some of the many possibilities within each range of colour. This they enjoyed immensely, especially when all those wearing anything blue, for instance, were asked to stand together in a group, to show some of the diversities of shade and texture that may be found within one colour. They discovered delicate light blues, pale turquoise blues, strong clear blues ranging to deeper greenish-blues, purplish blues, very dark indigo, prussian and blackish-blues. Each child excitedly produced his bit of blue, perhaps the colour of a narrow stripe in a sock, a hairband or a jersey. Looking at the more subtle colours, they found it difficult to decide where blue ended and green began —some colours it seemed could equally well belong to either group. Quite simple demonstrations of this kind can help children to become much more aware of varied yet kindred colours.

The interest introduced by looking for colours in this way was followed by a practical exercise in which the children were asked to paint small patches of as many different blues as they could make. They were working with the limited range of paints mentioned on page 160. Children will learn more about colour by discovering for themselves how great a range can be produced from a few basic colours than by being given a large number of different ready-mixed colours. They were soon absorbed by the exciting possibilities of colour mixing. They then cut out small pieces, about one inch square, from the different painted portions and these they pinned on to a piece of board (23 × 17 in.) so as to form a large oval of graded colour-tones, starting with a pale, nearly white centre, and working outwards to increasingly dark tones (No. 96). The children saw how many different deep blues could approximate to black in tones while yet retaining their own quality of colour, and similarly how other colours could link up with white or with the many greys ranging between black and white. The whole effect was one of great liveliness of subtle colour variations within each tonal-area, and after this exercise the children became more adventurous and also more sensitive in the use of colour in their own work.

For the next picture they imagined that after a long flight they had landed near a dense jungle. Some plants and carved wooden animals, placed on a small mirror (No. 93), aroused the children's interest in the structure and variety of forms and helped some to picture a scene more clearly. For instance, the girl who painted No. 94 used the visual material quite fully whereas some of the class depended on it rather less, each readily inventing his own scene.

But the results at the end of this session were still a little disappointing because the preliminary drawings, which should have consisted of little more than the lightest blocking-in, had become too set and detailed. In fact it would have been better if the children had been persuaded to paint directly on to the paper without any drawing. As it was they tended merely to tickle the paper with their brushes, keeping too much within the charcoal lines rather than enjoying the freedom of spontaneous brushwork.

Hoping to retrieve their paintings at this early stage, I began the next session by showing the children some reproductions and a few transparencies of landscape paintings, noting with them the directness and variety in the different artists' brushwork. These made a great impression on them.

They particularly liked Vincent van Gogh's *Yellow Wheat* (Cypress Trees) and his *Wheat Field with Crows*, Henri Rousseau's *Snake-Charmer*, Paul Klee's *Landscape with Yellow Birds*, a landscape by Soutine in which he had used long, swirling strokes to paint a large tree, Kokoschka's *Tower Bridge, London* and Graham Sutherland's *Entrance to Lane*.

Not only did they enjoy these as pictures, talking about them in a discerning way, but having seen them their own painting became much more vigorous and fresh. As the pictures were finished they were mounted on different coloured sheets of sugar paper and, when all available display space in the classroom had been used, some paintings were shown on separate pieces of insulating board. In this way it was possible to exhibit every child's painting.

In describing these aircraft and jungle paintings I have tried to indicate how the teacher can introduce exercises and experiences likely to be of benefit and of some inspiration to the children while their actual work is in progress.

We next studied some of the simplest forms of primitive pattern, noting the rhythm and power of many carved and painted African designs. To-day there is so great an interest in Primitive art that it is fairly easy to find good photographs and reproductions, and soon we had an interesting little exhibition that provided many helpful sources of reference.

The children then made and decorated shields cut out of thin card, working out full, well-balanced patterns. These were done in different media. Some children used candle and ebony stain (No. 95). Others engraved their patterns on a wax-base. This was done by preparing their card with two layers of wax-crayon, then scratching the patterns through the top darker layer so as to reveal the lighter colour beneath (see page 191). Another group concentrated on painting the shields, using mainly a range of earth colours—yellow ochre, raw sienna, burnt sienna, raw umber, burnt umber, light red —with black and white. This led to some discussion on the sources of different pigments, and an interest in the characteristics of different groups of colours.

Soon after the children had started their first paintings, their curiosity about some of the historical aspects of the theme was aroused. Gradually they spent more time on these studies and on making a variety of models. Their work in art could also have been carried further at this point and, had we worked together another term, they might have sketched and studied patterns directly from ethnological sources in a museum. Also they were now ready to enjoy seeing paintings in an art gallery. This was clearly shown by the fascination with which they looked at some original oil paintings, lent to me by friends, that I was able to bring to the school. As well as discussing the general effect of each painting, they wanted to examine closely the textures of paint and the character of the brush strokes.

History of Flight

Many other areas of interest connected with the central topic were developed. One group of children traced something of the history of flight, from the early legends of Icarus to developments of the present day. Other children made a model of Lillienthal's glider of 1890 and of biplanes of the 1910 period. There was also a model of a 1926 two-seater biplane DH 4A, a 1939 Spitfire and a 1963 VC 10 airliner. The children constructed models of hot-air and hydrogen balloons of 1783, an airship of 1900, helicopters, hover-craft and parachutes.

They kept written records of the work they did and made wide use of reference books. They experimented in order to discover their own ways of working out the constructions for their models, collecting their facts from various sources, with the help of diagrams and illustrations. Nos. 98 and 102 show the interest and thoroughness with which the children worked out their practical problems. Independent thought and initiative were needed and we felt that the individual approach was particularly useful for those who had been more accustomed to following the precise instructions often provided with aircraft kits.

Another group became very interested in the theory of flight. As they watched insects and birds they imagined how men may have studied birds as the earliest ways of flying were evolved. The children were able to discover similarities between the gliding, soaring and diving movements in the flight of birds and those of man's early flying machines.

They visited an airfield where they were able to see gliders at close quarters in the hangars. One glider had been stripped for repair, and the children were fascinated by the 'triangles and boxes' that could be seen in the section of the wing. Glider-pilots explained something of the elements of powerless flight and of the mechanical principles underlying forms of construction in which rigidity and strength must be combined with extreme lightness. But perhaps the children experienced some of their most exciting moments when they were allowed to sit in the cockpits and handle the controls, for they seemed at once to be transported to remote worlds of their own imagination.

The first-hand impressions gained through these visits contributed powerfully to the quality of their creative writing and to their work in speech and mime. Later the children wrote letters of thanks which, far more than bare acknowledgements of the visits, were expressive of their real sense of enjoyment; many of them described quite fully the work they were themselves attempting.

Wind Power

In the meantime some children studied man's use of wind power at different times. Nos. 99 and 100 show some of the models connected with this particular interest. Informative descriptions were written for the benefit of the rest of the class, in which the children explained the use and history of each model.

One aspect of the topic that came to life unexpectedly had to do with seed dispersal. One day the children noticed quantities of white fluff drifting across the school playground. They quickly collected this cotton-like poplar seed by the handful, and in this way became interested in a new study. They searched the library books for information on trees and plants and were fascinated to find how their own observations illustrated some of the principles of propagation. They then collected dandelion, thistle, sycamore and other fruits that had been dispersed by the wind, using lenses to see the finer details.

Geographical, Mathematical and Scientific Interests

During the course of the term the general geographical aspects were studied by the whole class. The children worked in twelve small groups and, from a large map of the world, each chose a country to study. The starting point was again an imaginary journey by air.

Many children chose countries they knew already. Groups variously wrote to travel agencies, collected stamps, photographs, posters and maps and each group of children generally found out as much as they could assimilate about the country they had chosen. They found many travel books in the library and read as much as they could about their subject. By the end of the term each small group was able to give a well-informed talk to the whole class.

They were enthusiastic in describing and discussing the different conditions and customs of the countries, and really began to think about some important world problems. Their talks were illustrated by large display sheets assembled round a map, linked to it by means of coloured wools representing the different air routes. The children enjoyed working out from airline brochures the fares for journeys by air and comparing the cost of different kinds of air travel. They also compared the speed of air and other types of transport. Measuring the distances between countries and the study of currency and exchange rates gave further opportunities for practical work in mathematics.

The topic of 'air' also aroused a curiosity about some elementary scientific laws, such as those of air pressure and wind currents. The children watched and carried out simple experiments with candles burning under large or small jars, and found out how long it was before the flames went out. They compared each other's rate of breathing, pumped up car tyres, and investigated the principle of the syphon. Soon they were ready to think about more complex topics such as rain cycles, cloud formations and the factors that influence weather. Here again a constant use of reference books supplemented the results of their own practical work and added to their understanding.

English

There were two main approaches to work in English. The children learned how to record precisely in their own words the information they had gathered about different aspects of the topic. They were encouraged also to talk freely and to write imaginatively about all sorts of experiences and ideas relating to the main theme.

Much of their creative writing had a freshness that sprang from the intensity of their personal interest. For instance, the experience gained through painting jungle themes seemed to lend greater depth to the children's imaginative writing and their expressive use of words frequently echoed qualities found in their paintings. The children's enjoyment of the colour transparencies also added to their feeling for descriptive language. This interaction of the different experiences is shown in these extracts from the children's writing on tropical forests or the jungle.

The atmosphere was humid and wet. Great clouds of steam rose from the ground in a rather eerie manner. Large spreading, trailing vines climbed and twined round the trees, strangling them in their attempts to reach the sky, far, far above the highest tree.

A large hippopotamus lumbered to the pool for a huge splash and to drink the cool, clear water. Its thick, hard skin shone in the water and beads of water rolled off its horny back. The heavy animal grunted with pleasure as it swam around.

The whole forest seemed to him like the Wembley Football Stadium on Cup Final day, with the occasional screech of a parrot ringing over and echoing round the whole place, like an angry spectator screaming at the other team. . . . I was dazzled by the reflection of sun rays gleaming on the shining pool. Round the edge of the pool there were thousands of footprints all mingled up, I noticed though that the elephant had been the last to drink. The middle of the pool was bubbling like a fountain, and as I looked to my right I saw a running stream. I knew then that I had found what I was looking for, for I had been sent by His Majesty the King to find the source of the River Shungi.

An unusual kind of bird came near me, I held out my hand and the bird remained still so that I had time to touch its rough back and to see the peculiar marking on its wing before it flew away.

The great shrubs in this dense jungle were twice as thick as a man's arm. We were not very far into this great jungle but already we had to hack our way through. All through the forest we could smell the dampness of the earth.

The aircraft we were flying in swooped down like a gigantic bird and came down to a rough landing on the bumpy surface of the jungle air-strip . . . the following morning we paddled downstream in a large canoe. We appeared to be in a dark, green tunnel, as the branches of the tropical plants met overhead. A puma stood on the bank, a blotch of yellow against a green wall. . . . I felt the roughness of leaves against my burning face. . . . The following morning we awoke in the steaming hotness of the tropical jungle. We went to a waterhole to watch and film the animals drinking.

The rain stopped as suddenly as it had begun and the constant beating of water falling from the heavy leaves made a queer noise.

Then I heard the whirring of the helicopter overhead, it had come to take me back. A rope ladder was dropped down into our clearing. I climbed up it and when I was at the top I looked down. All I could see were the green tree tops. Now we were so high I could only see specks.

Everything was trying to reach the sun. All the trees and ferns looked as though I was seeing them through a giant magnifying glass.

The children imagined themselves in their writing to be explorers, naturalists, photographers, missionaries, doctors and nurses; the stories of their imaginary flights and experiences were as personal and varied as their paintings had been.

Dramatic Work

In their dramatic work, too, they were able to launch into a really exciting programme on the theme of flight. They first considered the actual conditions of flight. After much introductory discussion the children began a series of mimes in the school hall. These were de-signed to help them to imagine the feel of different windforces. They then practised movement to a record of 'wind' (No. 7FX10, one of a number of very useful sound-effects, available in E.M.I. records). The idea was to give the children a vocabulary of movements, rather in the same way that the colour exercises introduced into their painting had helped them towards a fuller understanding of the use of colour. From this vocabulary they could then build up dance and drama.

After the class had felt how it was to move and work in a wind, they constructed a more ambitious drama based on the impact of a whirlwind on a community. They were now ready to do a considerable amount of group work, and often used the tape-recorder. In actual fact the children developed a good many of their ideas independently; for instance, during the last four weeks of the project a group of children were recording on their own nearly every day during the lunch hour, enjoying opportunities for spontaneous work. The value of allowing them to work and manage the tape-recorder away from adult supervision was fully justified when, as a result, many highly original and individual scenes were recorded on tape.

The children recorded their imaginary experiences on aeroplanes, their reactions to a flight, and their impressions of the different countries in which they landed. The fact that they were gaining a factual understanding about flight and travel by air in some of their other work brought a certain authenticity and a fresh depth to their imaginative expression in drama. As their teacher put it: 'We could only do this well when we had absorbed the information and were drawing from it quite naturally to give fullness and a new dimension to our work'.

Some groups developed more elaborate dramatic scenes in airports and foreign markets, and were learning to handle a variety of situations and character studies. This was all done without a sense of show or 'theatre'; there was no attempt to put anything across to an audience; the children were dramatizing their impressions and experiences by living them out in this way.

When reviewing the work at the end of the term, we felt it had proved that a number of subjects, each with particular qualities and disciplines, might be satisfyingly related to one theme which in this instance had been introduced through art. It was not only the information acquired that had been of value to these children. What was important was their excitement and their individual involvement in each fresh experience, as well as their appreciation of the diverse aspects of their topic.

'THE OLD ELM TREE'

All the integrated study arising from the aeroplanes was done by a class of thirty-seven children, about ten years old, in a Primary school of about two hundred and fifty children. A very different work, 'The Old Elm Tree' (Nos. 105–108), was a book written in a small, one-teacher, country school with about twenty-four children whose ages ranged from five to eleven years, and who worked and played in one big room. In this creative writing we see the quality that may spring spontaneously from ideas that are of immediate concern to children.

About three or four large books incorporating creative work from all the children are produced in this school each year, so that there is a certain tradition of communal activity. Whatever form the work may take, it is in the first instance suggested by some current interest.

This particular story movingly describes how an old elm tree, intimately known and loved by the children, had finally to be blown up and destroyed. Recently, when I visited the school, the children took me to the place where the elm tree had grown and, sitting near-by, they read their story to me. Some of the children who had worked on the book had in the meantime moved on to Secondary schools, but as far as possible each part was read out by the child who had written it. The older children were particularly helpful and patient as the younger ones read and talked about their pictures. A full page had been used for each sentence and another for each picture. Some of the illustrations were drawn with crayons, others were painted, yet others were built up in collage, and in some all these techniques were successfully combined.

This was the children's story:

The Old Elm Tree

About 200 years ago in a lovely green
meadow in the village of Madingley
there was a little seedling elm.
After a while it started to grow.
It grew bigger every year until it was a
hundred years old, and very very big.
The creatures who lived in it then have gone now.
Birds came to nest in its branches.
They built lovely nests and made them very
comfortable for their baby birds.

Snakes lived at the bottom of the Tree.
The squirrels paid friendly visits
now and then
Rabbits used to come and play near-by.
Swallows came and perched on the branches
for a rest.
The foxes came in the night to catch the rabbits.
Lots of beetles and little creatures lived in the tree
A tawny owl slept in the branches in the night time
Black-birds came to sing a song
Slimy worms wriggled round the roots
The cows rubbed their backs on its bark
Father Christmas peeped at it one day
When it was snowy and cold and the tree had
no leaves
Father Christmas was on his rounds, but the
school wasn't there
He only saw the robin looking for crumbs.
One summer day a kind friendly boy came to
the village. When he found the tree he played with
the creatures that lived there.
About that time the grown-ups decided a school
was needed
So they built a school with a little house joined on.
In the little house lived a very strict school master.
The school was small and it only had one room. The
school master slept in our Play-room
or Store-room.
The play room had no toys in it then.
After a while lots of children came to the school
so another school-room was built. Now it
is the dining room.
When school was over the children used to play in the
lofty branches of the tree.
Pussy cats came to visit the tree looking for mice.
It was still there when the soldiers came to camp
in the war.
As the tree got older big holes began to appear.
And the children played lovely games.
They played armies and cowboys and the holes got
bigger.
At last there came a big Hollow inside like
a room
The cricketers called it their pavilion and
wouldn't let the children play.
This made the children un-happy because only

the elm tree was good for their games.
One sad day a man with ginger hair came along
and said the tree must be pulled down.
Soon after there came a firm of wood cutters
in a shiny van with a tree painted on it
for advertisements.
First they lopped off the biggest branches.
Then they blew up the friendly elm making
a terrible bang which shook the school, cracked
a window and made plaster fall.
Lesley was in the Play-room with the little ones
and they thought the sky had fallen. First the
children were scared and then when they knew
about their friendly tree they were very sad.
All through the Easter Holidays the tree was left and
the children played on it secretly.
The end came very soon, for the wood-cutter thought
the lovely old tree was no good for cutting and
selling. So on one lovely May day when the
children were in school, they burnt it leaving
inquisitive cows gazing at the ashes.
Then all the children were very unhappy that their
lovely old tree had been destroyed
So they went into school and sadly wrote this
story.
Now no-body knows the tree was there—only the
children.

In printing the children's story we have kept to the exact arrangement and punctuation of each page of their book.

Every child contributed several pages of writing and pictures, and the whole book was completed in less than three weeks. Every afternoon, or sometimes for a whole day at a time, the work went on. This concentration enabled the children's first enthusiasm to be kept alive throughout the project.

The idea of writing the book arose in this way. One Thursday afternoon the children were shocked and distressed to see the remains of the elm tree being burned. As they sat on the grass watching, they talked about it freely—saying how quite soon there would be no one who knew about the elm tree, or where it had stood, or what had happened to it. Where would the squirrels and all the other creatures go? And where would the children play now? How old was the tree? And how many years would it take for another tree to grow so big? Another hundred years? Back in the classroom they decided they must make a book, so that their tree could never be forgotten, and the rest of the afternoon was spent in elaborating the story.

The children's impressions and recollections were expressed with intensity of feeling, their teacher quickly noting all that they said. The next morning she read the many fragments of conversation to the children and invited further suggestions about what they wanted to include in their book. During the week-end they were asked to think about the tree, while it was all fresh in their minds, and on Monday the book was started.

Each child wrote his own sentences, if necessary first referring to the teacher's note-book, in which his own statements were clearly recorded. Some began by writing, others started with a drawing or painting. Everyone worked at his own level and, knowing that his contributions were needed for the book, tried hard to produce his best work. When most of the book had been finished, a small group of older children became responsible for the final stages, which included assembling the book, sewing it together, planning, writing and decorating the title-page. After some experiments, they made an attractive bark-rubbing for the cover.

In the course of the work several of the children became interested in the earlier history of the school and of its surroundings. They were able to trace this back over the past hundred years. They were shown some of the early village records and Church documents and were fascinated by the first school log-books and by a very old 'punishment' book: '*In the little house lived a very strict school master*'.

During this time several other interests connected with the theme were also followed. The children made and dressed dolls and puppets which they were able to take home and keep.

The youngest children, working together on a large collage panel, made a special tree of their own. One or two older children had drawn a large tree shape for them, by lightly chalking an outline on to a piece of hessian. On to this base the five- and six-year-olds then freely pasted many leaves, nuts, seed-pods, twigs, fragments of materials and different kinds of papers. They worked at it spontaneously when they felt inclined. In the end they produced a panel that was exciting in colour and texture.

While the children were writing the story, they spent some of their time in preparing a short play about the tree and all the people. This was produced in mime form, among the trees in the school grounds. The children wore painted masks that they had made, and this approach gave even the most diffident child enough confidence to take part. The masks were made of canvas and paper, pasted on to structures of fairly stiff wire. It is true that some guidance was given by the teacher, but the children themselves were quick to discover the best methods of construction and were ready to help each other in the fitting and actual making of the masks.

The whole project, with its breadth of interest, had become one of major importance to the children, and through it they were able to re-create an experience affecting their own lives in terms of art and shared activity.

CHAPTER 7

Pattern

From early times man has expressed his feeling for ordered rhythm through the rich variety of pattern with which he has decorated the objects he has made.

There is the band of incised herring-bone lines on an Anglo-Saxon pot making such a satisfying pattern, with its position on the shoulder and the emphasis of its rhythms fitting in so well with the form of the pot. The broad simplicity of a dog-tooth design on an early Norman capital can be one of many carved patterns admired in a local church or cathedral. Or we may linger over the decorated line endings in a medieval manuscript, appreciating the flow of the quill-made strokes and the particular beauty of the illuminator's colours. We can find countless examples of art and craft forms that reflect this universal sense of pattern, in all parts of the world and from all ages.

In children's work, too, this inborn feeling for repetition and balance is an outstanding feature, and in Chapter 1 we noted how powerfully this sense of pattern is expressed in their drawing and painting.

This feeling for pattern is part of the child's whole being and can hardly be thought of in isolation; we find it as vividly expressed in his intuitive forms of speech, play and movement as in his many art activities. From his earliest years there should be opportunities for him to develop this sense of pattern in ways that are satisfying and meaningful to him.

In the Nursery and Infant schools children can become deeply absorbed in sorting out and arranging things of different shape, size, colour and texture, instinctively finding groupings that have a pleas-ing order. Throughout the Primary school years, this feeling and thinking creatively through the actual handling of objects continue to contribute to the child's aesthetic development as effectively as the practical work that may be introduced.

The making of specific collections, or the planning and arranging of small displays, should provide satisfying experiences for children.

Exploring pattern-forms of all countries and periods, and studying these in both man-made and natural forms, extends the range of the child's interests and builds up for him the essentials of a visual language. The teaching of pattern must, therefore, be wide in its interpretation, drawing its inspiration both from the traditions of the past and the trends underlying modern design. Taught in this spirit pattern making becomes an indispensable part of the art course, but without this breadth of interest it easily degenerates into a dull, undemanding occupation. Pattern making, then, should include wide ranges of activities, each of which leads to fresh adventures in searching, finding and looking.

Pattern Making and Picture Making

At every level there should be a close interaction between pattern and picture making; it will be found that qualities fundamental to pictorial expression naturally emerge through the making of patterns. For instance, the child who has painted a well-balanced band pattern, or worked out a well-related potato-print, will gain a feeling for space-filling and composition generally. When he makes a pattern, the child is not concerned with subject matter; his entire interest and thought can therefore be focused on the purely visual considerations of composition, shape, colour, tone and texture. Through a greater understanding of these qualities he is able, when he returns to picture making, to express the essentials of his subject more vividly than he might otherwise have done.

PRESERVING THE CHILD'S NATURAL FEELING FOR PATTERN

In the Primary school we look for a full but unforced development of the child's natural feeling for pattern. Neatness of execution is not the chief concern, nor should undue emphasis be placed on purely mechanical accuracy; in fact much of the life and sparkle in children's patterns comes from the many subtle variations and irregularities within an ordered system.

Brushwork repeat patterns, for example, should be painted freehand. If it seems necessary to have some guide for the placing of the main rhythms, then it is usually enough for the paper to be lightly folded into appropriate divisions. Elaborate tracing, complicated measurements, or the use of templates are likely to destroy the vitality and spontaneity of a pattern. They should be discarded in favour of more direct methods. Laborious drawings on paper, made before a pattern is worked out in another medium, should also, as a general rule, be avoided. In a few particular cases, for instance when printing on fabric, some preparatory work on paper may be necessary, though even this should be kept to a minimum. Whenever possible, children should be encouraged to work directly on the material, allowing the nature of the medium to dictate and decide the characteristics that emerge.

There is, however, a place for all sorts of pattern making on paper for its own sake, and designs in paint, pen and ink, pastel and collage, as well as a variety of patterns printed on paper, open out possibilities.

Patterns for a Purpose

As an alternative to the straightforward, all-over pattern, children also need opportunities to design for specific shapes and purposes. Through tackling different kinds of work, they meet fresh problems which have to be solved; the planning of a pattern for a particular shape calls on the kind of understanding that can recharge the work with a new sense of purpose and interest.

Borders, squares, rectangles, circles, ovals, shields and masks are some of the variations that can be introduced. No. 95, a shield design made with a candle resist, suggests the attractive pattern possibilities inherent in this shape; No. 104, collective work in mosaics, shows ways in which the square can be used; in No. 113, fish mobiles, the freely painted brush and ink patterns are well correlated to the simple shapes of the fish; in No. 132, the paper-bag heads, the painted patterns are made to fit the square shapes of the bags; and in No. 135, decorative masks, the patterns have been fully integrated with the mask forms.

Pattern making can have a strong functional appeal and the fact that something is being made and printed for a special purpose will stimulate fresh enthusiasm in the work. Infants like to paint or print mats, table-cloths and curtains for play-houses; children of all ages often need book-covers, not only for large scrap-books for the whole class, but for individual anthologies or for smaller note-books. Through this variety children learn to relate the scale of their patterns to the size of the objects on which they are to be used.

Children of nine and ten years of age enjoy making bags, ties, aprons, skirts, small cushions and pin cushions, and curtains out of fabric they have themselves printed or designed. They naturally get immense pleasure, and gain in confidence generally, when they see their own efforts satisfactorily used in these ways.

We can imagine the attractive skirts that were made out of the fabrics shown in No. 112. In fact most of the children in this particular class used their fabrics to make a variety of mats, tray-cloths, cushions, aprons and skirts. Some of their patterns were printed with Helizarin dyes; some were printed with a lemon discharge on material previously dyed in permanganate of potash; and some were painted with a wax resist, or were knotted and tied and dyed in indigo. Some of these processes are described more fully in the section on fabric design (pages 138–149); the point of interest here is that children in the Primary school, given encouragement and opportunity, can develop a real feeling for qualities of pattern and colour through such work. The techniques are well within their capabilities, and the equipment is simple and need not be expensive.

In order to avoid unnecessary repetition, I have fully described one process—that of the painted linear pattern. The general principles apply equally to other forms of pattern, in paint and other media, and can be adapted to suit the particular qualities of the medium or technique concerned. Each type of pattern work will need to be equally carefully planned; and every process will naturally suggest lines of interest suitable for classroom displays.

PAINTED LINEAR BAND PATTERNS

Materials
Papers to choose from:
    Kitchen paper
    Sugar paper
    Cartridge paper
    Carefully selected sheets of newspaper (size about 20 × 15 in.)
Painting equipment:
    Powder or tempera-block colours
    Mixing palettes
    Large hog-hair brushes, Nos. 8 or 9, and a few smaller brushes
    for finer work

The Four Main Stages of Work

I   A number of varied, simple, rhythmical lines are painted horizontally across the page, using one colour.

II   When the linear rhythms have been completed over the whole paper, the shapes between the lines are developed in terms of solids and textures.

III   Next there may be an enrichment of the pattern through further detail where this is needed.

IV   Practical work should be related to historic and primitive examples, and to contemporary industrial design, by means of collections or classroom displays.

TEACHING POINTS IN STAGE I

1   A rhythmical line, such as a wavy, scollop, or zig-zag line is painted across the top of the page in one colour. A second line is then painted close to it, after which a third is added, and so on until the paper is filled (see diagram on page 121).

2   As each fresh, rhythmical line is added, its relationship to the preceding one and to the pattern as a whole must be carefully considered.

3   The children should look for the shapes enclosed by the lines, so that these too are pleasing.

4   As a general rule, a combination of curved and straight shapes is especially satisfying.

5   It will also be found that a variety in scale, from deeper lines, about $1\frac{1}{2}$ in., to very narrow ones, about $\frac{1}{4}$ in., will contribute to the interest of the whole.

6   By holding small mirrors against the painted lines the children can see effects that would be produced by painting the lines in reverse.

Children enjoy looking for these different aspects and will combine them in original and individual ways so that no two patterns will be alike.

TEACHING POINTS IN STAGE II

1   The pattern is painted in a number of varied colours which should relate to the first colour that was chosen.

2   Just as in stage I each line was looked at as part of the whole pattern, similarly each space-shape is now considered as part of a well-balanced, unified design (see Fig. 1).

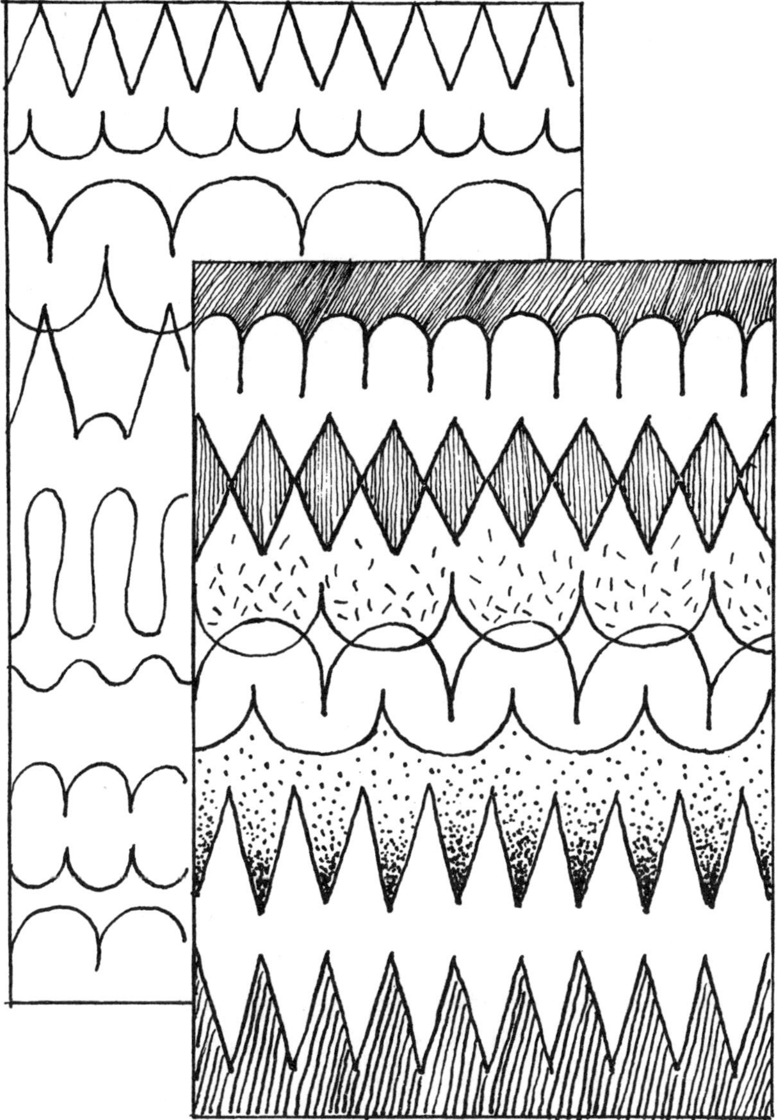

FIG. 1. Patterns made by relating simple, rhythmic lines, i.e. straight, curved-narrow, wide. The interest of the spaces between the lines is developed by means of colour, tone and texture (page 120).

3   The shapes between the lines are developed as solids or as textures of varying weight. At this point a brief demonstration (on blackboard or paper) will show how the solid shapes may

be painted in a flat colour, or how they may be graded from a light to a dark tone. Children will see that where tones are allowed to become too uniform the main shapes of a pattern will tend to disappear. Variation of tone will emphasize the impact of one shape on another.

Band patterns chosen from historic or contemporary sources can illustrate the beauty of a well-chosen juxtaposition of rhythms, colours and tones. Looking at and enjoying these qualities in other examples will help children to develop their own patterns with a greater insight.

Analytical appreciation of this kind, introduced while the actual work is in progress, is more appropriate for older than for younger children. The very young, and indeed some children throughout the Primary school, will be eager to follow their own impulses and should be allowed to develop their work intuitively. But the child who asks 'What shall I put here?' or 'What shall I do next?' will be better able to make his own decisions as a result of such guidance and stimulus.

TEACHING POINTS IN STAGE III

1   Some children will enjoy elaborating their patterns with quite intricate detail, perhaps by using smaller brushes. Textures in light colours may be painted on the darker parts and vice versa.

2   However richly the children may like to develop their patterns, they should not lose sight of the whole design. Embellishments should serve to bring out more fully the chief rhythms of the original design.

3   By studying the detailed patterns on natural forms children realize how in nature, too, these minute decorations often express the main rhythms of growth; for example, they may notice how organically the pattern made by the circles of growth on the cross-section of a tree trunk relates to its basic form.

TEACHING POINTS IN STAGE IV

1   Because of their interest in their own patterns children will appreciate examples of historic and primitive patterns, in which similar lines and bands have been used and placed together attractively. They may be fascinated to see how a particular

rhythm familiar to them—for example the zig-zag line—has been used decoratively in a number of different materials and crafts at other times. This can lead to a small exhibition devoted entirely to the zig-zag theme, the children discovering it in nature as well as in man-made objects. Many examples will be found in architectural and industrial forms of the present day. Classroom displays may include small patterns of dress and furnishing fabrics, in which similar motifs have been used, and they will also be found on stones, shells, feathers, shards of insects, leaves and tree bark.

2   Ideally, children should follow up their own classroom experiences with visits to museums or buildings, making sketches and collecting photographs. During a session on pattern making, children may also like to make a general book of samples of patterns. All these activities will encourage them to see their own work in a broader context.

Band Patterns in Other Media

The same principles of design followed in painting band patterns are involved when using many other media and processes. These may include:

Crayon
Pastels on light or dark paper
Paint combined with torn or cut paper
Candle and ebony stain
Printing with vegetables and with other blocks of different surfaces
Simple weaving in a wide variety of materials
Clay—simple pottery forms.

OTHER FORMS OF PATTERN MAKING

1. Patterns in Finger Painting

Finger painting—which may also be used pictorially—lends itself well to pattern making, and provides a particularly appropriate medium for Infants. A fairly thick cold-water paste is applied to the paper—this may be done by hand, with a large brush or with a piece of sponge. The child, after lightly dipping his fingers into the paste, picks up a little dry powder colour on them and applies the colour to the pasted surface of the paper in flowing pattern move-ments. The fingers push the colour along easily, while finer detail can be scratched into the pattern with the nails. (A fuller account of the technique is given on page 164.)

Finger painting can be used to paint compact linear or all-over designs for books or small folders. An alternative method is to scratch the pattern into the paste surface with various simple tools such as small sticks or pieces of balsa-wood. Coarse combs, cut out of stiff pieces of cardboard, make lines of varying thicknesses. But on the whole the direct contact between hand and medium will lead to the most worthwhile work, as in this approach the rhythm of movement is transferred directly through the sensitive finger-tips to the strokes that are made on the paper. As in clay work, the child experiences a direct satisfaction through this sense of touch.

2. *Painted Medallion Patterns*

These patterns should be painted free-hand on fairly large sheets of paper. The pattern is built up by a series of evergrowing concentric circles—of variously patterned lines—that spread outwards from a core near the centre of the page. A simple shape, about the size of a table tennis ball, forms the heart of the pattern—perhaps a star or a circle. Each additional painted linear circle should look well in re-lation to the rest of the pattern, as well as being of interest in itself. The design grows outwards until the edges of the paper are reached and a complete circular or oval pattern is produced. This is then de-veloped in a similar way to the linear band pattern. The corners of the paper may either be treated decoratively, becoming part of the whole design, or the circular medallions may be complete in themselves. They can look very attractive cut out and mounted for display.

Painted medallion patterns and painted band patterns can give the most diffident child confidence in his own creative powers. Each type of pattern is evolved through successive stages. At each step the work must be thought out, but the child need not have a conception of the final effect in his mind, and sooner or later the pattern will 'take over' and almost paint itself.

3. *Painted Repeat Patterns*

Patterns can also be developed through simple brush strokes repeated free-hand on paper that has been lightly folded into rectangles.

A fairly large, spontaneous stroke—probably combining curved and straight elements—is painted in the top left-hand division of the paper, touching three sides of the rectangle (patterns based on small isolated strokes tend to become thin and disconnected). This stroke is repeated rhythmically from left to right across the page in each rectangle, until the first stage has been completed over all the paper.

The strokes may be purely abstract or may be derived from letters or numerals. These should be chosen primarily for the interest of their shapes, which may need to be exaggerated or distorted to fit each folded rectangle. Too great a concentration on the actual letters is inclined to produce units that have little flow of movement.

The main rhythm of the pattern is then more fully developed, and the units are linked by brushwork. Some shapes may be treated in solid colour, others with brush textures (varied media, such as pastel, or pen and ink, can be combined with paint). Sometimes background shapes may be left plain, and it will be found that the interaction of figure and ground (the positive and negative) plays as important a part in patterns as in pictures.

Each stage of the pattern is completed before the next is introduced so that, from start to finish, the pattern is thought of as a whole.

4. *Repeat Patterns using Torn or Cut Shapes*

Another way to make repeat patterns is to tear a number of similar shapes out of a piece of coloured paper that has been folded over so as to produce about sixteen rectangles (roughly $5\frac{1}{2} \times 3\frac{1}{2}$ in. for units that are to be used on a page measuring about 22×15 in.). The torn or cut shapes should be kept fairly broad and simple, though a hole torn out of each coloured piece sometimes adds interest to the shapes. The pieces are then spread out on the large sheet of paper and various arrangements are tried out. The units can be placed together so that they touch, or a more open distribution may be preferred. One advantage of this method is that the child can move the pieces about experimentally before deciding on the final arrangement.

The pasted shapes often stand out too strongly as separate blocks of colour, and they then need to be more fully integrated to obtain a harmonious pattern. This can be done by rhythmical brushwork, some of which may be superimposed on the shapes themselves; again each decision is made in relation to the whole effect. Patterns based on an arrangement of flat, pasted paper-shapes may be developed in a variety of media; if powder colour is used it should be thick enough in consistency for the palest colours to show up well on a dark—even on a black—ground. This form of pattern making encourages a feeling for mass and larger shapes, and can be a helpful means of counteracting work that has become over-linear.

5. *Patterns made with Candle and Ebony Stain*

Several ways of working with candles and ebony stain are described in Chapter 9. The emphasis here is on their use in pattern making.

Patterns made in this way have marked contrasts of light and dark, as well as interestingly broken surface textures. Briefly, the drawing is first done with a candle so that the greasy candle surface acts as a resist when dark stain is finally brushed over the drawing (No. 95). The technique fascinates children, for whom it has an element of magic when the completed pattern suddenly emerges from the paper.

MATERIALS. Similar to those needed for candle-rubbing technique, see page 192. Paper should be cut fairly small, about 10 × 7 in., as it is less easy for children to press firmly enough with the candle over a larger area, and in any case full, compact patterns on small paper will probably produce the most successful results.

METHOD

a.   For band patterns some guiding lines may be ruled lightly over the paper, at fairly close but irregular intervals. This is not essential and many children manage good spacing and produce adequately straight lines by eye.

b.   With firm pressure, and using variously shaped pieces of candle, different types of lines—straight and curved, wide and narrow, thick and thin—are drawn in a well-related arrangement at closely spaced intervals across the paper (see linear band patterns, page 119).

c.   The lines themselves may be elaborated and the spaces between the lines developed with candle textures, though some paper should be left plain.

d.   From time to time the paper is held horizontally at eye-level in order to check that a fairly generous amount of candle-work is distributed over its surface. Patterns in which the candle-drawing has been too sparsely applied are apt to appear over-dark and heavy when finally painted over with the stain.

e. Ebony stain is lightly brushed over all the paper, and the pattern is placed flat on old newspaper to dry.

6. *Candle Patterns with Colour*

Once the basic technique is understood, further patterns may be made using colour. This involves an additional process, introduced at the beginning of the work.

a. Apply coloured ink with a brush, planning for the coloured areas to come at fairly frequent intervals. Different effects should be tried out on small, spare pieces of paper first. On the whole, fairly broad bands of colour are most effective. The placing of the coloured areas should be carefully planned, but the actual painting on of the ink needs to be done freely, leaving quite roughly painted edges. If the coloured inks are applied too neatly, the final design may appear disappointingly hard and rigid.

b. The coloured ink must be allowed to dry thoroughly.

c. When it is quite dry, the drawing is made, as already described, with the candle. The candle-work should be placed so that it comes partly on the inked portions, partly on the plain paper.

d. When the candle-drawing is finished, ebony stain is brushed over the whole and allowed to dry.

e. A rich effect will result, the colour adding depth to the whole pattern.

f. After one or two experiments the process will be readily understood. Full attention can then be given to obtaining a good integration of colour with the general movement of the pattern. The colour should not cut across the main feeling of the design but should emphasize its essential rhythms. It may sometimes be helpful first to try out the pattern in candle and black stain, then to decide where the colour will be needed and what kind of shapes or bands of colour will best fit in with the pattern as a whole.

g. Patterns made in this way provide attractive covers for small note-books and reading-books. The scale of the pattern must be adapted to suit the size of the book. A large, straggling design would look lost on a small cover. On paper 10 × 7 in., the lines should probably be placed at intervals of about half an inch to one inch. Wider bands of pattern should be used on larger pieces of paper. Covers suitable for simply sewn or stapled scrap-books and folders can be made in this way.

h.   A dull sheen may be given to the surface of a completed pattern by polishing the paper lightly with a white shoe polish or a special wax polish for paper. This provides a serviceable surface for book covers.

i.   It should be stressed that full, varied work with differently shaped pieces of candle produces the most satisfying results; children should therefore be encouraged to draw as generously as possible with the candle, spending a good deal of time on this stage of the work. Once the ebony stain has been applied the pattern cannot be made lighter.

It is possible, however, to draw with coloured crayons on top of the black ebony-stained surfaces, once these are dry. Younger children particularly may find this the most practicable way of introducing colour.

Floor and tree rubbings (how to make these is described on page 194) and textures from a number of other surfaces, such as frosted glass and fibre-matting, also offer possibilities for rubbed patterns which can be combined with colour. The rubbed and drawn candle-surfaces in No. 116, a pictorial subject, show a variety of textures (fine and coarse, light and dark, regular and irregular) that could also be satisfactorily used for book covers.

PATTERNS PRINTED WITH VEGETABLES AND OTHER SURFACES

In this process patterns are built up by means of rhythmical printing with a unit arranged or repeated so as to produce an all-over design. Potato printing, particularly, is a technique that can be used successfully throughout the Primary school. Apart from printing on paper, various forms of printing on fabric can be introduced. The dyes that are used are reasonably easy to handle and can be satisfactorily fixed by ironing, so as to be fast to light and water (No. 112).

The simplest forms of potato printing are used in the Infant school. From the earliest stages the functional interest has a strong appeal, and Infants enjoy using their patterns for small mats, book covers, Christmas wrapping papers and for wall-papers for playhouses.

Seven- and eight-year-old children are able to print material for puppet clothes; curtains for a theatre or Wendy-house can be produced as a combined effort, each child printing a few rows which contribute to the design of the whole material. Older children who are able to print fabrics for ties, scarves and skirts will become really interested in qualities of design and will be ready to enjoy further experiments in textile printing and dyeing at the Secondary stages.

Potato printing may also be developed pictorially and can be effectively combined with other techniques, such as candle-rubbings and leaf-rubbings, Nos. 109 and 111.

TWO METHODS OF PRINTING WITH VEGETABLES

Printing with vegetables can be done either with a printing pad or by applying the colour to the printing surface with a brush. I would particularly recommend the former, because the regular movement of printing lends a rhythm to the pattern as a whole. On the other hand, the second method may be easier to organize in some schools and can also produce very satisfactory results.

A. *Printing with the use of a Pad*

MATERIALS

Vegetables:

Small potatoes, medium sized carrots, small turnips or swedes.

Tools:

An old, thin, sharp kitchen knife

A lino-tool handle

A v-shaped lino-cutter, size 2

A gouge lino-cutter, size 3. The end of a metal penholder, without the nib, makes a very adequate gouge, especially for Infants; a piece of old umbrella-spoke, with a cork at one end serving as a handle, also makes an excellent gouge.

A penknife is useful, but not essential.

Papers:

Good quality newspaper, cut to pieces of about 10 × 8 in. The newsprint should be of an even grey and dark pictures should be avoided.

Sugar paper

Kitchen paper

Any slightly absorbent paper—very smooth, shiny papers are
less satisfactory—can be experimented with, such as tissue
paper (white and coloured), Chinese printing paper, paper
handkerchiefs or towels

Newspaper for pads under the printing.

Stain:

Ebony stain

Small squares (approximately 4 in.) of undercarpet felt for
printing pads

A mixing tin on which to place the printing pad

Water with which to dilute the ink on the printing pad

Plenty of old, soft rag

Old newspaper for wrapping up waste bits and pieces.

STAGES OF WORK

1   Prepare a pad of two or three thicknesses of newspaper, on top
of which the paper to be printed is placed.

2   Prepare the felt pad for the stain. First moisten the felt with
water, then squeeze it out so that it remains just damp—by no
means saturated, but wet enough for the ink to be picked up
easily. This ensures satisfactory, even printing. Next add several
drops of stain which will quickly spread out evenly on the
moistened pad. The proportion of stain to water determines the
depth of tone for printing.

3   Cut the potato in half smoothly, to get a flat printing surface. A
simple 'handle' can be cut out of the rounded end of the potato.

4   Press the cut surface of one half of the potato on to the inked felt
pad, so as to pick up an even layer of stain.

5   Press the inked potato-surface firmly on to the top left-hand
corner of the paper to be printed, then lift the potato carefully
off the paper.

6   Re-ink the potato and make a second print level with the top
of the first print, and just touching it at the left-hand side. Continue to print across the top of the paper in this way, from left
to right, until the potato has been printed four or five times.
Start a second row immediately under the first row, then a third
row, so continuing until enough has been printed to show the
effect of the pattern as whole. Probably four or five rows (a block
of at least sixteen prints) will be needed. Re-ink for each print.

7 When putting the potato in position it is helpful to check the placing each time by looking at the top and at the left-hand side of the potato, just before it is pressed down on the paper. Let the prints touch each other so that these first experiments produce full, all-over effects.

Newspaper columns provide useful printing guides. If plain paper is used a line should be ruled at the top of the paper and another on the left-hand side, to help keep the printing straight and regular.

8 Note the pattern of light produced by the spaces left between the prints. These portions form a vital part of the pattern and often make as strong an impact as the printed surfaces. This is particularly easily seen if one looks at the pattern through half-closed eyes. As a child, who was making a potato-print pattern said: 'Look at the shapes I didn't make.'

9 Prints from the same block can be tried out in different arrangements (see Fig. 2, page 133). For instance, having printed the first row of shapes, the second row can be moved slightly to the right instead of being put immediately underneath the first one, so that each print fits compactly in between the prints in the row above. Several variations may be tried—long, narrow-shaped potatoes lend themselves to herring-bone patterns—and each arrangement will produce a new rhythm of dark and light, or figure and ground.

After one or two experiments the child gets used to the feeling of printing and learns how the simplest unit can be placed in different ways so as to produce various effects. This approach encourages sound standards of printing, though naturally too much time should not be spent on these preliminary stages.

10 A simple pattern is then cut on the printing surface of the potato. The slightly irregular shape of the potato itself often makes an interesting unit, or the potato surface can be cut into other shapes such as squares, rectangles or triangles.

The pattern should be cut freely, and fairly deeply, with the lino-tools—or with the end of the penholder or umbrella-spoke. The simplest patterns, consisting of a few curved or straight cuts, are likely to produce better results than more complex designs. An asymmetrical arrangement, which in places will cut into the outer shape of the unit, usually produces designs that are interesting when repeated. Symmetrical patterns can also be successful, though these more easily lead to over-formal, rather rigid designs.

The children themselves soon discover how to make their patterns and there is no need to help them with the cutting of the designs. I have seen a lesson in which the children were wearily queueing to have their patterns cut by the teacher. This may be an extreme instance of misplaced help, yet it is only too easy for us to underrate children's creative resources and withhold from them the opportunities they need. Once children understand the technique of cutting, they will be eager to experiment, often evolving patterns of unexpected beauty which they have built up from the simplest motifs.

The youngest children in the Infant school can quite safely gouge a few holes and shapes out of the soft potato surface, and will thoroughly enjoy stamping their prints on to the paper or fabric. At first they may do little more than enjoy the sheer rhythm of the printing, moving their whole bodies as they work. The results they produce may seem clumsy and haphazard, but are as important and necessary for them as their crude explorations in paint and colour. Gradually their exuberance in printing is channelled towards the making of more deliberately ordered arrangements, and their natural feeling for pattern has had the chance to develop through the pleasure and freedom of these introductory experiments.

B. *Applying the Colour with a Brush*

MATERIALS

Papers:
Vegetables: } as for printing with a pad
Tools:
Powder colour or tempera-block colours
Water colour thickened with a little starch or Polycell
Dyes and inks
A fairly large hog-hair brush for applying the colour
Mixing tin
Rags.

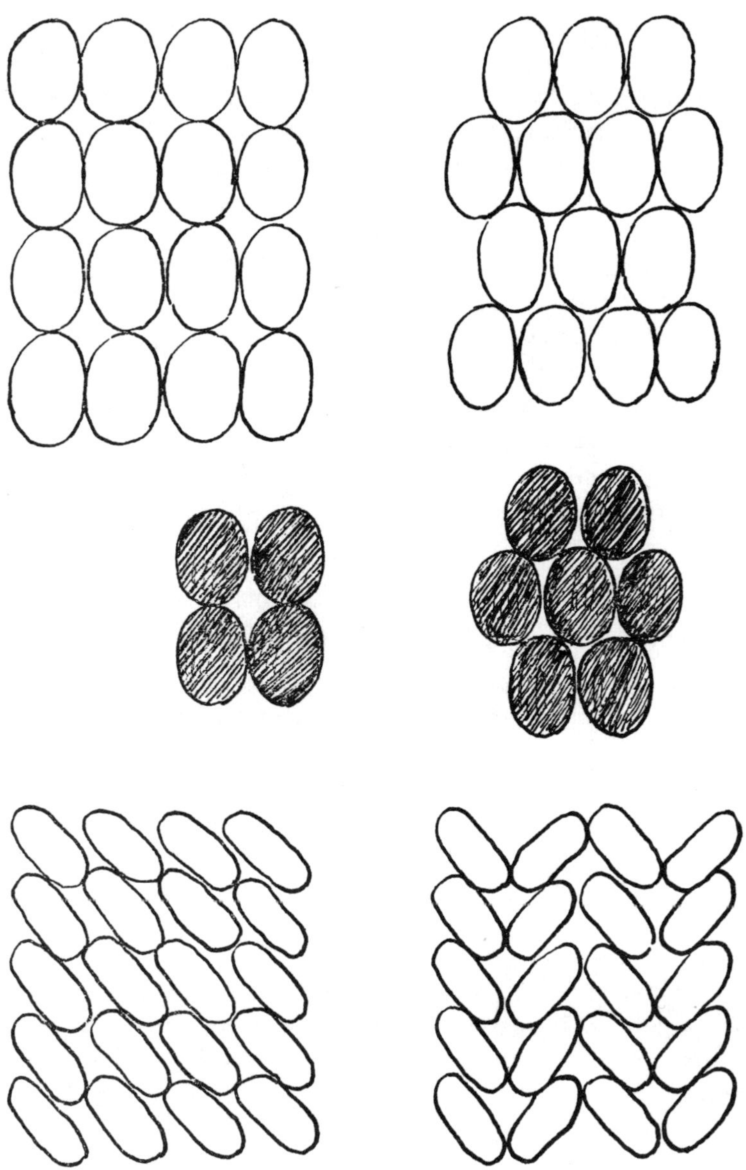

FIG. 2. Potato prints: different arrangements of the same unit produce varying rhythms and relationships of figure to ground (page 131).

SETTING TO WORK. The actual printing and pattern making are done in much the same way as in the first method.

In the second method, however, the paint is applied to the printing surface of the potato with a brush. Fresh paint is applied each time a print is made. The paint is mixed on the tin and, for the printing to be satisfactory, it is essential that the paint be of just the right consistency—neither too wet nor too dry.

The potato itself, when it is first cut, has a good deal of moisture and the paint at this stage should therefore not be too watery. A firm, rhythmic pressure of the hand is needed each time the potato is pressed on to the paper. A certain unevenness, caused by the starch in the potato, is a characteristic of the medium and provides a pleasant quality of surface variation in a pattern.

More than one colour may be used in successive stages of printing. Attractive effects of depth and richness of colour can be produced by superimposing one colour partly over another. The palest colours are printed first and the paint is usually allowed to dry between the stages.

General Points about Methods A and B and the
Use of Other Materials in Printing

Potato printing has been described fully because it provides a sound approach to printing in a school, and the general technique is approximately the same, whatever materials are used.

Printing methods A and B can be freely combined; at times one process may be more suitable for use with a particular paint or ink than another. Patterns started with paint can be completed with stain, just as an ebony-stain print can be developed by means of superimposed brushwork.

Ebony stain—used on a printing pad—is a very suitable medium for introducing potato prints, because the dark tone of its grey or black colour seen against a light paper immediately reveals the rhythm and balance of a pattern. But coloured inks, dyes and even powder colour—mixed to a suitable consistency—can equally well be used on the printing pad.

Felt printing pads must always be well washed after use. Inexpensive off-cuts of foam-rubber also make excellent pads and are easily rinsed.

The varying effects produced by printing with different types of colour on different thicknesses and kinds of paper should be tried out. Apart from stain, inks and paint, the remains of mixed liquid dyes (such as Helizarin or Procion dyes), that are no longer suitable for fabric printing can be used on paper. Procion dyes have a particular brilliance and translucency on paper. All kinds of commercial dyes can be experimented with in various strengths. One mixture—especially useful for younger children who wish to print on fabric—is easy to prepare. Add the contents of a small Drummer or Dylon dye container to a large cupful of Polycell, which has been mixed to its double strength. This makes a dye-paste that can be brushed on to the printing pad and that is easy to print with. It is not absolutely fast to washing but, although a small amount of colour runs, the definition of the pattern remains clear enough and the washed result is not unpleasant.

Children will gain a feeling for quality by experimenting with these possibilities over a period of time. Limiting them to one approach or to one range of materials would inevitably restrict the growth of personal initiative and understanding that should result from these experiences.

A VARIETY OF PRINTING SURFACES

Stick printing is sometimes done in a school but, although this way of making patterns may have an occupational appeal, it is of relatively little value educationally. In this process small printing sticks, which are bought with their ends already cut into a variety of geometric shapes, are used for stamping patterns. Although there is some scope for experimenting with different arrangements, there is little real challenge to creative thought. (Supplying children with a range of ready-cut-out paper shapes for pattern making, usually on squared paper, is equally restricting.)

Rather than provide such ready-made motifs, we should allow children the excitement, both of cutting the patterns of their own blocks and of discovering other surfaces from which to print.

As soon as they have become used to printing with vegetables, they should look for other substances. They may try out the effects of coarsely grained blocks of wood, an open-mesh canvas, heavily embossed wall-papers, fragments of old tyres, corrugated papers, or small pieces of loofah and sponges. Sometimes they can make their own printing blocks by gluing pieces of heavy cord, or shapes of thick felt or other scrap material, on to the ends of cotton-reels or small blocks of wood. These units can be used experimentally and children may combine them with other surfaces or processes in building up printed patterns or pictures. They will come to realize that it is not the unit alone that provides the pattern, but the way in which it is spaced and arranged in relation to other factors in the design.

Chance, too, plays a part in pattern making, and some of the most interesting effects may be produced accidentally. The child should be receptive to these different possibilities, and should be prepared to make use of them in his work.

FURTHER PRINTING POSSIBILITIES

1. *Variations in All-over Prints*

A plain colour unit is printed regularly as a basis. A cut-out design is then printed on to this foundation. The block with the pattern should be of approximately the same size as the plain colour unit, so that the one fits closely over the other. Alternatively, the cut-out print can be placed so that it stretches from the middle of one plain colour print to the middle of the next one, either moving along horizontally, or vertically downwards. This overlapping can lead to interesting patterns which have both movement and depth.

2. *Cut and Print Again Patterns*

a. In this type of pattern, the first stage consists of a regular, foundation print in which little, if anything, is cut out of the printing surface. Usually a pale colour is used.

b. A few cuts are made in the potato surface, which is then printed in a different colour over the first layer of printing.

c. The block surface is then elaborated with a little more cutting, after which it is printed in a yet darker colour over the second layer.

d. This process may be repeated as often as seems necessary for the effect of the pattern. Three or four printings usually produce a full, pleasing design.

Because each additional stage of cutting is done on the same printing surface, the results when printed naturally relate together. For the colours to be effective the tones should be built up from pale to dark ones. The variety of subtle colours produced by the super-imposed layers of ink or paint adds to the quality of the pattern.

Once a stage has been completed and the block has been re-cut, it cannot of course be repeated. This means that only relatively small areas can be printed in this way.

3. *Printed Circles and Medallions*

Circular or oval medallions, printed with a combination of potato and other vegetables, make attractive patterns. These designs grow outwards from the centre in the same way as I have described the painting of medallions (see page 124). Matters of balance, rhythm, colour and the variety of tone and scale are equally relevant to printing as to painting (see Fig. 3, page 139).

4. *Borders*

Borders and bands of varying widths—4 in. to 6 in.—give further opportunities of creating a pattern for a specific shape.

5. *Squares and Rectangles*

Nine-inch squares and rectangles of about 9×6 in. are evocative shapes for patterns. The areas may be broken up in various ways. A border of heavy weight can be contrasted with a lightly treated centre, or a small central square of intricate design may be surrounded by a plain space, outlined by a narrow border. Countless designs that are well integrated with the basic square or rectangle can be evolved. The planning and working out of a satisfactory corner pattern will also be important. Children who have thought about these problems will tackle the designing of a head-scarf, for example, with some real understanding.

6. *Pictorial Design*

A number of potatoes of varying sizes and shapes are cut into different textures or patterns, and then combined freely to build up a pictorial idea. No. 87, the owl, shows how different prints have made up the varying characteristics of the feathers and how the concentrated arrangements of small, overlapping textural prints have been used to express the smooth solidity of the bird's head. Nos. 109, 110 and 111 are further examples of potato prints in which the pattern units have been used pictorially.

In No. 110, a panel made collectively by boys and girls of nine and ten years old, the different textures of the potato prints have been used to suggest the textures on the scales of the fish. The children in this particular group became immensely interested in everything to do with under-water life and, with their teacher, they collected photographs and made many studies of the patterns and markings on fish. They had a large pattern reference-book into which they pasted their individual findings, and 'The Fish in Art and Nature' became the theme for a classroom exhibition.

They kept and watched fish in aquaria, and whilst they were making the frieze their teacher produced mackerel, plaice and other fish for them to study closely. These, together with many books that were available, provided their sources of reference. The children had then to translate their knowledge into the particular terms of the medium, and we see how its very limitations served to stimulate their powers of invention.

FABRIC PRINTING AND DYEING

Fabric printing grows naturally from the work we have been considering and is related to it in all essentials of design and approach. Traditional ways of making patterns on fabric can be adapted to suit the particular needs and interests of children from the Infant to the Secondary stages.

Helizarin Dyes

I would particularly recommend Helizarin dyes for the Primary school as they are straightforward to prepare and use. The dye pigment is bought in paste form. A small amount of dye-paste is mixed with an emulsion, called Binder D, and with a chemical known as Condensol A. The dyes and chemicals are obtainable from Skilbeck Brothers (see page 276).

A RECIPE FOR THE PREPARATION OF HELIZARIN DYES

INGREDIENTS

1   Condensol A—a coarse, granular substance
2   Binder D—a white, creamy emulsion
     Each of these chemicals can be bought in a minimum quantity of one pound.
3   The dye pigment—available in one-ounce jars.

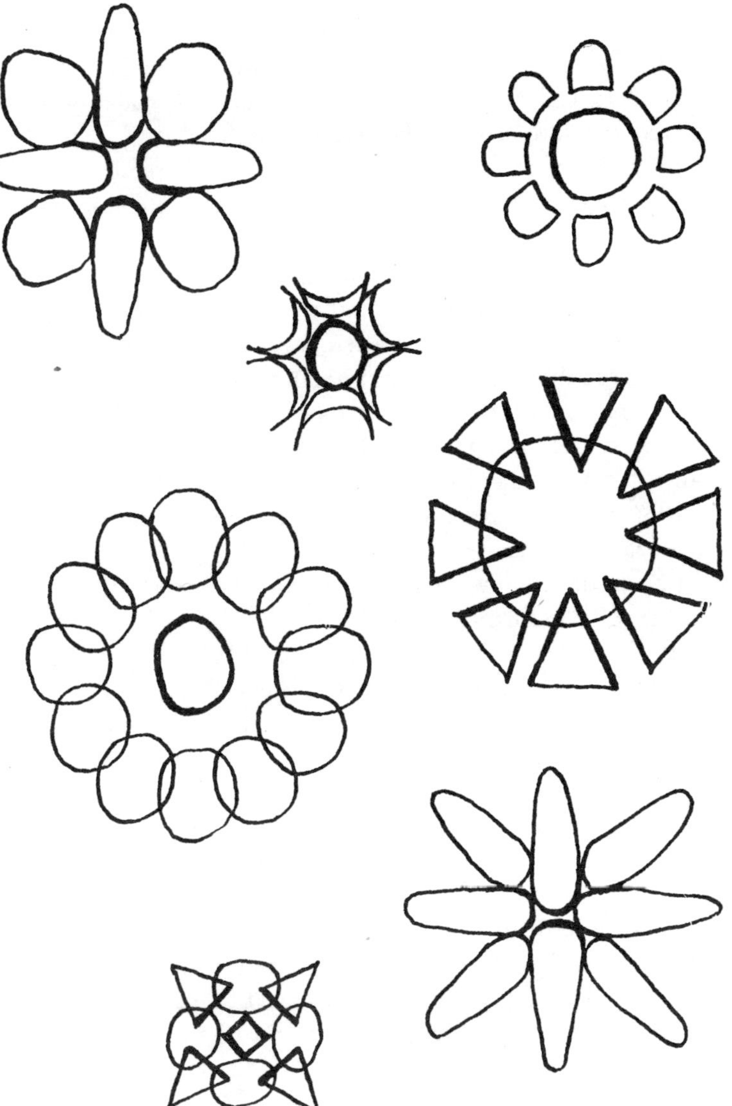

FIG. 3. Medallions printed with vegetable sections. The natural shapes of the sections can be used without any additional cutting. A group of well related shapes may provide a useful basis for various forms of superimposed printing (page 137).

METHOD

1 Half-fill a one-pound screw-top jar with Binder D.
2 To this emulsion add a small teaspoonful of Condensol A, dissolved in a few drops of hot water. Stir well.
3 Then add two or three teaspoonfuls of dye pigment—according to the strength of colour that is needed—stirring thoroughly.

If the prepared mixture is kept in an air-tight jar, it will remain in a satisfactory condition for several weeks. Once a skin is allowed to form, or the dye becomes solidified, it is no longer suitable for use.

The prepared dyes may be intermixed, producing a wide range of colours so that only a few essential ones need be ordered from the manufacturer. Helizarin grey should be included in even the smallest selection; it is a good colour on its own and can also add depth to other colours. Paler tones are produced by adding more Binder D to the prepared mixture.

After an initial outlay on the dyes and the necessary chemicals, there need be little further expense.

The dye is applied to the printing pad with a brush and the printing process is the same as for printing on paper.

Clearing up is easy as only water is needed for rinsing the printing pads and for washing the spoons, brushes, mixing palettes and utensils.

Helizarin dyes are made fast by exposure to heat. Small pieces of printed fabric can be pressed by hand with a very hot iron; larger pieces of material are folded in a piece of newspaper, and baked in an ordinary domestic oven at a temperature of approximately 250° F. The heat penetrates a piece of folded material in about half an hour. The ironed or baked printed material may become rather stiff, but this hardness disappears when the fabric is washed. Material printed with Helizarin dyes can be washed repeatedly without any loss of colour.

Procion Dyes

Procion dyes are also excellent for printing, though they are rather less simple to handle in a Junior school.

They have an intense brilliance of colour and, as they are translucent, produce very rich effects when one colour is printed over another. Procion dyes are bought in powder form—in four-ounce jars—and although expensive in the first place, they will last for several weeks once they have been prepared.

The dyes are mixed, in certain proportions, with Urea and Resist Salt L, and the mixture is thickened with a Manutex binder. A recipe for a Procion printing paste, together with working instructions, will be found on page 73 of *Textile Printing and Dyeing*,[1] by Nora Proud. Mayborn Products Limited (see page 275) supply Procion dyes and the chemicals that are used with them; they also issue a useful booklet of information on the preparation and use of Procions.[2]

The dyes can be fixed by ironing the printed fabrics at a temperature of 140° C. or by baking the material in an oven set at 140° C. (285° F.), for about five minutes.

Various kinds of cotton materials, such as lawn, poplin, pillow-cotton and unbleached calico, are suitable for fabric printing. It is generally advisable to wash new material before it is used. This removes some of the dressing so that the cloth will absorb the dye or printing pigment more readily, as well as becoming easier to handle.

Children should have opportunities of working on materials of different thicknesses and textures, and should think about the suitability of a fabric for the purpose for which it is intended. A head-scarf suggests a fine lawn, whereas a skirt that is to be gathered will need a rather heavier material that falls well in folds. For a cushion, on the other hand, quite a stiff calico may be the most suitable material.

DISCHARGE PATTERNS

Effective discharge patterns can be made by printing with lemon juice on material, or paper, that has been previously dyed in a solution of permanganate of potash (also known as potassium permanganate). The patterns, in which the whitened parts stand out against the soft brown of the permanganate, are very pleasant in colour. They can also be expanded by overprinting with a potato-block or with some other kind of printing surface (lino, cork). A fairly dark colour, such as a Helizarin grey, is particularly effective with the permanganate and white.

[1] *Textile Printing and Dyeing*, by Nora Proud (Batsford, London, 1965).
[2] *Textile Dyeing and Printing with Procion Dyestuffs* (Mayborn Products).

Preparing the Dye

Thoroughly dissolve one dessertspoonful of the permanganate crystals in about two pints of hot water. If a little of the hot water is poured on to the permanganate crystals first, it will be found easier to dissolve. The same solution of dye can be used repeatedly. It should be kept in a bucket with a lid, in which it can conveniently be stored for several weeks.

Dyeing the Material

To dye the material plunge it for a moment or so in the solution, rinse it and hang it up to dry. One dip will produce a pleasant, but rather pale brown. To obtain deeper tones put the material into the dye several times, allowing it to dry between each dip (it is inadvisable to use a stronger solution of permanganate because this may easily rot the fabric).

Printing

One can print on the material as soon as it has been dyed and is dry. The dyed fabric should be pinned out flat, over a thin pad of newspaper. The lemon juice can be used as a printing ink, or it may be brushed directly on to the dyed material. If the pattern is to be printed pour a little undiluted lemon juice on to a pad (about three inches square) of foam rubber, under-carpet felt or thick flannel. The pad, which is placed on a mixing tin, needs to be evenly saturated.

The printed pattern, which at first is hardly visible on the material, gradually emerges as a white design on the permanganate brown. Producing patterns in this way appeals to children, for whom the process seems as magical as that of making designs with candle-wax and ebony stain.

Making discharge patterns is not only one of the most interesting kinds of pattern making, but is also easy to take with a class. The materials needed are easily obtained and the practical organization presents few problems. Before introducing this work to children, however, it is as well to check that everything is in good working order by making a few quick preliminary experiments oneself. The material must be one that takes the dye well; the permanganate solution needs to be strong enough to produce a reasonable depth of colour, without weakening or rotting the material; the consistency of the lemon juice has to be just right for printing and the juice itself must be concentrated enough to discharge the colour from the dyed material.

TIE AND DYE

Tie-dyeing, which is one of the oldest and most primitive methods of patterning material, is a craft that has been practised extensively in Japan, China and India, and that is still much used in several West African countries. The Victoria and Albert Museum, the Imperial Institute and the British Museum have many samples of traditional forms of tie and dye. Even a brief study of some of these enables one to appreciate the fascination and variety of this craft, which may range from the most delicate, small-scale patterns on lengths of finest Indian muslins and silks, to the much bolder, robust designs on the indigo-dyed cloths of Nigeria.

Tie-dyeing is one of the most direct methods of making patterns on material and in its simplest forms it can be used successfully throughout the Primary school. It is a process closely allied in principle to that of candle and wax resists on paper (see page 192). Certain parts of the cloth are knotted, or are firmly bound and tied, so that when the material is dyed, the dye cannot penetrate these areas. After the fabric has been dyed and rinsed, it is then untied, revealing a pattern of white or pale shapes on a dyed ground.

In *Tie and Dye as a Present-day Craft*,[1] by Anne Maile (pages 13–14), there are clear descriptions of the various stages of the process, together with recipes for dyes, notes on equipment and abundant diagrams and illustrations. Nora Proud, in *Textile Printing and Dyeing*[2] (pages 40–6), shows the unique characteristics of tie-dyeing in a series of photographs, each of which is accompanied by a description of the method used. *Fabric Printing by Hand*,[3] by Stephen Russ (pages 96–8), has an interesting and practical section on tie-dyeing; Teachers will also find reliable approaches to tie-dyeing in *Simple Fabric Printing*,[4] by S. and P. Robinson, and *Dyed and Printed Fabrics*,[5] by June Hobson.

[1] *Tie and Dye as a Present-day Craft*, by Anne Maile (Mills and Boon, 1963).
[2] *Textile Printing and Dyeing*, by Nora Proud (Batsford).
[3] *Fabric Printing by Hand*, by Stephen Russ (Studio Vista).
[4] *Simple Fabric Printing*, by S. and P. Robinson (Mills and Boon).
[5] *Dyed and Printed Fabrics*, by June Hobson (The Dryad Press, Leicester).

Very satisfactory results in tie-dyeing can be obtained by using household dyes, such as Drummer or Dylon.

The simplest patterns that grow naturally out of the way in which the materials are used are generally the most pleasing. Because the quality of the pattern depends on chance effects, it is inappropriate to introduce preliminary paper work. Sometimes, however, it may be helpful to indicate where the pleats are to come, or where the objects are to be tied into the material, by marking the positions lightly on the fabric with a soft pencil. But on the whole children should use the material in as direct a way as possible, accepting the qualities of shape and texture produced by the various methods of knotting, pleating, twisting, binding and tying the cloth.

Small pieces of fabric—about six inches square—should be provided, so that the children can try out a number of experiments and see the different results fairly quickly. Small, old handkerchiefs can also be used for tie-dyeing, and lend themselves especially well to medallion designs. For bolder band patterns lengths of a good quality butter muslin are recommended. First fold or pleat the length of the muslin, concertina fashion; then bind the pleats at intervals with tape, string or raffia, making bands of varying widths.

After trying out some of the methods demonstrated by the teacher, the children will quickly master the techniques of binding and tying. The keynote of the work should then be independent experiment.

But although the patterns should be the outcome of the child's spontaneous handling of the materials, the composition of a pattern, that is to say its general balance and the relationship of its shapes, texture and colours, should in some measure be deliberately planned. Each time the child makes a fresh visual decision, he becomes more discerning. This is of course particularly true of older children; we must remember that at the Infant stage, and frequently in the younger Junior groups, many patterns are produced quite intuitively.

In *Textile Printing and Dyeing*,[1] Nora Proud gives a fascinating all-over view of the development of fabric printing and dyeing throughout a school. She outlines the steady growth from the first efforts on fabric in the Infant school, through the many attractive forms of printing and dyeing appropriate to the Junior school, to the more

---

[1] *Textile Printing and Dyeing*, by Nora Proud (Batsford)

complex batik work that can be done by boys and girls in the Secondary school (pages 102–15).

Children who are able to learn through such a planned continuity will grow in confidence and understanding as, at each stage, they achieve worthwhile standards that are well within their capabilities. Each range of work should provide the child with immediate creative pleasure, and should also give him the kind of practical experience that will naturally lead on to subsequent stages of the work.

The Infant School

Many five- and six-year-old children are able to pleat or fold small pieces of material with reasonable accuracy, and to tie them up strongly enough to make effective striped patterns. If cold-water dyes are used, it may be possible to arrange for each child to dip his own material into the pan of dye. In any case, the children should have the opportunity of watching the different dyeing processes. Young children generally find raffia or string the easiest materials to manage for binding and tying their patterns.

Medallion patterns in a variety of media have already been mentioned. They can also be made by tying small objects such as pennies, buttons, marbles, corks, conkers, pebbles and shells securely into the material before it is dyed. When the binding is removed, irregular circles or ovals of a broken white will be seen against the dyed background colour. The youngest children often find it easiest to wind small rubber bands round the objects.

No two patterns are ever identical and much of the delight of dyeing these patterns lies in this surprise element.

The Junior School

Older children, as well as using tie-dyeing on its own, may like to combine it with simple block printing.

They will also want to put their experiments to some use. Tie-dyed samples can be made up into cushions or mats. Belts and neckties can be planned directly on pieces of material that have already been cut to the necessary shape and size. Children often find it easier to make skirts and aprons out of several strips of material than out of one large piece. When the dyed patterns are finished the pieces are joined together by machine. Some preliminary planning will be necessary. This can be done by drawing the proposed arrangement of the tied shapes, or pleats, very freely in charcoal on kitchen paper that has been cut into strips of the same size as the material. This kind of rough-and-ready, direct planning gives the child some idea of the finished effect.

He can move the pieces of paper around and see which arrangement he likes best.

It is also possible to overprint tied and dyed fabrics with potato or other blocks. In this case the child starts with a basis for his printed pattern. He has then to think how he can best integrate the superimposed print with the dyed foundation. By finding successful ways of enriching a pattern, without losing sight of the over-all unity, the child begins to understand some of the fundamentals of sound composition.

The Secondary School

In the Secondary school, the interest and range of design can be extended by introducing methods of stitching and pulling up the cloth, as an alternative to binding and tying it, before it is dyed.

Older children also enjoy working in batik. In this process the pattern is first painted on to the material with very hot wax. When the wax has cooled and hardened, the fabric is dipped in a cold-water dye (Dylon, Procion, indigo, permanganate of potash). The waxed areas resist the dye. Then the wax is removed, and the reserved parts that were covered by it appear as light shapes against the dyed background.

Removing the wax can be a rather laborious process. One method is to boil the material for a few minutes in water to which some detergent or a small quantity of household soda has been added. As soon as the water boils, lift the material out with tongs, and plunge it immediately into a bowl of cold water. This causes all the loose wax to solidify on the surface of the material, from which it can then easily be washed off or lightly scraped away. In any case the material may need to be washed and rinsed several times before it is completely clear of wax.

Great care has to be taken not to rinse any wax down the drain, as it may solidify and cause a blocked sink. Hot water which has wax in it should be allowed to cool. When cold it can be poured through a sieve, which will retain the wax particles. These can either be used again or thrown away.

Some people prefer another method (though I personally find it less easy to use successfully). Put the waxed materials between sheets of blotting-paper or layers of newspaper, then press it firmly, using a very hot iron. The wax melts and is absorbed into the paper, which must be renewed frequently. The material has to be ironed repeatedly until all the wax has been removed.

These processes are by no means simple, and it is usually neither easy nor, perhaps, desirable to use them in the Junior school. It is true that sometimes a teacher, who is himself especially interested in this work, will successfully introduce the technique of wax resists to small groups of older children. Boys and girls of ten and eleven are certainly able to do such work extremely well, and I know of one or two Primary schools where wax resists form a special feature of the pattern course, and where fine traditions in this branch of design have been established. The technique does, however, involve so many problems of organization that, on the whole, it seems as well to keep it for older children in the Secondary school. Very hot wax has to be used, so the most carefully controlled working conditions are essential to ensure complete safety and to rule out the risk of accidents.

Illustrated descriptions of batik processes, with working instructions are given in *Textile Printing and Dyeing*,[1] by Nora Proud and *Fabric Printing by Hand*,[2] by Stephen Russ.

INDIGO (COLD DYEING)

'Indigo is the oldest and still the most magnificent cold dye.'[3] Anyone who has used this dye will agree that it is indeed 'magnificent', and that the beauty of its blue, in all its tones, can hardly be exaggerated.

In its natural form indigo is a blue powder obtained from plants belonging to the genus Indigofera. It cannot be used in its powder form and has first to be converted into a soluble form in a vat. The making of an indigo vat naturally requires considerable expert knowledge. But it is a process by no means beyond the scope of the non-specialist teacher who has become an enthusiast in dyeing, and who is prepared to go to some trouble to make a beginning in the use of indigo.

---

[1] *Textile Printing and Dyeing*, by Nora Proud (Batsford), pp. 40, 47–53.
[2] *Fabric Printing by Hand*, by Stephen Russ (Studio Vista), pp. 98–100.
[3] Ibid., p. 26.

Most forms of dyeing are fascinating, but indigo provides some of the most immediately rewarding experiences for children—and for others—because the process itself is so absorbing to watch. After the fabric has been immersed in the vat for a certain period of time (this may vary from about three minutes to fifteen minutes, according to the recipe which is being used) it is lifted out and exposed to the air. When it first comes out it is yellowish-green in colour, but within seconds this changes to an emerald green, then to a dark greenish blue and finally, as complete oxidation takes place, to a pure indigo blue. Greater depth of tone is obtained by reimmersion in the vat, after which the material is again brought into the air. These alternating processes are repeated until the required depth of colour is obtained.

However accustomed one may become to using indigo, the sense of enchantment at seeing the full blue emerge on the material always remains.

It is beyond the scope of this book to describe the actual making of a vat, or to discuss the properties of the chemicals that are used. Stephen Russ, in *Fabric Printing by Hand*, describes several methods of making a vat, gives lists of the chemicals that are needed, and provides a selection of recipes (pages 26–9).

Mrs. Susan Boscence (see page 275), who has herself made an intensive first-hand study of the traditional methods of textile designing and dyeing used in West African countries, organizes short courses, in which she gives a full, practical introduction to indigo dyeing and textile printing.

Such a course can be an ideal means of gaining a preliminary understanding, and even a few days will help to give one the confidence needed to make a beginning in a school. Once an indigo vat has been made, the children's whole conception of pattern making will receive a fresh impetus.

A vat, to hold about five gallons, can be made in a small dustbin. It has to be kept at a temperature of approximately 60° F. for it to remain active. One way of preventing the vat from becoming too cold is to place it near some hot floor-pipes, or by a radiator. The necessary temperature may also be maintained by lagging the bin with under-carpet felt.

If it is practicable, the vat should be kept reasonably near an outside yard, so that the dyed material can be hung out in the air to dry. In several country schools I have seen a corner of the playground used for this purpose. Finding a suitable place out of doors, where the material can drip and be dried, considerably reduces problems of undue messiness in the classroom. It is usually possible, however, to arrange for some dyeing to be done indoors, even if the general conditions for practical work are inadequate. For instance, if a small length of clothes-line is hung across one corner of the room, an area can be reserved for dyeing and drying the children's work. Protect the floor with sheets of polythene; it is also advisable to place some underneath the vat. An old zinc bath provides a useful receptacle for catching drips.

If a sink is not available, it is essential to have one or two plastic buckets in the classroom. In any case there should always be a deep bowl or bucket of water with a cloth to be used for cleaning and washing up, both while the work is in progress and at the end of a session. The children will need overalls, and the teacher should provide one or two pairs of rubber gloves for those who are actually using the dyes.

I have tried to show how lively in interest these various aspects of printing and dyeing are, and how they can be adapted to the teaching situation. It is hoped that the non-specialist teacher particularly may be tempted to try out some of the suggestions. Only a few recipes for making dyes and printing-pastes have been included, as this information is readily available in the books mentioned on page 279. These books are essentially practical in approach, dealing as fully with matters of equipment, materials and organization as with the more general aspects of design. The various crafts are considered in relation to home and school facilities, so that teachers will find a sound basis both for their own work and for the teaching of fabric printing and dyeing. Without some such guidance on the technical side, the results in the early stages could easily be unsatisfactory and disappointing. Invaluable, however, as these sources of reference are to the teacher, no one system should be followed exclusively. Nor is it desirable to copy slavishly the actual designs that are used as illustrations. At each level of work there is ample opportunity for personal interpretation and invention. Having made an experimental start in a school, the teacher can then go on to develop those aspects which appeal most strongly to his own and to the children's tastes, according to the facilities open to him.

CHAPTER 8

Working with Paint

PAINTING AND THE 'TEACHING' OF COLOUR

The majority of children in the Infant school paint freely and intuitively, so that teaching at this stage is largely a matter of preserving this spontaneity. The actual conditions for painting may quite considerably influence the quality of the work. Children can stand at low, flat tables to paint, but ideally they should paint standing at easels so that they can use the large arm movements that come naturally to them. Nos. 19 and 20 show the freedom of movement and rhythm of brushwork achieved by children standing freely as they work.

Many schools have easels at which children work in pairs. The number of easels and the floor space for them may be limited and, in order that more can paint at the same time, it may be possible to clip paper on to hardboard that is either propped up against a wall or blackboard or supported against the back of a chair. It may even be necessary for one or two children to have their paper on the floor.

I know of one small nursery school where a firm easel at which three children can stand to paint has been made from a three-sided clothes-horse. This has been done by altering one set of hinges so that the sides can be folded inwards to form a triangle. Hardboard has been fitted into the upper panels, providing a firm base for paper that is clipped on to the top rung. A wire milk-bottle container has been fixed on to the front of each side to hold the pots of paint at a convenient height for the children to reach.

The school itself had an interesting beginning. A small group of children—their ages ranging from two to five years—used to play together in each other's houses and gardens, the parents looking after them in turn. One of the mothers, who happened to be a trained teacher, became increasingly involved in thinking out ways of interesting the children, until she finally started a small school for them.

Twelve children now attend the school, and their varied indoor activities take place in one large room. The painting corner is in constant use throughout the school day. The children's paintings are dated and filed, so that it is possible to see the change in an individual child's work during the course of a few months, and to note how this links up with his general intellectual, emotional and physical development.

Younger children should have inexpensive, slightly absorbent paper to work on (glossy papers are less satisfactory). Most painting in the early stages should be done on comparatively large sheets of paper, about 20 × 15 in. This will encourage a free rhythm of movement, whereas painting on a smaller area is likely to demand too great a precision in the control of the brush. Such work need not however be entirely ruled out; and when children really want to work on a smaller scale they should be able to use smaller pieces of paper, and brushes that are also suited to the scale of the painting. Sometimes children should be allowed to draw on small paper with monster wax crayons or pencils with thick lead.

Little mention has been made of the pencil for drawing, because on the whole it is less suitable for younger children than other drawing media, such as crayon and charcoal. Pencil drawing has in the past been so abused that one is very conscious of its possible dangers. We may have memories of drawings made with hard pencils pressed relentlessly into the paper; laborious lines that were made only to be rubbed out again, until the surface of the paper became irreparably roughened or even broken as a result of the constant rubbing and scrubbing.

Yet a well-sharpened B or 2B pencil can be most satisfying and expressive to draw with. A sensitively drawn pencil line has lively qualities of contrasting delicacy and strength; and a great variety of freely drawn textures, as well as tones ranging from pale greys to black, can be produced by pencil. Pencil work leads chiefly to an interest in linear qualities, and is therefore especially suited to subjects in which there is an emphasis on detail.

Pencil is essentially a medium for older children, who should be encouraged to discover and try out its possibilities as spontaneously as they would those of any tool. It is less easy for younger children to work freely with pencil, because of the muscular control needed to use such a relatively fine point. The separate parts of the drawing may easily appear disconnected and the feeling of the composition as a whole be lost.

A fairly strong paper, such as cartridge paper, provides a better base for pencil work than a thinner paper. Drawings that are to be complete in their own right should, because of the richness and interest of detail, be kept fairly small in size—about 8 × 10 in.

When painting pictures, all children should be encouraged to start with a brush. Young children do this naturally, but some older children feel the need to draw before they paint. This can have a cramping effect on their work, and when they reach the painting stage they have often become so preoccupied with the drawing that they are unable to paint spontaneously. They then tend to tighten up, become over-careful, and miss the essential experience of using brush and colour freely. Painting is not a matter of filling in shapes with colour, but of actually creating areas of colour and brush textures that relate together. If children, however, do need the security of some preliminary drawing they should use charcoal very lightly or even block the main lines in with brush and paint. Even so there need be little attempt to keep slavishly to the drawing, which should be regarded as little more than a general indication of the main shapes. Sometimes the brush outline can be vigorously painted in a strong colour or, if the painting is on dark paper, in a very light colour (see No. 3), so that it becomes a vital part of the whole picture. Nos. 3, 4, 47, 50, 63, 89 and 101 are paintings that show these possibilities.

From the earliest stage painting is a personal matter and a teacher will soon recognize the individual characteristics of each child's work. The illustrations in this book suggest something of the range of style and approach.

Children in the middle and upper Junior school will benefit by occasional periods of experimental brushwork in which they try out a variety of effects that can be produced by different brush strokes. This can provide a helpful means of loosening up and of increasing the children's confidence. Brushwork can range from delicate flecks through a series of textures to large, vigorous strokes. There are also many different ways of painting large areas of colour. The paint may be applied thickly or thinly; in close, broad strokes; in large rhythms or in stippled textures; in flat colour or in graded tones.

Some limitation of colour in this exploratory work may make it easier for children to concentrate on qualities of brushwork. This does not mean that the colour need be dull or lifeless; in fact by keeping within the range of one predominant colour a greater richness of result can be achieved than by using a larger number of colours indiscriminately.

Through experimenting with these different ways of using paint the child will evolve his personal techniques.

Colour

Children also enjoy occasional exercises on colour mixing, in which the emphasis is on the sensation of experiencing colour rather than on its theoretical analysis. It is important to remember that however much we learn about colour, it remains in essence an inexplicable miracle through which the personal feelings of the artist—whether child or not—are expressed.

For children in the Junior school, matching colours in paint can become an absorbing and exciting game. Using only the basic paints (see page 160) they will delight in finding out how, by mixing, they can match the precise colours of various objects, specially selected for their colour-interest by the teacher.

Suggestions for Colour Mixing

Only a few broad brush strokes of each colour need be painted. The small patches of colour produced (about 3 × 2 in.), can later be used in collages and mosaics. If a hand-painted paper is used it will be found to have a vitality often lacking in bought papers.

1   Oranges. The teacher produces an orange. When the children have successfully matched and painted a patch of the colour, they make several variations of orange—some yellow-orange and some red-orange.
2   Pale colours. The children find out how to make a number of pale, nearly white colours—some will be warm, some cool.
3   Pinks.
    a.   The children visualize and try to mix the pale pink colour of icing sugar on a birthday cake.
    b.   They then make quite a different pink, using another red with the white.
4   Blues.
    a.   The children discover how to make a number of very pale blues, using white with the smallest additions of blues and other colours. For example, a soft turquoise can be made by

first mixing a little ultramarine with white, and then by adding a very little lemon-yellow or yellow-ochre.

b.   After making these pale blues the children can mix several really dark, almost black, blues.

5   The teacher produces four or five examples of quite different greens:

a.   A pale lime green—nearly a yellow.
b.   A deep blue-green.
c.   A green in which the proportions of yellow and blue are equally balanced.
d.   A soft olive green.
e.   A pale, silvery blue-green (the leaves of a pineapple).

By using combinations of the different yellows and blues in varying proportions, with the addition of small amounts of other colours—for example, reds—an infinite range of greens may be produced.

6   Each child in the class selects the colour of a particular piece of his clothing and tries to match it in paint. It should be so successfully matched that the teacher can easily recognize the bit of clothing.

7   Different children in turn choose a particular colour in the classroom, which is mixed in paint by everyone in the class.

8   Each child selects a postcard reproduction, finds in it a mixed colour, which he then matches in paint.

9   The teacher may tell a story, in which certain colours are mentioned. As each fresh one is described the children mix it in paint.

In these ways the teacher gives the children an opportunity of mixing variations of yellows, reds and blues; of making oranges, greens and purples; and of learning how to produce different browns and greys.

Both white and black paint are essential for these colour experiments. Variations of white, grey and very dark paper can be used; such a range of papers will show how colours are influenced by the ground on which they are placed.

Children who have begun to look at colours closely will also become aware of the way colours affect each other. They may already have experimented with these possibilities in weaving and collage. If a red is placed next to a complementary green, it becomes more intensely red than before; the green, too, seems to become a more dynamic colour.

Children will see how dominant some colours are in certain arrangements—how they seem to expand and push forward, while others seem to recede. Different arrangements will produce fresh emphases of colour.

Subjects in Relation to Colour

Fantastic subjects encourage imaginative expression through colour. Magic flowers, beautifully patterned butterflies, birds, fish and strange make-believe creatures are some of the subjects likely to build up a personal feeling towards colour. Themes of this kind are so far removed from representational associations of colour that they allow the child to be inventive.

A realistic theme can also be interpreted in an intensely individual way, so that the colours little resemble the actual colours of the subject. Some children, on the other hand, respond immediately to the colours they see in real life, wanting to translate these as closely as they can in their paintings.

Biblical passages often inspire a very personal reaction to colour:

And I saw another mighty angel come down from heaven, clothed with a cloud: and a rainbow was upon his head, and his face was as it were the sun, and his feet as pillars of fire:

Revelation X, 1

And there appeared another wonder in heaven; and behold a great red dragon, having seven heads and ten horns, and seven crowns upon his head, and his tail drew the third part of the stars of heaven, and did cast them to the earth:

Revelation XII, 3–4

These descriptions can evoke dreamlike shapes of colour. An even greater sense of atmosphere is sometimes suggested if the pictures are painted on moistened paper. Paints which have run or merged on damp paper may provide a basis of broad colour areas into which details can then be worked. By trying out different thicknesses of paint on dry or wet paper unlimited colour effects can be produced; older children especially should be encouraged to make use of the fortuitous qualities that result from these experiments.

Children who have become familiar with particular ranges of colour will be ready to use these in paintings. Themes of rain, storm, flood, wild seas and hurricanes will bring to mind some of the subtle, as well as the rich, dark colours they have learned to mix. Again, children who have discovered a number of reds and closely related warm tones will be able to imagine fires, fireworks, firelight and night scenes with a greater sense of colour. Subjects of this kind may be most effective on dark paper, so that the colours can really glow.

Children in our art club find these various colour experiments both exciting and satisfying. We do not make too much of these exercises, but through them we hope to give each child a fuller enjoyment and realization of colour. We may be able to provide the essential colours, we may even teach a child how to mix them (though it is much better for him to discover this for himself), but we cannot show him how actually to use colour—this can only be the outcome of his own personality. Each child will have an individual sense of colour. Some may use it symbolically or emotionally, as a means of expressing their own reactions to a subject or to an idea; others will show a feeling for rich decoration in the way they select and put colours together; and yet others will use colours more representationally.

MATERIALS AND ORGANIZATION FOR PAINTING

As teachers we have to remember how completely dependent children are on the materials we requisition for them to use. The teacher's initial choice of colours can largely determine the character of the work produced by a class; the importance of selecting appropriate materials can therefore hardly be over-emphasized. The recurring uniformity of colours sometimes seen in the work displayed on a classroom wall may serve as a salutary reminder of the inescapable influence of these personal preferences. The practical organization for painting and the need to ensure satisfactory working conditions for the children are as important as the provision of suitable paints and colours, for it is only too easy for a potentially good art lesson to come to grief because of weak administration. This section therefore provides some factual suggestions which may help the non-specialist teacher.

Powder Colour, Tempera Blocks and Poster Colour

Opaque colours are most suitable for the Primary school and several types are available. Powder colour and tempera blocks are especially useful and both kinds should be requisitioned for a class. Powder colour can be satisfactorily used in its dry form, if there are adequate facilities for mixing the colours.

It may even be used in this way in the Nursery school, though for very young children many teachers prefer to provide the paint ready mixed in liquid form. In this case the paint should be thick enough for it to be opaque and creamy in consistency. It is otherwise likely to run too easily—especially if the children are standing at upright easels—so that the main shapes become blurred or lost in the general wetness of thin paint trickling down the almost vertical surface of the paper. This can be frustrating for the child who, at this early stage, needs to express himself through clearly defined shapes and colours.

To mix the liquid paint, take a heaped dessertspoonful of powder and stir it with a little water into a smooth, thick paste, gradually adding more water until the required consistency is obtained. A small amount of household starch or Polycell (approximately a heaped tablespoonful to two or three tablespoonfuls of liquid paint) can be added to the mixed paint to ensure this consistency. The different colours are then put into small jars (which must be heavy enough to stand firmly), a separate brush is provided for each colour, and the paints are ready for the children to use. Easels for painting usually have a metal ledge on which jars may be kept. Alternatively, if they are put on a tray on a low stool or chair by the easel, two children can share a set of paints and reach them conveniently.

Poster paints of a thick, creamy consistency can be bought, ready for use, in jars. They are brilliant in colour and can be intermixed, but they are expensive and tend to harden if left open to the air. Tempera-block colours are therefore preferable for the Primary school. These are circular cakes of solid, opaque colour; they are straightforward to use, and the colours are intense and usually remain soluble to the end of the cake. Tempera-block colours are sold in various sizes, in polystyrene or metal containers which fit into holes or compartments in trays especially designed for this purpose. A tray may be shared by several children, and at the end of a lesson the trays of colour can be conveniently stacked in piles. Colours can be replenished when necessary with refills supplied to fit into the trays.

All varieties of tempera-block colours have basically the same properties. They produce smooth, brilliant colours—probably more vivid than powder colour—and they can be freely intermixed. Many teachers find them less messy in use than powder colour, and they certainly require less preparation at the beginning of an art period.

In spite of these advantages I personally prefer powder colour for most of the painting in the Junior school, and find that, of all the paints available, this kind most readily encourages an interest in colour mixing. We often have both powder colour and tempera blocks available, so that either type can be chosen; the two can also be combined satisfactorily in the same painting. Individual mixing palettes with generous mixing space must be provided whatever type of paint is used.

Dry Powder Colour

We have found that even the youngest children in the Infant school quickly learn to use the colour in its dry form: the brush is dipped into water and any excess water removed by lightly pressing the brush against the side of the water container. Some dry powder colour is then picked up on the moistened brush and mixed on the palette. More powder, of the same or even of another colour, can be picked up on the same brush; a certain amount will readily adhere to the wet bristles while the rest of the powder in the compartment remains unaffected. More powder can be added to the mixture on the palette until the child is satisfied with the colour and the consistency is suitable for painting. It is then applied to the paper, after which the brush is well rinsed before the next colour is mixed.

In practice the whole process is quite simple, and its advantages are twofold. First, the dry powders are so easily mixed that unlimited colours for painting can be made from a few basic colours; secondly, this method enables the child to control the wetness or dryness of the paint, adapting it to suit the particular part he is painting. These are essential considerations in painting, and to my mind they fully justify the use of the paint in its dry form.

It is unwise to assume that 'all young children love bright colours'. This generalization may be true of the majority, yet there are many Infants who, given the opportunity, will thoroughly enjoy mixing and using quite subtle colours as well as pure, unmixed ones. It is important for each child to have the chance to discover and make a wide variety of colours, so that he can develop his own feeling for colour.

Containers for Powder Colour

Bun tins with nine compartments provide useful containers for the different colours. One tin may be shared by two children, or by four if it is placed in the centre of four desks or small work-tables arranged to form a larger working area. Bun tins are best stored in piles of about eight or nine, stacked criss-cross on one another to keep them clean underneath.

When buying powder colour for general use it is probably most convenient to order containers of 700 c.c. Those in use can be kept on an enamel tray that is easily cleaned, with a separate teaspoon provided for each container. Only one flat spoonful of powder should be placed in each compartment of the bun tin. If too much powder is put out the colour inevitably spills over into adjacent compartments, so that pure colours become difficult to retain and a good deal of paint is wasted.

If the paints are used with reasonable care, it should be possible to keep the bun tins fairly clean, but an over-fussy attitude can easily spoil the children's enjoyment and the spontaneity of their painting. In any case the tins will need special attention from time to time, depending on the extent to which they are used. This is a routine task that can be done quite quickly with the help of the older children. Place the tin on a piece of newspaper, lightly brush the clean colours back into the appropriate compartments and sweep the remainder gently on to the newspaper, so that the top of the tin is left clean. Sometimes the colour becomes caked into lumps in the containers, and these can be neatly lifted out with a penknife.

Water Containers

Fairly large enamel or plastic mugs, tins with smooth rims, or 1 lb. jam jars can be used to hold water. If table space is limited, two children can share one jar, but whether or not the jars are shared, it must be possible for children to change their paint-water when it becomes dirty. This is important because only when the water is clear will pure, singing colours become a possibility. If there is no water supply in the classroom, two buckets—placed on a plastic or polythene sheet—will be necessary, one filled with clean water and one for the dirty water. (Even in a crowded classroom it should be possible for about two children at a time to empty their jars and refill them with clean water.)

The quality of colour in a painting will quickly deteriorate if the supply of clean water is inadequate or the water containers are too small. Small potted-meat jars are unsatisfactory because a No. 8 hog-hair brush has only to be rinsed once in such a jar for the water to become muddy.

Mixing Palettes

Plenty of space for mixing colours is essential and each child will need his own palette. Enamel plates or round sandwich tins, about eight inches in diameter, make useful palettes. A thin coat of white enamel painted over the tins makes it easier for the colours to be seen and prevents the tins from becoming rusty. There may not be enough room for the mixing palettes to be placed on the tables or desks and in any case it is as well for children to hold them as they work. If possible they should be shown an artist's palette, as well as some reproductions of self-portraits in which the artists are seen holding their palettes.

The quality of colour in children's paintings will to a great extent depend on adequate mixing facilities (small tin lids and saucers are not big enough); children must also be able to clean their own palettes from time to time as they work. One or two old sponges and a basin of warm water should be available for this purpose, and the teacher can also carry around a soft, damp cloth with which he can easily wipe a palette clean.

The Choice of Colours

The non-specialist teacher or beginner may well be bewildered by the vast numbers of different colours listed in catalogues. There can be no one correct set of colours, and individual teachers and children will have their own preferences. We have, however, found that the following seven colours provide a sound basis for most general work:

> White
> Lemon or chrome yellow
> Yellow ochre

Vermilion
Crimson
Ultramarine
Black.

There can be several alternatives for most of these colours. It is, however, essential to include the three primary colours—yellow, red and blue—in some form, as well as black and white. From these colours all kinds of oranges, greens, purples, browns and greys can be made.

Colours for Infants could be reduced to six:

White
Lemon or chrome yellow
Vermilion
Crimson
Ultramarine
Black.

Children will gain an understanding of colour through using mainly primary colours, from which they will learn to mix the exact colours and tones they need.

There should always be one clear, brilliant yellow. Yellow ochre is a more subtle colour invaluable for mixing oranges, greens and browns; it is less necessary for Infants.

Ultramarine is a blue of great intensity and is indispensable. Prussian blue—a darker, rather more greenish blue—is another beautiful colour that may be used as well as, or sometimes instead of, ultramarine. Prussian blue mixed with some of the earth colours, such as raw umber or burnt sienna, makes rich, soft greens that are appreciated by older children painting out of doors.

Vermilion and crimson lake can be regarded as indispensable reds, both to be included in even the most limited ranges of colours. Red No. 8 (Winsor and Newton) is also an attractive colour—a vivid, pinkish red, rather lighter in tone than crimson.

Other useful colours could be added to these lists, such as viridian green and turquoise, but as a general rule it is wise to keep to a fairly limited range.

Earth colours can profitably be used as a change at times—the possibility of introducing them for sketching has already been mentioned—and these colours also lend themselves to patterns on shields and masks.

A range of paints with an emphasis on earth colours:

White
Raw sienna (similar to yellow ochre but more transparent)
Burnt sienna
Raw umber
Burnt umber
Light red
Prussian blue
Black.

Black may occasionally be withdrawn for a time, so that children can, by mixing other colours, make all manner of deep shades that are approximately as dark in tone. Prussian blue and burnt sienna, for instance, together produce a colour of intense depth.

Water Colour

On the whole this medium is suitable only for children in the top classes of the Junior school. Water colour is technically a difficult medium for younger children to manage well and they are usually better able to handle the opaque brilliance of powder or tempera-block colour. Used freely and in its full strength, water colour has a translucency unobtainable in any other medium. Individual children who have a special feeling for painting may enjoy using it in the Junior school, but the majority are likely to use it more successfully at the Secondary school stage, especially if they have gained a general sense of confidence and enjoyment through painting with powder colours.

When buying water-colour paints it is advisable to select a few colours of a really high quality, rather than a larger number of colours of an inferior quality which tend to produce thin, anaemic results. Tubes of water colour may be the most practicable, as only a small amount of paint, to be used immediately, need be squeezed out at one time.

Children's Water-Colour Boxes

Parents who want to buy paints for their children to use at home might welcome some advice on the different possibilities.

Quite young children are often provided with rather costly, elaborate boxes of water colours, which within a few months become too hard to use. Instead of these they can be set up with some quite simple equipment for painting with powder colour or tempera blocks at a very reasonable cost. On an Open Day the teacher might arrange a small display of painting equipment to show the materials suitable for young children, together with some information as to cost and where such materials can be obtained.

Inks and Dyes

Waterproof inks and old dyes (no longer suitable for printing on fabric) may also be used for painting. They can, for instance, be sponged on to the paper as a basis for painting, so that their brilliance sparkles behind the thicker layers of superimposed colour.

Brushes

Medium sized (No. 8 or 9) hog-hair brushes are recommended for use with powder colour or tempera-block colours. For general painting this type of brush, with its stiff bristles, is most likely to encourage vitality and character of brushwork. Nos. 47, 56, 86 and 94 each show some of the distinctive qualities produced by painting with hog-hair brushes.

Children should also have access to other kinds of brushes, so that they can select those appropriate for different purposes. The range should include: round and flat-ended hog-hair brushes, smaller ones for finer work and a few sable or squirrel brushes for small scale work or for water colours. A child is dependent not only on the type of brushes provided, but also on their general condition; he cannot be expected to work sensitively with poor tools.

The Care of Brushes

Children should from the first be trained to look after their brushes —or any other tools—carefully. But as well as showing children how to wash their brushes and how to protect the ends from damage, the teacher himself should from time to time wash them all thoroughly in warm, soapy water. If care is taken, a set of brushes in constant use should remain in a satisfactory condition for at least a year. Then new brushes may have to be added to the stock and those that are really worn can be used for ebony stain, or for pasting and gluing.

We find it convenient to store our hog-hair brushes, the bristle ends exposed to the air, in two jugs, one for larger brushes and one for smaller ones. Each jug is labelled in a different colour, and the handle end of every brush in each of the jars is painted in the same colour, thus indicating its size and showing which jug it belongs to. As well as the main supplies of hog-hair brushes, we keep a few squirrel or sable brushes upright in a jam jar. Old brushes, for rough work, are placed separately in a clearly labelled box. A child can therefore quickly find the kind of brush he needs and easily return it to its correct place.

FINGER PAINTING

Materials

1　Cartridge paper, or any strong, non-absorbent paper, preferably white.
2　Tapwater paste, or a flour paste mixed with cold water to a fairly stiff consistency. Flour paste may also be made by adding rather more water in the first instance, stirring the mixture well, then boiling it in a saucepan until it thickens. Care must be taken to stir the paste frequently while it is being heated.
    Children may work more easily with a paste that is slightly warm to the touch; a basin of cold paste can usually be warmed over a radiator before the lesson.
3　A mixing palette, or some suitable container for paste, for each child.
4　A bun tin with the usual range of dry powder colours.
5　A generous supply of soft rags. Each child will need a piece of rag as he works. (Rags should be washed and dried after each finger-painting session.)
6　Drawing-pins.

Before starting to paint, it is useful to find somewhere where the wet paintings can be pinned out flat, or left on boards to dry overnight. Part of an old, wooden classroom floor may be available, or a piece of insulating board may be found. When finished, each wet painting should be fastened down with about eight drawing-pins. Thick paste contracts as it dries and will cause some shrinkage of the paper. Unless the painting is securely pinned the edges will curl up and be difficult to manage when the paint is dry.

Stages of Work

1   Each child is provided with a heaped tablespoonful of paste on a mixing tin, together with the other materials already mentioned. The paper should be pinned on to a board or laid on several layers of newspaper.

2   The first time finger painting is done a brief demonstration of the technique will be necessary. It is important that the subject chosen by the teacher should be different from the one to be painted by the children, as they may otherwise be over-influenced by the teacher's work and find it difficult to work out their own ideas. Once the children have seen how it is done, the teacher's painting should be removed.

3   The children's subject is then discussed. One consisting of a few shapes that will fill the paper well is likely to be most successful: for example, a close-up portrait, or a picture of someone holding flowers or balloons, a cat or a bird. One large animal, perhaps a fabulous dragon, or an animal that can be studied direct from life, such as a tortoise or hedgehog—imagined in a characteristic setting—provide suitable themes for finger painting. Subjects that suggest a variety of surface textures will lend themselves especially well to this medium.

4   As soon as the subject matter has been agreed upon, each child spreads the thick paste all over his sheet of paper, using his fingers or any part of his hands and gently pushing the paste to within half an inch of the edge of the paper. Already at this early stage, a sense of pleasure and freedom is experienced through this direct contact with the material.

5   The children next trace the main shapes of their pictures freely with their fingers over the pasted surface, before any colour is applied. This stage is invaluable, because adaptations and alterations can be easily tried out before the final arrangement of the composition is drawn.

   Children who for various reasons think that they 'can't draw' gain assurance through the flowing ease with which they find their hands move over the paper.

6   As soon as the main rhythms and areas are established—only a few minutes need be spent on this stage—the pictures should be developed as fully as possible in colour.

To use colour, the child picks up a little of the fresh paste on the tips of his fingers, which he next dips lightly into one of the colours in the bun tin, so that a small quantity of powder sticks to them. He then applies the colour direct to the pasted surface of the paper. Hands must be wiped on the paint rag between the use of each colour.

7   Children quickly discover different ways of putting the colour on to their pictures: for instance, they may spread it on thickly or thinly, with little dabs of their fingers or with bigger drawn-out movements. The side of the hand can be used for broad, blurred effects; or sharp flecks and lines may be made with the nails. No. 88 shows how satisfactorily the feathery characteristics of the owl have been expressed through a variety of crisp textures made with the nails and finger-tips. All the colours in this picture were applied broadly first, in areas of tone that emphasized the solidity of the bird. The background, except for the incised signature, has been left unbroken. As a general rule it is advisable to complete the main parts of a painting before elaborating the picture with finer detail, so that the unity of the composition is kept in mind.

8   When finished, the paintings are pinned out flat and left to dry.

9   The dry paintings usually need to be pressed under boards, or weights, to keep them quite flat.

10   If necessary, the edges can be trimmed before the paintings are pinned on to mounting paper.

One of the chief interests of finger painting lies in the beauty of the broken colour, which is a natural outcome of the technique. The colours are actually mixed on the paper, and they therefore retain much of their original purity and brilliance. For example, to produce green, small amounts of both yellow and blue are picked up on the fingers and allowed to merge together lightly on the paper; to turn the green into an olive green a little vermilion is added to the blue and yellow already on the paper. Colour used in this way will shimmer, and children should be encouraged to preserve and enjoy this quality.

Once the colour has been applied, it should as far as possible be left undisturbed; an overworked finger painting quickly becomes lifeless and drab. The whole process is therefore a fairly quick one, and even older children will rarely need to spend longer than half an hour on a painting.

The value of finger painting as a tactile experience has already been mentioned and certainly the intense satisfaction that children experience through this activity can become a liberating influence that affects all their creative work.

Thus a child who finds it difficult to organize his images into a meaningful whole may, through finger painting, discover an unaccustomed creative fluency that enables him to translate his ideas into satisfying visual relationships. His success is immensely significant and important to him, so much so that his whole approach to painting becomes more buoyant and the next picture he paints with a brush is tackled with a sense of release and greater confidence. The value of his success is not only therapeutic, but is also reflected in his growing understanding of visual qualities. In our painting club we often encourage a child to make a brush painting immediately after he has completed a rhythmical finger painting, and time and again we are struck by the real progress that seems to be an outcome of the freedom of expression experienced in finger painting.

Finger paintings, especially when they are still wet and glowing, have a marked affinity with some oil paintings. It should not be difficult to find reproductions of paintings in which the actual surface of the paint and the kinds of brush strokes used are clearly visible. The children will study the heavy impasto of a Van Gogh painting with some real insight and, closer to their own time, will discover work in which artists have used paint really thickly or with particularly striking varieties of texture. One or two reproductions of Jackson Pollock's work may provide the nucleus of a small display that is directly related in its interest to the children's paintings.

Older boys and girls will readily appreciate the pointillist technique used by some of the Impressionists. Children who have an opportunity of looking really closely at a painting by Seurat, for example *Les Baigneuses* at the National Gallery, will at first be astonished by the juxtaposition of countless minute specks of vivid primary colours on the canvas. As they stand away from it, they will be equally fascinated by the way in which these myriads of spots merge into luminous, vibrating greens, purples and cool greys.

Finger painting is a technique that requires very careful organization and a fair amount of space—especially when the paintings are drying. It is therefore usually more practicable to take it with a small group than with a large class.

CHAPTER 9

Working with Other Materials

COLLAGE

Collage (from the French word 'coller', to glue) opens up a further range of creative activities. A great variety of materials can be used: paper, cloth, fabric, as well as miscellaneous objects such as beads, buttons, string, cord, matches, old tickets and stamps. Wood-shavings and small off-cuts of wood, fragments of stone, gravel, coal, slate, brick and glass can also be used, though many of these heavier materials should be set in a cement rather than secured with glue.

The basic process, whatever the materials, consists of assembling, arranging and pasting the various pieces in a well-related, unified composition (Nos. 12, 15 and 16). Experience of collage in paper and fabric stimulates children's imaginative powers in the selection and use of materials and, by trial and error, they can experiment with different ways of using the simplest remnants of paper and cloth. The collage portraits, Nos. 15 and 16, show the sensitivity with which each child has used the available materials.

Paper Collage

MATERIALS

1. An extensive collection of papers. Remnants of wallpaper and old pattern-books provide a diversity of textures and good ranges of colour and tone. Pages from magazines will add to the variety of colours and surfaces. Similar considerations to those governing the provision of papers for torn and cut paper friezes (page 94) will influence the teacher's choice of papers for the children to use in collage.
2. Strong card or thick paper of various neutral and fairly pale colours to serve as the foundation. Used wrapping-paper, well flattened or even ironed out, can provide a useful base to work on.

3   Paste: either a tapwater paste or any effective adhesive, such as Polycell.
4   Old, clean brushes for pasting.
5   Newspaper for working on.

SUBJECTS. A theme based on one large figure or design is best suited to this technique. Any subject that is chosen, whether it is purely abstract or figurative, should depend for its main interest on broad effects of mass and colour.

Picasso and Braque, in the early part of the century, were among the first to experiment with the juxtaposition of quite common-place wallpapers, embossed papers and fragments of newspaper in a composition. Schwitters, a modern German artist, composed intricate panels of haphazard bits and pieces he collected in the streets around him, frequently incorporating small objects in a collage panel. The Tate Gallery has an immense collage by Matisse in which large shapes of paper, painted in pure, intense colours, are assembled to make a composition that is illuminated from the back. Its dynamic quality is brought to life by the exact relationship of each colour to the whole.

Older children, who may themselves use collage for abstract compositions, will enjoy looking at the work of these artists.

STAGES OF WORK
1   If the class is not too large, children should collect their own supplies of paper from boxes placed around the room. For bigger classes each pair of children can be given a newspaper folder containing a fair selection of colours and textures. These folders need not take long to prepare or to fill, especially if the twenty or so separate piles are spread out so that each fresh colour can be dealt out systematically and the ranges of papers within each little pile can be seen at a glance. It is well worth taking this extra trouble beforehand, as each child, in even the largest class, is then able to make an immediate start. Small groups of children can meanwhile leave their places to supplement their own supplies from the remaining papers.
Children need plenty of materials from which to choose, if they are to try out alternative arrangements of colours and textures. Only in this way can they benefit fully from the opportunities inherent in this work.

2   The main shapes are then torn or cut out of the papers and, after they have been tried out in several arrangements, are pasted on to the foundation. The respective characteristics of cutting and tearing have been discussed in relation to collective work (see page 94 and also Nos. 83 and 84). Either method, or a combination of the two, may be used in collage; the important thing is for the tearing or cutting to be done spontaneously, without preliminary drawing. The attraction of the work lies partly in the quality of the cut or torn shapes, and any attempt to follow the precision of pencil-drawn lines would inhibit the direct freshness of the work.

Some children may want to have their compositions, or pictures, fairly complete before they begin to paste the shapes; others may build up their panels gradually, step by step, relating each fresh piece to what is already in position. There is no one 'right' way and it is important that each child should use his own method.

3   Once the main pieces are in position more detail may be introduced. It is helpful to have a collection of varied smaller scraps and pieces, which can give children renewed interest in carrying the work through to the final stages. No. 16 shows how a figure may be embellished with all sorts of odds and ends.

A good collection of strings, wools, cords and braids is essential, as these can be used to provide the linear rhythms that link the broad masses of a collage composition (No. 12).

Sometimes the main form of a picture may be established by starting with an outline of wool or braid, freely pasted into position before any paper is used (No. 114). In this case Rosalind first pasted a thin layer of Polycell over the whole cardboard foundation. She then 'drew' the main shape and decorative details of the fish with soft braids, pushing them gently into place on the pasted card as she worked out her ideas. Finally she enriched it with overlapping layers of coloured tissue papers. The finished result had great vitality of design and colour.

It is generally best for the background in a collage panel to be left as a plain background colour; otherwise the effect may become too confused and the salient image or design is lost.

Fabric Collage

A fabric collage is basically an extension of a paper collage and the same working principles are therefore relevant. Fabric and paper can very satisfactorily be combined and, as in other forms of creative expression, there are no set rules laid down. Children need every encouragement to try out their own, perhaps quite unorthodox, methods.

MATERIALS

1   A variety of pieces of silks, velvets, cottons, ginghams, wools, furs, nets, tarlatans and American cloth. Plain and patterned materials will be useful, and any collection for collage should include both the lightest and darkest tones.
    Many of the miscellaneous objects that have already been mentioned may be incorporated in a fabric collage and there should also be a collection of feathers, ribbons, coarse and fine yarns, braids and sequins.

2   Strong card, hessian, coarse sacking, calico or any reasonably thick material to serve as a foundation.

3   Scissors, though it is by no means necessary for all the shapes to be cut out. Often the chance shapes of bits of fabric or paper themselves suggest a starting point and stimulate a child's imagination.

4   A glue or paste that is used for paper is usually satisfactory for pasting fabrics.

5   Old newspaper for working on.

In collage, as much as in any other medium, children can gain a greater feeling for colour by sometimes working within certain limits. Fabrics can be used particularly well in this way, provided that the basic collection covers a wide range of textures and colours. Within each colour group children should be able to find countless surfaces and variations of tone.

There is no advantage in hurrying children over the initial stages of collage work; their first response to the colours and textures is important and they should be allowed time to handle the bits and to put them together in all sorts of unexpected combinations. Even if the children have less to show at the end of a period they will, by enjoying the materials for their own sake, have sensed the real essence of the work.

MOSAICS

Mosaic patterns and pictures can be made in many materials, the methods of working being basically the same. A mosaic panel is built up of a number of small pieces, or tesserae, arranged and fixed together so as to make a composite whole. This technique naturally produces formal shapes with flat, two-dimensional qualities, and is therefore less suitable for purely representational forms of expression.

Paper mosaics are pasted on to a foundation of thick paper or card, while mosaics made of heavier materials need to be set in plasticine, clay or in some kind of cement.

In the Junior school mosaics can be made from all sorts of materials:

Papers: newspaper, coloured papers of all kinds, tissue papers, gold, silver and coloured metal papers.

Natural materials: twigs, small leaves, tiny pebbles, sand.

Seeds: peas, lentils, and beans of different colours and sizes, rice and other grains. Displays of such products in large stores offer a wide choice.

Larger fragments: chips of broken tiles and crockery, bits of broken mirror, small stones, shells, fragments of fired clay, small pieces of coal.

Oddments: all kinds of small objects—beads, buttons, wood shavings, match sticks, etc.

Paper Mosaics

MATERIALS

1   Various bits of paper. These can either cover a wide choice of colours and textures, or a more limited, carefully selected range may be provided, especially if the individual mosaic panels are to be incorporated in a communal piece of work.

Papers should include those collected by the teacher and the children (for instance, from sweet wrappings or glossy magazines) as well as paper bought for the purpose. Sheets of paper painted by the children themselves have a liveliness of surface which stands out in contrast to the flat perfection of manufactured papers.

2   Scissors

3   Strong paper or card for the base (fairly small-sized pieces, about 10 × 8 in., or even smaller, are most suitable)

4   Polycell, or a similar type of adhesive
5   Brushes for pasting
6   Saucers, small jars or mixing palettes for the paste
7   Spare newspaper for pasting on, and for protecting working surfaces.

METHOD

1   Cut a number of small squares with sides about half an inch long out of differently coloured papers, so as to include a considerable range of colour and tone. The children themselves will enjoy cutting and preparing the pieces and the teacher can speedily produce further supplies by cutting the paper on a guillotine.

Smooth organization should enable children, in even the largest classes, to have ample ranges of colours and textures easily accessible. One method of distribution is to place the cut pieces in small boxes, each containing either assorted colours or variations of a single colour. Small groups of children share two or three boxes, which are placed on newspaper that has been spread over the desk or table-tops. Thus the children have their materials readily to hand, the room is kept reasonably tidy, and clearing up at the end of the lesson is easily done.

2   Choose and arrange some of the pieces to form the main outlines of the mosaic on the foundation-card or paper, and paste them into position.

3   Next paste further small squares into the empty areas, until the whole panel is complete. Tiny gaps are inevitably left between the squares. Such gaps add to the vitality of the work, having something of the same effect as the interstices between the tesserae of a Byzantine or Roman mosaic.

Subjects in which large shapes and background areas predominate provide the best scope for interesting use of colour. All sorts of subtle variations can be introduced within a main block of colour, thus producing the lively movement of tone and shade that is so characteristic a feature of mosaics.

Tissue Paper Mosaics

This material also provides good opportunities for using colour freely and imaginatively. Pictures are built up of small fragments of coloured tissue papers, the results combining some of the decorative qualities of a collage with the sparkle of a mosaic.

The main parts of the picture are developed by tearing up and pasting down innumerable little pieces of coloured tissue paper on to the base, letting the colour scheme grow spontaneously. Cartridge paper should be used for the base, so that the fullest brilliance and translucency of the colours are preserved. If a wide range of tissue paper is supplied it is possible for the children to explore the subtlest gradations as well as the strongest contrasts of colour. By using small bits of paper they will discover some of the unexpected effects that can be produced by overlapping one piece of paper on another. 'The Fire', 'Huge Waves', 'The Heart of the Forest', 'The Sun'—such titles suggest the kind of subjects in which the atmosphere can be expressed through the glowing depths of superimposed colours.

On the whole, subjects that are fairly simple in form and large in scale compared with the size of the paper are best for this medium— a close-up, decorative fish, a large bird, and so on.

Paper mosaics and paper collage can have much the same character, the difference between them chiefly depending on the sizes of the pieces used. One method of making a tissue paper mosaic consists of dabbing each separate piece of paper with paste before it is placed in position. Or one can brush some paste over a small area of the base paper, immediately applying the dry pieces to the sticky surface. The latter method will probably produce greater freedom in working, whereas pasting each piece separately may easily lead to an over-precise approach. Another advantage of pasting the base paper, rather than each individual piece, is that the work is bound to grow more rapidly, thus encouraging a greater spontaneity and direct response to the actual qualities of the materials.

Newspaper Mosaics

Mosaics in this medium are especially suitable for the older children in the Junior school, whereas mosaics in coloured paper can be satisfactorily adapted to suit schoolchildren of any age. Made up of small rectangles of newsprint, newspaper mosaics particular emphasize qualities of tone; they depend on a controlled use of light and dark rather than on the interest of a range of colours.

Prepare three piles of torn or cut bits of newspaper (about half an inch wide), selecting very dark pieces for one heap; very light, or even white, pieces for another; and medium tones of grey for the third group. A variety of surfaces, both glossy and matt, add to the interest of this basic material, which is then used to build up a mosaic picture in which the contrast of tones plays an essential part.

The method of working is similar to that used for most other mosaics on paper or card: the main outlines of the composition are pasted down, after which the remaining areas are filled in with further pieces.

Subjects that include extremes of light and dark, or that suggest clearly defined patterns in blacks, whites and greys, are well suited to this medium (zebras, tigers, cats, cows, tortoises, patterned fish, moths with patterned wings, and so on). Imaginative portraits also provide good subject-matter, and older children, using newspaper, enjoy tackling self-portraits by candle- or torch-light. They will discover the possibilities of setting the individual pieces in varying directions, which discovery will lead to an interest in studying re-productions of the details of Byzantine mosaic portraits or patterns.

Mosaics made with Natural Objects and Oddments

In these panels objects such as small pebbles, dried vegetables and various odds and ends are set into a firm base of plasticine or clay. This is a technique that quite young children can manage successfully. It is worth trying out several substances as bases, the object being to find something that sets reasonably hard yet not too quickly, so that the many small pieces of mosaic need not be pressed into position too hurriedly.

BASES

1   Sand, mixed with a strong adhesive paste to a consistency that can just be poured, provides an effective base. The mixture is poured into a shallow wooden mould, lined with greaseproof paper to prevent sticking. This mould can be made quite simply by fencing in a shape with rulers and flat sticks, kept in position by small wedges of plasticine. Various pieces of differently coloured stone, coal, chips of flower pots, sticks and so on are then gently pressed into the soft surface.

2   It is also possible to use a fairly stiff mixture of sawdust and Poly-cell for the base of a mosaic. The small objects are pushed down

into the soft sawdust mixture, which usually takes several days to dry out and harden. It is advisable to make a few preliminary experiments, using various proportions of Polycell to sawdust, so as to ensure an effective consistency that will hold together as the base hardens. A fair amount of Polycell is needed to bind the sawdust and to make the mixture set firmly. In any case this is not a very permanent material, but it does provide a useful working foundation for small tiles, flat, circular or oval plaques, or masks that are needed only for short periods.

3   For more durable results a cement of some kind is probably most suitable. To make a cement, mix equal parts of cement powder and sand with water until a fairly thick consistency is obtained. Pour this mixture into a shallow mould. Square or rectangular moulds can be made of wood; if an irregular oval or circular shape is required, curve a narrow strip of linoleum into the necessary shape. The separate pieces of the mosaic are then embedded into the surface, before the cement has set.

4   Marley cement is an inexpensive substance now on the market that can be used for making bases for heavier panels composed of small pebbles, pieces of coal, fragments of china or fired clay. It costs 10s. 6d. a hundredweight, and is reasonably economical in use, as only a small amount is needed for each mosaic panel. This material is particularly suitable for older children.

Method of setting a Mosaic in Marley Cement

1   Plan the subject, by arranging a number of small pieces of stone and other materials on a piece of paper that is roughly the same shape and size as the intended mosaic. There should naturally be a wide range of appropriate materials to hand, so that an interesting selection of pieces can be made.

2   Next place a piece of greaseproof paper—rather larger than the mosaic will be—on to a base of wood or very stiff card. This will prevent the cement from sticking to the wood or card.

3   Mix some cement powder with enough water to make a smooth, heavy paste, thick enough to keep its own shape when it is dropped from a spoon.

4   With a spoon put some of this mixture on to the greaseproof paper, patting and flattening it into the required shape, about half an inch in depth.

5   Take the stones singly from the preliminary paper-plan and
    place each in its corresponding position on the cement slab,
    embedding it into the surface.

The final mosaic may differ considerably from the first plan, which
is only meant to serve as a working guide. It may, for instance, be
necessary to place the stones rather farther apart in the cement than
on the paper; they should not, however, be so separated that the
design becomes too bitty. The aim is to make the patterns or pictures as interesting and closely packed as the technique allows. It is
of course essential to leave some cement between the stones, so as
not to lose the clarity of the design and the character peculiar to the
technique. The soft cement tends to spread. It is necessary from time
to time to push its edges back into shape with a ruler, or flat stick.
Remove, with a small sponge, any excess water that may ooze out
at the edges, so that the outer shape remains firm and of an even
thickness.

If a panel is to be eventually hung up, insert into the top of the
slab, when the cement is still soft, a small piece of looped wire with
its ends splayed apart, to make a projecting loop.

Pasting the Mosaic on to a Base

Another simple method of building up decorative patterns or pictures in mosaic is to glue the separate pieces directly on to a base made
of a piece of linoleum or really stiff cardboard. No. 103 shows a
symmetrical pattern in which dried beans, lentils, peas, rice and areas
of coarse sand have been stuck on to a tile made of a dark synthetic
material. This particular tile was one of a number placed together to
form a larger, decorative panel, incorporating several people's work
(No. 104). The students working on this project decided on a certain
range of materials, so that there was an overall unity of colour and
texture.

The outlines of each design were lightly chalked on to the base,
after which the patterns grew freely through a direct use of the
materials.

In any mosaics in which materials other than paper are used, it is
important to be sure that the glue is strong enough to hold the
heavier objects, such as small pebbles, securely in position. A number of satisfactory glues are available and a little experiment will
avoid the disappointment of patterns being spoilt by pieces falling off.

Some General Considerations

All sorts of materials, and combinations of materials, can be used experimentally. In work of this kind the emphasis should be on the interplay of shapes and on the relationship of various colours, tones and textures. Certain questions must be kept in mind by the teacher.

COMPOSITION. Is the general design or picture pleasing as a whole? Do the different parts look right in relation both to each other and to the whole? Are the various aspects well balanced? This should be considered in both symmetrical and asymmetrical designs.

COLOUR. Do the colours make an important contribution to the total effect? Are they used instinctively or is the selection mainly an outcome of conscious planning? This will differ with individual children. Have the materials and colours supplied for the work provided the children with an adequate means of expression? Has the most been made of minute colour changes within an area? (See No. 96.) Is there an interplay between warm and cool colours? Or has the interest been limited mainly to one range of colours? Has a focal area been established by introducing a few brilliant colours, perhaps quite different from the rest? Is there an interplay between smaller patches of vivid colour and larger areas of quieter colour? Does the general distribution of colour work in with the rhythm of the composition as a whole?

TONE. Have dark and light colours been used together effectively? Do the variations of tone help to emphasize the clarity of the picture or pattern? (See Nos. 103 and 104.)

TEXTURE. Are the different surfaces interesting in themselves and in relation to each other? Has enough variety of texture been provided in the working materials?

SCALE. Is there enough contrast between the relative scale of the different objects and materials introduced? (See No. 103.) This is obviously important in panels depending on groupings of stones and other materials. An interest in differences of scale can also be introduced in paper mosaics, by slightly varying the size of the cut squares.

Collective Mosaics

Mosaics can be used for group projects, such as classroom decorations for Christmas. Parts of a classroom—perhaps the panels of a cupboard or the jambs of a door—can be decorated by making individual units as small as four or five inches square, which, combined, make an attractive whole. Small pieces of radiant-metal paper, interspersed among matt colours, add to the richness of a mosaic panel. It should be realized that assembling the finished mosaics in a well-balanced and pleasant arrangement is as important a part of the work as the actual making of the mosaics.

It is helpful to show children carefully chosen pictures of tiled mosaic pavements, so that they see how the simplest forms of pattern can be the most effective.

Reproductions in books and on postcards of Roman, Byzantine and Early Christian mosaics are fairly easily obtained, as well as reproductions of the work of modern artists, for example, the mosaics of Coventry Cathedral. At every stage of the Junior school the enjoyment of both traditional and contemporary mosaics can be related to the children's practical experience in this field.

WEAVING

Simple weaving in the Primary school can bring fresh interest to the use of colour and texture. It is a fundamental craft that children of all ages enjoy.

Experimental approaches can be introduced by teachers who have had little previous experience of the craft. They themselves will learn as the work develops. Taught sensitively, weaving provides a basis for imaginative thinking; at this stage it is a creative rather than a technical process, and weaving in the Infant and Junior school may be regarded more as a means to an end than an end in itself.

Weaving in essence consists of the intersection of one set of strands or threads (the warp) with another set of threads (the weft). It should be started on a really primitive basis, the children making the simplest forms of loom and using all sorts of yarns experimentally for the weft. A warp of fine string can be very successful. The emphasis should be on increasing the children's understanding of the relationships of colour and texture and on freedom in designing rather than on the acquisition of technical skill or on the production of material. An experimental approach in the Junior school not only provides creative experiences of immediate significance to the child, but also establishes a foundation for the development of technically more advanced work at the Secondary stages.

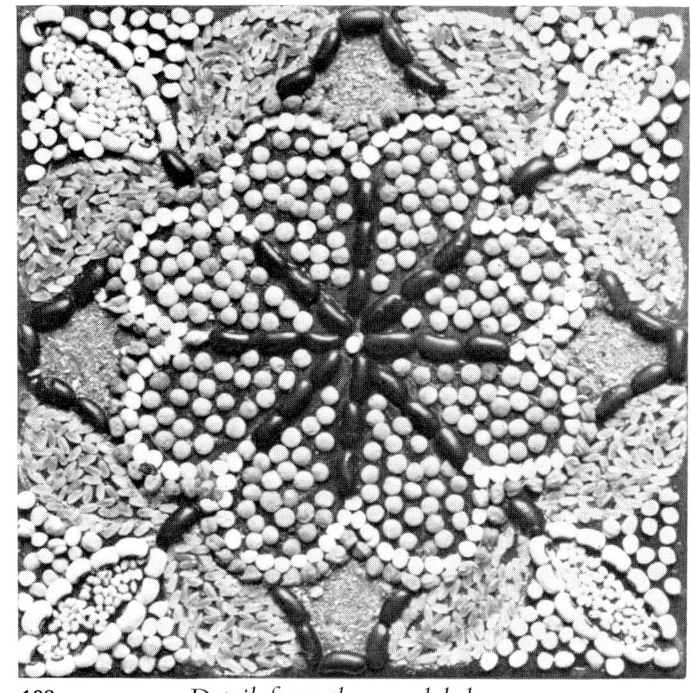

103   *Detail from the panel below.*

104   *Collective work by a group of students in which 'mosaic' squares, each 9″ × 9″, were built up from peas, beans, rice-grains, straws, sticks, gravel, small pieces of coal, etc., see page* 178.

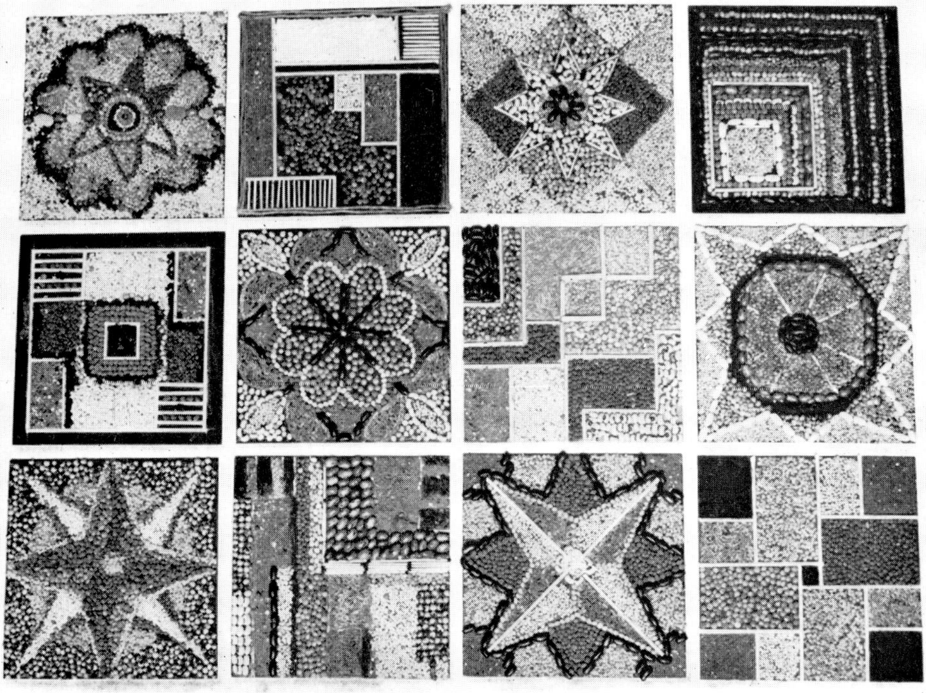

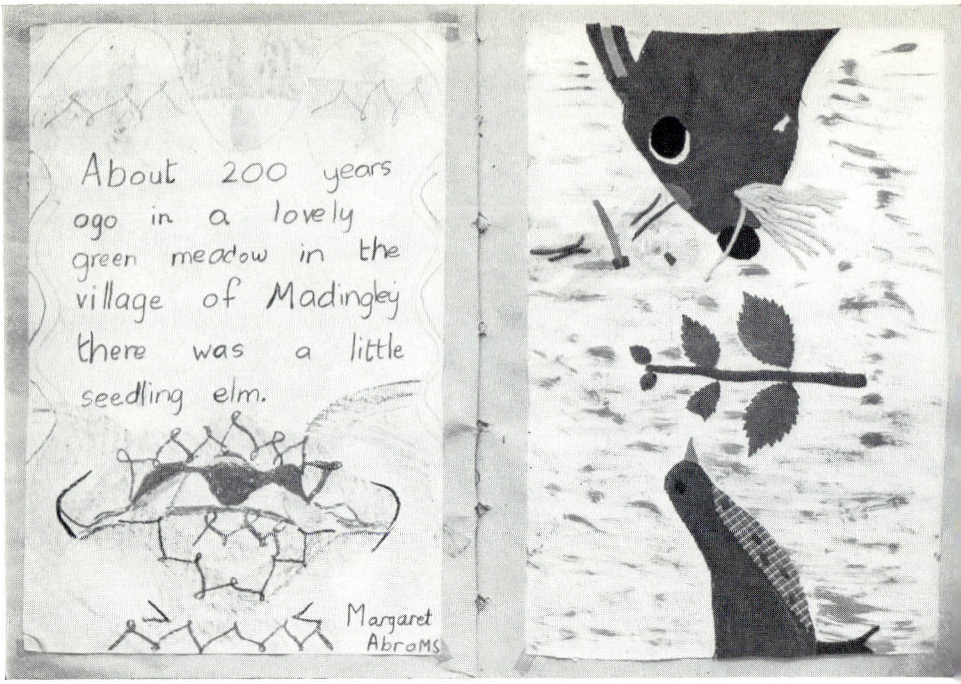

105

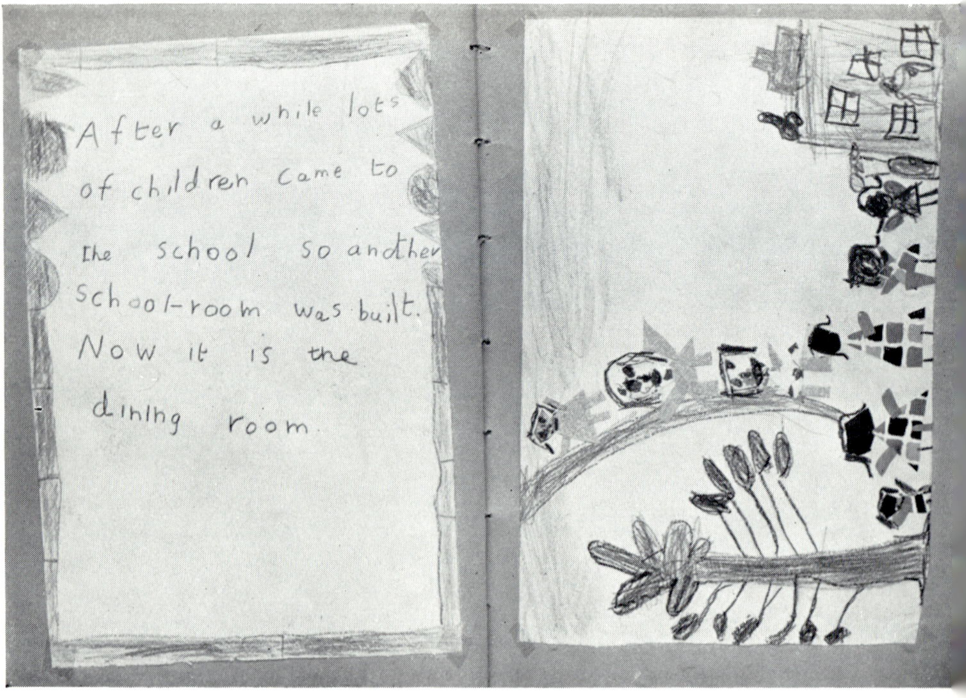

106

Pages from 'The Old Elm Tree', 25" × 20" when open, ma

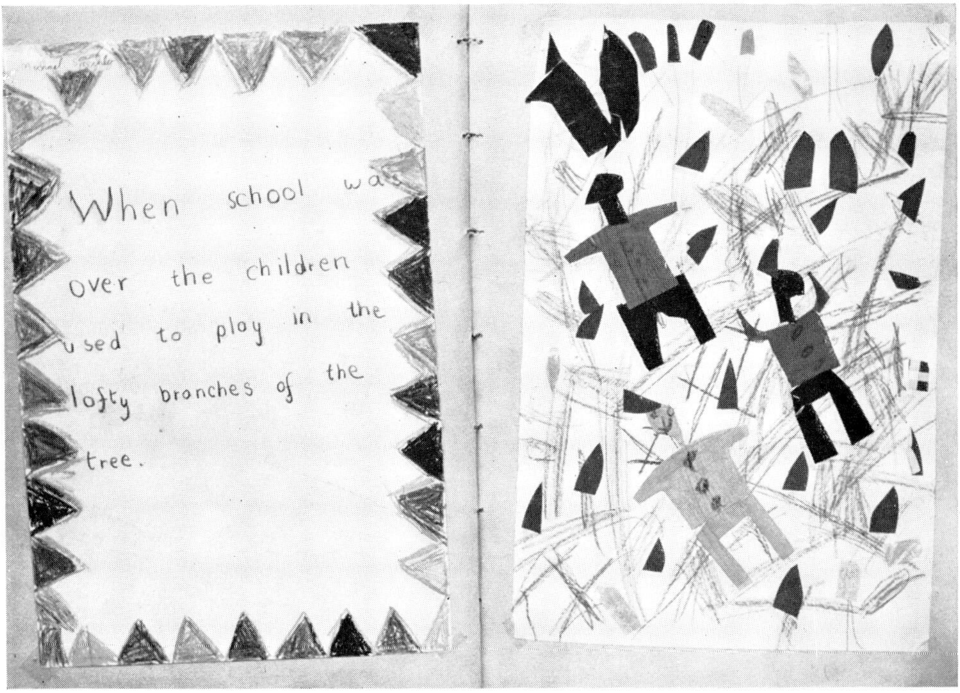

When school was
over the children
used to play in the
lofty branches of the
tree.

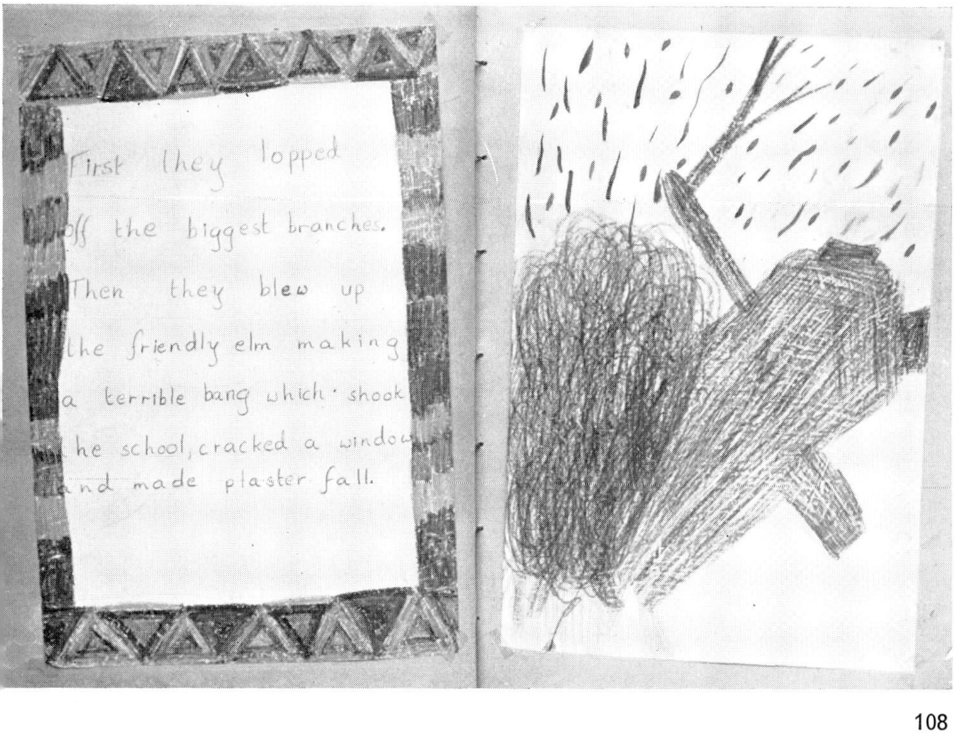

First they lopped
off the biggest branches.
Then they blew up
the friendly elm making
a terrible bang which shook
the school, cracked a window
and made plaster fall.

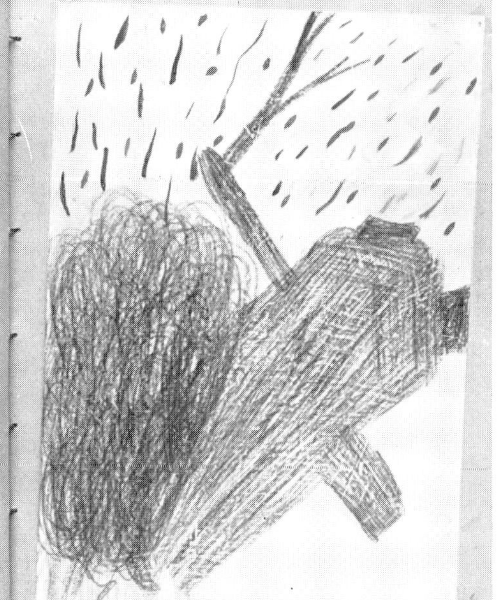

y 5 to 10 year old children in a village school, see page III.

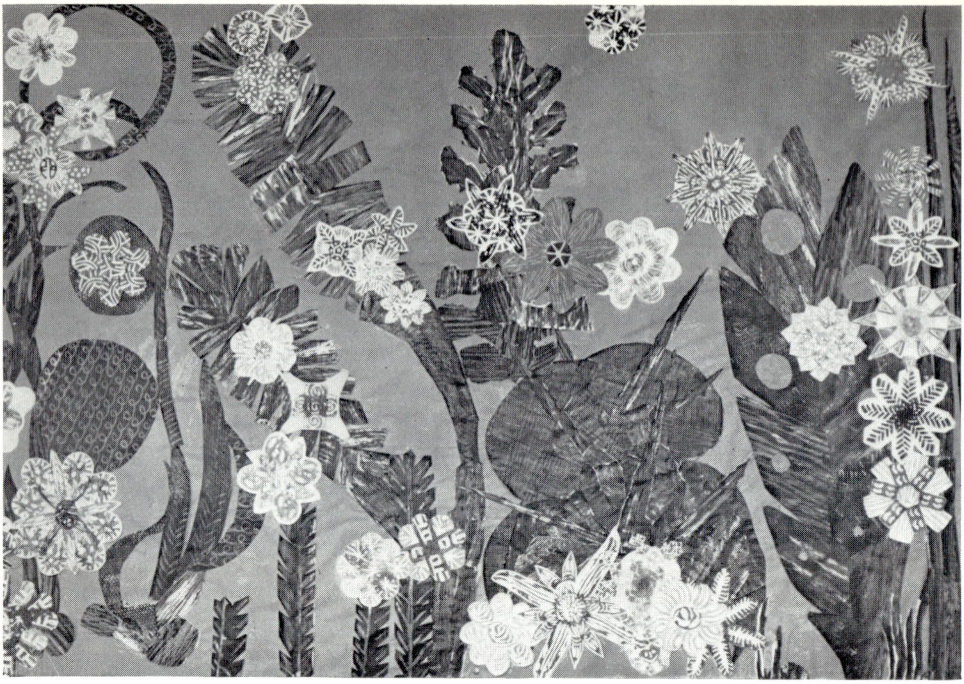

109   *Panel, 4 ft. × 3 ft., made by a group of students, using potato cuts with candle and ebony stain rubbings, see pages 129, 137.*

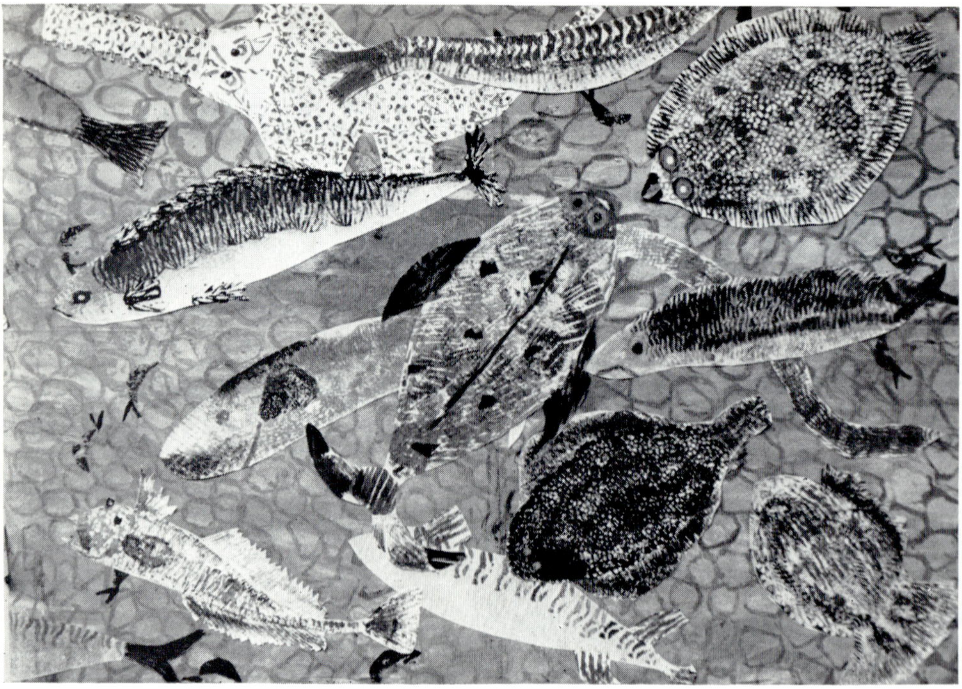

110   *A group of 9 and 10 year old children produced this potato-print panel, about 4 ft. × 3 ft., based on their observations of real fish, see page 137.*

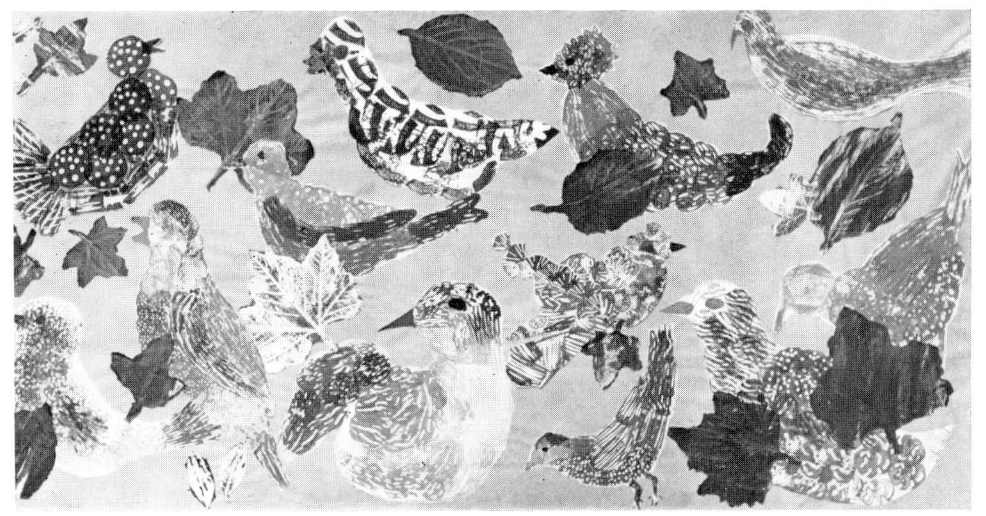

111 *A bird panel, about 4 ft. × 2 ft., built up by a group of students, using potato prints and leaf rubbings, see pages* 129, 137.

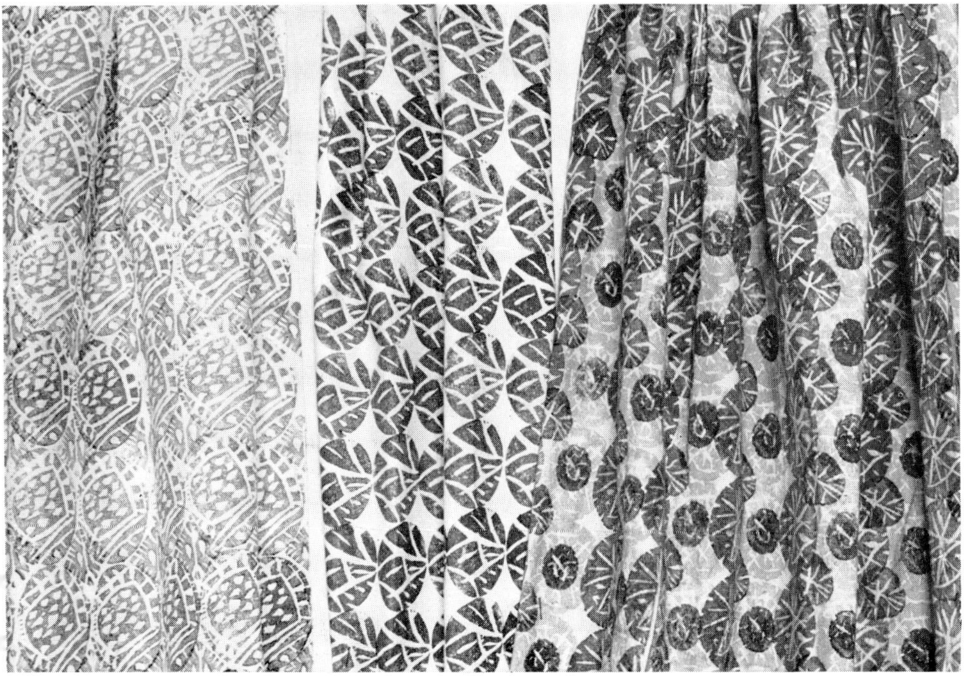

112 *Potato printing on fabric, by* 10 *year old children in a primary school, see pages* 15, 73, 119.

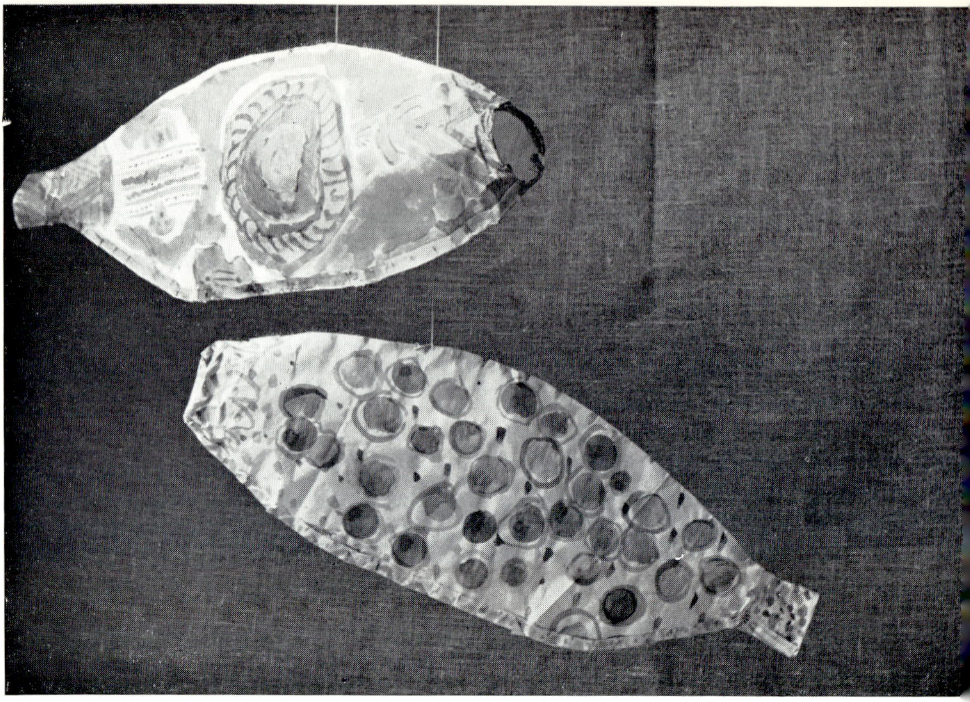

113 *Fish mobiles, length 16″, painted in coloured inks on thin paper by 9 and 10 year old children, see page 118.*

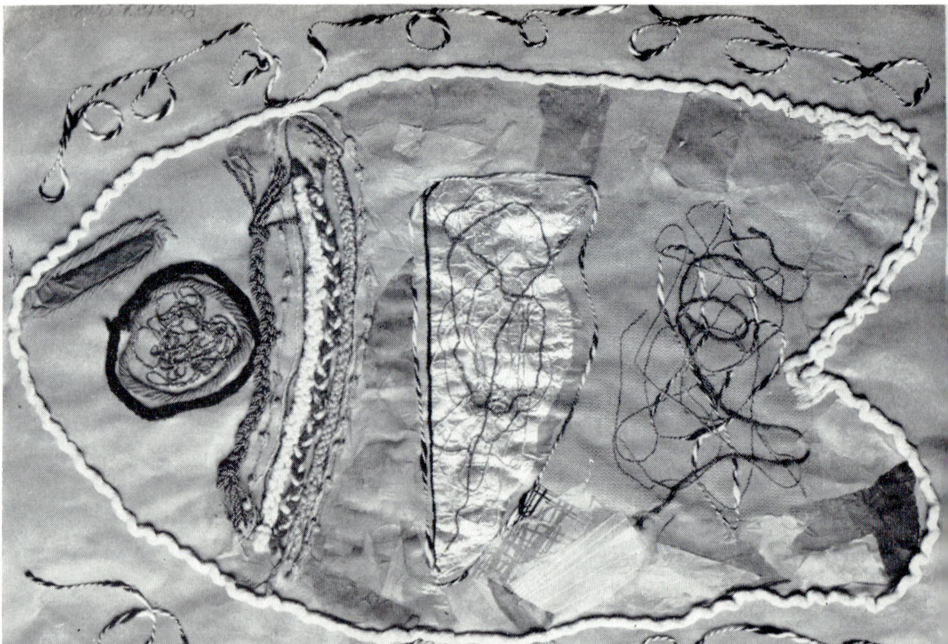

114 *A collage, 18″ × 14″, made in a variety of papers and wools by Rosalind, aged 10 see page 171.*

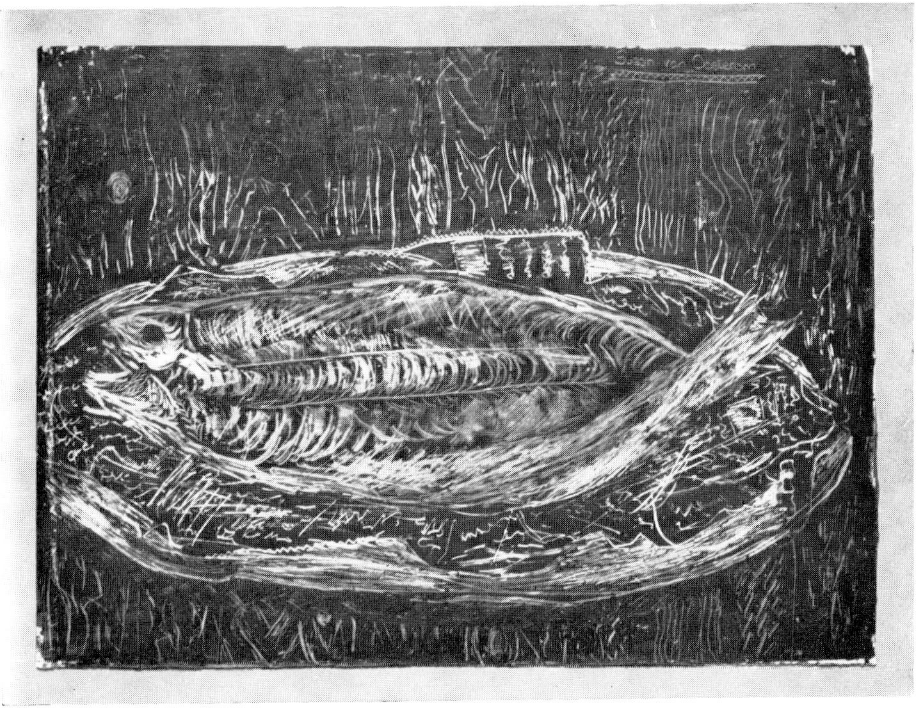

115   'Kippers', a wax-crayon engraving, 17″ × 12″, by Susan, aged 12, see pages 61, 191.

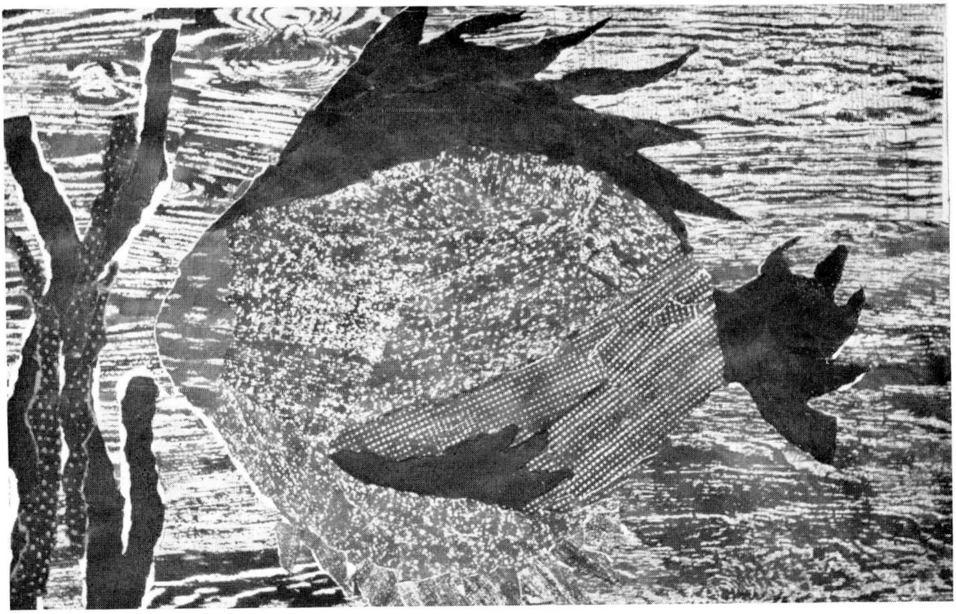

116   A torn-paper composition, 21″ × 15″, made by a student using candle and ebony stain rubbings of various textures and tones, see pages 128, 195.

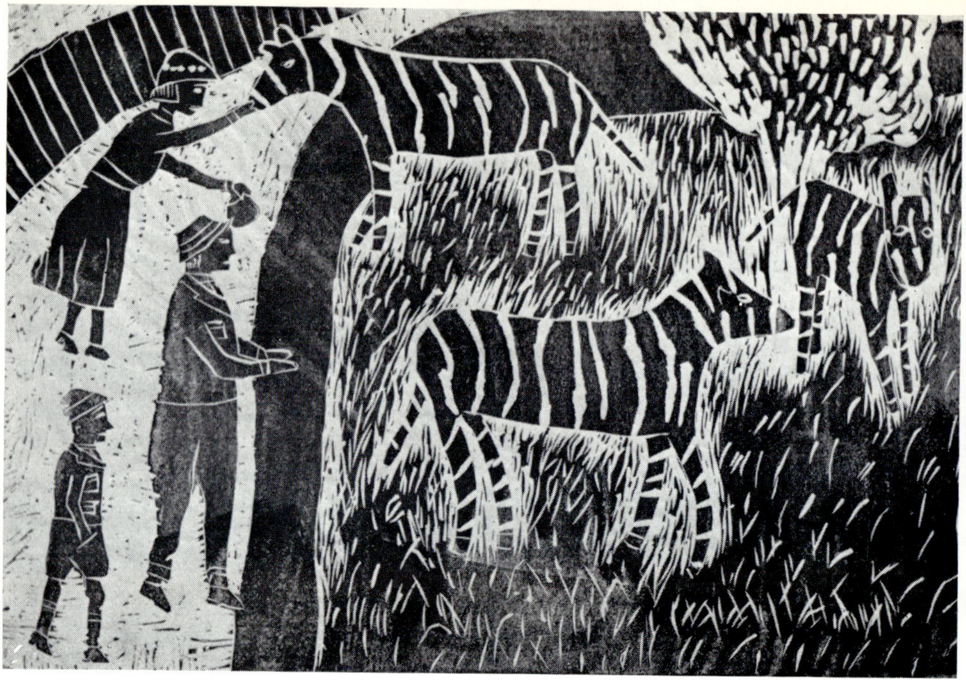

117

Lino-cuts, 15″ × 10″, by 10 year old girls, following a visit to the Zoo, see page 186

118

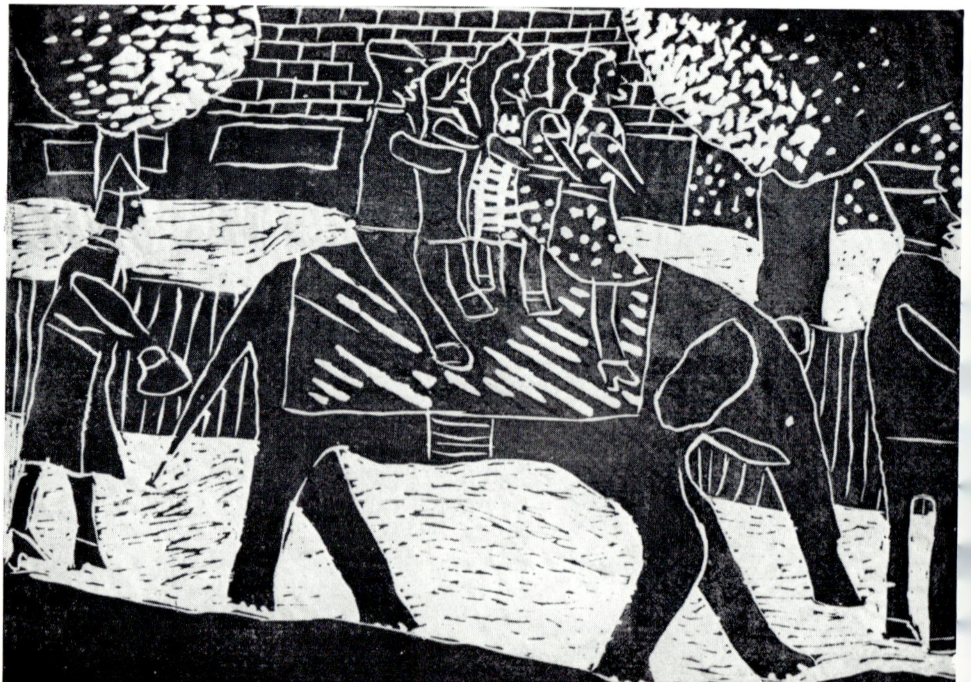

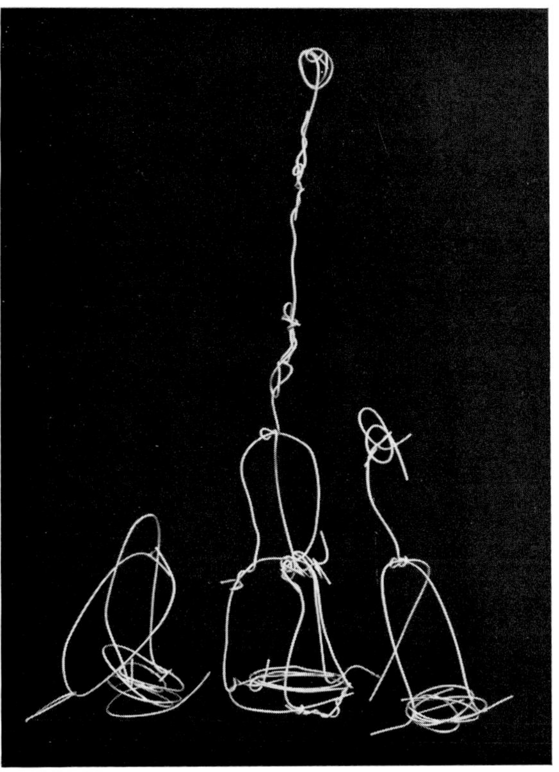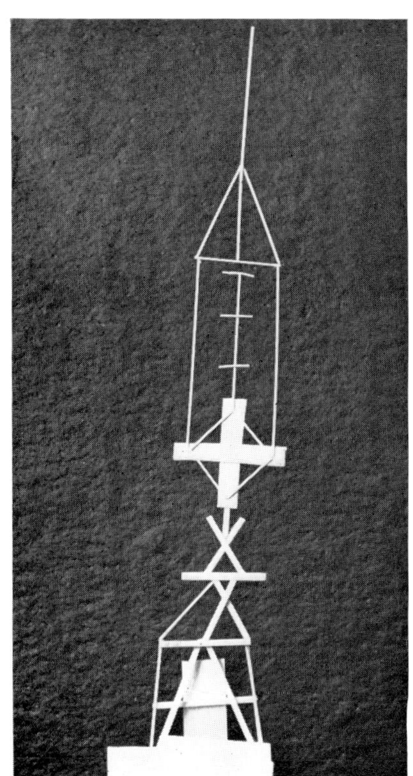

119   *Three-dimensional work in varied media by* 10 *year old children;*   120
121   *models about* 18 *inches high, see page* 210.   122

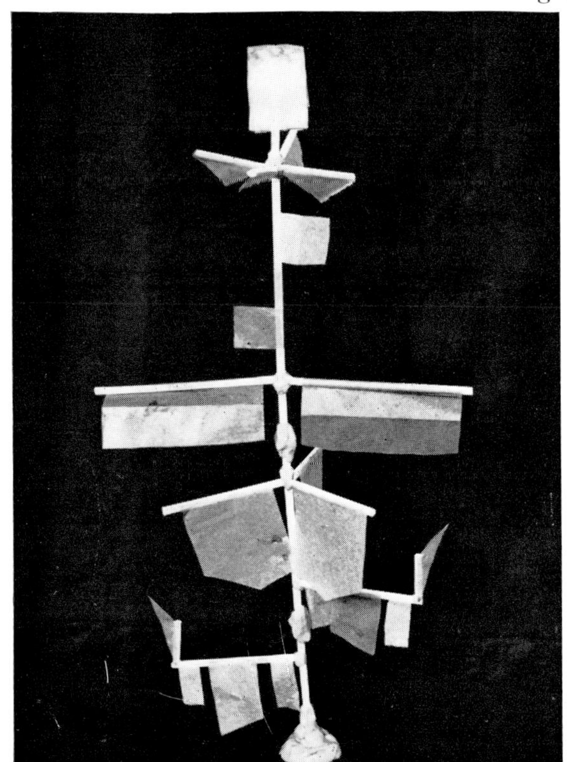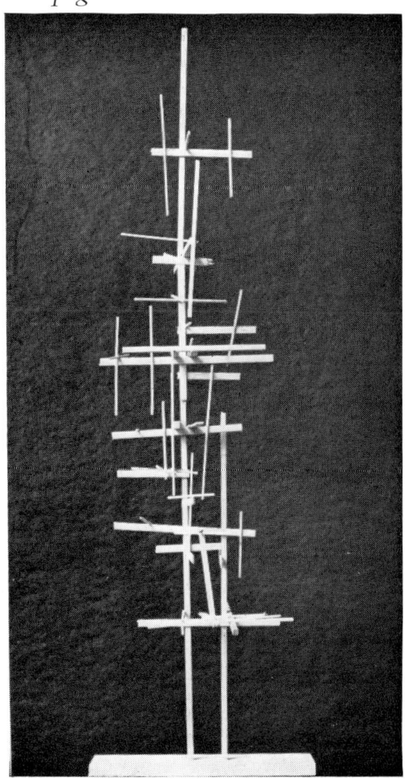

123

Weaving by 10 year old boys in a village school. They put string warps on looms they
had made themselves, and used a variety of materials for the weft, see page 181.

124

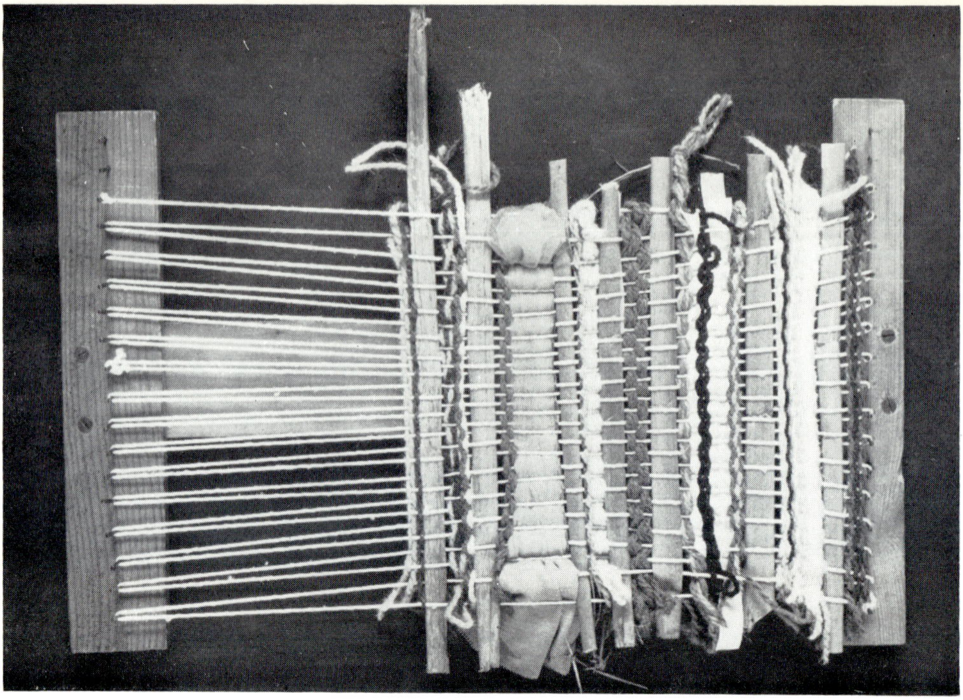

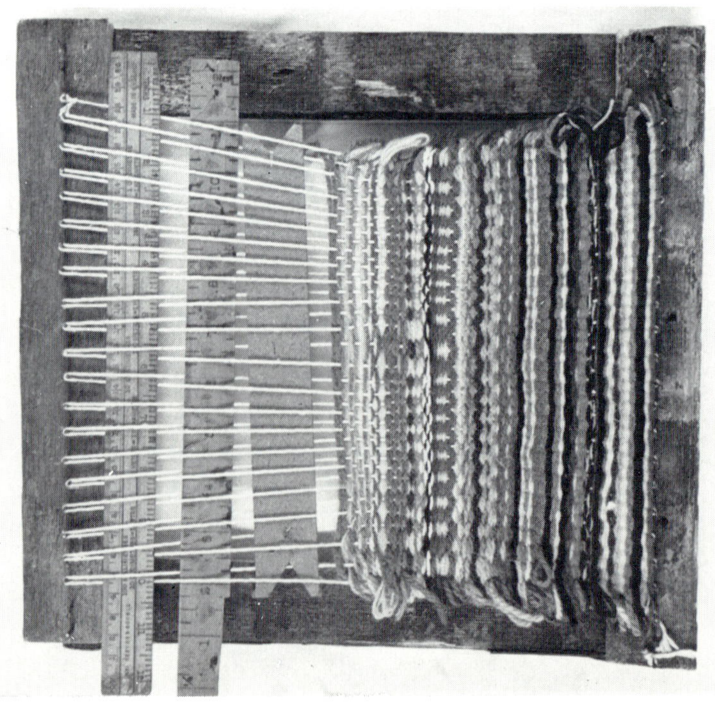

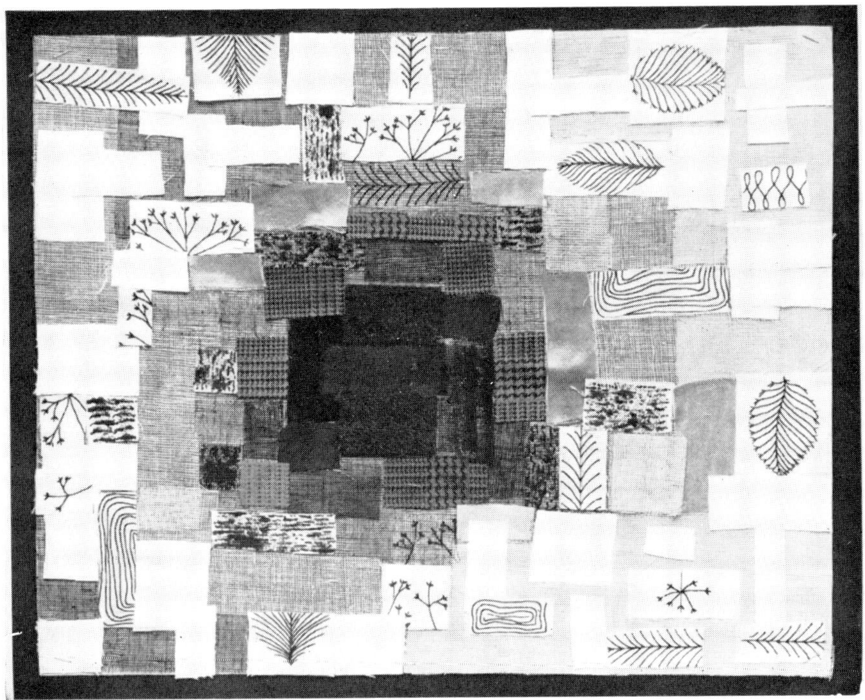

125

Fabric collages, 12″ × 9″, made by students, using feathers and scraps of fabric to show possible arrangements and relationships of tones, see page 172.

126

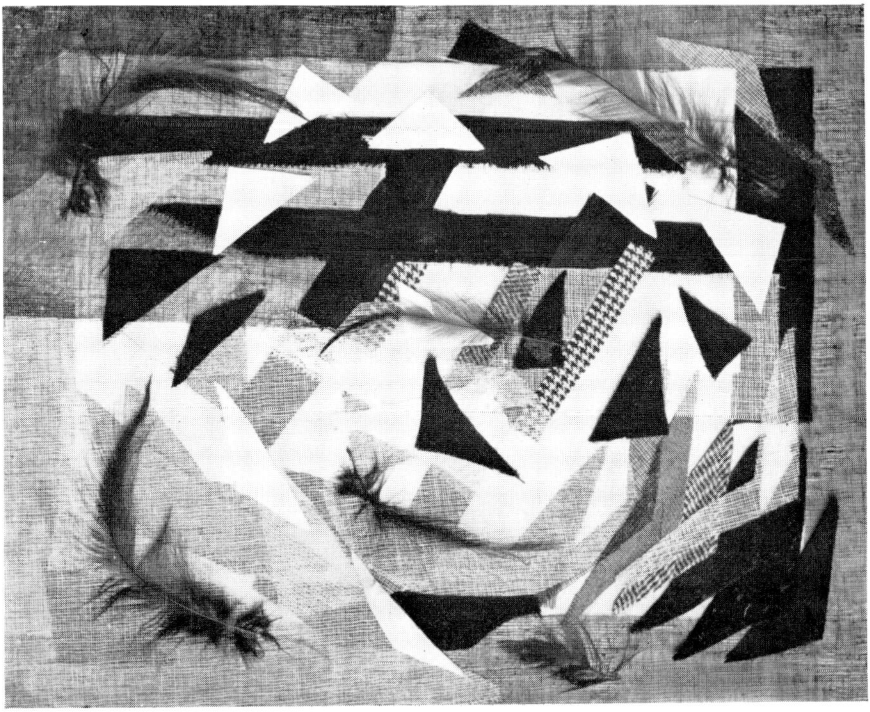

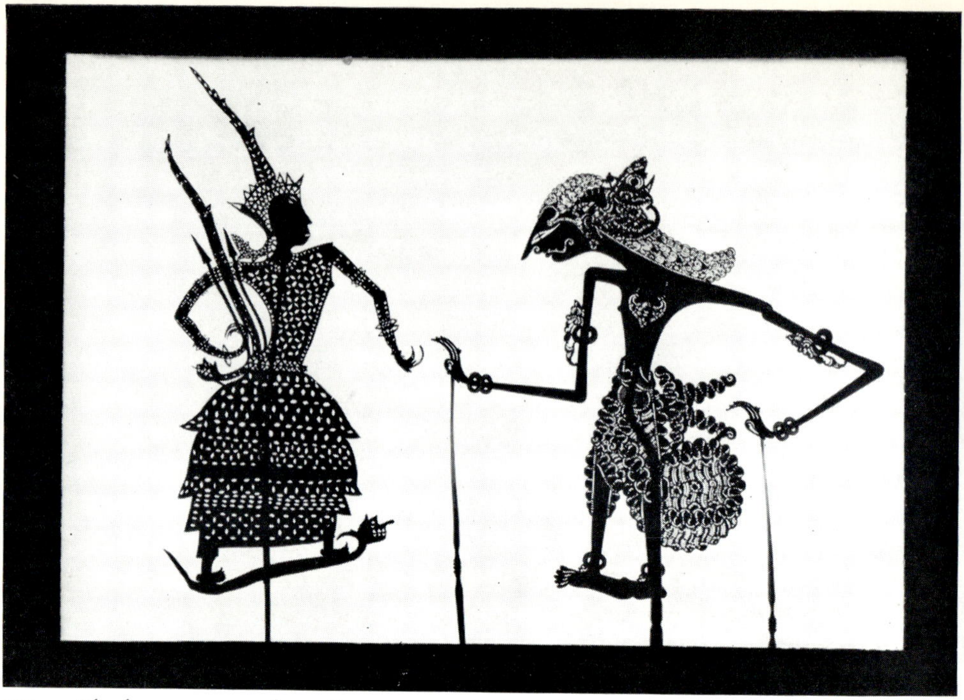

127 *Shadow puppets from Java, as used there for ritualistic display. Size of screen 32″ × 22″, see pages 101, 204.*

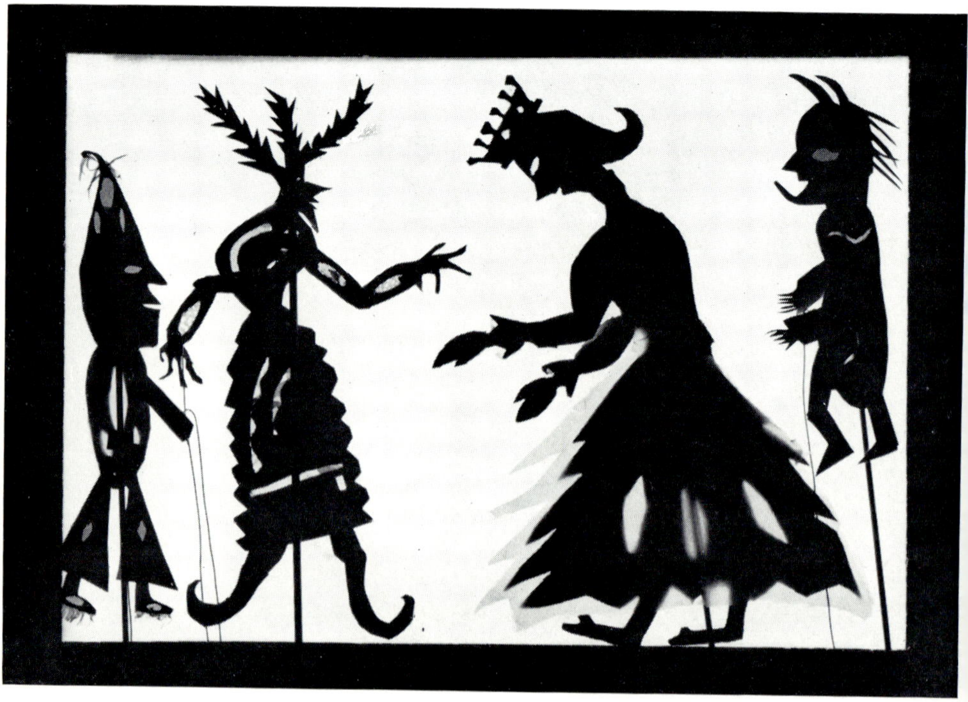

128 *Examples of shadow puppets produced by students working*

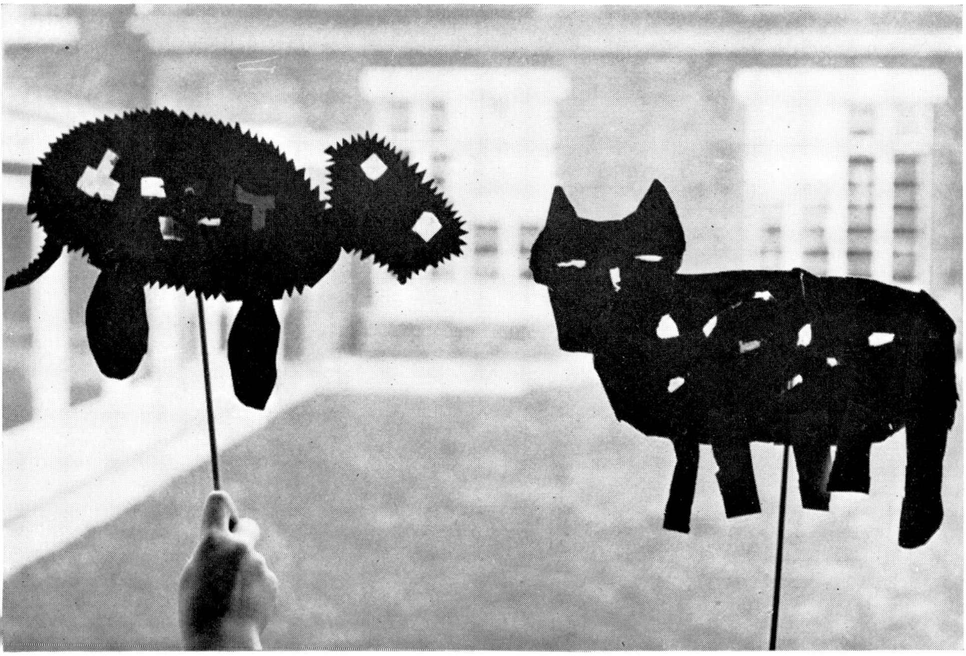

129   *Shadow puppets made and used by 6 year old children in a country primary school,
see pages 101, 204.*

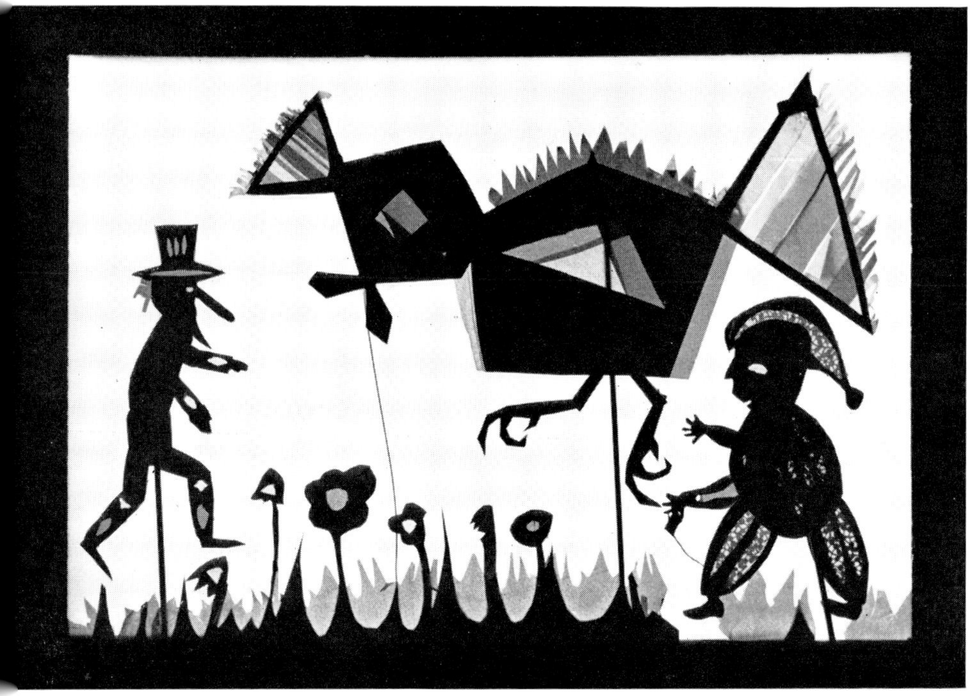

...ith 11 and 12 year old children. Screen 32" × 22", see page 205.   130

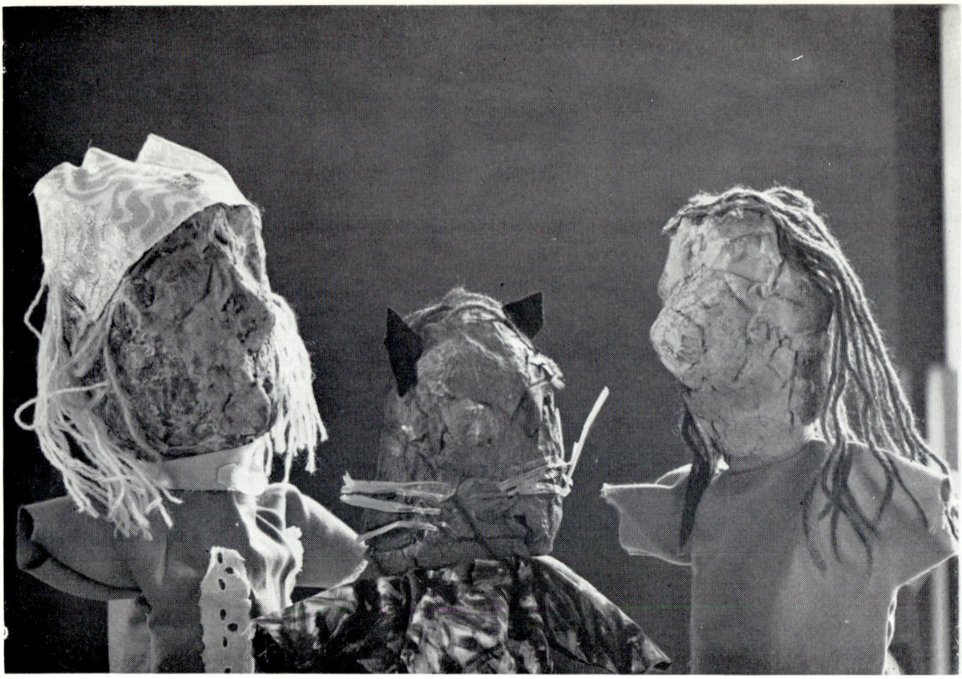

131   *Glove puppets with papier mâché heads, made and used by 6 year old children, see pages 77, 100, 199.*

132   *Paper-bag masks made by children of 7 to 10 years, see page 118.*

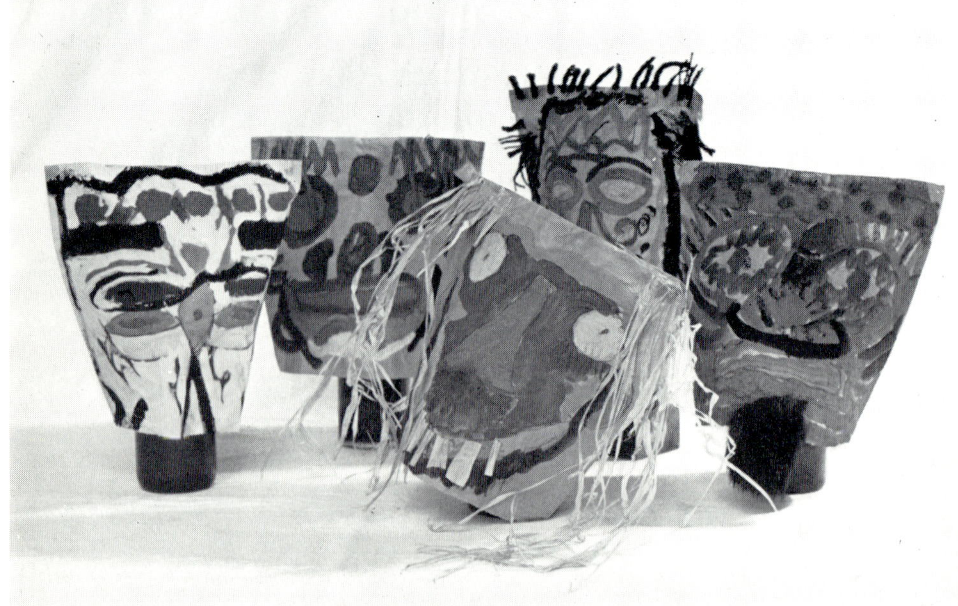

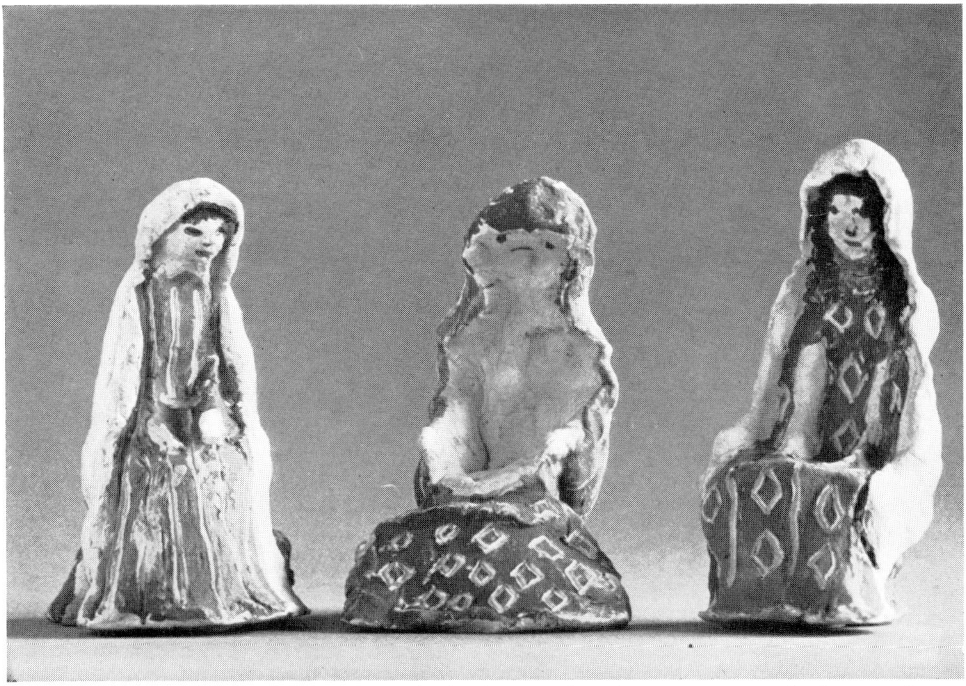

133   *Clay models, each about 4 in. high, decorated with patterns scratched into coloured slip, made by 10 year old children as part of a nativity group, see pages 15, 99, 214.*

134   *Glazed clay models, about 5 in. high, made as part of a farm project by 10 year old children, see pages 99, 210.*

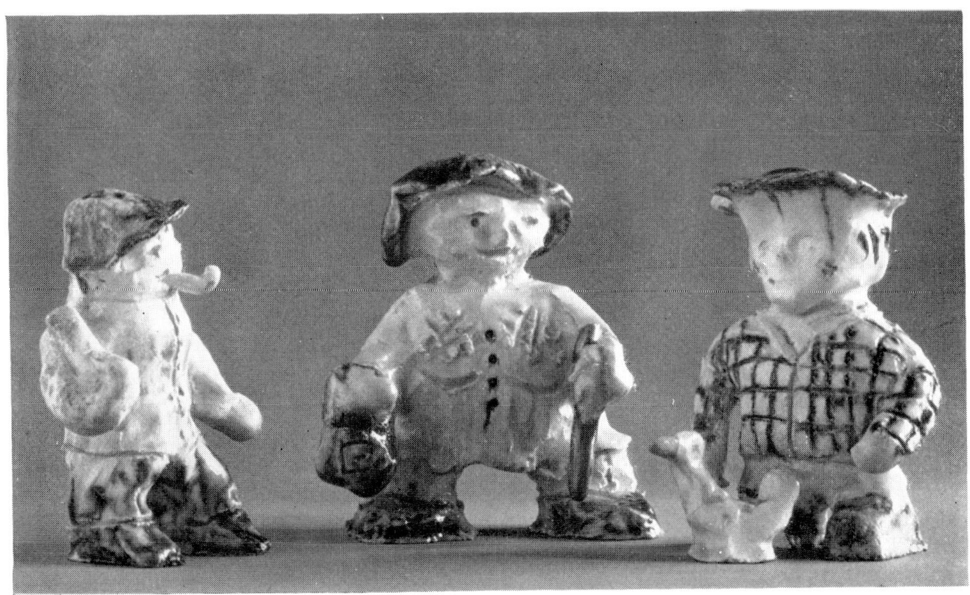

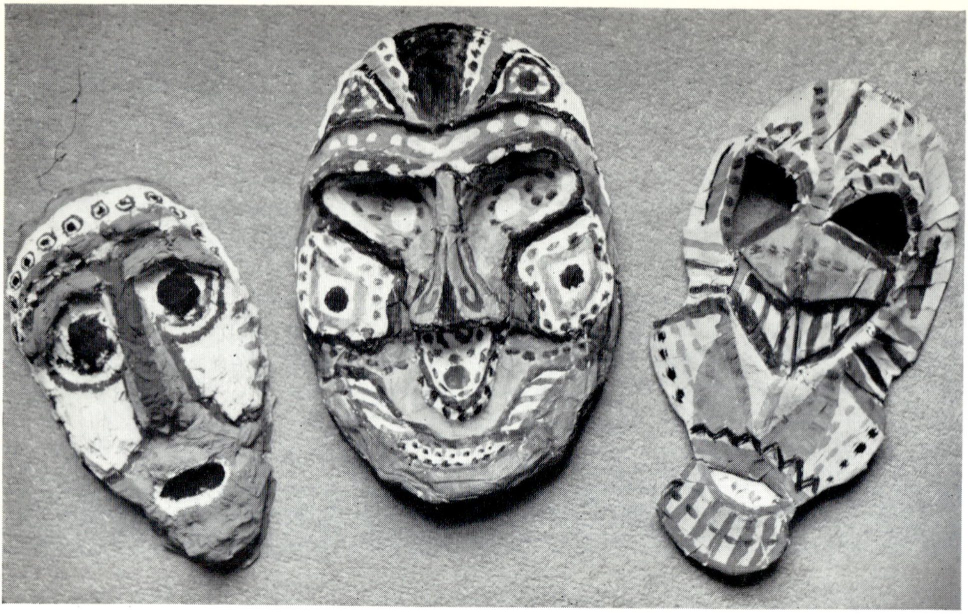

135   *Decorated papier mâché and wire masks, about 12 in. long, made by children of 10 to 12 years, see page 223.*

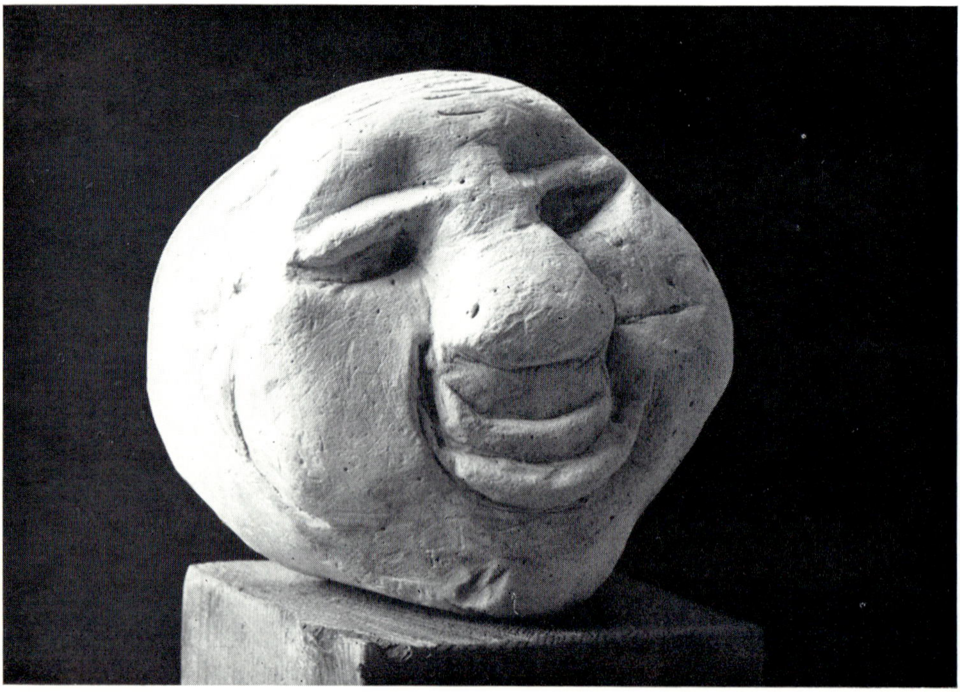

136   *A carving in chalk, about 4 in. high, by a boy of 12, see pages 77, 210.*

Materials for Weaving

1   Machine-spun threads of various thicknesses and kinds: wools, silks, cottons and man-made fibres. Shiny and matt, smooth and rough, warm and cool-coloured, and light and dark-toned yarns should be available.

  Plying, plaiting, mixing and twisting threads or materials will produce a vitality of colour and texture in the composite threads or strips. Narrow lengths of dyed sheeting can also be twisted or plaited into thicker cords or bands of varied colour. Through these processes the children will become interested in the effects produced by their threads, and will look at both their own and manufactured fabrics with greater understanding.

2   A selection of natural materials: rushes, reeds, grasses, straw, raffia, hemp, etc.

3   Synthetic products: strips of nylon, plastic, rayon, cellophane.

4   Coloured rags and scrap material, old stockings (which may be dyed), gimp, ribbons and wrapping-string.

5   Sheets dyed in commercial dyes—including black. Rich blues can be produced by dyeing cotton material in indigo (see Chapter 7, pages 147–8).

Looms

Looms can be made from old strong picture-frames—although unfortunately these are becoming less easy to procure—or a simple frame can be constructed by joining together four fairly stout pieces of wood. No. 124 illustrates a loom of this kind, made by a ten-year-old boy.

  A row of nails, about half an inch apart, is hammered in at either end of the frame. The warp—in a continuous thread—is then wound over the nails, up and down the length of the loom, and fastened to a nail at each end. A fairly strong yarn should be used for the warp. As soon as it has been wound on to the loom the actual weaving can be started.

  The weft is woven over and under alternate warp threads or groups of warp threads. One method is to insert a flat stick or ruler, weaving it in and out of the warp threads; by turning the ruler up on its side, alternate rows of warp threads are effectively separated so that the weft thread can be passed through quite easily, either on its own or on a shuttle. The weft thread may be held in a safety-pin or Kirby grip, or a simple shuttle may be made out of a piece of card, see No. 124.

The rows of weaving are pushed down with a stick so that a piece of fabric is produced. Care has to be taken not to pull the weft threads across the warp too tightly, so that no unsightly waist is made in the weaving. Experience will enable children to gauge the tension correctly. It helps if each weft thread is left lying rather loosely, at an angle of about forty-five degrees between the warp threads, before it is pushed into place. When very young children are weaving it is often best to cut the ends of the weft threads, so that the problem of pulled-in sides will not arise. Thick grasses or reeds, or wide rags, will in any case have to be left free at the ends (No. 123).

The finished weaving is lifted off the nails and the two ends of yarn used for the warp are securely fastened. On a longer loom an extra length of warp is sometimes left at either end, which can be knotted so as to form a fringe. A very loosely woven piece of fabric may need to be strengthened by a line of loose machine stitching at each end.

This approach to weaving is so simple technically that the child's creative energy can be directed towards discovering ways in which colours and textures relate well in a woven fabric. Many patterns can be produced quite simply: by using blocks of different colours in the weft, by going over and under groups of warp threads, or by introducing tufts or loops in the weaving.

Through a lively, experimental attitude towards weaving, it should be possible to counteract the effect of the monotonous regularity of some commercial fabrics, in which interest is limited entirely to the mechanical repetition of stripes of colour. Even when the proportion and colour of the stripes are well combined, there is often singularly little life or character in the body of the material. This is naturally by no means true of all manufactured fabrics, and in many designs imaginative use is made of mechanical methods of production, with very beautiful results.

As an outcome of their introduction to weaving and textile designing, limited though these experiences will inevitably be, children should become sensitive to some of the more satisfying forms of industrial textile design.

Colour, Texture and Tone

In weaving, as in other forms of art, children can discover effective colour combinations by keeping within the limits of a specific colour group. The only rule might be that the full tonal range of a colour must be included.

A piece of weaving in the red group will therefore contain the palest pinks as well as very dark, nearly black, reds, with countless tones between. Apart from a wide tonal range each sampler of weaving should express as fully as possible the intrinsic qualities of a colour. Red, for instance, will range fully from orange-red to purple-reds. A movement of colour is achieved partly by the vibration of subtly related colours, partly by the interaction of opposites. A cochineal pink by the side of a vermilion will intensify the orange quality of the vermilion. Children will find this reaction of one colour on another exciting in weaving especially when, for instance, two colours crossing each other produce a third, quite different colour.

Once colours have been painted in a pattern they are not easily changed, whereas dozens of actual threads and textures can be put together and quickly altered. In a matter of minutes new arrangements and proportions can be tried out, some to be used straight away on a warp, others to be discarded in favour of fresh juxtapositions of colour. The child needs time to enjoy fully the sparkle and glow of these different arrangements, so he should have the chance to linger over them without being pressed to 'get on'.

The Small Table-loom

Relatively little expense need be involved in the craft at this stage, An enthusiastic teacher, who has some specialist knowledge of weaving, may plan to extend the scope of the work by setting up a small table-loom, with a warp on which individual children can try out a number of variations of simple weaving, selecting their weft threads from a wide choice of materials. A number of short lengths can be woven on one warp, so that each child is able to complete an individual piece of weaving reasonably quickly. The emphasis is on the understanding gained by the children through this further opportunity for experiment.

The use of Heddles

Instead of introducing a table-loom, the teacher may prefer to make a simpler type of loom, in which the warp is controlled by solid heddles. These may be bought at a reasonable cost, and can be used on a string warp that has been wound and tied round a smooth, wooden box.

Such looms, on which children of ten and eleven years are well able to weave attractive pieces of cloth, may be regarded as a half-way house between the technically rather more elaborate table-loom and the primitive looms made by the children themselves (Nos. 123 and 124).

Children who have painted linear patterns and made band patterns with candle and ebony stain, or who have impressed bands of pattern on a pot, will find themselves dealing with much the same problems in their weaving. In each medium, the placing, balance and proportions of the various parts to each other and to the whole will be of chief importance.

A Free Approach in Design

Weaving can be so freely and imaginatively treated that the somewhat formal structure of ordered bands may be completely abandoned. A string warp provides the support or scaffolding for weaving of this kind, allowing the weft to be used with extreme flexibility. The weft, selected from a variety of threads and materials, can be allowed to wander about the string structure. It may be loosely pushed together into partially open shapes or in parts it can be compressed into quite solid blocks. In places maybe the warp is left untouched, becoming the dominant pattern, in other parts meandering strands of weft are interwoven with a filigree lightness.

Whether the composition is abstract or an adaptation of a particular theme, the result is as much a personal expression of the individual as any painting. This kind of weaving, which older children in the Junior school can enjoy, is primarily a creative experience. While the results may be of little functional use in the generally accepted sense, they lead to the discovery of fresh visual and tactile qualities, and sometimes these freely woven panels make very attractive wall-hangings.

Tapestry Weaving

Tapestry weaving also brings out the creative elements of the craft. In this type of weaving the weft threads—or strips of rag—are pressed or beaten very closely together on a fairly widely spaced string warp, so that hardly any warp remains visible in the firmly woven fabric. Dyed strips of rag can be used for the weft, as well as thick wools.

Simple patterns and formalized two-dimensional figures, their angularity rightly reflecting the characteristics of the technique, will be produced in this way.

Dyeing and Spinning

Some mention must be made of dyeing because this activity goes hand in hand with weaving, textile printing and designing. Dyeing, either with vegetable or with synthetic dyes, may well become an absorbing aspect of work with textiles. Some sources of information on chemical dyes have been given in Chapter 7. Natural dyes are very different in character and have their own distinctive beauty. Ideally, older children who have become interested in this subject should have opportunities of getting to know something of both kinds of dye.

A variety of natural dyes, such as those obtained from onion skins, privet or elderberries, walnut husks or lichens can be used and will be particularly appreciated by children in the country who can make their own collections. Some technical knowledge is of course necessary for preparing and using these dyes, and a practical approach is given in *The Use of Vegetable Dyes*, by V. Thurstan (Dryad Press), together with a number of recipes.

Hand-spinning is another craft that many older children find absorbing and those who have had even a brief experience of using a simple spindle will become more sensitive to the quality and texture of threads and fabrics. Descriptions of various ways of spinning are included in several of the books on general crafts mentioned on page 280.

To get the most out of weaving and any of these related activities in the Primary school, a teacher should be prepared to waive the more technical considerations and concentrate on the creative aspect of the work. Children should enjoy the feeling of weaving, without being cramped or overwhelmed by problems which are better studied at a later stage.

LINO-PRINTS

Lino cutting is an exciting technique that is especially suitable for older children, who will enjoy the processes of cutting and printing.

A fair amount of preparation is needed and, as it may not be possible to organize equipment for large numbers, lino cutting is probably more appropriate for small groups. All the same, if it can be arranged, there is something very invigorating when a whole class is working simultaneously at making prints, and the results are often particularly rewarding.

Children who have had some experience of potato-printing and of printing from other surfaces will readily understand the general principles of lino cutting and printing. There are countless variations and children should be encouraged to experiment with as many of the related techniques as possible.

It will probably be most useful to describe one method in detail, that of making a one-colour block, as this type of print provides a good starting point for further experiment. Nos. 117 and 118 are lino-prints made in this way. In each of these white line engravings the lines and textures were cut directly into the lino, with the minimum of preliminary drawing. The interest lies largely in the pattern made by the light and dark shapes and by the juxtaposition of the different textures. In both Nos. 117 and 118 the pictures have been built up from dark to light—in contrast to a black and white drawing which is usually developed from light to dark (No. 66). Each print contains areas of black and white as well as a number of intermediate greys. Much of their success lies in this range of tone. The prints also have a spontaneity characteristic of direct, unafraid cutting, although the work has in no sense been carelessly handled. No. 117 has some especially varied cutting, in which the markings on the zebras and the textures of the grass and trees are expressively related.

There were over thirty girls—ten years old—in the class, and each made a lino-cut of a Zoo subject, while her impressions of a recent visit were still fresh. The blocks were large, and three afternoons—each a period of seventy minutes—were spent on the work; by the end of the third week each girl had finished the cutting and taken a print. Several prints were taken during lunch hours, and in the fourth week the printing table was again available for individual girls to use, though the class as a whole had started a new subject.

Equipment

Plain linoleum

Lino tools: a handle, a gouge and a V-shaped nib

Indian ink and an old brush

Black and coloured printing inks. An oil-bound printing ink is recommended; printing water colours are generally less successful

A dessertspoon or wooden spoon for rubbing the print through

A tile or slab of glass on which to roll out the ink

Absorbent paper for printing: a variety of surfaces and colours should be tried—kitchen paper, good quality newsprint, tissue paper, Japanese paper, thin fabrics

A small rubber roller

Plenty of loose newspaper

Old absorbent rags

Turpentine, for general cleaning.

Method

The use of fairly large blocks is recommended, in order to encourage broad, vigorous work. The block is first painted with a thin coat of Indian ink. This black surface is invaluable when the block is actually being cut, as every cut made on the lino will be seen as a light mark on a dark ground, much as it will appear in the final print.

Subjects with a few main forms are most suitable and complicated scenes should be avoided. Close-ups usually have big shapes that lend themselves to this technique.

The aim is for the children to start cutting as soon as possible, so that their interest is sustained and they have not to wait too long before printing. Some will start cutting directly; others may need to make a sketch and transfer it to the block. If the sketch is drawn on paper of the same size as the block this is easily done. The back of the drawing is lightly covered with white chalk, which is then well rubbed into the paper. The drawing is then placed on to the block, the chalked side downwards against the inked surface. It can be kept in position with drawing-pins or Sellotape. The main parts of the drawing are then traced through with a sharp, fairly hard pencil. When the paper is removed, the essentials of the drawing appear as a white outline on the black ink surface.

If the children have not already used lino they may need to spend a little time practising on scraps of lino, so that they learn how to hold and use the tools and what kind of cuts each tool makes. Children soon find their own ways of working. Many start by outlining the main shapes, which makes a good basis for the further development of a block.

The next stage is to indicate where the lightest parts are to be by lightly chalking them in, in white, on the black surface. In this way children can see at once what the final effect will be. The chalk can easily be flicked off with a rag and one or two different possibilities tried out.

Cutting is done directly on the lino, using the V tools and the gouge tools, and the picture is developed through the textures produced by the tool strokes. The block is held in position for cutting with one hand and, for curved strokes, is turned round as the cut is being made. The child should direct the tool away from himself as he works, as this both allows greater freedom of movement and prevents accidents. Blocks that are kept warm by being placed on a radiator from time to time will be softer for cutting; if they become too hard, the tools easily slip and the rhythm is lost.

However careful the children may be, small pieces of lino inevitably accumulate on the classroom floor, which should therefore be swept carefully at the end of a period.

Printing

A table should be prepared, on which printing equipment is methodically set out. As the children will need individual supervision, it is advisable for only a few at a time to be printing, while the rest of the class does other work needing less organization.

Printing has to be carefully planned if there is not to be considerable mess and muddle, and black or coloured printing ink is even more difficult to remove from the classroom than clay. The teacher's desk makes a useful printing table, providing a convenient working area for about four children. More than this tend to get in each other's way, with the result that the standard of printing is lowered, work is spoilt and the general atmosphere becomes one of frustration.

PRINTING METHOD

1   Prepare a space—insulating board serves well—where finished

prints can be pinned up; printing ink is sticky and takes about twelve hours to dry.

2   Cut the printing paper into pieces rather larger than the lino blocks. This paper should be kept near but not on the printing table.

3   Cover the printing table with several layers of newspaper.

4   Place the lino block ready on the table on top of some extra pieces of newspaper.

5   Squeeze a small amount of printing ink on to a corner of the tile—avoid putting out too much at a time. Take some ink on to the centre of the roller and roll it out thinly on the tile. This is done by pushing the roller along, lifting it up and letting it spin round on itself, before it is again pushed across the tile. In this way the ink is evenly distributed over the roller—too much ink clogs the finer cuts of a block, too little produces a patchy print.

6   Next roll the ink on to the cut surface of the lino block, taking it from the tile on to the block, until its surface is covered with a thin, even layer of ink.

7   When the block has been inked, throw away the stained top sheet of newspaper, so that the edges of the print remain clean.

8   Holding the printing paper with both hands in the form of a U, lower it slowly over the block. Let the printing paper rest on the centre of the block first, then lower the edges of the printing paper carefully, so that the whole paper lies flat on the block.

9   With the palms of the hands gently smooth the paper from the centre outwards to prevent creases, pressing it evenly on to the block.

10   Using the back of the dessertspoon as a burnisher, gently rub over the back of the printing paper. Very thin tissue paper or Japanese printing paper will need to be protected by an extra layer before rubbing.

11   Check that the whole surface has been well rubbed, by gently lifting a corner of the paper to see if the print is clear enough.

12   When the print is ready, take it gently off the block by lifting the corners of one edge of the paper and by pulling the paper away from the surface of the lino.

13   Pin the print up to dry.

14   The block will need to be re-inked for each print taken.
15   When printing is finished clean the block gently with a soft rag, if necessary moistened with a little turpentine.
16   The roller and tile should be cleaned with turpentine immediately after use, as once the ink is dry it cannot easily be removed.

Cutting on a black surface will give a clear idea of how the print will look—in reverse—and children should be encouraged to cut a fair amount before taking a print. When they have made a first print, however, they may decide that some parts need to be lightened or taken out entirely, and further cutting can easily be done when the block has been cleaned. All cutting should be done well away from the printing table, or the small pieces of lino will get into the ink and spoil the prints.

GENERAL POINTS. Once the method of taking a straightforward print is understood, all sorts of variations and developments of the printing process can be tried out. Many printing methods and allied techniques are described in *150 Techniques in Art*,[1] by Hans Meyers. Here are a few suggestions:

1   Interesting and varied effects can be produced by rolling the ink on to the block unevenly, or in gradations of tone.
2   Before a print is taken blocks of colour can be applied to the printing paper, by means of pastels, coloured waterproof inks, or by pasting coloured paper on to the paper to be printed.
3   Various combinations of coloured printing inks and coloured papers should be tried. Pale inks on dark paper provide an interesting reversal of tone.
4   The prints themselves, when they are dry, may be developed by pastel drawing, or by superimposed blocks of texture.

Children working on lino-cuts will enjoy seeing examples of medieval wood-cuts, and will like to learn something of the early forms of wood engraving. Thomas Bewick's engravings of animals and birds provide special delight.

More recent work may include engravings by Eric Ravilious, Clare Leighton and Gwen Raverat—to mention only a few—and the enjoyment of these will naturally lead to an interest in different types of book illustration, perhaps with an emphasis on children's books. Material for small, attractive classroom exhibitions can be

[1] *150 Techniques in Art*, by Hans Meyer (B. J. Batsford).

collected and arranged by the children and the teacher. These could include examples of all sorts of prints and engravings, scraper board, pen and ink drawings and water colours. Examples of engravings and prints, that are reasonably well reproduced, can be carefully selected from Christmas cards.

If possible one or two actual wood engravings or prints should be obtained, and children who have some first-hand knowledge of lino cutting will also like to see a wood engraver's equipment—particularly the finely, cross-grained boxwood blocks and the different graver tools.

WAX ENGRAVINGS

Drawing—or engraving—on a waxed surface is especially suitable for detailed work on fairly small pieces of card, although it can also be used successfully for drawing on a larger scale (see Nos. 81 and 115).

Materials

1   A variety of white and other light coloured wax crayons and a plentiful supply of black wax crayons. There are many different makes and qualities of crayon on the market, and it is as well to check that the kinds selected can be used together satisfactorily.
    Softer crayons produce the best surfaces for engraving, and it should be possible to scratch lines and marks into the crayon surface easily, so that clear incisions are made.
2   Shiny white card. Paper is not tough enough to stand up to the vigorous rubbing and scratching processes that are involved.
3   Any scratching or scraping tools, such as large nails, wire of different thicknesses, knitting needles and fragments of slate.

Method

1   Protect the desks (or table tops) and the floor with newspaper, so that wax fragments are not trodden in (greasy wax marks can be removed from most surfaces with turpentine).
2   Rub a thick layer of white, or light coloured, crayon over the entire surface of the card. This layer may include several colours but they should not overlap.

3   Cover completely the first layer of crayon with a thick layer of black wax crayon.

4   Engrave the picture or pattern into this top surface of dark wax, revealing the colours that are underneath. A variety of lines and marks can be made by using the tools in different ways and much of the interest of the technique lies in these varying textures, and in the lighter colours that are allowed to show through the darker tones of the top surface.

Subjects

Imaginary creatures, animals, birds, fish, close-up flowers, portraits, self-portraits and simple still-life groups are some of the subjects suited to this medium. The subject should consist of a few large shapes in which there is considerable scope for the use of detail.

Those who have become interested in looking closely at natural forms will be able to make precise and detailed drawings in the wax; for example, feathers, fir-cones and shells can be studied, their actual sizes fitting comfortably on to quite small pieces of card.

Sometimes a slight pencil indication of where the main form and areas of underlying colours are to come—later to be 'rediscovered'—may be helpful, though this can lead to difficulties and be too confining, especially if the pencil plan is allowed to become over-detailed.

The technique is easily understood and may be enjoyed by quite young children. For older children it relates well to lino cutting and also to an interest in scraperboard.

Scraperboard—which may be black or white in colour—can be bought in various sizes, together with special cutting tools for engraving. The board, which is especially prepared for engraving, has a top surface which is smooth and velvety, making it possible for a wide range of textures—including the very finest—to be made, revealing the opposite tone of the layer beneath. The materials are fairly expensive so that scraperboard is most suitable for a small group of children at a time. Wax engraving provides a cheaper alternative, and on the whole children will gain more from the work by preparing their own surfaces and using improvised tools.

CANDLE RUBBINGS

Materials

A selection of strong papers: cartridge paper, wrapping paper, sugar paper, a firm 'detail' paper. ('Detail' is an architect's paper obtainable as 'office equipment'.)

Ordinary candles which may be cut in half. Each child needs at least one piece. Quite small pieces of candle can be used, but they should previously have been cut into a variety of shapes: flatended, chisel-shaped, and with both fine and coarse points.

A sharp, thin knife for cutting the candle through and for shaping the ends.

Ebony stain. Paint may also be used with some success, but by far the most satisfactory results are produced with stain.

Old hog-hair brushes—they cannot afterwards be used for general painting.

Newspaper: for the general protection of floor and desks; for placing underneath the wet rubbings as they are completed; for waste candle-shavings, and as an occasional surface for an actual rubbing—though on the whole newspaper is too soft for this purpose.

Waterproof coloured inks, if colour is to be introduced.

I. *Drawn or Scribbled all-over Textures*

Small pieces of paper, about 7 × 5 in., are recommended for the first drawings.

1   A rhythmical texture is drawn with a candle, firmly, closely and evenly over the whole piece of paper. Variously shaped candles produce different marks: broad strokes, square strokes, spots of different sizes, lines of various thicknesses. A firm pressure is needed and the candle should be used quite thickly. Several sheets of different textures may be drawn, each with a different piece of candle.

2   It is at first difficult to see the work but if the paper is held horizontally at eye-level, the candle marks can be seen and one can check that the drawing is spread reasonably evenly over the paper.

3   The completed drawing is placed on a large piece of newspaper.

4   Pour a little stain into a broad-based jar, which should be placed on a circular, enamel mixing palette for extra safety. One jar can be shared by two or four children.

The stain is then lightly brushed across the drawing, so that each stroke is joined to the previous one, leaving no gaps. The actual direction of the brush strokes can emphasize the main movement of texture or pattern. Only the smallest amount of stain should be used—too much easily results in a heavy, unattractive effect.

With careful organization it should be possible to take this work with quite large classes. If, however, working conditions are particularly cramped it may be easier to have the stain on the teacher's table only, the children coming out in turn—perhaps two at a time—to paint their drawings.

5   The painted candle drawing is left flat on the newspaper to dry.

II. *Wood Rubbings*

1   Select an area of wooden floor, table or desk top, in which the grain can be clearly seen and even felt by the hand—a knot adds to the interest. Rough, scrubbed wood produces a more interesting texture than polished wood.

2   Hold the paper firmly over the area of wood and rub the whole surface of the paper with the candle, taking care not to move the paper until the rubbing is completed.

3   By selecting different pieces of wood, a collection of tones, ranging from nearly white to nearly black, according to the grain, may be made.

III. *Tree Rubbings*

1   The technique is similar to that used in I and II.

2   The bark surface of a tree trunk is carefully chosen, bearing in mind the character and scale of the pattern in relation to the size of the paper. Rather bigger paper, 14 × 10 in., is an appropriate size for this work.

3   In order to achieve clear, firm rubbings it may be helpful for the children to work in pairs, so that one can hold the paper in position while the other rubs with the candle.

4   Children will become interested in finding a variety of bark textures, from those with fine markings to those with broader patterns.

5   The direction of the brush strokes should again be related to the main movement of the texture.

IV. *Rubbings from Other Surfaces*

Children may be encouraged to make rubbings from other surfaces, such as frosted glass, bricks, concrete, baskets, matting and so on. A collection of such rubbings, covering a wide range of texture and tone, provides excellent material for use in pictorial collage compositions. No. 116 shows this effectively.

V. *Ebony Stain and Colour Rubbings*

As a further development colour may be combined with an ebony-stained candle rubbing. This process is fully described on page 127.

BRASS RUBBINGS

Children who have enjoyed making candle rubbings will find great satisfaction in learning how to make brass rubbings, and will be fascinated to discover how close in technique and in some of their more general characteristics these two processes are.

It is sometimes possible to take a small group of older children on a brass-rubbing expedition, perhaps during a weekend; their rubbing can be displayed in the classroom so that they can describe some of its special points of interest to the rest of the class. They can also explain how a brass rubbing is made and show the class the materials they used.

Materials

1   White lining or ceiling paper, 22 in. wide, obtainable in rolls of 12 yards from a decorator's shop; or 'detail' paper, 22 in. wide, from art stores or office equipment departments.
2   Heelball—a mixture of beeswax, tallow and lamp black used by cobblers and leather cutters—is usually obtainable at their shops. This black or dark brown substance is sold in small cakes of varying consistencies, hard, medium and soft. It is generally useful to have some of each variety.
3   A soft duster or small soft brush.

To Make a Brass Rubbing

1   Permission should first be obtained from the vicar or verger of the church. This may sometimes be done at the time but it is usually safer to get permission beforehand. A convenient time

to make a rubbing may need to be booked and in many instances a small payment has first to be made.

2 Carefully dust or gently brush the surface of the brass plate, so as to remove any small bits of grit or dust.

3 If the brass is in a horizontal position, lay one end of the paper on one end of the brass and fix this end of the paper with weights. Some churches provide small weights especially for this purpose, but books or hassocks can be used.

4 Unroll a little of the paper, gently pressing it down by hand so as to feel the edges of the brass, and smooth the paper into the incised lines. Put further weights to hold this part of the paper steady.

5 Rub the heelball evenly over the surface of the paper. Gradually unroll the rest of the paper, readjust the weights, and continue to rub over the whole length of the figure until its impression on the paper is complete. The incised lines will appear white on the dark surface. (Effective rubbings of lino blocks can be made in a similar way, by rubbing a rather soft pencil over a thin paper placed on the block.)

6 The hardest heelball makes it possible to get really clear impressions of intricately engraved brasses, whereas a softer heelball is more suitable for covering large areas of unbroken surfaces.

7 The rubbing is now finished. One method of displaying a brass rubbing is to fix the top end over a dowel rod, so that it can be suspended from this. The name and date of the brass should be noted.

GENERAL POINTS. It is sometimes easier to place the paper over the whole brass in the first instance, though care must then be taken to fix the paper so firmly that it cannot shift as the rubbing is being made.

A brass effigy on a wall is less easy to rub clearly; several people will have to hold the paper firmly in position, while one or two people make the rubbing (very much in the manner that a tree rubbing is taken).

It is sometimes interesting to make a rubbing of a church brass with a small piece of candle. In this case the completed rubbing is brought back to school, where its whole surface is brushed over with ebony stain. This method produces a reverse effect from a heelball rubbing, the engraving appearing as a design of black lines on a white ground, so that the children will see both a positive and a negative rubbing of the same brass.

Several books on brasses are mentioned on page 280. *Monumental Brasses*, by the Rev. Herbert W. Macklin, is a particularly helpful one. In it the author gives some account of the history of brasses, as well as practical instructions for making rubbings; he also provides lists of the most interesting brasses to be found in each county.

BAMBOO PENS

Excellent pens can be made very simply from bamboo canes. These pens are pleasant and smooth to use, and can be given to the youngest children in the Junior school.

1   Choose fairly thin bamboo canes—obtainable from a nursery or general gardening store—or from one's own tool shed.

2   Several pens can be made from each cane, by cutting it into short lengths, using the natural joints as divisions.

3   With a sharp knife cut one end of the cane into a bevelled slant to form the pen.

4   Remove the pith from inside the end of the cane and from the back of the pen, which should be hollowed out and left quite smooth.

5   Trim the sides of the nib and make a clean cut across the end of the nib. To obtain a clean cut use a sharp knife, cutting on to the surface of an old penny or slab of glass.

6   Carefully make a slit, about half an inch in length, down the centre of the nib. It should then be ready for use. A pen that has been well cut moves smoothly, has no scratchy edges and rarely blots. Fine or thick lines (depending on the width of the pen) can be made, together with a great variety of textures.

CHAPTER 10

Puppets and Three-dimensional Work

PUPPETS

Puppetry as a means of creative expression has been discussed in relation to co-operative work (Chapter 6); this section deals more particularly with the practical side.

Subjects

Puppets may either be made with a certain play in mind, or a play may be built around the finished puppets. The way the activity is carried through will depend largely on the age and interests of the children; but puppetry at all levels should be a creative experience that, as much as any other art form, offers children a satisfying outlet for their own imaginative interpretation.

Older children particularly may like to think in terms of a complete planned production, and may wish to work in groups from the beginning. For instance, they may prepare the narrative or dialogue for the play, make puppets, make scenery, plan music, organize lighting, and improvise simple stage-arrangements. Younger children, on the other hand, will probably want to use their puppets quite spontaneously, each inventing his own story and extemporizing as soon as the puppet is made.

Themes for plays can be based on fables, legends and fairy stories from different countries, on folk songs and ballads, on ideas suggested by music, on Biblical episodes or on the children's own creative writing. The sources are infinite. As a rule we have found that stories with simple plots produce the best results. Puppet plays lend themselves especially well to purely imaginative conceptions, in which images from the world of fantasy are freely used. For the shadow play particularly, weird make-believe creatures, strange dragons, witches, giants, magic animals, huge caterpillars and insects suggest ideas for a variety of shapes that cast exciting shadows.

Music

Choosing music and relating it to the plays is an important part of puppetry. Sound, movement, form and colour become virtually one, each contributing its particular quality to the whole effect. Music made by the children themselves is perhaps most in keeping with the spirit of their own productions. They can sing, and make music on piano, guitar, violin, recorder or percussion instruments, each adding to the atmosphere of the scene. In a school or class where there is a strong interest in music, the use of records or tape-recorded music is a further possibility.

GLOVE PUPPETS

All sorts of odds and ends—clothes pegs, paper bags, potatoes carved into puppet heads—can be used in the Infant school to make simple forms of puppets. These can, already at this stage, inspire the children to enjoy inventive play. These introductory forms naturally lead on to glove puppets, which provide excellent opportunities for creative work at every stage in the Primary school (No. 131).

Making a Glove Puppet

MATERIALS

Thin cardboard
Newspaper
Papier mâché
White tissue paper
Powder colour or tempera-block colours and the usual painting
    equipment
A strong glue
A cold-water paste
Scraps of materials for costumes—in a variety of tones, colours and
    textures. Calicos are particularly suitable, also soft jersey cloth.
Odds and ends like feathers, pipe-cleaners, buttons, beads, sequins.
Material for hair, such as coarse and fine wools, raffia, cords, string,
    partially unravelled hemp, twine.
Push-on paper clips
Bottles—the modelled heads may be placed over slender bottle-
    necks to dry.

METHOD. A cylinder of thin card—big enough to fit over the index finger—is made and joined together by push-on paper clips or fine string. A piece of crumpled newspaper is next wrapped firmly round the cylinder, some of which is left free at one end for the puppet's neck. A head shape, about the size of a child's fist, is roughly formed in the crumpled newspaper. Some cold-water paste may be brushed into the crushed paper and, to help it become quite firm, fine string can be also wound a few times round the rough head shape.

The papier mâché is then modelled on this firm foundation of paper. Whatever character is to be made, the child should aim at bold, strong effects and should avoid unnecessary detail. The different planes of the head and the features are emphasized and even exaggerated. The nose is formed and hollows are made for the eyes, then the cheekbones, jawbones, ears, mouth, lips and eyebrows are modelled. The modelling is best done with the hands alone, although sometimes small, flat pieces of wood may be used as tools. Small pieces of tissue paper can be worked smoothly into the sticky surface of the papier mâché as a final layer, when the main modelling is complete. This provides a good surface for painting. A small ridge of papier mâché, to which the dress will later be fastened, is left at the base of the neck.

The heads may be placed on the necks of bottles to dry or, if the cylinders are not wide enough, on to pieces of dowel rod or pencils supported vertically in plasticine. Heat will help the papier mâché to dry out more quickly.

PAINTING. The puppet heads are painted either with powder or with tempera-block colours in clearly defined areas that show up the form of the head. Features should be emphasized through the painting and sometimes beads or buttons may be used for the eyes—in fact all sorts of scrap material may be utilized effectively. The puppet should frequently be held in a strong light, to see how this affects the shapes and colours.

HAIR. Hair is glued directly on to the head and may be applied thickly or in straggling wisps. The type of hair selected and the way in which it is stuck on will help to express the character of the puppet.

COSTUME. Clothes are based on an almost square magyar pattern and must be cut large enough for the puppeteer's hand to fit inside the dress and for his thumb and third finger to move in the two sleeves. Different kinds of materials can be used; jersey cloth drapes well and falls smoothly over the hand; calicos are suitable for direct painting, for potato-prints or for stencilled patterns. The basic costume can be elaborated by adding cloaks, sashes, hats, feathers, beads and sequins.

Children should try to bring out the distinctive qualities of a particular character through the dress, and they should be encouraged to be adventurous in choosing the colours and textures of the costumes. But however grotesque or strange a puppet may be, the general effects of head, hair and costume must be well integrated in terms of shape, colour and tone.

Puppets have little to do with realistic representation; rather they open doors into worlds of fantasy. Original interpretations should be welcomed and the teacher will try to discourage subjects and characters that are likely to be expressed in terms of clichés or preconceived ideas.

When the sewing is reasonably secure, the dress is fixed over the ridge on the neck cylinder with glue, or it can be firmly tied with fine string. Very young children may find rubber bands easier to use for this purpose. As soon as the dress is complete, the puppet should be tried in action.

This simple and straightforward method of making a glove puppet can provide a starting point with quite small children. Many other suitable approaches—some of which take the work further— are described in the books on puppetry recommended in the bibliography, page 279.

SHADOW PUPPETS

Many of us will have early memories of using our hands to make shadows on a wall—we may recall the different animal-heads, whose ears could be made to move or whose mouths to open and shut—a few movements of our fingers and our rabbit had become a crocodile. Perhaps these shadow images held for us something of the magic of shadow puppets.

These, as we see in Nos. 127 to 130, can be either of the simplest or of the most complex shapes. Shadow puppets originated in China, spreading to Java towards the end of the fourteenth century. They were closely associated with the religious traditions and ritual of the community, and remain significant to Indonesian thought and customs today.

Older children, who have become enthusiastic about puppetry through their own work, will like to find out something about the background and history of the different types of puppets and plays. Travel books and geographical magazines, as well as books on puppetry (page 279), provide sources of information.

The simplest forms of shadow puppet are made of cardboard and are held flat against a rigid screen consisting of a piece of thin material, such as lawn, tightly stretched over a frame. A light is fixed fairly high up behind the screen, so as to be a little distance behind the puppets when they are moved about against it. By doing this their shadows are clearly cast on its surface.

The onlookers watch the puppets from the other side of the screen. If the puppets are pressed firmly and flatly against the screen's surface, sharp silhouettes are produced, whereas if the puppets are moved slowly backwards the outlines of their images become blurred. These different effects can be successfully used as a means of making mysterious arrivals and departures.

The shadows cast on the screen will appear flat and in profile, so that the character of each puppet must be expressed by means of clear, effective contours and by basically simple shapes; rather formal side-views should be encouraged while realistic, foreshortened positions of the body are best avoided.

Essential characteristics should be over-emphasized and each feature should be shown in its most telling position; thus, in No. 127, the Javanese puppets, we see how, in one of the figures, the elongated front-view eye is strikingly large in proportion to the head (which is shown in a side-view position). Such exaggerations—and even distortions—are necessary to bring out the distinctive character of a puppet. Chins, noses, eyebrows, finger-nails and hair should be treated with strong emphasis.

Making a Shadow Puppet

MATERIALS

1   Thin card—black card will produce the best shadows. If light card is used it can be painted black on both sides. The thin cardboard obtained from cereal packets provides a suitable material, especially for younger children.

2 Dowel rod—about ¼ in. in diameter. This is needed to provide both a rigid support and a handle by which the puppet is held and worked.

3 Wire—of a 16 gauge—to be attached to a limb or particular part of the body so that it can be moved.

4 A pair of wire cutters.

5 A pair of scissors for cutting the card—or cutting knives and boards if the card is too stiff for scissors.

6 Push-through paper clips for fixing the joints together.

7 Insulating tape for holding the dowel rod firmly in position against the cardboard.

8 Coloured tissue papers, or scraps of colour filters (gelatines) used for stage productions.

9 Oddments of lace, paper doilies, raffia, coarse string and feathers can be used to add interest to the shadow.

METHOD

1 Twelve inches is usually a suitable height for a puppet, though its size must naturally be considered in relation to the size of the screen.

2 A simple silhouette form of the puppet is roughly sketched. The character of a puppet will be expressed mainly through the impression given by the contour: straight, spiky shapes may look well contrasted with curves, and larger shapes with smaller ones.

3 Additional pieces of card are needed where two shapes overlap at a joint. Therefore the different limbs and parts of the body have to be drawn separately—on tracing paper—in order to include these overlapping portions in the shapes.

4 The separate parts of the puppet are then cut out of the card or other material.
Interesting colour effects can be produced by making shadow figures out of a semi-transparent material—such as lampshade parchment—which can be painted with coloured inks. If thick cartridge paper is used, the paper shapes may be coloured on both sides, then painted with linseed oil and, when this has fully penetrated, be given a coat of colourless varnish.
Shadow puppets offer particular scope for decorative effects, as the edges of the cardboard may be cut quite intricately and all

sorts of open inset patterns can also be cut out of the cardboard shapes themselves (Nos. 127–130). Oriental puppets, made of buffalo hide or thin donkey-skin, are usually perforated with ornate pierced designs, which are left as open patterns. Puppets made by children will obviously be very much simpler, indeed quite crude by comparison, but may also be decorated with inset patterns on headgear and costumes.

Rich colour effects can be produced by placing coloured cellophanes over the openings—using a clear adhesive or Sellotape. Scraps of 'cinemoid' colour filters, which allow the full brilliance of the light to shine through the colours, are excellent for this purpose. Beautiful qualities of colour may also be obtained by overlapping layers of coloured tissue paper. In these different ways, crowns, shields, sashes and swords may be richly jewelled; or the wings of birds and dragons and the scales of fish and insects may be enlivened with inset colours.

5   Overlapping joints are fastened together with push-through paper clips. One clip is inserted rather loosely in a place where movement is required; two clips will firmly secure the joints that are not intended to move. The children should experiment with the relative angles and positions of the individual parts before they are fixed together with the clips.

6   At this stage the partly completed puppets should frequently be held up against a screen, lit from behind, so that the shadow effects can be fully exploited as the work progresses.

7   On the whole it is advisable to limit the flexibility of a shadow puppet to one—or possibly two—really characteristic movements. For instance, a leg or arm may be made to move; a wing to sway to and fro; or an animal's mouth to open wide and close again. In No. 130, the head of the large bird was the only part that could be moved. Children who become really fascinated by their puppets will discover ingenious ways of introducing some quite subtle movements, such as the closing of an eye or the movement of eyebrows. But on the whole a few simple gestures are likely to be most effective. The looseness or tightness of the clips will to some extent control the flexibility of the joints and, by keeping the joints fairly slack, it is possible for slow, graceful rhythms, as well as jerky movements, to be practised.

8   Fixing the dowel rod in position:
    The dowel rod must be firmly secured at the back of the puppet
    to keep it rigid. Use several pieces of insulating tape, placed at
    frequent intervals, to fix the rod to the cardboard puppet. The
    dowel rod is usually fixed vertically, covering nearly the full
    length of the puppet, but for creatures designed to move side-
    ways, such as fish, swans and other birds, it is generally more
    convenient to fix the rod horizontally. In this case the child
    manipulates the puppet from the side rather than from the
    bottom of the screen.

9   Fixing the wires:
    Movement of an arm, for example, is achieved by attaching a
    piece of wire to the extreme tip of the hand, the other end of the
    wire being held and moved about by the manipulator. Alter-
    natively, the unattached end of wire can be looped around the
    lower free end of the rod, and the movement of the puppet's
    arm controlled by pushing the wire up and down the rod.
    Various ways of attaching the wire to the moving part may be
    devised. One satisfactory method is to bend the end of the wire
    sharply into a small hook and to fasten this into position by
    means of a thread. The wires and rod are functional parts of a
    puppet and should be accepted as features of the whole effect
    (Nos. 128 and 130).

Once the puppets are finished, each child will want to experiment
to find out how best to work his own. It is important, indeed essential, that every child who has made a puppet has the opportunity to
work it himself in any production that may be given. This personal
involvement, so vital to the real spirit of creative work, is often felt
by children taking part in a co-operative production of a shadow
play. The shy child especially may feel an unwonted security and
confidence when, unseen himself, he can speak and improvise
through his puppet. The assurance he gains in this way may be reflected not only in the rest of his creative work but in his whole attitude towards new experiences.

Scenery

Scenery that is to be used two-dimensionally and that is to relate
well to shadow figures should be kept to silhouette forms. Children

can cut out simple yet effective shapes to suggest different settings—perhaps a scene of turreted castles, modern city forms, foliage and flower structures, mountain peaks, submarine caverns or purely abstract forms. The scenery must not, however, be allowed to take up too much space on the screen, or it will interfere with the movement of the puppets; whole areas of the screen should, in fact, be left blank. A really large screen has obvious advantages, because there is room for the puppets to be made to move freely between the pieces of scenery.

To make the scenery all sorts of materials may be used, such as thin card, thin metal, gauze, nets of different meshes and coloured tissue papers. Scenery is usually pinned to the screen, though it can be suspended from a wooden lath fixed into position above it.

Properties, too, should have shapes and textures that are particularly expressive when seen as shadows. Children should be encouraged to experiment with the use of natural forms, such as twigs, ferns, grasses, leaves and feathers, and to find other types of objects that cast effective shadows on the screen. Experimenting with these different aspects can open up new visual worlds for the children, and we should remember that, however attractive the end-product may be, it is chiefly through the interest and excitement felt at every stage of the work that the children derive the greatest benefit.

The Screen

Several kinds of screens are suitable for shadow plays. A piece of lawn, organdie or any other semi-transparent material can be stretched tautly over a large, old picture frame and fixed with drawing-pins. The frame is then supported vertically on a table, held in place by various weights such as heavy blocks or boxes, so that it stands firmly. There must be enough room behind the table for the children to work the puppets, and the level of the table top should be high enough for the children to be able to work comfortably from below the bottom of the screen. The space on either side of the screen must be blocked out with rugs or other material, so that the light is focused on the screen alone.

Where a school or class already possesses a theatre for glove puppets, a shadow-puppet screen may be hung over the proscenium opening.

A three-sided clothes-horse can also provide a useful basis for an improvised theatre. The clothes-horse is opened out and securely propped up on the top of a fairly large table. The screen is hung over the central division and the two wings are covered with material that is thick enough to exclude the light.

We have also successfully used a thin, old sheet pinned firmly over a door opening, behind which a standard lamp provided the source of light.

Best of all, part of a school stage may be used, as this leaves enough room for several people to work the puppets behind a spacious screen. Quite a large, wooden framework can be very simply constructed and covered with white material. An appropriate portion at the base is blocked out with dark material leaving the white screen above.

The ordinary stage curtains are drawn level with either side of the screen, and can of course be pulled right across between the scenes.

A PUPPET THEATRE MADE OUT OF INSULATING BOARD

Children of ten or eleven years should be able to make a simple puppet theatre out of stout board, and several methods of construction are given in the books recommended on page 279. It may be useful here to describe one simple construction that has proved satisfactory for both glove and shadow puppets. A group of students who were making puppets worked out the plans and, after a good deal of experiment, decided on the measurements.

The theatre stands 6½ ft. high and is made out of three pieces of soft insulating board. The two side pieces are each 2 ft. wide and these are hinged to the central panel, which is 4 ft. wide. The hinged wing pieces fold inwards and the whole theatre can be stored flat against a wall.

Only a small amount of board, 6 in. deep, has been left above the proscenium opening, which measures 2 ft. 8 in. across by 1 ft. 10 in. down.

If these measurements are used children can stand inside the theatre and work their puppets easily, without themselves being seen. When the side-wings are opened out there is a reasonable amount of working area behind the front of the theatre. A slotted lath of wood is fixed from the top of one side to the top of the other side, to keep the wings firmly in position when they are open (see Fig. 4, page 209).

In their design the students concentrated on the essentials of a basic structure, leaving the details of fixtures for lighting, scenery and curtains to be thought out for each production. Scenery can be hung from laths placed across the top of the theatre, and for shadow puppets the lights are fixed on to a strut of wood also held in position across the top.

The theatre therefore offers scope for working out the various problems connected with a simple production. It may also stimulate an interest in pattern making, as it is easy to try out various kinds of decoration for the outside, by pinning cut paper and other materials directly on to the insulating board. All sorts of simple patterns or formalized pictorial schemes, perhaps cut out of coloured paper and combined with rug wool or cords, may be pinned on to the soft insulating board and changed from time to time.

This theatre has been described in some detail because, although the students had had no previous experience in puppetry, their theatre proved to be most suitable for simple productions. It was cheap—the material cost less than £2—and could hardly have been easier to construct. Other types of theatre construction may well be equally, indeed more, satisfactory and the best solutions will be found by individual teachers and children working experimentally with their own particular needs and facilities in mind.

Useful though it may be to have a simple theatre in the classroom, it is by no means essential; and some of the most lively, worthwhile work may be done with a rough-and-ready stage improvised for an occasion. The important thing is for children to be able to try out their puppets as they make and dress them, so that from the start they get a real sense of the theatre.

THREE-DIMENSIONAL WORK

Three-dimensional work involves handling materials and actual things, and this in itself stimulates creative expression. Few children in the Primary school are likely to set to work with fully formed visual images in their minds, but these take shape through a sensuous response to the nature of the materials. The very young child may be concerned solely with the possibilities of exploratory play suggested by each material, or by using a number of media together. An experimental approach is important at every stage, although for older children it should lead on to work that is more consciously and deliberately evolved. The nature of the medium provides inspiration, and aesthetic and technical solutions are discovered through working freely and adventurously with it.

Modelling and carving encourage sensitivity toward the qualities

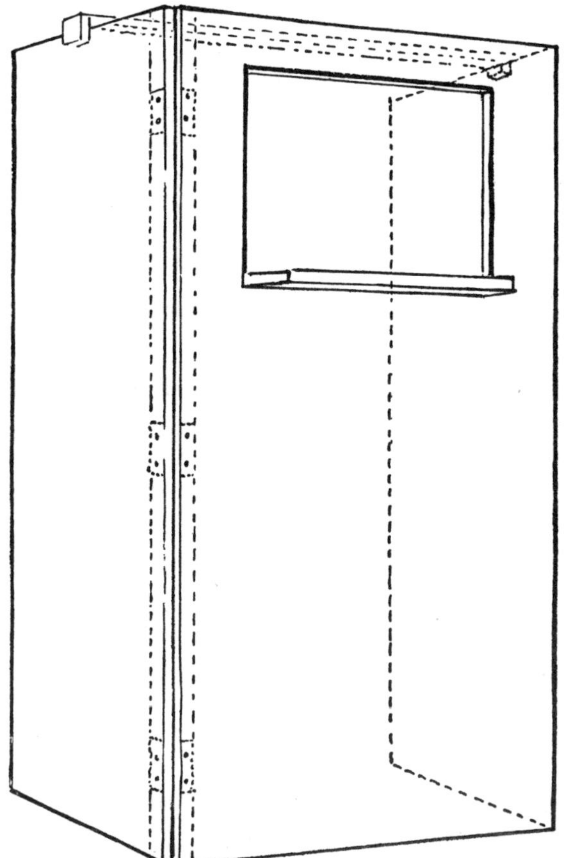

FIG. 4. Diagram of the theatre for glove puppets. When open the structure is held in a rigid position by means of the wooden lath, slotted over the top of the wings. The small wooden ledge for properties is fixed on to the lower edge of the proscenium opening (page 207).

inherent in materials; powers of imagination, invention and constructive thought are developed too, through making things experimentally with card, wood, metal and other kinds of materials.

In drawing and painting each part has to fit in to the proportions and limits of the two-dimensional paper. Younger children—who are natural pattern makers—usually produce work in which the flat, two-dimensional qualities relate closely to the flat surface of the paper; but when older children want to introduce depth into their work they have to find ways of creating an illusion of depth on the two-dimensional paper. It is, therefore, particularly satisfying for them to experience a sense of volume and space through modelling, carving and making constructions in actual depth.

Only after experience with a number of materials can children discover that each has its particular disciplines. Simple pottery techniques, for instance, will help the child towards an understanding of some of the distinctive possibilities of clay and to respect the limitations it imposes. It will be realized that models and free-standing constructions must be made strong enough to stand firmly. When modelling in clay and other plastic materials this may mean that the legs or feet of a figure have to be considerably emphasized in order to provide a foundation solid enough for the whole model (Nos. 45 and 134). Straggling, spindly shapes in clay break easily and should give place to more solid forms. Sometimes the necessary support is provided by a solid base incorporated into the whole composition; this has been done in both the models illustrated in No. 44.

A simple carving depends for its beauty and interest on the balance and movement of its forms, and on the effect of light and shadow on its broadly treated areas (No. 136). Intricate, realistic detail would be out of keeping with the compact strength of the material. In carving and modelling we expect to find distortions of realistic appearances, which are simplified or exaggerated to meet the demands of the materials and to communicate a personal conception.

Nos. 119–122, constructions in soft wire and in balsa wood, show how an interest in spatial relationships may be stimulated by three-dimensional work. The boy who made No. 121 and the girl who constructed No. 122 both enjoyed exploring space, cutting into it in different directions, enclosing it by planes or grids. During the process of construction each child frequently turned the structure round, to see if it looked right from all sides. While No. 122 is a linear design in three dimensions, No. 120, also made out of balsa wood, is essentially two-dimensional in conception. As a rule we try to encourage children who are working in these materials to think in terms of depth, but the purely front-view design of No. 120 is so well resolved that we can enjoy it as a very satisfying, flat structure, in which each part is related two-dimensionally to the whole. Actually the boy who made this model was working on his own during a period of convalescence. He was given some scraps of balsa wood and cement, and in one afternoon produced this tower-like erection —reminiscent in its delicacy of a Paul Klee drawing. The children who made Nos. 121 and 122, on the other hand, were members of large classes. The teacher had indicated how the models could grow upwards and outwards into the space all round, but each child was then left free to evolve his work in a personal way.

CLAY

Teachers who have specialized in sculpture or pottery will have their own ways of introducing three-dimensional work in clay. But even the quite inexperienced teacher can learn with the children, whose enthusiasm and immediate response to this medium should give him the confidence to use it with small groups from time to time.

It is essential, naturally, to know about the storage and care of clay, and how it should be prepared for classroom use. Provided the organization is well planned, clay should be as successful and convenient a material to use in school as any other medium introduced in art teaching.

There are a number of good books, written by experts, describing, much more fully than I can, the possibilities of clay work and related crafts in schools. The aim here has been to give the non-specialist teacher who has become convinced of the need for clay work just enough practical information to make a beginning. *Creative Crafts in Education*,[1] by Seonaid M. Robertson, can be recommended as an imaginative and thoughtful survey, which traces the fundamental nature of crafts as vital forces in a child's education. Miss Robertson describes many aspects of three-dimensional work, discussing approaches to teaching and problems of organization. *Crafts for All*,[2] by Karl Hils, a book that deals with a wide range of crafts and media, has some excellent chapters on work in clay and related materials. Ernst Röttger, in *Creative Clay Craft*,[3] describes many possibilities

---

[1] *Creative Crafts in Education*, by Seonaid M. Robertson (Routledge & Kegan Paul).

[2] *Crafts for All*, by Karl Hils (Routledge & Kegan Paul).

[3] *Creative Clay Craft*, by Ernst Röttger (Batsford).

with clay and plaster, and includes a number of concise practical and technical notes.

Modelling with clay provides children with tactile experiences that are immensely important to them; plasticine and papier mâché, though useful, are less satisfactory media. Children have a highly developed sense of touch, and we have only to watch their absorbed satisfaction as they handle the clay or squeeze the papier mâché slowly through their fingers to realize how impelling this faculty can be.

Some forms, particularly abstract ones, may be modelled without looking at them at all, the internal and external forms being linked exclusively through the sense of touch.

To use this tactual sense as fully as possible, children should be encouraged to hold the clay in the hand as they work, rather than have it on a board. It will then seem natural to them to turn their models round as they shape them and really to feel the volume of the clay. But older children may prefer to use boards, which should be about six inches square. A few modelling tools may also be available, though actually touching, smoothing, patting and pinching the clay are in themselves such satisfying experiences that tools may detract too much from the directness of this contact. When children do want to scratch and indent patterns they can themselves cut flat or pointed tools out of small sticks.

To work in the round with clay each child will need a fair-sized lump (at least the size of a cricket ball), which he pulls outs, squeezes or pushes into different shapes until a form emerges. Smaller parts, such as animals' ears and tails, should be pulled out of the head and body forms so that they remain part of the main lump of clay. This will make a stronger and more unified form than one on to which fragments have been stuck.

Children should look at their work from all sides so that they see it in the round—sometimes a slight turn or twist of the clay can give a greater sense of movement or bring out a particular rhythm made by the related forms. This dynamic quality is seen in No. 45, 'Horse and Rider', modelled in plasticine by a six-year-old girl. For some children, however, depth may have little meaning; they look at their models consistently from one angle and produce two- rather than three-dimensional forms (No. 46). In clay modelling, then, as in drawing, we find different kinds of visual expression, corresponding to each child's way of seeing.

Frequently the child's need to model goes hand in hand with the urge to make pots; even the youngest children in the Nursery school will find their own ways of making plates and cups and saucers, if they have access to clay or plasticine.

Thumb Pots

One of the basic forms of pottery, the making of a thumb pot, is so closely related to modelling in clay that a brief description of the technique may be appropriate here.

A lump of clay, about the size of a tennis ball, is held in one hand —usually the left—and is rhythmically turned around with the right hand until the clay becomes a smooth, spherical ball. By inserting the right-hand thumb and by pressing it down into the clay, a hole is made in it. As the clay is rotated the hole is made larger and becomes a hollow. This is done by increasing the pressure of the thumb on the clay inside, whilst the fingers of the same hand push the clay against the thumb, from the outside. The wall of the pot is gradually drawn upwards from the base and can be firmly squeezed and stroked into various shapes. It may, for instance, be sloped slightly outwards to form a shallow dish, or it can be pulled upwards to make a taller pot or, by turning it in at the top, a compact form with curved shoulders is produced. The rim of the pot should be kept fairly thick, as otherwise it easily cracks.

Through seeing their own, and each other's efforts, the children will discover that the most satisfactory pots are generally fairly simple in form and that more elaborate shapes tend to be less successful. A critical appreciation and discussion of the work is only suitable for older children who are beginning to be consciously interested in aesthetic qualities and standards. The younger child will be happy in making a pot or modelling a figure in his own instinctive way. For him the sheer satisfaction of handling the clay is the important thing; that his pot may be lopsided in shape, or too thick or too thin to be practicable, is of little concern to him at this stage.

Thumb pots may be decorated with incised or impressed patterns, or with patterns painted in a slip of a different coloured clay (slip is a clay of a thick, creamy consistency). Or the pot can be painted all over with a slip of another colour and, while this is still moist, a pattern can be scratched on to the painted surface, revealing the colour of the clay underneath. The figures in No. 133 have been decorated in this way.

Coiled Pots

An interest in other ways of making pots grows quite naturally out of the children's first attempts at thumb pots. Perhaps one of the thumb pots seems to need the finish of a heavier and more emphatic rim, so a small coil of clay is made and joined to the top. Having seen the effect of this, another child may decide to increase the height of his pot by adding several coils to the neck, and before long some children in the group will be eager to make pots that are built up entirely of coils.

How to make coiled pots is described in the books already mentioned on page 211. Briefly, the pot is built up of a series of coils (thin cylinders of clay, about the thickness of a finger, rolled out by hand) which are joined together one above the other to form the pot.

The coils are rhythmically and firmly joined and smoothed together on the inside with the fingers or with a small, flat tool. Sometimes the marks made with the tool or thumb are left to make a simple pattern on the coils. This kind of decoration emphasizes the construction of the pot and is, in fact, part of it—a principle appertaining to the use of pattern generally.

Sometimes the coils are completely smoothed over, on the outside as well as on the inside, so that the pot has an uninterrupted surface. Children who in their clay modelling have possibly been concerned with two or three related figures will become interested in the single form of a pot in relation to the surrounding space.

This awareness of form and volume will probably lead to thinking about the functional demands which influence the shapes of pots that are in daily use. The finish or surface treatment can also be looked at from a practical point of view: Will the jug or pot be constantly washed? How will it be used? To what extent will it be handled? How will such considerations influence the choice of glaze on a cup, for example, or for a tea-pot? When is it appropriate to use the matt surface of earthenware clay?

Questions such as these, that arise naturally from the children's first-hand interest, will direct their thoughts to wider aspects of design. In an approach of this kind there is no attempt to train 'taste', nor to label things arbitrarily as 'good' or 'bad' in design; but there may arise opportunities for spontaneous discussions during which the children can be encouraged to look and think for themselves about these matters. Photographs of pots can be obtained and if possible children should see actual examples in a museum: some of the simplest and most direct forms of primitive hand-built pottery will be closer to their own interests than pottery that is more sophisticated.

Models built up of Smaller Pieces of Clay

Pulling the form out of one lump of clay is probably the most satisfactory method of modelling in the Primary school, though models can also be made of smaller pieces of clay built up together to make the main form. It is important to press the pieces together tightly so that they are firmly joined. If this is not done small air pockets may be left and these air bubbles expand when heated in the kiln and cause breakages.

Working in Relief

Attractive results can be produced by decorating flat surfaces of clay with imprinted textures. The clay is rolled out—with a rolling pin—into a slab of even thickness, between a quarter and half an inch in depth. It is then pressed or cut into a simple shape—for example, a bird, fish or animal; or a circular, oval or rectangular shape. The surface is next decorated in low relief with textures that are impressed in the clay while it is still fairly soft. Effective marks can be made with all sorts of things—natural and manufactured objects—sticks, shells, buttons, wire-meshes, combs, string and cord; a great variety of patterns can also be pressed down into the clay with the fingers.

Children discover how to select and combine various surface-textures, and through experiment learn how to relate the patterned and plain areas satisfactorily. They also see how important the proportion of each part is in relation to the whole. Textures produced by stamping or pressing objects into the clay surface can be used either to make patterns, for example, on slabs or pots, or to suggest particular qualities in modelling, such as the texture of the hens' feathers in No. 43.

If incised or impressed bands of decoration are used on a pot they should be placed so as to become an integrated part of the whole.

'Where shall the pattern be placed on a pot? Half-way up? Higher on the shoulder? Or will it look best as a block at the base? How wide should each band of pattern be in relation to the pot? If several patterns are to be incised, how much space should be left between them? Should all the patterns be the same width? If of varying widths, where should the broadest bands be placed? Would the imprinted pattern look better as an all-over design over the whole pot?'

Such questions will need to be considered for each individual pot, and children, in finding their answers, will become increasingly sensitive to principles of design.

These methods of making patterns will add to the interest of the pots without destroying the natural quality and texture of the clay. They are therefore preferable to those forms of decoration in which patterns are painted on to pots with poster colour, and 'finished off' with a coat of glossy varnish or lacquer. Such processes are quite alien to the genuine qualities of the material.

PRACTICAL PROBLEMS

Types of Clay

Different kinds of clay for modelling and pottery—grey and terra cotta—can be bought by the hundredweight ready for use.

Clay can also be bought in powder form, but this is less satisfactory for school use because of the excessive work involved in its preparation.

Prepared clay is sometimes obtainable from local sources, or from drainpipe works, as well as from most suppliers of educational art materials and potteries.

In some districts clay can be dug out of the ground and prepared from local deposits. If possible, the children themselves should take part in finding it and getting it ready for use. Some clay that is found locally is pure and clean enough to be used direct. If it is obviously mixed with impurities it should be dried out completely, then broken up and bashed or hammered to powder. Soak the powder in water and pass it through an ordinary domestic sieve, so that stones and impurities can be removed. Drain excess water off the top of the clay residue and let the surplus moisture evaporate until the clay reaches a workable consistency. It can then be squeezed and worked by hand until it is free from lumps and ready for use.

Any old, used clay that has become dry and hard has to be dealt with in a similar way to get it back to a plastic condition. The drying out process can be accelerated if the wet clay is spread out by the handful on a slab of plaster of Paris. The plaster draws the moisture from the clay so that it quickly becomes firm enough to use (recipe for plaster of Paris is given on page 221).

Storage

A zinc or galvanized dust bin, with a lid, provides a convenient receptacle for storing clay. It should be kept in a cool place, away from direct heat or radiators.

The clay rests on a board which is supported by a few bricks at the bottom of the bin. This allows excess water or moisture to drain down under the level of the clay. Clay that is too sloppy and wet is as unsatisfactory for use as clay that has become too dry and hard. If a damp cloth or piece of sacking, frequently remoistened, is kept over it the clay remains in good working condition. A layer of polythene may be tucked round the cloth. The aim is to keep the clay air-tight so that it retains its moisture. Clay quickly dries out and hardens if it is exposed to air or heat.

It is worth while to check the consistency of the clay from time to time: with reasonable care it can be kept in a satisfactory condition from one term to another.

Used Clay

A separate bin should be available for clay that is to be re-used. Discarded models and pieces of clay that are still fairly soft can be returned to this bin. Keep the clay well covered with a damp cloth and store it in the same way as fresh clay. Provided the cloth is kept well moistened, the clay will be ready for immediate use.

Dry, hard clay has already been mentioned. Collect and keep it in a separate bucket or bin until there is enough to be broken up and resoaked, as described on page 216.

Classroom Organization for Clay Modelling

One of the practical considerations in preparing for clay work must be to protect the classroom from mess, and to prevent the clay-dust being trodden in to other parts of the school. From this point of view alone clay modelling is ideally done out of doors, and may well be planned for the summer term. But with forethought it is also quite possible to organize it satisfactorily in the classroom. Certain precautions must naturally be taken. Children should wear aprons or overalls; desk or table tops should be covered with American cloth. Newspaper should be available so that at the end of the period powdered crumbs of clay are easily swept up and thrown away in the paper.

The floor by each desk must be similarly protected, each child being responsible for his own working area. A broom, dust-pan and brush, and a cloth and bowl of water should be available for final cleaning up. All the working materials should be to hand so that, once the children have settled, there need be relatively little movement about the room.

The clay should be well kneaded before the children use it, to get rid of air pockets and to ensure that it is all of a fairly even consistency. Balls, about the size of a clenched fist, are then pulled off the main piece of clay. These can be kept moist in a polythene bag until the children are ready to start modelling.

KILNS

Older boys and girls who want their models to last should be able to fire them in a simple kiln they have themselves made. For younger children the most important aspect is their personal involvement in the actual handling of the clay. Once this is over, they are less concerned with the results. But for older children the absorbing interest of following through the various stages of a primitive firing is so great that, even where gas or electric kilns are available, children should still have the opportunity of making and firing their own kiln. Where it has also been possible for the children to find and use local clay, the total range of these experiences will have particular significance for them. Many wider interests connected with other subjects such as geography and history may grow through these activities.

A Kiln for Sawdust Firing

Several kinds of primitive kilns can be made, but basically all follow the same principles in providing conditions suitable for a safe, slow firing at a low temperature. Information on the various types and their suitability for use in schools can be found in some of the books recommended. The kiln described here works well and is simple to make; children, under supervision, could help their teacher in its preparation and in the actual firing.

Use an old can or bin or an old metal oil drum, with holes punched in the sides and base to form an incinerator.

Partly fill the can, or 'kiln', with sawdust. Place the clay models or pots—which must have been thoroughly and slowly dried—in the sawdust, so that they do not touch each other. Several layers may be packed in the kiln, according to its size, but quite a thick covering of sawdust should be put over each lot of models. Sometimes it is useful to wedge a piece of wire netting between the layers to prevent the models from falling on each other as the sawdust burns down. Leave enough space above the top models so that they can be well covered by a thick layer of sawdust, which has then to be packed to the top of the can.

The sawdust is lit from the *top*—by means of a small fire of paper and sticks, or with a dash of turpentine. The heat should travel downwards very gradually, and the sawdust must be allowed to burn slowly for twelve hours or longer. The kiln should be refuelled with sawdust continuously, a few handfuls at a time. The sawdust in a kiln lit first thing in the morning should still be very near the top by the end of the school day. It may be left to burn slowly all night and even during part of the following day. The top of the kiln can be protected from rain by a dustbin lid, wedged open on one side by a brick so as to allow for draught.

Slow-burning kilns of this kind have no flames, but even the glowing embers from the sawdust can be dangerous to nearby wooden buildings. Therefore the kiln should be set up in an open space or if possible placed in an old, partially bricked-in area. A corner of a playground may provide some protection from strong winds and encourage a slow, even firing. It is sometimes advisable to build a brick floor, about eighteen inches square—this will serve as a base and will also prevent the ground from becoming blackened. Nearby walls may need some extra protection; it is also well to ensure that neighbours will not be worried by persistent smoke. These difficulties can sometimes be avoided if the packed container stands on two bricks inside a dustbin. The lid would of course need to be propped open to allow for the circulation of air.

Hollowing out Clay Models

A clay model that is to be fired usually needs to be hollowed out, so that its wall is roughly the same thickness throughout. Otherwise cracks may be caused by the uneven shrinkage of the thinner and thicker parts. The excess clay can be carefully scooped out with an improvised wire loop from underneath the model, leaving it partly hollow inside. This process is done when the clay is 'leather' hard, that is, not fully dry but already well set and quite firm.

Leather-hard clay can also be burnished, or polished, with the bone handle of a knife; this may be done several times before the model or pot is dry and will produce a pleasant surface quality especially suitable for pots.

Models and pots that have been fired in a primitive kiln will appear black, or may be mottled white or red, according to the colour of the clay that has been used. If a pot has been well burnished before firing, at the leather-hard stage, an attractive dull sheen can be produced by rubbing a candle over the sides of a pot while it is still warm from the firing. The pots and models must, of course, be lifted out of the kiln most carefully, as it will retain its heat for some time.

CARVING

Carving in various materials is a technique more suited to older children in the Primary school. Natural substances such as chalk, clunch or soft stone can be found locally in some districts. The natural forms of these materials are often in themselves visually stimulating; a piece of chalk may suggest an abstract or figurative subject that needs a minimum of cutting. Just to feel and stroke and look at the forms of the stones can afford immense pleasure and awaken perception.

Children can also collect pieces of wood, such as pine or willow, which are soft enough for whittling or carving. In some seaside districts the carving of driftwood offers further possibilities. Work of this kind is appropriate for groups of three or four children who have become especially interested in carving.

The simplest tools should be used and, as a rule, a sharp pocket-knife, a cutting board, one or two coarse files and some sandpaper are all that will be needed at this stage.

Large, simple forms, in keeping with the volume of the material, should be preserved in the carving. Children are encouraged to look at their work from different angles and to develop the various aspects simultaneously, so that they realize the forms as a whole. In general, carving should be treated broadly, though parts can be enriched with finer detail scratched or cut into the surface with a nail or knife—probably during the final stages of work.

The finished carving is arrived at by a process of cutting away the excess parts of the substance so as to reveal a form dormant in, or 'seen' within, the material. This is quite different from modelling, where the form is built up from the mass of clay. Children should therefore have some experience of both techniques, as each way of working can contribute to the child's powers of creative thought.

The same general principles hold good in carving, whatever material is used: stone, chalk, clunch, plaster, block salt or soap.

Careful planning of work and of materials is always necessary, as carving inevitably produces waste—or cut-away—substance, and this can lead to considerable mess, especially on the floor. The same precautions for the care of the room as those suggested for clay work are recommended. If it is at all possible the children should do carving outside during the summer term.

Carving in Plaster of Paris

This material provides a most useful medium for carving, especially in districts where natural substances are not available. Plaster is bought by the hundredweight from a builder's stores.

Various qualities can be obtained; dental plaster probably provides the most suitable texture for carving though it is also the most expensive kind.

The teacher prepares for this work by casting a variety of both rectangular and irregular shaped blocks of plaster of different sizes. This will take some time, but the children's enjoyment in using the plaster blocks will fully justify the trouble. As each child must have a separate block, plaster carving is more conveniently undertaken by a few children at a time.

STAGES OF WORK

1   Boxes and moulds:
Before mixing the plaster collect and put ready a number of fairly small cardboard boxes. Variously shaped moulds can also be made out of lengths of corrugated card: curve a strip of the card (about 4 in. deep) round on itself in an oval or irregular

shape, overlapping and joining the ends firmly. Stand the mould upright on a stout cardboard base, supporting its sides with lumps of plasticine pressed firmly against the outside of the card.

2   Mixing the plaster:
Mix the plaster of Paris in a basin or bucket—in the proportion of $1\frac{1}{2}$ or $1\frac{3}{4}$ pounds of plaster to 1 pint of cold water. Sprinkle the plaster—which is in powder form—into the water until it appears above the water's surface. The creamy mixture, which can be stirred lightly with a stick, will now begin to thicken and should be poured fairly quickly into the cardboard boxes or moulds, to a depth of two or three inches.

3   When the plaster has set hard the cardboard sides of the containers are peeled away, leaving the plaster ready for carving. The plaster can be poured into a large dress-box but in this case it should be cut into smaller blocks before it has had time to set too hard. It sets in a matter of five or ten minutes and carving can be begun while the plaster is still slightly soft.
Slabs of plaster—to be used for drying out clay—can also be cast in cardboard dress-boxes.

4   Put the plaster block on a piece of stout cardboard—which can be easily turned round—for carving. A strong pocket-knife is used for most of the work, and the children must learn to cut away from themselves so as to avoid accidents. A 'Junior' book-binding knife, which has a rigid blade embedded right through the wooden handle, is also suitable for carving.

Because of the nature of the material the carving will be strong and sturdy in character; and each part of the carving will be directly related to the form of the original block.

Cleaning and Clearing up

Spoons, sticks, bowls or buckets that have been used in making the casts should be washed and well rinsed immediately after use—before the plaster has set—and any small pieces of plaster collected in a sieve so as not to block the drains. Working surfaces must be well covered with strong brown paper so that chippings of plaster can easily be kept together and thrown away.

Other Carving Materials

Block salt and cakes of kitchen soap are also interesting substances for carving and, although the expense of these materials makes them impracticable for use with large numbers, they can sometimes be given to a small group.

PAPIER MÂCHÉ

Papier mâché is another modelling material that is almost as indispensable as clay in the Primary school. It is inexpensive and can be used for many purposes. It does, however, take some time and trouble to prepare and the children's success in using it will depend on the consistency of the papier mâché being just right.

No. 131, the puppet heads, were modelled in the round with papier mâché, and the two masks on the left in No. 135 were modelled with it in low relief. Papier mâché dries very hard and, as can be seen in the masks (No. 135), it takes paint well. But as a material it is rather coarse in texture and usually the final effect is—rightly—correspondingly rough and crude. The natural qualities of clay encourage a greater subtlety of form and delicacy of handling, as we see in the modelling in Nos. 43, 44 and Nos. 133 and 134. Papier mâché cannot, therefore, be regarded as a substitute for clay, but it certainly provides an admirable additional material in the Primary school. It is especially appropriate for puppets, models connected with projects, decorative masks and shields, and for heads built up three-dimensionally on wire for play productions.

One method of making papier mâché is to soak quantities of small pieces of newspaper, less than an inch square, in water for two or three days. A number of children tearing paper for a short period of time can quickly produce a good bulk of paper. To speed up the pulping process the paper can be boiled in a zinc container for about half an hour. After one or two days the paper becomes a soft pulp from which the excess water is then drained.

The pulped paper is next taken by the handful, squeezed as dry as possible, and placed in an empty bowl. A stiff paste (a mixture with a high proportion of Polycell to very little water) is added to the pulp and thoroughly kneaded in with it. It is repeatedly squeezed through the fingers until it becomes firm, smooth and pliable. Alternatively, a cold-water paste can be worked into the pulp in dry powder form. The aim in either case is to soften the paper, eliminate excess water, and, by adding a strong paste in some form, to produce a well-mixed substance suitable for modelling. Papier mâché dries slowly, though this process may be accelerated by placing the damp models near radiators.

Quicker results may be obtained by crumpling and rolling dry newspaper into shapes. These are then covered with strips of pasted newspaper and tied around with fine string so that they dry in the required shape.

PLASTICINE

Plasticine is another material which, though excellent within certain limits, can in no sense take the place of clay. Because plasticine has to be handled in small amounts the results are usually small in scale, and the breadth of treatment that comes so naturally when using clay is less easily achieved. Plasticine also tends to harden easily, becoming too stiff to be readily pliable. All the same, it has countless uses in the Primary school and some should always be to hand. Nos. 45 and 46 were modelled by two six-year-old girls, who selected plasticine out of several materials that were available in an activity period.

CARDBOARD CONSTRUCTIONS

Materials

Thin white cardboard
Small pieces of stout waste cardboard for cutting on
Scissors
Swan-Morton cutting knife or penknife
Pencil
Ruler
Set square
Sellotape.

A variety of three-dimensional card constructions—rather reminiscent of children's 'card-houses'—can be made and, in spite of certain limitations imposed by the material, can stimulate initiative in design.

A number of card units are cut out. These may all be of one width but of different lengths (often a very satisfactory result is produced in this way), or a number of rectangular pieces of card of varying sizes and proportions may be cut. Corners should be exact right-angles so that the whole construction fits together accurately. It is worth first preparing a good number of building units, so that there are plenty of pieces to experiment with and the construction, once started, can grow quickly.

Small slots are cut, either vertically or horizontally, into most of the pieces of card. An interlocking structure is then dovetailed together by means of inserting other pieces of card, either vertically or horizontally, into the slots. Experiment will show how long the slots should be in relation to the size of each piece of card; the aim is to achieve a firm, reasonably strong construction.

The character of the material produces a predominantly vertical and horizontal emphasis. Variety in the relative scale and proportion of the pieces can lead to countless ramifications of structure. On the whole bigger, rather than smaller, units are recommended. Children enjoy building towers or tall erections well over 12 in. in height, and constructions that spread into space laterally can be equal fun to make. The interrelation of each part to the whole structure must be considered from various view-points.

Hollow spaces and rectangular blocks are linked by means of the different positions of the pieces of cardboard. The proportion of solid to space also becomes important. The slot-and-insertion method of construction enables the child to try out several different possibilities as he works out his design. If necessary, small pieces of Sellotape can be added to some of the corners, to make the structures more rigid.

The models show up particularly well if they are placed against a strong colour—perhaps white card against ultramarine. Experiments with different kinds and source of lighting bring out particular aspects of the composition. Torches shining through openings provide changing effects of shadows, adding a greater sense of depth to a construction.

These card constructions are composed mainly of hollow spaces contained within flat planes in contrast to the more open balsa wood structures.

The interest of such experiments in spatial composition will encourage older children to look thoughtfully at contemporary architecture and to think about some of the more general principles of planning.

BALSA WOOD CONSTRUCTIONS

Balsa wood is an extremely lightweight, easily handled wood, very familiar to boys as a medium for the making of aircraft models. Because of its flexibility, balsa wood is also suitable for imaginatively evolved free-standing constructions (Nos. 120 and 122).

Materials

1   A selection of lengths of balsa wood of varying thicknesses and sections[1]
2   Small tubes of balsa wood cement, for example, Britfix[1]
3   A Swan-Morton or similar thin cutting knife[1]
4   Scissors
5   Small, waste pieces of stout cardboard, for cutting boards
6   A steel rule
7   A bench-hook
8   A fine, balsa wood saw.
   Nos. 6, 7 and 8 are useful, but not essential.

Prices for balsa wood range from 1½d. for the thinnest strips, to 3d., 4d., 5d. and upwards for thicker pieces.

Once the initial outlay has been made, it should be possible to maintain a reasonable stock—without undue expense—by adding small amounts of wood to the basic supply from time to time.

Method of working

The wood is so soft that it is easily cut to the required lengths. Separate pieces are fixed together, piece by piece, usually starting from the base of the construction which consists of a small, fairly thick, flat piece of balsa wood. The base should have enough substance to stand firmly.

The pieces are joined by cement, each joint being firmly held in position until the cement has set. This usually takes a moment or so, but once the first joint is secure, the structure begins to grow rapidly. Constructions should be turned round frequently so that the balance of linear and spatial relationships can be seen from different viewpoints.

Direction of planes may be emphasized by the addition of tissue paper, by fine threads of cotton, or by sheets of very thin balsa wood (which may be gently bent with the grain, for curved surfaces). Children quickly invent their own methods of working.

[1] Obtainable at most hobby or model-making shops.

The completed constructions look well displayed together against a dark coloured background: the delicate lines and spaces may also be sharpened by different lighting effects.

WIRE CONSTRUCTIONS

A few coils of wire of different gauges and some wire-cutters are useful additions to the class art materials. The wire should be flexible enough to be easily bent but thick enough for the constructions to be firm (a 20 gauge is a useful thickness). It can be used in a variety of ways, either quite freely, as in the structures in No. 119; or to form a rigid skeleton foundation over which strips of paper may be pasted. The mask on the right of No. 135 was made in this way.

Masks and Shields

To make a construction of this kind set up a wire framework of the main shapes, by bending, shaping and joining together various pieces of wire. These are joined by twisting the ends tightly over one another, firmly nipping them together with wire pliers. Some-times one end of wire can be wound round a piece of wire that is already in position.

Next, brush strips of newspaper (about one inch wide) with Poly-cell paste, and wrap or fold them over the wire construction, until all the surfaces of the form have been built up as a series of facets. Edges and ridges should be left sharp and precise so that the directions of the planes are clearly defined. A number of these narrow strips of torn paper can be prepared beforehand by placing them flat on some spare newspaper and pasting them lightly with Polycell on both sides. They are then ready for use and the work can go ahead quite quickly, full attention being given to the design of the construction.

This technique, as well as being suitable for the construction of masks or shields in low relief, provides an excellent method of con-structing hollow masks or headgear in the round. A dramatic pro-duction may need heads of animals, or perhaps giants; these can be made to fit individual children.

When the constructions have dried out the paper surfaces become hard and taut, so that they can easily be painted. Tempera-block or powder colour should be used.

Shields or masks in which the angularity of the various facets has been emphasized look well if displayed in different kinds of lighting. Interesting colour effects can be achieved by placing coloured cellophane over a lamp or by using a plain coloured transparency in a projector. It may be possible to arrange different coloured lights to shine on a shield or mask simultaneously, so that the interest of a design is brought out in unexpected ways. Other methods of making masks are described in *Masks and How to Make Them*, by Richard Slade.[1]

Wire Models

Wire is also suitable for making free-standing constructions and, provided it is soft and pliable enough, its use will encourage designs that are flowing and rhythmical in character (No. 119). These models were made in a class that was being taught by a student, the children's ages ranging from seven to eleven years. She had planned a month's work, during which the children were to explore space in a variety of ways, both in their art and in their movement lessons. The children who made the models in No. 119 were consciously working upwards into space, whereas the child who constructed No. 121 worked in a downward direction as well, with pieces of paper hanging from horizontal bars.

During these weeks the children used various materials: wire, cardboard, straw, small boxes, tissue paper and coloured threads. Through their related experiences in movement and art they became very much aware of different dimensions. In the same way that they themselves moved in different spatial directions they discovered that they could emphasize upward, downward, sideway, inward and outward directions in their constructions and models.

The student arranged small displays of photographs of industrial constructions together with reproductions of paintings and sculpture that fitted in with the children's interest in space. She had collected pictures of motorway-bridges, pylons, cranes and aerials, and she also included some photographs, taken especially for this project, of swings and climbing frames, and of the interlacing branches of bare trees.

SCRAP-IRON AND METAL CONSTRUCTIONS

Children from the earliest days in the Infant school use scrap-material and oddments of all kinds to make things. By handling and exploring

[1] *Masks and How to Make Them*, by Richard Slade (Faber & Faber).

these materials they become familiar with the nature of their physical environment, using it freely to serve their own imagination. A piece of wood may as easily be a train or a doll, according to the need of the moment. Equally, the shapes and qualities of different objects may be the means of awakening the imagination. To a child the lid of a date-box can suggest the idea of a ship; perhaps he then gives this mental image actual form, by adding smaller boxes to represent cabins, and by fixing cotton-reels on top for funnels. In the first instance the box provided the stimulus for the expression of a personal idea.

This need for creative expression exists at every stage of the Primary school and the teacher should try to provide satisfying forms of outlet by introducing materials appropriate to the child's changing interests and skills.

Making constructions out of scrap-iron and oddments of metal, for instance, provides older children with intense satisfaction. The materials, some of which can be collected by the children themselves, are neither too costly nor too difficult to obtain and store, especially if we gather only enough for one small group at a time.

Materials

1   A selection of small, strong blocks of wood, suitable for bases—a sack of such wood is sometimes obtainable at little cost from a local wood merchant.
2   A collection of oddments and small pieces of old scrap-iron, wire, springs, bolts and so on (the weathered surfaces and colours found in old iron are particularly attractive).
3   Off-cuts of soft metal, scraps of aluminium, varying wire-meshes—obtainable from an ironmonger dealing in engineering equipment.
4   A selection of panel-pins and small nails, tacks, bronze and dark-coloured nails, staples and push-on paper clips.
5   A hammer.
6   A bradawl.
7   A pair of pliers.
8   Metal-scissors or tin-nippers—useful, but not essential.
9   An adhesive strong enough to stick metal, e.g. Evo-stik.

The general principles of composition applying to other forms of three-dimensional construction provide a working basis. Pieces of metal, wire-mesh, wire, cogs and small scrap-iron are placed together, and joined or twisted so as to form a well-related whole. There is no one correct way of working and children will soon discover how to use these materials. Their results will be as individual in character as in any other work. Some constructions may be graceful, delicate and airy in feeling, while robust, solid shapes produce a sense of weight in others; or perhaps open wire-meshes alternate with solid pieces of iron. The constructions may be simple or complex; some will represent a particular subject, in others the interest may lie in the humorous juxtaposition of the unexpected.

The materials themselves are exciting and challenging to use and may, by their particular qualities, suggest the next move in a construction. Thin pieces of tin can be gently twisted or bent into different shapes. Many forms just 'happen', for instance a perfect spiral is produced when a small strip of thin metal is cut from a larger sheet.

Problems of construction, balance, contrasts, rhythms and movement have to be resolved as each fresh step is considered. The total effect of a composition should be three-dimensional.

The child's intuitive response to the materials provides an initial impulse, which is then developed through his powers of imagination and thought.

CHAPTER 11

Displays and Exhibitions

All through this book I have tried to show the value of having frequent exhibitions of the children's work. Inevitably displays will be overcrowded, because we must try to show the work of as many different children as possible. But despite this overcrowding the exhibition should be pleasant to look at as a whole; there must be resting-places for the eye and a few areas or spaces should be left empty, to create order and serve as quiet background for the lively work.

Teachers may well ask how this is to be done allowing for the pressures of an ordinary school timetable. In fact it need not take undue time, as there are some quite simple yet effective ways of mounting paintings and displaying other work. The first essential is to have supplies of different coloured mounting papers.

Pictures can be mounted by pinning rather than sticking them on to the background paper, using ordinary dressmakers' pins. In this way the teacher—or the children—can easily and quickly mount the pictures, and the same mounting paper can be used several times.

The children themselves should frequently have the opportunity of looking at their paintings against differently coloured backgrounds. This is a worthwhile aesthetic experience through which children learn to discriminate between the effects of different colour relationships, and to choose mounts that seem to them to enhance the colour of their own paintings.

One painting may look best on a mount that echoes its own predominant colour; another may be more effective on a colour which contrasts with the general tone, but which re-echoes one of the smaller but important focal notes. For instance, a picture that is painted mainly in grey-greens, but that has a small patch of vivid orange, may be seen to advantage on a terra-cotta that relates to the orange, or it may be even more effective on a grey that merges closely with the greens and that does not compete with the splash of orange. Each painting needs to be considered separately so that its most telling qualities of colour may be brought out.

On the other hand, a teacher can also display paintings effectively by placing a whole series on mounts that are similar in colour, preferably a neutral shade. Contrasting tones of pale and dark grey papers may sometimes provide a suitable background for a whole set of paintings.

A roll of frieze paper, fixed to the wall as background, offers another means of unifying a display of individual paintings. But in every case the grouping of the coloured mounts, or the effect of a general background colour, is of importance to the whole display.

The background wall, or the area on which the mounts are pinned, must also be considered. Does it provide a setting of pleasant colour and texture or has it a prevailing drabness that will need to be somehow transformed? Much can be done by pinning different coloured materials, such as hessians, black or white scrims and tarlatans, over part of a classroom wall, or over the door to the room or to a cupboard. Rolls of wide, coloured paper (see page 267) are useful for this purpose. As well as these materials, we have found that large pieces of insulating board are invaluable as a means of exhibiting work, especially in classrooms in which little wall space is available. The board can be bought in several stock sizes, or in sizes especially cut to required measurements. Several boards, each painted a different colour, may be propped up in a classroom to provide additional display space. The children will enjoy painting the boards, first with size, then with emulsion paint. Various clear colours can make attractive backgrounds, although on the whole we find that children's paintings look particularly well seen against a white ground.

Apart from mounting their own individual work, older children should sometimes be able to help arrange a series of paintings in their classroom; in this way they come to appreciate different types of painting and to look with interest at each other's work.

Sometimes the teacher should privately arrange a simple display of the children's work after school hours. This need not take very long to prepare and yet the result will be infinitely worth while; for the children's surprised delight when they first see the display invariably leads to all sorts of animated discussions and to a more responsive enjoyment of the work.

Lettering and layout are also of vital importance in the presentation of all visual material. Acceptable standards need to be rigorously maintained by the teacher at every stage of the Primary school; the cumulative—and often indirect—influence on children of the appearance of the visual material put before them daily cannot be overemphasized.

Lettering used on labels, flash-cards, charts and all visual aids should be simple and clear in form, and of course legible. The function of margins, spaces and the satisfactory relationship of each part to the whole is as important in the simplest labels (as on a nature table) as in the more complex charts and maps that may be made for history or geography.

There are many varieties of lettering and each teacher will have his own style. In the lower classes of the Primary school the lettering used and displayed in the classroom should, ideally, provide a good example of the kind of handwriting that is currently being taught. This will avoid confusion in the child's mind.

Handwriting usually starts as a form of script in the Infant school, to be replaced—at the appropriate time—by a cursive writing. The Marion Richardson system of handwriting or one of the various forms of italic handwriting, such as the Beacon Writing, is most commonly used in schools.

Teachers who are not familiar with these systems and wish to acquire a good personal hand, can consult some of the books in the bibliography (page 281).

For lettering the use of a felt pen or a flat-ended brush is recommended. With these it is possible to produce writing of good standard reasonably quickly, without too much practice. Elaborate, laborious methods are not only inexpedient, they are also unsatisfactory aesthetically.

For labels and other visual aids, teachers themselves may need a good source of reference, a pattern for well-proportioned capital letters. The standard example is still that of the Roman alphabet, taken from the Trajan's Column, about A.D. 114. The most satisfying proportions and forms of capitals in use today are usually derived from these letters. This is not to recommend a course of study on the refinements of Roman lettering with its serifs and thin and thick strokes which followed the stone-cutter's chisel. The teacher must simply acquire a general feeling for proportion and for the relative widths of the letters and the spacing, so that he can reproduce these with the simplest brush-strokes.

Admirable stencils for lettering can be bought, but these are usually expensive. When available, they should be used only by the teacher. Children must learn to form their own letters.

Lettering, as such, should not be taught in the Junior school. But if children are constantly looking at good lettering they unconsciously acquire standards which can later be applied when they do lettering themselves in the Secondary school.

Displays of any visual material, including painting or other art work, should not be kept on show for too long a period. The really important impact occurs when the children first see the display; after this, their initial enthusiasm becomes less marked on each successive day, until all their interest evaporates.

In short, the classroom should be a place of intensely satisfying visual experiences. Frequent changes of displays and variety of arrangement help to keep alive the children's involvement in what is going on, without which the children are apt to lapse into that all too familiar state of apathy in which they are no longer aware of their surroundings.

CHAPTER 12

Some General Principles and Schemes of Work

PLANNING AHEAD

Teachers hold differing views as to the value of keeping to a scheme of work in art teaching. Some maintain that a scheme provides an essential structure for the work, and that it should be followed closely; others argue that any scheme is far too limiting and that it may actually prevent the free development of a child's spontaneous creative expression. For me a sound working basis for art teaching is to be found somewhere between these extremes of attitude.

A planned programme is essential to ensure good timing when introducing different kinds of work during the course of a term, or of a year.

We also need to be able to see at a glance whether the plans we have made for a class will provide the children with well-balanced opportunities for creative expression.

MATERIALS

A wide range of media and techniques encourages children to remain creatively alert; our scheme should therefore include changes of medium from time to time. The materials introduced must of course be suitable; that is to say they must be well related to the natural interests of the children, to their technical ability and particular needs. The age of the children will also determine the kinds of materials that are used. Many of these are illustrated in the plates included in this book, yet they are only some of the countless possibilities.

But we have also to decide whether the variety of media we envisage is likely to be satisfying and stimulating to the children, or whether we are merely introducing variety for variety's sake. There is no particular virtue in using many different materials, unless the experiences gained through taking part in these planned activities help the child's development.

It has been stressed that much of the value of using many media lies in the child's recognition of the qualities peculiar to each one. Through the interplay of different creative experiences he (both consciously and unconsciously) absorbs underlying aesthetic principles and gradually—as he gets older—builds up firm standards.

Materials need not necessarily be expensive; in fact frequent reference has been made to the possibilities inherent in all sorts of odds and ends, and in scrap materials. But there should always be some intrinsic interest and character in the materials provided, so that the children can respond to these qualities and enjoy the particular challenge they offer. By working experimentally with different materials the child learns to make his own judgements, especially if he is allowed to work out for himself the problems that crop up during the successive stages of the work. The work must, however, be well within his capacity, so that he attains the security given by successful achievement.

Another reason for including a variety of media is that only in this way will each child be able to discover those materials for which he has a special feeling. Needs may change quickly and each child should therefore frequently be allowed to choose his own working materials. It is the teacher's responsibility to provide an appropriate and inviting initial selection of media, although it is generally advisable to limit the number of materials offered for use at one time. Too great a choice can be bewildering for a child.

Expediency may also partly influence the choice of materials. Finger painting, for example, demands rather special organization; while this is going on, other groups are best engaged in activities that require less time spent on preparation and clearing up. Drawing in pastels or painting with tempera-block colours are examples of techniques involving simple materials that need less organization.

A CHANGE OF MEDIUM

A change of medium can do much to re-establish confidence that has been lost, and a child who fails to make headway in one medium may be able to work more freely and successfully in another. An instance of this occurred in one of our first-year art groups. A student whose previous experience in art had been very brief and limited in range, had enjoyed working experimentally with all sorts of materials

She had tackled each aspect of the course readily, but as soon as painting was introduced she became so inhibited that she was unable to do anything that satisfied her. As she put it: 'I was all right until I had to hold a paint brush.' Feelings of uncertainty and memories of earlier inadequacies crowded in upon her, robbing her of the spontaneity and assurance she had been enjoying. It was difficult to help her and she naturally became disappointed in her work and despondent.

Fortunately she regained her confidence when she started to make a glove puppet. Puppetry was new to her; she chose to make a witch and soon produced a vigorous figure of grotesque aspect. It was certainly one of the most effective puppets in her group. The face and head, already distorted in the modelling to add emphasis to the features, were crudely painted in strong greens, purples and blacks, the colours and shapes contributing to the originality of her interpretation. The witch, with straggling hair of emerald-green wool, was clothed in jagged strips of coloured nets and painted calico. Finally she made a striking appearance as, intensified by a spot-light, she took her part in a short dramatic performance of *Hansel and Gretel*.

While making, painting and clothing this puppet, the student had been concerned only to deal with the matter in hand as effectively as possible, in actual fact achieving a most satisfying result aesthetically. While the mere idea of 'painting a picture' had awakened anxieties about how to convey the realistic appearance of things, a change of medium had restored her confidence and proved an important factor in the development of her future creative work.

I have touched on this student's experience at some length as such blocking of progress is by no means rare. Perhaps we underestimate the damaging effect that recurring failure, or even implied failure, may have on the children we teach if, week after week and possibly term after term, they are allowed to feel unable to reach the standards of achievement imposed by the teacher.

TRYING OUT NEW MATERIALS

Sometimes a new medium, combined with others that are quite familiar, can add liveliness to children's work. For instance, while some 'storm' subjects were being painted, I suggested to the children that they might like to use a really thick, different type of paint in parts of their pictures. I had provided a fair-sized tin of a leadless white distemper, some small plastic saucers and various improvised tools with which the children could apply the paint. They used the distemper instead of the customary white powder colour, which would of course have been much thinner in consistency. They very much enjoyed trying out some of the effects produced by using the thicker paint, mixing the distemper with their other powder colours, and applying it with old brushes, knives or pieces of wood. Some of the children quite spontaneously applied the paint directly with their fingers in order, through the sense of touch, to express the surface textures as richly as possible.

Paul, aged ten—whose painting has already been mentioned in Chapter 3, see No. 63—was particularly fascinated by the thicker distemper and eagerly experimented in several successive paintings. He often enjoyed finding new ways of painting, and in this case he obviously liked the feel as well as the look of the pigment surfaces, which he finally linked with coarse lines drawn in pen and ink.

I remember the urgency of his request: 'Come and look at the new technique I've invented.' He was spreading paint thickly on to the paper with a flat stick, and then with various tools scraping and scratching different textures into the deep layers of the moist paint. When he saw his painting displayed on the wall his first reaction was to run his fingers gently over the raised surfaces of paint, enchanted by the feeling of the textures.

THE SUBJECT AND THE MEDIUM

These are generally so closely related as to be virtually inseparable. In choosing our working materials we have to ask ourselves both 'What will be the most appropriate medium for interpreting this subject?' and 'What subjects will lend themselves especially well to the use of such and such a medium?' Such considerations must influence the choice of themes and media in any scheme.

A RANGE OF ART ACTIVITIES

In planning sequences of work for a particular group of children we must also vary the type of work itself—picture making, direct observation, pattern making and communal work—so that the children can enjoy a reasonable balance between these different yet interdependent areas of practical work. It is only by putting the child in touch with a real breadth of experience that he can discover sources from which he may satisfactorily build up his own special forms of expression. Here again, each child's response is intensely personal and it is important that each individual should frequently be able to enjoy the kind of work that most appeals to him.

THE CARRY OVER OF EXPERIENCE

We have also to consider whether the sequences of work that we plan to follow will encourage progress in the children's work. Will there be a useful carry over from one form of expression to another? For example, the understanding gained through making a tissue-paper collage—in which the child has been very conscious of colours in relation to each other—should extend his feeling for colour when he is painting.

Or again a child—in the upper Primary school—who is going to make a coloured-paper collage, may benefit by first making a small abstract in torn paper, using a restricted range of black, white and grey paper. After this exercise he will be able to relate what he has learned about tone variations to his collage in coloured papers.

An awareness of this kind of interaction of experience will help us to decide on specific sequences of work.

ART AND HANDWORK

Throughout this book art and handwork have been considered as one subject, integrated parts of a total experience. This would usually occupy two double periods a week in the timetable, allowing for sequences of work to be completed and carried through on the crest of the children's enthusiasm. Though the term art can be used to cover all painting and handwork activities, too much importance need not be attached to giving a label to the course, provided that, where there are separate timetabled periods known as art and handwork, the children are still allowed to complete one range of experience at a time, using all the periods available. There is otherwise the danger that the work may become too fragmented and that the children's understanding of it will become confused by a series of seemingly unconnected experiences. The teacher should therefore plan to spend fairly concentrated blocks of time on each aspect of the work.

In some schools where art and handwork are taken as separate subjects, boys and girls are segregated for these lessons. Often the girls have needlework while the boys paint or do woodwork. But if we are really concerned with the contribution art makes to the education of the whole person and believe that this is in part achieved by working freely in a stimulating range of materials, then we can hardly think it right for certain children to be consistently deprived of these opportunities.

Needlework rightly becomes an increasingly important subject for girls in the upper Junior school, but even so it should not take the place of art. It remains important to find ways whereby girls and boys can—at this stage and in mixed classes—follow the same basic work in art. It is as desirable for girls to be able to use a hammer and nails and to make simple constructions in wood, as it is for boys to use a needle and coarse thread and to work with yarns and fabrics.

A friend of mine who was doing some part-time teaching tackled glove puppets with a class of very backward eight-year-old children. She found the boys were as eager to sew as the girls. They made their stitches with great deliberation, to the accompaniment of a little chant: 'In, out, bottle of stout', and, as they became more skilled: 'Out, in, bottle of gin.' I imagine it was a demanding session, as most of the children needed help in ending off their threads: 'Please Miss, I can do "in, out" but I can't cast off.' Finally each child had the satisfaction of producing a dress he had himself sewn for his puppet, even if it had been necessary for the most badly frayed edges to be reinforced with Copydex.

VARIETY OF EXPERIENCE

As well as allowing for a carry over of experience, we must alternate the work in such a way that the children's interest is kept alive partly through the element of change. Is there enough interplay between two- and three-dimensional work during the course of a term or year? Are aspects of pattern and picture making interspersed so as to be of mutual benefit? Are the more precise techniques, such as lino cutting, wax engraving and pen and ink, balanced by broader processes, such as collage and modelling? Have we allowed scope both for themes related to the daily environment and to the world of fantasy? Are we planning for a variety of stimuli but remaining alive to the dangers of becoming too stimulus-bound? Is the balance between freely chosen work on their own and more specifically guided work likely to be a useful one for the children we have in mind?

COLLECTIVE WORK

We have also to make good use of the interaction between individual work and communal projects. A programme of work should allow time to be spent on planned collective work—perhaps two or three projects in the year—at the same time ensuring that each child has ample opportunity to develop his own powers at a personal level.

This brings us back to the individual child, or group of children, and to the extent that their needs should influence our planning.

SCHEMES OF WORK

Ready-made schemes, only too easily to be found in some of the current educational journals, may at first seem tempting. Yet however good any one of these may be, it cannot in any sense provide a satisfactory substitute for one that has been planned by a teacher to meet the demands of an actual situation. A scheme, to be valid, must be the outcome of the teacher's personal thinking and sensitivity towards the children in his class.

It should also be of significance to him personally, drawing on his own resources, gifts and enthusiasms, through which he will best be able to teach. The teacher must regard his own scheme of work as flexible, so flexible that he can alter or modify it or even abandon it should unexpected developments and interests occur. The nature of the children's work will inevitably be dependent on their own changing preoccupations which may follow quite unforeseen courses. Children should never be forced into doing work arbitrarily imposed by the demands of a scheme that has lost its relevance. The teacher may have to sacrifice his original ideas in order to use the children's new enthusiasms. A scheme that is allowed to become too dominant an influence can quickly destroy spontaneous delight in the work, both for the children and for the teacher. Its only real justification is that it should serve the children, and provide a light framework for the teacher's general planning.

Sybil Marshall, in *An Experiment in Education*,[1] remembers her reactions as a young teacher to the use of schemes of work in her own one-teacher school. She writes:

My new schemes of work for example: they had at last been returned from the education office approved and even commended. But in the interval of time we had found freedom of approach to education, and to attempt now to use set schemes of work based on a rigid four-year cycle with these living children would have been like trying to tie up water in a false-line.[2]

Later she says:

But in any case, a three- or four-year scheme defeats itself by the very nature of what it is intended it shall do. It lays down plans of work for a hypothetical class which it is supposed will exist in three or four years' time. As every teacher knows, no two classes are ever alike, nor the same class alike on two separate occasions, or under two different teachers. Plans can only be made for the class as it is, and only then to cover a period of time easily foreseeable—at the most I would say six weeks at a time.[3]

While I fully agree with the whole spirit of Mrs. Marshall's viewpoint, I would myself think it desirable to work out a balanced range of activities that could be grouped and dovetailed into the continuity of a year.

The plans of work set out in this chapter are only meant to suggest ways in which the many aspects of art and the wealth of materials at our disposal could be used. It cannot, therefore, be over-emphasized that these are *not* intended as model schemes—plans of work are essentially the personal concern of individual teachers. Perhaps to venture to include any schemes seems something of a contradiction to what has already been said, yet it may be helpful to see how satisfactorily the various activities that have been touched on can slip into place in a variety of planned sequences. With this object in view I have included a scheme for upper Juniors, and one for Infants;

---

[1] *An Experiment in Education*, by Sybil Marshall (Cambridge University Press).
[2] Ibid., page 38.
[3] Ibid., page 39.

these will I hope show how we can set about planning schemes of work, and will illustrate an application of the various points that have been considered in this chapter.

The plans of work cover three terms, each of twelve weeks, and in all cases art and handwork have been thought of as one subject.

Somewhat detailed subject-matter has been referred to in the scheme of work for upper Juniors, because it is difficult to envisage work for children of this age without thinking in terms of actual themes. The subjects I have chosen could readily be changed for others that would contribute as successfully to each particular sequence of creative experience. Headings, such as 'Picture making' and 'Pattern making' are too generalized to be useful in a scheme; they both include so large a number of possibilities that it has been necessary to be fairly specific.

I have tried to show by actual examples how the children's practical work can be seen against a wider, yet related background. All such work can lead to an expansion of interest. The suggestions made in these schemes are simply intended as a few examples to show how this might work out in practice. Information about available sources of material will be found on pages 265–74.

A small, relevant display of work has been suggested as a means of concluding each short period of practical work that the children spend on a particular theme. Exhibitions of this kind can be attractive without being large. Quite small, unpretentious collections can be pleasantly arranged on a black-board—previously covered with paper—or on the top of a table. A few appropriate cards—well mounted on a sheet of sugar paper—placed by the children's own work may be enough to encourage an appreciation of other aspects of art.

At other times it will be a valuable experience for the children, working with the teacher, to arrange a rather bigger display that is in itself satisfyingly composed and presented.

THE SCHEME FOR INFANTS

The suggested plan of work shows one way in which the various creative activities suitable for older Infants could be distributed over the course of a year. Infinite variations and adaptations are possible, and each working plan, to be satisfactory, must be resolved by the teacher concerned.

Little emphasis has been placed on collective work because younger children are on the whole chiefly concerned with their individual efforts. It is generally not until they reach the middle Junior school that they become interested in combining their results with those of other children, and in working for a common purpose. In the Infant school they like to feel that they are one of a group, but tend to remain fully absorbed in their personal worlds.

Classroom displays have not been mentioned in connection with Infants' work, because children at this stage are not usually ready to connect these consciously to their own results. But Infants should have the constant delight of visual material to absorb. Things likely to appeal to them, or which have some bearing on their current interests, can be displayed in many attractive ways—always well related to the children's view-point. The small arrangements must be changed frequently, different parts of the classroom being used for these displays, so that an element of surprise may sharpen the children's pleasure in looking. Sometimes only few objects should be used, such as one or two carefully selected shells, which the children can study minutely. Even if the shells are linked with the work in the classroom, their pattern and form will impart an indirect, rather than a conscious, source of inspiration.

It will be noted that few specific subjects have been suggested for the top Infant—or it could be lower Junior—group; because at this stage children usually decide quite spontaneously what subjects they want to draw or paint. On the other hand there may be instances when some children will welcome a lead; there are also occasions, already at this stage, where it is stimulating for a whole class to be sharing the interest of one and the same subject, however different their individual interpretations of it may be. The most suitable subject matter centres around the child himself and around the people and things most closely connected with his life and personal world:

> Myself
> Me and my Mummy
> My family
> Our house
> Our dog
> My pet.

Subjects of this kind enable the child to express his growing awareness of himself and of his own relationship and reaction to people and to his environment. The idea of movement or action may add further significance to his ideas:

> I am playing with my brother
> Mummy and I are taking our dog for a walk
> I am carrying my Teddy.

In many Infant schools painting, drawing or modelling are included as one of a number of activities, in which play materials such as water, sand and dough are introduced. Excellent as this is, I think there is also a place for an activity period devoted purely to art pursuits, and I would like to put in a plea for supplementary art periods in the upper Infant school. Through these the child's range of creative expression will be extended so that he is able to communicate more fully when he selects to paint—or use clay or make a collage—in a general-activity period.

Some children may otherwise hardly become aware of the possibilities offered by the different materials. Or we may find that the child who frequently chooses to paint produces a similar picture time after time—perhaps of a house—until his interpretation tends to lose its meaning and become careless through constant repetition. Such a child will benefit by some guidance on the use of media and will find it helpful to be given specific suggestions from time to time.

But when we do introduce subjects in the Infant and lower Junior school, there will usually be some children who are clearly eager to choose their own subjects. In such cases their own ideas will be the more vivid and they should be encouraged to use them.

SOME GENERAL POINTS

Through experiences in art we hope to give the child an outlet for his feelings and reactions, both to the world around him and to the world of fantasy.

We allow him the freedom essential for genuinely creative expression and provide him with materials to use experimentally. From the earliest school years we hope to liberate his powers of communication through visual means, to safeguard his own modes of expression and to avoid influences likely to impair his honesty of vision.

Tracing is sometimes introduced as a means of ensuring accurate recording when children—in an art activity—make friezes or pictorial charts connected with another subject, say history. While reference to various—and if possible direct—sources of historical information must be an essential part of such an activity the children should also be free to re-create in their own way their impressions of Norman castles, dwellings, people and costumes. Their finished frieze may appear crude and even incorrect to adult eyes, yet for the children their imaginative interpretation will catch something of the character and vitality of the Norman scene.

When it is necessary to have quite precise, factually accurate records—to be used in connection with a specific subject—duplicated illustrations may be more useful than tracings. Here again the children's own pencil or pen and ink sketches will have a vitality usually lost in a tracing; and children will be more inclined to remember essential features that they have understood and searched out for themselves in their sketches. By encouraging the child to trace his shapes we imply that he is unable to draw satisfactorily without this aid. He loses confidence in his own ability to draw free hand and before long becomes inhibited in his whole approach to working creatively. As he traces he concentrates on each small line, unable to take in the whole concept, which may in any case differ from the forms of expression natural to him.

Colouring books for younger children also tend to cut across their own way of using colour. The young child makes his own shapes with firm outlines. These he may leave as linear forms or he may fill them in vigorously with colour, using paint or crayon with broad movements. Sometimes he starts by painting or crayoning areas of colour, letting the edges of the strokes produce the shape. By asking him to work within the confines of an imposed outline and by offering him schemes of colours to copy (probably unrelated to his personal way of using colour) we inevitably restrict his natural movements and spontaneity. Moreover, the traced forms (often of a representational sophistication) may become the child's main criteria of visual standards, undermining his readiness to accept the quite different forms of painting and pictorial expression that come naturally to him.

The child's standards should be the result of his own intuition and —as he gets older—of his own judgements about work that has been the outcome of a really personal expression.

Work that is produced solely to please a teacher will have little lasting value for the child. Each teacher naturally has a different approach and emphasis of interest and, right as it is for the child to be stimulated by these varying influences, it is also essential that he should be sure of his own values.

In summing up it may be helpful to remind ourselves of some of the essentials of art teaching, in which our chief concerns must be for the development of the child as a whole person. We offer him a range of experiences to which he can respond both with his senses and his mind. For many children the emotional content of their work may be most significant. But we hope also to arouse the child's curiosity, so that he brings a sense of wonder and inquiry to his work, as he makes his decisions and finds the best ways of working out his ideas visually. This fusion of feeling and thought has been an important element in most of the work that has been described in this book. In children's art—as in art generally—we value qualities of feeling, sensitivity, imagination and original thought more highly than skills and techniques. Yet we have seen that these too play a part if children are to find effective means of expression. At every stage of the Primary school the teacher attempts to equate these aspects satisfactorily for the child.

Through pattern making alone the child acquires—consciously or unconsciously—a basic vocabulary of shapes and relationships. He builds up a visual language with which to speak; equally—or even more important—he should have something to say through this language. He may have resources within himself that the lightest touch will bring to life; or he may need a visual stimulant before his own ideas take shape.

The teacher concentrates on providing a range of satisfying visual experiences, and recognizes too the importance of the classroom setting which, at its best, can offer vital sources of inspiration. These influences will become part of the children's aesthetic awareness and cannot really be divorced from life.

Art is a vital, growing affair. Growth means change, an unfolding that reveals new forms which relate to the children's world of tomorrow. They are the people who will in part create the visual world of the future. The teacher has at his disposal materials and processes that can extend the whole range of visual expression. Many of the techniques described, in which experimental approaches have been emphasized, are close to modern trends in painting, sculpture and architecture. Yet in exploring new possibilities the teacher has to guard against following fashion for fashion's sake. The criterion of the work must always be directed towards the fulfilment of the child's needs. New forms of art teaching could otherwise easily degenerate into superficial mannerisms, as remote from the children's natural ways of expression as were former systems of over-academical instruction. Whatever work is being undertaken, and we have seen how wide the range of subject, approach and media can be, the children should feel an initial excitement. Work of real creative value can only happen where the atmosphere is charged with a sense of enjoyment and purpose that equally involves the children and the teacher. Work born of a shared enthusiasm will thrive and develop well; suitable materials, although very important, will not take its place.

THE NON-SPECIALIST TEACHER

Non-specialist teachers sometimes question their own ability to teach art successfully. In reality a non-specialist teacher with a deep feeling for children and a determination to work out ways of art teaching that really meet their needs is sometimes more successful than the art specialist. The latter may be so subject-minded that he tends to judge the children's work too much from the specialist's view-point, thereby sacrificing something of the children's natural interests and characteristics of work.

Successful art teaching depends to a very great extent on the understanding existing between the teacher and the children, and the importance of a really sympathetic partnership cannot be too strongly emphasized. The necessity of a right balance between freedom and security for the child has been stressed as vital to art teaching. Security will be an outcome of the mutual affection and respect experienced between child and teacher; each child must know that he counts as an individual and should feel the assurance of his teacher's basic friendliness of attitude. This sense of security will also depend on quite practical aspects, such as the way a subject is introduced, the kind of guidance given in the use of materials and tools, and on the positive, constructive nature of any criticism that may be given.

A quotation from one of the concluding chapters in *Education through Art*, by Herbert Read, underlines some of the essential factors that relate to art teaching:

I have been enormously impressed by the fact, at first puzzling, that the best results could not be correlated with any system of teaching or any academic qualifications in the teacher. Sometimes the best work comes from schools where an art-master or mistress as such does not exist. It was equally evident that the good results did not come from a particular type of school. A collection of the best work would come in arbitrary proportions from public, elementary, secondary and private schools. My first conclusion was that good results depended on the creation, in the school or class, of a sympathetic atmosphere, and to a certain extent I still think this is true. But if by 'atmosphere' one means the amenities which money can buy, it is not true. The right atmosphere can exist in a village school, or in a dingy barracks in some industrial city. The atmosphere is the creation of the teacher, and to create an atmosphere of spontaneity, of happy childish industry, is the main and perhaps the only secret of successful teaching.

Most Secondary schools—and also many Primary schools—are well equipped for most forms of art and craft. But there are still large numbers of Infant and Junior schools that have few real facilities for practical work. A teacher in such a school is inevitably faced with countless difficulties and frustrations. Perhaps we can find some comfort in the points made by Sir Herbert Read. The most important elements in art teaching reveal values other than those dependent on the purely physical conditions of buildings and equipment. (This should not, however, suggest that we give up struggling to improve conditions that are obviously unsatisfactory.)

Finally, some words of Marion Richardson's come to mind:

Art [she once wrote] is not an effort of will but a gift of grace—to the child, at least, the simplest and most natural thing in the world. Wherever people are sincere and free, art can spring up. That is why the child's happiness or otherwise in the presence of the teacher is all important, and why the school of to-day is, or should be, the perfect setting for children's art. It is not too much to say that unless a relationship amounting to love exists between teacher and children, children's art, as it is now understood, is impossible.[1]

This passage, written many years ago, still stands for values that provide the basis of enlightened art teaching.

[1] Marion Richardson, 1892–1946, *Athene, The Journal of the Society for Education in Art*, Summer 1947, Vol. 4, No. 1.

UPPER JUNIORS

A scheme to show how some of the principles discussed in Chapter 12 might work out in practice. These are only suggestions; by no means all types of work are included and for each sequence of work or theme there could be many alternatives.

AUTUMN TERM	SPRING TERM	SUMMER TERM
1 and 2: SIMPLE WEAVING—free use of colour and texture in design.	1: PAINTING—imaginative subject introduced by means of discussion.	1: CANDLE RUBBINGS—a collection of candle rubbings painted with ebony stain.
	2: OBSERVATION—either a series of sketches of animals or an imaginative painting based on direct observation of an animal.	2: COLLAGES—the rubbed candle-made textures are torn into shapes, which are arranged in a tonal and textural composition.
3: TORN PAPER COMPOSITION—using shapes of coloured tissue-paper, combined with threads of different thicknesses. Abstract themes, clowns, imagined flowers, make-believe birds, fish or dragons, simple shaped objects: bottles, fruit, etc.		*Exhibition relating to 1 and 2* Display of the children's panels, together with a variety of prints, brass rubbings and other relevant material.
	3: WAX ENGRAVINGS—study of smaller creatures: for instance, a tortoise, hedgehog or frog.	3: PAINTING—self portraits.
	Exhibition relating to 2 and 3 Animals in art. Examples to include reproductions of paintings and illuminated manuscripts, as well as illustrations of animals depicted in pottery, carving, weaving and embroidery.	
4: COLLAGE—using a variety of matt and shiny papers, also nets, coarse canvas, etc. This work relates to many of the points considered in the weaving of weeks 1 and 2.		4: DRAWING FROM LIFE—a person dressed up, someone holding an animal or child, or carrying a basket filled with things of interest: flowers, fish, large apples; or balloons may be attached to the handle of the basket.
Exhibition relating to 2, 3 and 4 A range of examples on the theme of collage	4: MOSAICS—in a range of papers.	*Exhibition relating to 2, 3 and 4* Display of postcard reproductions on the theme of portraits and people.
	5: MOSAICS—in pebbles and various small objects set in plaster or cement.	
5: FINGER PAINTING—the subject chosen to encourage free, rhythmic treatment, and a personal use of colour.	*Exhibition relating to 4 and 5* Small display on the theme of mosaics.	5: IMAGINATIVE PICTURE—a poem or description in which a person, or people, may be introduced. The choice of media to include paint, pastel or collage.

6: PAINTING—(a) experimental brushwork, linking the freedom of finger painting to the sensitive use of the brush, followed by (b) the main subject, to bring out further interest in the use of texture and colour: for instance, a coloured light shining on to a large bunch of mixed flowers.

7: PAINTING—a tonal exercise: (a) a collective collage of small pieces of painted paper or fabric, covering a full tonal range, (b) subsequent individual work to be a picture painted chiefly in a range of one colour.

8: DRAWING OR PAINTING—sparklers or fireworks, drawn and painted on dark paper, ideas to be clarified by means of a visual starting point.

9: DRAWING OR PAINTING—an imaginative interpretation of light: candlelight, torch light, the light of a hurricane lamp—with practical experiment and demonstration.

Exhibition relating to 8 and 9
The children's work supplemented by a range of paintings showing different treatments of light.

10: DECORATIVE LANTERNS—circular or rectangular-sided lanterns made of black paper. Insets of coloured tissue or cellophane papers are pasted behind geometric shapes cut out of the black paper. The height of a lantern to be about 6 in. so that it can be placed over a 1 lb. jam jar in which a small candle or night-light has been lighted.

Exhibition relating to 10
Display of children's lamps together with reproductions of stained glass, or small arrangements of actual fragments of coloured glass.

11 and 12: COLLECTIVE ACTIVITY—a Christmas theme: a frieze, a rectangular panel, a large collage of a tree, or a project of paper decorations planned for a particular room or place in the school.

6: PAINTING—preliminary experiments in colour mixing—followed by individual paintings, through which a personal interest in colour can be developed.

7: PAINTING

8: PATTERN—oval or circular painted medallions.

9: MEDALLION PATTERNS (or designs for squares or oblongs)—using a medium other than paint: pastel; potato, turnip and carrot prints; wax engravings.

Exhibition relating to 8 and 9
Display built around the medallion theme. Examples to be selected from historical and contemporary sources, covering a range of media. The exhibits to include natural as well as man-made forms; patterns made by hand and by machine.

10: DRAWING—a session based on observation, rediscovering possibilities of a range of media such as brush and ink, charcoal, crayon, conté, pastel and bamboo pen. Themes to depend on prevalent interest of children, for instance, industrial (wheels, cogs, springs and bolts) or rural (bushes, growing plants, vegetables, fruit).

11 and 12: GLOVE PUPPETS—leading to a simple production.
OR
POTTERY—thumb pots and coiled pots.

6 and 7: STILL-LIFE PAINTING—a large collection of objects, which the children use imaginatively as the basis for their own interpretations.
Still-life—a change in approach: the children (working in small groups) assemble their own arrangements, selecting objects from a collection of things provided in the classroom by the teacher.

Exhibition relating to 6 and 7
Interpretations of the still-life theme: for instance, realistic, impressionist, expressionist, decorative and cubist.

8 and 9: PAINTING out of doors—using the school environment.
Sketching—any out-door subject matter that is practicable: recording actual places and things—outhouses, greenhouses, workshops, trees and plants. Opportunities for sketching animals to be included. Reference to the different drawing materials experimented with in the spring term, week 10, may be useful.

10, 11 and 12: (a) MODELLING
OR (b) CARVING
Primitive firing—some of the thumb pots and coiled pots made at the end of the spring term can be included in the firings.

Exhibition relating to 10, 11 and 12
Photographs of pottery, sculpture and carving, including primitive and medieval pottery, together with some examples of contemporary work.

A SUGGESTED SCHEME FOR UPPER INFANTS TO LOWER JUNIORS

AUTUMN TERM	SPRING TERM	SUMMER TERM
I: PAINTING	I: WHITE AND LIGHT PASTELS—on dark paper (snowflakes). Separate circular patterns cut out and mounted as a collective panel.	I: PAINTING—huge flowers.
2: (a) FINGER PAINTING (b) DRAWING IN CRAYONS (c) PAPER COLLAGE	2: PAINTING—a choice of different coloured papers (medallion pattern-pictures).	2: PAINTS OR CRAYONS
3: PATTERN-PICTURES—using rug wools and yarns on a paste-covered surface.	3: PAINTED AND CUT-OUT BUTTERFLIES OR MOTHS—mounted as a large panel or pinned on to an actual branch.	3: TISSUE-PAPER COLLAGE—magic birds.
4: (a) PAINTS—pictures of people. (b) CLAY—modelling.	4: PAPER OR FABRIC COLLAGE—abstracts or pictures of people.	4: (a) FINGER PAINTING (b) DRAWING IN CRAYONS
5: PAINTS OR CRAYONS—patterns for book-covers.	5: PAPER-BAG HEADS	5: (a) CLAY (b) WOOD AND SCRAP MATERIAL
6: COLLAGE—paper or fabric.	6 and 7: PAPIER MÂCHÉ PUPPETS	6 and 7: SHADOW PUPPETS—to be used individually or collectively.
7: (a) CLAY OR PAPIER MÂCHÉ—modelling or making pots, making masks. (b) WOOD AND SCRAP MATERIAL—making simple constructions.		
8: COLOURED TISSUE-PAPER COLLAGE	8. PAINTING—preceded by short period on colour mixing.	8 and 9: (a) PAPIER MÂCHÉ—ovals, shields or faces. (b) PAINTING OR DRAWING in crayons.

9: PAINTS OR PASTELS—on dark paper.

10: (*a*) PAINTS—Christmas theme.
(*b*) CLAY—Christmas theme.

11: CARROT-PRINTS—on coloured tissue-paper (Christmas wrapping paper).

12: COLLAGE—fabric and small oddments stuck on to card.

9: COLLAGE—in a variety of materials—feathers, braids, buttons, etc.

10: (*a*) CLAY—modelling and making pots.
(*b*) WOOD—making simple constructions.

11: (*a*) PAINTS
(*b*) CARDBOARD, WOOD AND SCRAP MATERIAL—simple constructions.

12: PAINTING—preceded by short colour-mixing game.

10: PAINTING—preceded by short period spent on colour-mixing game.

11: (*a*) CLAY—rabbit or other pet.
(*b*) CRAYONS OR PASTELS

12: FABRIC COLLAGE—large animal.

The Children's Art Club

Many of the illustrations in this book are photographs of work produced on Saturday mornings by children of the Homerton Art Club. A description of a particular morning, with some account of the children's activities, may be of general interest.

Although it is not yet nine o'clock, several children have already arrived. Everything has been left ready the evening before. It is rather like preparing for a large party, which in a sense it is, with the materials invitingly set out for use. How attractive it all looks, each desk with its mug of water, mixing palette, brush and bun tin with colours. One or two kinds of paper have been left on a separate table, ready for the morning, so that the children may make their own choice.

To-day, as usual, we check the paints and, with the help of the first arrivals, replenish the tins with teaspoons of powder colour, a job much enjoyed by the children, who do it quickly and efficiently. Most of the children know and enjoy using the full, lovely sounding names of the colours —lemon-yellow, yellow ochre, vermilion, crimson and ultramarine.

We usually make preparations for some painting each week, although we may also offer an alternative; on this occasion the children had the choice of painting or of making a fabric collage.

In the meantime the studio is filling up with groups of boys and girls, waiting expectantly. We have two sessions each Saturday. The first, from 9.00 a.m. to 10.00 a.m., is for the younger members, whose ages range from about four years to eleven years. The older group, which includes young people up to about sixteen years, follows on from 10.30 a.m. until noon. There are over forty children in each group and the demand for places is so great that we have had to close our waiting list. We do not keep an official register, but parents, or the children themselves, let us know of any absences. Apart from this the work itself provides a record as to who is present each Saturday.

The children pay 5s. a term towards the expense of materials and the club is largely self-supporting. Members sometimes pay small additional amounts for activities involving extra expense, such as the cost of material for fabric printing.

Parents usually bring and fetch the younger children, and we enjoy this contact. The children like it too, as they are then able to show their morning's work to their parents. Outdoor clothes are left in another room, where the big tables are soon hidden beneath piles of coats. Admittedly it looks rather a confusion and often I mean to evolve some more orderly system. Only very occasionally, however, has a child gone away in someone else's coat. Scarves and gloves are sometimes left behind and, if these are unnamed, it is almost as difficult to find the owner as it is to have nameless paintings claimed. For weeks, once, a small Fair-Isle glove was pinned inquiringly to our notice board.

We begin at about 9.00 a.m.; the children group themselves around any visual material that we may have prepared, ready to take part in an introductory discussion. Some members will still be arriving. There are no bells to mark the sessions; the general atmosphere is informal and rarely does everyone begin or stop at quite the same time.

Though the children are of course free to choose their own subjects, we find that, with the exception of the youngest, most like to be given a theme, with some guidance as to the use of materials and the general treatment. Sometimes even the youngest children listen to the introduction with rapt attention, nodding, smiling and taking an animated part in the general talk; they then return happily to their places, immediately setting to work on a quite different subject.

On the other hand, I remember one occasion when Mark, aged six, not only attached himself to the older children of the group, but made a vigorous charcoal drawing of their subject. We had collected a number of musical instruments: a violin, guitar, tambourine, drum, triangle and cymbals. These attractive shapes were to provide a basis for individual interpretation, each child using them in his own way. Mark, in his drawing, not only expressed the form and character of each instrument, but showed the relative scale of each with realistic accuracy. While some young children, like Mark, may respond eagerly to a stimulus that excites their growing powers of observation, other children of six and often much older remain absorbed with what they 'know' and are less concerned with the representational expression of what they 'see'.

On this particular Saturday most of the children chose to make collage portraits. We had collected an exciting assortment of scraps and remnants of material. These we ironed and spread out invitingly in main colour groups and in sequence ranging from pale to dark. The children were soon stroking the various pieces appreciatively, loving this abundance of colour and texture. They were just ready for a change of medium.

With portraits in mind, we had also provided some larger pieces of material big enough for the shapes of faces and heads. We wanted the children to respond particularly to decorative and imaginative qualities rather than to representational ones. We therefore offered them colours by no means limited to the purely realistic. These included pale yellows, pinks, blues and greens, as well as strong reds and oranges. There were also patterned ginghams and spotted muslins, in fact any textures and colours likely to appeal to the children and set them working imaginatively and spontaneously through the direct interest of the materials. We had one or two large colour-swatches recently given to us by a local furnishing shop; these contained patterns of heavier cloth in many different colours and tones.

The variety of materials available made it possible for the children to select and use all sorts of colours, and because they were not restricted by ideas of representational accuracy, they could enjoy colour freely in its own right. It is disappointing that the whole gallery of portraits cannot be reproduced in colour. The results were lively and personal and often we were amazed by the unexpected beauty of the colour combinations that the children used intuitively.

We started with a brief talk about portraits—how these might be pictures of the head and shoulders, or of the full-length figure. We discussed front-view and side-view portraits and, as the children looked at each other, they noticed some of the different positions of the head.

A few direct experiments proved useful to those who were tending towards greater realism of representation. For instance, a boy might place his hands against the sides of his head, then move them outwards to touch his shoulders, in this way actually feeling the relationship of one part to the other. As these portraits were likely to be most successful if the children used fairly large shapes, the question of the scale of the main forms in relation to the size of the paper became important. By holding a piece of card similar in size to that being used (22 × 15 in.) behind a child's head and shoulders, the children easily saw that the heads in their portraits could actually be life-size.

Some children thought of someone they knew—perhaps someone at home; others chose an imaginary character. We also offered two suggestions, likely to encourage interest in colour and texture:

1   A lady, wearing the most beautiful hat they could think of, perhaps Mother in her best clothes. Who might it be? Where might she be going? How could they make the hat look really fine? The dress would be beautiful too. Would there be jewellery? This was a lively discussion in which boys and girls were equally ready to describe, or invent, details of clothing.

2   The Chief of an Indian tribe, with a full and splendid head-dress. Again, what kind of person would he be? Was his time spent

mainly in the sun and wind? What colours might they use for his face? Or for the lady's face?

We were not trying to impose an idea, but to feel our way towards stimulating a personal response from the children (Nos. 15 and 16).

After this introduction the children were divided into groups. Those who wanted to paint moved to desks already prepared for this. About ten of the other children (those working on the near side of the studio) came to the table of fabrics to make a quick preliminary selection of materials, while another ten (those in the centre) collected paste (previously put out on to mixing palettes), paste brushes, newspaper and scissors. The last group (children on the far side) selected card for the background of their collages. The groups then changed over and very soon everyone had the essential equipment and enough material to make a beginning. Throughout the session a few children—not more than two at a time—continued to come up to the table of fabrics, either to make further selections or just to look at the materials again.

Once the children had selected their pieces of material they spent some time experimenting with the different colours and textures, placing first these, then those together, until their portraits took shape. Some of the children tried out several arrangements before pasting the main pieces into position. Others pasted the pieces into place as they selected them, letting their portraits grow bit by bit.

Often the original shapes of the materials were kept and used without being cut at all, the pieces themselves suggesting and determining the nature of the composition. Whatever medium is used, we try to let the materials 'speak to us', so that the character of the work grows naturally through these inherent qualities.

Soon buttons, sequins, lace and feathers were being added freely, the children being quick and ruthless in their search for suitable embellishments. For instance, a piece of fur, which I had recently bought for a small sum at a jumble sale and cherished as a special addition to our stock, was pounced upon eagerly and almost entirely used up during the morning. One of our youngest boys, Colin, aged six, who was doing a full-length figure, came across a piece of webbing with a buckle, which immediately suggested to him the idea of a belt; it was securely fixed to his work and he was immensely pleased with the effect (No. 16). The children became absorbed in the possibilities of these fabric-collages, developing them into rich panels on which they spent two or even three weeks.

There is always a certain amount of clearing up to do at the end of the first session. The children put away their own things and a few of the older ones usually stay on to wash the palettes and brushes. We either pin up the children's work or put it away in their individual folders.

We have then to make preparations for the next session at half-past ten. On the morning I have in mind the older members made wax-crayon engravings on card, using themes based on a direct study of fish. We had bought kippers, plaice, mackerel, sprats and one or two complete fish skeletons, the fishmonger allowing us to choose fish with specially clear markings. Fortunately we were able to keep the fish in a college refrigerator overnight. Just before the children arrived we placed the fish, together with a collection of plates, saucers, newspaper and greaseproof paper, on a table, so that the children could make their own selections. Working together in small groups, they arranged their subjects in different parts of the room. The skeletons were hung up near the windows where the structure of the bones showed up clearly against the light. The other fish were placed on newspaper or plates, in as good a light as possible.

Once settled, each child had first to cover his piece of card with a closely scribbled layer of light crayon; over this went a thick layer of black crayon. The drawings were then scratched on the dark surface with small pieces of slate. Hardly any children had used this process before, and they were intrigued by these preliminary stages of work. The actual technique (described on page 191), fascinated them and, as small pieces of extra card were available, the children often stopped their main work to try out different effects that could be scratched into a wax surface.

Having the actual fish as a basis for the work ensured that each 'engraving' was the outcome of some quite searching observation. Some children emphasized the solid form of the fish; others the patterns on the fishes' skins, perhaps seen against the print of crumpled newspaper (Nos. 81 and 115). Whatever the individual slant might be, each interpretation was based on direct study. Without some such understanding, the drawings of fish could easily have degenerated into weak, inexpressive shapes lacking in real character.

By the end of the morning, however, we had all become uncomfortably conscious of the fish, and it was with some relief that we wrapped them up in newspaper, and presented them to various members to take home for their pet cats.

Although, on this occasion, we happened to be working with children of twelve years and over, the same principles would hold good for the older ranges in the Primary school.

This, then, is a typical morning in the art club, which gives some idea of our approach as a whole and of the varied ways in which the children work.

More difficult to define is the general mood and atmosphere of the club. The children come because they really want to paint and work creatively. They may or may not be particularly gifted, but all have enthusiasm and work seriously. We are told that for many the art club stands out as one of the peak points of the week. We like having children of different ages at the same time; all contribute something, as well as gaining something themselves. The children are tolerant with each other; frequently the older ones are seen helping younger children in various practical ways—for instance, fetching clean water with an air of benevolent encouragement.

The children work where they like and there are no set places; some move around from week to week, others like the security of the same place, which soon is regarded as their own. Once a small boy asked, 'I suppose there's no chance of my ever working on the platform?' It had never occurred to me that, in the children's eyes, different parts of the studio could represent varying degrees of importance, and that for them the platform might stand for promotion.

Something special also seems to happen to children when they have the opportunity of working at an upright painting easel. There was Roger, ten years old, who found it less easy than some to settle and lose himself in his work, but who became absorbed for long periods of time when standing at an easel, palette in hand, 'like a grown-up artist'. Little smiles of satisfaction would pass across his face and for several weeks his first request on arrival would be, 'May I work at an easel again?'

The children come from a number of state and independent schools, in which they may have experienced widely differing approaches to creative work. Sometimes there is a close relationship between the work done at school and at the club, but there are also instances when school and club stress very different values. In spite of these differences, there is a remarkable feeling of unity, the children quickly adapting themselves to the club's particular outlook and opportunities.

Children who come to us from schools where the art teaching is especially formal (the main emphasis being on neatness and representational accuracy) tend at first to lack confidence in their own powers of creative expression. Once we had an eight-year-old girl who had been affected in this way. She was convinced of her own inadequacy in art; in fact, she had been told that she was 'no good' at drawing. On her first visit to the club she was very diffident and unsure of herself. The student helping that morning made it her special concern to give this girl as much encouragement as possible. The first painting, though very tentative, was much like many other paintings produced by eight-year-old children. She was still at the stage of 'schematic' drawing, using symbols, with little or no overlapping of forms. She enjoyed mixing colours but was not at all concerned with using colour representationally. Her painting—of a group of people holding up umbrellas—while not remarkable, looked very adequate mounted and pinned on the wall. I remember her well on that first morning. She was very small and very quiet; the studio—with all its colour and movement—must have seemed overwhelming to her. But she felt that her work was acceptable and knew that it was regarded seriously. She was allowed to take her painting home and, as she left us, she glowed with the pleasure of her unexpected success. After this her painting developed well, and she soon found real fulfilment in creative work. She told her father that she 'couldn't paint on Wednesdays', but that she was 'all right on Saturdays'.

The children, of course, are really fascinating and the club takes its life from the interplay of their many individual qualities.

There is Tony, for instance, his sensitive face sometimes grave in concentration, sometimes breaking into smiles of pleasure. When he was a very small boy he had a passion for pastels and, however enticing the other materials might be, he still asked to be given these. Not only that, he soon refused to be fobbed off with anything other than our best artists' pastels, smooth as velvet, delicious in colour and also very expensive. I had once, rather unwisely as I later realized, introduced these as a treat so that some of the colours less easily obtainable in paint could be enjoyed. After that, no matter how briskly I handed Tony the ordinary pastels appropriate for six-year-olds, he would follow me around the room persistently, saying politely but firmly, 'These are the wrong ones, can I have the soft pastels, please?' He was, of course, absolutely right; in any case, I found him irresistible and it would not be long before he had a box of best quality artists' pastels on a chair by his side, with a drum of fixative also within reach. He used them with the greatest affection and care.

Then there is Anna, quickly absorbed in her work, who already, as a little girl, talked about all kinds of aesthetic matters with interest. For many terms she had the engaging habit of keeping on her hat all the time she was in the studio. It was a Norwegian hat, brightly coloured and richly embroidered. Anna looked charming in it and she and her hat belonged together perfectly.

We often have brothers and sisters coming together. James, for instance, was the first member of his family to join the club. He was an independent boy, sturdily built, self-contained and silent. He was very gifted, and there was imagination and originality in all his work. From time to time he had flashes of inspiration and then his pictures became strangely moving in their expressiveness (No. 10). After a while he was joined by his sisters—first Josephine, then Jane; they, too, are of the same sturdy build and there is a strong family likeness between the three. They always seemed united by a bond of understanding silence. Josephine and Jane still come to the club, though James has now left us and is being trained as an engraver. The two girls sit together and, although they are quite at ease, they seldom speak and they remain as solemn as when they first came. Once I asked, 'Do you ever argue or quarrel together when you are at home?' at which they nodded and Josephine gave a quick, little smile. Their mother says they love coming to the art club and we certainly enjoy having them.

Then we have two small Anglo-Indian boys, Paul and Pompey, brothers who come and go together but who are usually to be found working in different parts of the room. Paul first came to us when he was six years old. He was very able academically but had had little opportunity of working creatively. He soon made great strides in his work, deriving satisfaction through his own painting and through the general atmosphere of the club. He and Pompey have pale, fine faces, deep brown eyes and swiftly changing expressions. Paul's sensitivity is seen in his use of colour, too. His pinks and reds, often intermingled with earth-colours, vibrate together, producing effects of exceptional richness.

Paul, who was well established in the club by the time Pompey started coming, at first seemed weighed down by the sense of responsibility for his younger brother. Pompey, four years old, was an extremely lively little boy, full of curiosity and energy. Paul helped him over matters of general routine, and regarded Pompey's paintings, which usually consisted of brushwork scribbles and splashes of colour, with an amused, but kindly tolerance. But he became worried and apologetic when Pompey, with complete unconcern, started shouting loudly as he painted or darted freely here and there about the studio. Soon, however, Pompey was able to look after himself and I think it was with considerable relief that Paul felt free once more to devote himself wholeheartedly to his own work.

Derek, aged 5, gained his independence less readily. So devoted was Alison, his older sister, that he was at first rarely allowed to do much for himself or venture far alone. 'I'll show you how this goes' or 'What colour do you want? I'll mix it for you'. When I suggested, 'Let Derek do it, he'll be all right', Alison would answer, 'I was just doing this part for him because he couldn't do it very well'. Gradually we were able to persuade Alison that it really was all right for him to have a little fling, even if the result did look a 'terrible mess'.

During the course of a term or so, a number of activities are introduced: painting and drawing with different media, collage and mosaics in all sorts of materials, work in clay, modelling in papier mâché, balsa wood constructions and puppets.

A few children sometimes follow a special course of work, introduced by a colleague. In this way the older children gain some experience of modelling and pottery, plaster and scrap-metal constructions, spinning, dyeing and weaving, lino cutting, fabric printing and appliqué.

Painting and drawing form the core of the work. Themes are often presented by means of a visual stimulus: a friend posing—perhaps with an animal—as in No. 85, or animals on their own, Nos. 77, 80, 82.

Groups of objects, or one particular object, often provide our starting point. No. 5 is an example of such an approach. The children were shown a small Persian rug; the richness of its colour, its geometric pattern and silky texture immediately appealed to them. Someone thought it would be a lovely rug for a cat to sleep on, and soon many of the children began to visualize their own pets on its patterned softness.

Sometimes we find an idea for a painting in a poem or description. Often a general discussion is enough to launch a subject, as with the 'Towers' (Nos. 1 and 2). The children imagined tall, beautiful towers, perhaps part of a great castle. Their own powers of invention were heightened by brief preliminary references to illustrations and photographs. We found early French and Flemish manuscripts and paintings of particular interest, for example, the illuminated *Très Riches Heures du Duc de Berry*, by Pol de Limbourg, and Memlinc's *Shrine of St. Ursula*; these, and some photographs of French Medieval and Baroque architecture, provided the visual atmosphere. We see this interest reflected in No. 2, whereas the imaginative quality of No. 1 calls to mind the fantasy of Hieronymous Bosch.

No. 4 is a painting stimulated partly by a description, which was made with Matisse's *Still-Life with Goldfish* in mind. The children took turns at standing on a raised platform from which they looked down on to a circular table. They imagined themselves coming down a staircase, seeing just the top of the table and visualizing on it a bowl containing several goldfish. I suggested that the table top might be surrounded by a variety of plants. Several growing plants had been lent to us and these I had placed in a different part of the room, so that if they wished the children could refer to actual structures of growth.

When they had finished their own pictures, the children were shown a reproduction of the Matisse painting, and it was interesting to notice how close some of their paintings were in viewpoint, rhythm and movement. The suitability of introducing pictorial work by means of a description has been discussed in Chapter 4; in this instance the idea worked well, largely, I think, because the children used the suggestions only as a general structure on which to build their own interpretations.

When, on occasion, the children have been left free to select and develop their own subjects without further stimulus, the results have usually been disappointing. It would seem that some guidance is needed if children are to experience really satisfying levels of creative activities that, nevertheless, express their own intuitions and judgements. At the same time we are prepared for the few who may depend far less, if at all, on any external stimulus; whose visual imagery may be so vivid that all they need is the freedom necessary to fulfil their creative ideas.

From time to time we change from painting to experimental, three-dimensional work in various materials. The children meet these opportunities with initiative and are quick to realize the potentialities of a new material.

I shall not forget the sight of the studio one morning, as, with remarkable speed, innumerable constructions in balsa wood sprang into being on all sides. There was a great sense of concentration as imaginative structures grew freely in space, delicately cutting into the air in all directions.

Twentieth-century children seem to have an immediate response to these abstract forms, which may be accepted less readily by members of an older generation. The children were quick to sense the rightness of spatial relations in which each plane and each space was satisfyingly balanced in relation to the whole. Eagerly they explored the nature of the materials, learning how to use particular qualities without forcing the material beyond its limits. The complete erections, massed together in a strong light at one end of the studio, seemed to relate quite naturally with mid-twentieth-century industrial and architectural forms.

In our work in the art club, as with all art activities in a school, one area of experience plays usefully into another. This means that the children come to recognize principles that are fundamental to most forms of creative expression. Thus, after our children had attempted to relate areas three-dimensionally in space, similar ideas were tried out two-dimensionally, through the interplay and juxtaposition of different textures and colour-tones, by means of papers, fabrics and rubbed surfaces assembled and pasted on to a flat base (see page 169).

A number of the children's current paintings are pinned up each week and often we try to show a complete set of work. There is usually some special interest in each painting, or some positive criticism can usefully be made. Thus the children acquire a sense of standard and enjoy looking at their own and other people's work. The youngest children, we find, are less aware of results, once their work has been completed. Certainly they will want to show their paintings to Mother or Father but the main value and interest, for them, will have been experienced in the actual doing of the work.

From time to time we frame the children's work and, by keeping a number of standard-sized frames with removable backs, the pictures can be changed easily and quickly. Many children, not used to thinking of their painting in this category, will at first pass by their own work without recognizing it; then their incredulity gradually gives way to a warmth of pleasure.

Our annual exhibitions are necessarily overcrowded, as we include a fair amount of work from each member. Apart from these general displays we try to ensure that each child's work is put up at least once every two or three weeks. At times a small group of paintings or collages is carefully mounted, perhaps on coloured tissue paper, and displayed for longer.

The children's enthusiasm is kept alive by an interest in the work for its own sake and competition plays little part in maintaining their interest. This is not to say that they are unaware of standards; and often they may compare their present work with that of a little time past and themselves see the improvement. In any case, they begin to look critically at their work, deciding which painting, of several, they prefer and which are the qualities they particularly like.

The club originated during the early war years for London children evacuated to Cambridge. Problems of overcrowding in local schools and in the evacuees' billets were acute and there seemed to be a need for greater facilities for painting and other creative activities. This we tried to meet, and the success of the club was immediate and dramatic. The children, covering the same age-range then as to-day, responded warmly and it was initially through the children themselves that the distinctive atmosphere of the club was set.

To me, and I think to all students and friends who have worked with the children, either in the early days or more recently, the quality of these experiences will remain an outstanding source of inspiration.

Materials

The following lists of materials are necessarily limited and are not intended to cover all the materials that could suitably be used in a school. The items listed have been chosen because in our experience they have proved satisfactory and because they cover the range of work considered in this book.

The amounts of materials needed for general art work cannot be specified, as these vary from school to school and from class to class. The quantities needed are determined by the age and number of children in a class, the frequency and length of art periods, and the nature of the schemes of work.

In some instances catalogue reference numbers of specific materials, obtainable from particular firms, have been given. This has been done only when we happen to have some special working knowledge of the materials, and in no way implies that other firms do not sell similar, and equally good, materials.

Prices have not been quoted because these may change so quickly. Most suppliers of art materials will send up-to-date catalogues, in which current prices are given.

PAPERS

This section lists the papers most useful for general work. Each teacher will have personal preferences but, whatever type of paper is provided, the children should whenever possible be allowed some scope for individual selection. Decisions about the choice of colour, tone, size and proportion in relation to the work in hand can contribute much to the children's interest and feeling of personal involvement in the work.

Sugar Paper
25 × 20 in.

A thick, absorbent paper, suitable for paintings in powder colour, tempera-block colour and poster colour; it can also be used for all kinds of printing in paint, ebony stain and inks. An ideal paper for drawings in charcoal, crayons, conté, pastel and for brush and ink work (it is less satisfactory for pencil drawing, owing to its rather spongy surface).

The price varies according to the thickness of the paper; the thinner varieties are fairly slight in substance so that it is advisable to order at least some of a stronger quality.

Off-white and grey are particularly useful colours for most forms of picture and pattern making; the original 'sugar bag' blue is a pleasant colour, and some black should also be available.

'Charcoal grey' sugar paper, obtainable from Hunt & Broadhurst Ltd., has an attractive colour, less hard than a pure black. It makes a suitable foundation for pictures drawn in pale-coloured chalks or white conté, and provides an effective background for paintings in pale colours or in extremes of light and dark. It is an extremely useful mounting paper. Colour samples of Hunt & Broadhurst's range of Oxford sugar papers are sent on request.

Brushwork Paper, Newsprint or Kitchen Paper
30 × 20 in.

There are several fairly similar, thin, off-white papers sold under various trade names. A matt, absorbent surface is usually better than a shiny finish. A fair amount of this paper should be ordered, as it is ideal for most forms of direct painting (especially for Infants), for charcoal drawing, brush and ink work and print-making.

Unprinted newspaper may sometimes be obtained from a local paper mill.

Newspaper

Carefully selected smooth, flat newspaper provides an attractively textured surface for drawing, painting, print-making and work in collage. Indispensable for constructions made of wire and paper (masks and shields). Bundles of unsold papers are sometimes obtainable from a newsagent. Old torn and crumpled papers can be kept for making papier mâché. A generous supply of old paper is also needed for covering table-tops and floor during practical sessions.

Brown Wrapping Paper

Strong wrapping paper provides another useful surface for drawing and painting. A stout paper will take most paints including distemper and emulsions. The middle tone of brown or grey wrapping paper shows up extremes of light and dark colours particularly well. Old, crinkled paper may need to be ironed before it is smooth enough for use.

Cartridge Paper

Although cartridge paper is too expensive for constant use, a small amount of one of the least costly varieties should be included in each term's stock, especially for upper Juniors. Apart from considerations of cost, the exclusive use of cartridge paper would be too limiting for children, and could easily lead to an undue uniformity in the work.

It is particularly suitable for pencil drawing, pen and ink work and water-colour painting, although it also provides a good foundation for most paints used in school. Cartridge paper, which is white or pale cream in colour, brings out the intensity of colours used on it—colours sometimes 'sink' into toned, absorbent papers and become disappointingly dull, especially if rather wet paint is used. Cartridge paper gives full value to the translucency of water-colours; it also makes an excellent background for transparent, coloured inks and dyes. It is strong enough to stand up well to the more vigorous techniques, such as finger painting and making patterns with candle resists.

Most firms sell cartridge paper cut to various sizes (see catalogues); it is useful to order some that is quite small in size, for instance 10×6 in., as well as some half imperial (22×15 in.) and some quarter imperial (15×11 in.). Quarter imperial is especially convenient for use in the Junior school.

Poster Paper (Dryad K1)
30×20 in.

A smooth, matt-surfaced paper available in a wide range of colours—useful for collage and for torn or cut-paper work. These poster papers need to be added to by all sorts of other papers, collected for the interest of their textures and colours.

Some teachers may prefer to use poster papers with gummed backs, but we have found that an ungummed paper, used with a cold-water paste or with Polycell, is easier for children to manage and leads to better results.

Rolls of Poster Paper (F. G. Kettle)

These rolls—approximately 12 yards long by 30 inches wide—are available in a number of colours (samples sent on request). They provide attractive background colours for displays of work and can be used to cover the flat surfaces of doors, cupboards, display boards and table tops, so that even quite unpromising classroom facilities may be transformed and used to good advantage.

Frieze Paper (Dryad K39)

An inexpensive paper which is obtainable in rolls, approximately 12 yards long by 20 inches wide. Samples of colours available on request.

Oxford Paper (Dryad B35)
30 × 20 in.

A useful mounting paper, also invaluable for classroom displays.

Tissue Paper (F. G. Kettle)

This firm offers an excellent range of over thirty colours. As many as possible should be ordered, including subtle as well as brilliant colours, pale as well as deep shades. Tissue paper is not bulky to store and an initial supply of about a quire of most of the colours should last several classes well over a year. Coloured tissues are useful for many forms of practical work as well as for display purposes.

Japanese Printing Paper

A hand-made printing paper, obtainable in various thicknesses and qualities. In spite of the expense, it is worth stocking a small amount of one of the thinner varieties, for occasional prints. Children enjoy the stimulus of using paper of a really special quality from time to time.

Scrap Paper

Each class should collect scraps of paper of different colours and textures: matt, glossy—thick, thin—rough, smooth—transparent, opaque—plain, patterned. Collections should include corrugated papers, labels, printed fragments, metallic papers, fancy papers, cellophanes, lace papers and doilies.

Wallpaper Books

It is usually possible to buy pattern-books of discontinued wallpapers at a very low cost. Local building firms or decorators are often glad to find a use for these books and may even give them away. The papers, which are varied in colour and texture, can make a useful basis for collage. The stronger varieties also provide a suitable paper for painting. The back hinges of a pattern-book should be carefully prised open, so that the sheets remain undamaged and complete (about 20 × 16 in.).

Old Magazines

Glossy magazine illustrations contain wide ranges of colours and textures for collage, torn-paper work, paper mosaics and colour experiments.

Collections of coloured papers can conveniently be kept in cardboard boxes, using a separate one for each colour group. Boxes that are about 10 in. long, 6 in. wide, and 4 or 5 in. deep are usually obtainable from a chemist or grocer. When not in use, the boxes may be stacked on top of one another, so as to take up as little space as possible. The outside ends of each box can be pasted over with pieces of paper corresponding in colour to those inside, so that the children can quickly find the colours they need, and can easily return any unwanted pieces to the appropriate box.

White Card

A small amount of fairly thin card should be stocked for cardboard models, shadow puppets, wax engravings and fabric- or paper-collage. Cereal packets, cardboard cylinders and boxes provide useful additions to the general stock.

PAINTS

Powder Colour

Fairly large amounts of powder colour have to be ordered each year. No. 16 containers (500 cc.) are convenient in size for classroom use and storage. About three containers of each of the essential colours—white, lemon-yellow, yellow ochre, vermilion tint, crimson lake, ultramarine and black—should last a class for a year, although it is advisable to order more of white and lemon-yellow, as these colours tend to be used most quickly.

The powder colour is distributed for the children's use in bun tins with nine circular wells.

Tempera-block Colours

This list gives some of the trade names used by different firms to describe their own varieties of opaque, solid colour.

> Dryad Handicrafts, 'Temperablock' Colours
> Margros Ltd., Colour Cakes
> Reeves & Sons Ltd., 'Tempera block' Colours
> Rowney & Co. Ltd., 'Opake' Colour Cakes
> Winsor & Newton Ltd., Postablocks and Postacakes

Prices of individual cakes of colour vary according to size and packing. Any of these kinds can be recommended. Further details, together with information about palettes designed for use with these paints, are given in the various firms' catalogues. Colour charts are sent on request—a fairly limited range of colours (see powder colours) should be chosen.

BRUSHES

Hog-hair Brushes

These are suitable for use with powder colour or tempera-block paints. They vary considerably in price, and should be of a reasonably good quality if they are to stand up to constant use and retain their flexibility and shape over a long period of time.

Hog-hair brushes are made with round, flat or filbert-shaped ends and, although a round-ended brush is most useful for general work, some variety of shapes is recommended. In addition to a set of fairly large brushes, for example Nos. 8, 9 or 10—allowing one brush for each child—a few smaller bristle brushes should also be available for each class.

Water-colour Brushes

Soft-haired brushes, suitable for water colours, are sometimes useful for detailed work in powder colour or tempera-block colours (particularly for upper Juniors). Sable brushes are too expensive for school use, but most suppliers of art materials offer a variety of satisfactory substitutes. Fairly large brushes (Nos. 7, 8 or 9) are most appropriate in the Junior school. It is advisable to examine a few sample brushes (sent on request) before ordering a whole set. A water-colour brush should have a reasonable amount of spring and a round-shaped brush should come to a good point when dipped in water.

Old Brushes

Worn brushes, no longer suitable for painting, can be used for paste and glue, ebony stain and dyes.

DRAWING MATERIALS

Crayon and Pastels

Most suppliers stock a wide range of crayons, pastels and coloured pencils, and send samples on request. Many of these varieties, as well as other kinds, can be bought from the Educational Supply Association.

Finart Crayons, K552	Dryad Handicrafts
Freart Monster Crayons, K593	Dryad Handicrafts
Iris Pastels, K531	Dryad Handicrafts
'Roman City' M105	Margros Ltd.
(Non-smear wax crayons)	
'Frexon', M106	Margros Ltd.
(Giant-size wax crayons)	

Assorted Wax Crayons	Reeves & Sons Ltd.
'Non-Smudge' Wax Crayons	Reeves & Sons Ltd.
'Terrachrome' Non-wax Crayons	Reeves & Sons Ltd.
'Greyhound' School Pastels	Reeves & Sons Ltd.

'Greyhound' School Pastels
(Pastels are smooth and soft in texture, and, as they are more chalky than wax crayons, need to be fixed to prevent smudging)

Oil Pastels	Reeves & Sons Ltd.
Rowney New Art Crayons	George Rowney & Co. Ltd.

Rowney New Art Crayons
(These, like some of the Dryad Finart wax crayons, are big enough for young children to hold easily ($4\frac{1}{2}$ in. long by 2 in. thick))

Cray-Pas Round Oil Crayons	George Rowney & Co. Ltd.
'Filia' Oil Crayons	Winsor & Newton Ltd.

'Filia' Oil Crayons
(These are suitable for wax engraving as well as for direct drawing)

Superchrome Crayons	Winsor & Newton Ltd.
Conté Crayons (No. 3 Soft Black)	Winsor & Newton Ltd.

Conté Crayons (No. 3 Soft Black)
(A pleasant though not essential drawing medium for upper Juniors)

Charcoal

Pencils

A good make of soft, blacklead pencils (2B) should be available, as well as some with an extra thick lead, such as 'Black Beauty' or 'Black Master' pencils.

Fixative

For use on chalk, crayon, pastel, charcoal and pencil work. This can be bought in bottles and used with a small *Spray Diffuser*, but it is easier and quicker to fix drawings by means of an aerosol pressure spray container.

Waterproof Drawing Ink

A few bottles of assorted coloured inks (colour charts available) should form part of the general stock, especially in the upper Junior school.

Ebony Stain P260	Dryad Handicrafts

Penholders
An assortment of pens
Felt pens of varying widths
Magic markers.

LINO CUTTING AND PRINTING

Handles

A graver type of handle is best—one for each child.

Lino-cutting Tools

Elaborate sets of tools are unnecessary and it is more economical to buy essential cutters in separate boxes, each box containing twelve cutting tools, of any one pattern.

The most useful cutters for Juniors are:
No. 2, a large V-shaped tool
No. 4, a gouge.

Rubber-covered Roller

2 in. or 3 in. wide.

Printing Inks and Materials

Oil printing colours, rather than water printing colours, are recommended. Black and a few colours, which can be intermixed, should be available.
A thin, *kitchen knife* or *palette knife* for mixing printing colours on tile
Tile or *small plate-glass slab* for ink
Dessertspoon, or *small wooden spoon*, for rubbing prints
Turpentine substitute for cleaning blocks and printing apparatus.

Black Scraperboard

This can be bought in various sizes—fairly small pieces, about $6 \times 4\frac{1}{2}$ in., are generally most convenient.

Scraper Cutter Handles

Boxes of Cutters
Assorted or of one pattern.

OTHER MATERIALS

Balsa Wood

An assortment of 3 ft. lengths of stripwood, ranging from $\frac{1}{16} \times \frac{1}{16}$ in. to $\frac{1}{4} \times \frac{1}{4}$ in. A few 3 ft. lengths of sheet wood, ranging from $\frac{1}{32} \times 3$ in. to $\frac{1}{4} \times 3$ in.

Balsa Cement

The smallest tubes (one shared by two children) are most economical for general use. The cement quickly hardens if the tubes are not closed after use and larger tubes of cement are easily wasted in this way.

Cutting Knives (Swann–Morton)

Small, strong *cutting-boards*, about 12 × 8 in.

Plasticine

Dryad Handicrafts. The Educational Supply Association Limited. Obtainable in 1 lb. packets, in a wide range of colours.

Clay

Most conveniently bought by the hundredweight.

Plaster of Paris

A 7 lb. bag provides a useful amount.

Flexible Wire

Tools

Hammer
Tenon saw
Bench hook
Try square
Steel rule
Wire cutters
Pincers
An assortment of nails and panel pins.

Adhesives

A cold-water *paste powder*, obtainable from decorators and from suppliers of art materials; 1 lb. packets are convenient in size. *Dryad paste powder* (B196) is quick and easy to mix and satisfactory for all general pasting purposes.

Polycell Paste Powder

A clean adhesive suitable for most work with paper or fabrics.
Evo-Stik, Bostik and vegetable glues are strong adhesives, for sticking heavy materials and solid substances.

Miscellaneous

Remnants of undercarpet felting or foam rubber for printing pads
Candles
Plastic funnel, for ebony stain
Plastic or enamel mugs, for paint-water
Circular mixing tins (one for each child, whatever type of colour is used)
Easel paper–clips
Small sponges
Rags
Steel dressmaking-pins, for mounting paintings
A stapler, for tacking papers to wallboards
A few small pieces of insulating board (about 42 × 24 in.) for classroom displays.

Addresses

PAPERS, PAINTING AND DRAWING MATERIALS, AND OTHER
ART EQUIPMENT

J. Bryce Smith Ltd., 117 Hampstead Road, London, N.W.1.

Dryad Handicrafts, Northgates, Leicester. *Showroom at 22 Bloomsbury
Street, London, W.C.1.*

The Educational Supply Association Ltd., School Materials Division:
Pinnacles, Harlow, Essex. *Showrooms:* 233 Shaftesbury Avenue,
London, W.C.2.

Margros Ltd., Monument House, Monument Way West, Woking,
Surrey.

Reeves & Sons Ltd., Enfield, Middlesex.

George Rowney & Co. Ltd., 10–11 Percy Street, London, W.1.

Winsor & Newton Ltd., Wealdstone, Harrow, Middlesex. *London
Showroom:* 51–52 Rathbone Place, London, W.1.

SPECIFIC PAPERS AND FABRICS

Hunt & Broadhurst Ltd.; Botley Road, Oxford. (*Oxford sugar papers:*
25 × 20 *in., colour patterns sent on request.*)

F. G. Kettle, 127 High Holborn, London, W.C.1. (*Coloured tissues, rolls
of poster paper, metallic papers.*)

MacCullach & Wallis Ltd., 25–26 New Bond Street, London, W.1.
(*White and black tarlatan—useful for display purposes.*)

TEXTILE PRINTING AND DYEING

Mrs. Susan Boscence, Oxenham, Sigford, Bickerton, Newton Abbot,
Devon (Offers short courses on indigo dyeing etc.)

T. N. Lawrence & Son, 2–4 Bleeding Heart Yard, Greville Street, Hatton
Gardens, London, E.C.1. (*Printing papers and all equipment for
lino-cuts and print-making.*)

Mayborn Products Ltd., Dylon Works, 139–147 Sydenham Road,
London, S.E.26. (*Procion dyestuffs and necessary chemicals—leaflet of
instructions sent on request.*)

Skilbeck Bros. Ltd., Bagnall House, 55–57 Glengall Road, London, S.E.15.
   (*Helizarin dyes and necessary chemicals.*)
Tootal Broadhurst Lee & Co. Ltd., 56 Oxford Street, Manchester, 1.
   (*Inexpensive cotton fabrics—ready for printing and dyeing—patterns sent
   on request.*)

CLAY

Podmores & Son, Shelton, Stoke-on-Trent.
Potclays, Copland Street, Stoke-on-Trent.

MISCELLANEOUS

T. Gerrard & Co. Ltd., Worthing Road, East Preston, Littlehampton,
   Sussex. (*Inexpensive magnifiers on tripod stands—ideal for inspection of
   small objects of all kinds; also small, moderately priced microscopes.*)

GALLERIES, MUSEUMS AND OTHER INSTITUTIONS

Up-to-date information, describing collections in all the museums and
galleries in Great Britain and Ireland, is given in the annual publication
Museums and Galleries in Great Britain and Ireland. This extremely useful
reference book gives details of the type of exhibits and of the periods
covered by each collection. Collections are listed in alphabetical order of
cities and towns, with a subject index. Many museums have excellent
archaeological and ethnological sections, rich in sources of pattern.

Most galleries, libraries and museums issue descriptive catalogues of
collections, as well as annual lists of current material available for sale
(e.g. postcards, illustrated booklets, colour-transparencies).

Postcards, available on most aspects of art, are useful for classroom
displays; also for showing pictures to a class by means of an epidiascope.

Some institutions are prepared to lend pictures, museum exhibits and
models to local schools: particulars are available from the School Loan
Services, Museums Association, 33 Fitzroy Street, Fitzroy Square,
London, W.1.

Slides and Transparencies

Facilities for showing transparencies are available in some schools, and it
is worth while building up small collections of transparencies. These are
obtainable (sometimes quite inexpensively) from many galleries and
museums in the United Kingdom and abroad.

Several of the larger galleries and museums are prepared to lend slides,
free of charge, for use in schools.

Most teachers are likely to be within reasonable travelling distance of a local gallery or museum; the following list, which represents only a very limited selection, gives some idea of the widely distributed range of places in which collections of art (including contemporary painting) can be studied at first hand: Birmingham, Brighton (also the Toy Museum, The Grange, Rottingdean), Bristol, Cambridge, Cirencester (Corinium Museum: Roman mosaics), Colchester, Derby, Durham, Hull, Ipswich, Leeds, Leicester, Lincoln, Liverpool, London, Manchester, Newcastle-upon-Tyne, Norwich, Nottingham, Oldham, Oxford, Reading, St. Albans (The Verulamium Museum: Roman mosaics), Sheffield, Southampton, Stoke-on-Trent, Wakefield, York.

Institutions in the London Area

Many of the London galleries and museums, some of which are listed below, are useful as sources of illustrative material.

Arts Council of Great Britain, 4 St. James's Square, S.W.1. (*Temporary exhibitions of British and foreign art.*)

British Museum, Great Russell Street, W.C.1.

Commonwealth Institute, Kensington High Street, W.8. (*Frequent exhibitions of work of Commonwealth artists.*)

Geoffrye Museum, Kingsland Road, Shoreditch, E.2. (*Special facilities for children's visits.*)

Guildhall Museum, Royal Exchange, E.C.3. (*Roman and some medieval London.*)

Horniman Museum, London Road, Forest Hill, S.E.23. (*The ethnological section includes a wide selection of primitive art.*)

Imperial War Museum, Lambeth Road, S.E.1. (*Contains a large collection of twentieth-century painting and sculpture.*)

London Museum, Kensington Place, W.8. (*Emphasis on prehistoric, Anglo-Saxon and medieval London.*)

National Gallery, Trafalgar Square, W.C.2.

National Maritime Museum, Greenwich, S.E.10. (*The collection includes maritime paintings and ship models.*)

National Portrait Gallery, St. Martin's Place, W.C.2.

Science Museum, South Kensington, S.W.7.

Tate Gallery, Millbank, S.W.1. (*Mainly work of artists of ninteeenth and twentieth centuries.*)

Victoria and Albert Museum, South Kensington, S.W.7.

Wallace Collection, Hertford House, Manchester Square, W.1.

Whitechapel Art Gallery, Whitechapel High Street, E.1. (*Changing exhibitions of contemporary work.*)

Bibliography

CHILDREN'S ART AND THE TEACHING OF ART

ENG, HELGA, *The Psychology of Children's Drawings: From the First Stroke to the Coloured Drawing*, 2nd edition, Routledge & Kegan Paul, 1954.

GIBBS, EVELYN, *The Teaching of Art in Schools*, 5th edition, Ernest Benn, 1958.

HARRISON, MOLLY, *Museum Adventure, The story of the Geoffrye Museum*, University of London Press, 1950.

HILS, KARL, *Crafts for All*, Routledge & Kegan Paul, 1960.

LAWLEY, LESLIE W., *A Basic Course in Art*, Lund Humphries, 1962.

LOWENFELD, VIKTOR and BRITTAIN, W. LAMBERT, *Creative Art and Mental Growth*, 4th edition, New York, The Macmillan Company; London, Collier-Macmillan Ltd., 1964.

LOWENFELD, VIKTOR, *The Nature of Creative Activity*, 2nd edition, Routledge & Kegan Paul, 1952.

MARSHALL, SYBIL, *An Experiment in Education*, Cambridge University Press, 1963.

MEYERS, HANS, *150 Techniques in Art*, B. T. Batsford, 1963.

MEYERS, HANS, *150 Themes in Art*, B. T. Batsford, 1965.

MOCK, RUTH, *Principles of Art Teaching*, 2nd edition, University of London Press, 1955.

PLASKOW, DAPHNE, *Art with Children*, Studio Vista, 1968.

READ, SIR HERBERT, *Education through Art*, 3rd edition, Faber & Faber, 1958. First paper-covered edition, 1961.

RICHARDSON, MARION, *Art and the Child*, University of London Press, 1948.

ROBERTSON, SEONAID M., *Creative Crafts in Education*, Routledge & Kegan Paul, 1952.

DE SAUSMAREZ, MAURICE, *Basic Design: The Dynamics of Visual Form*, Studio Vista, 1964.

TOMLINSON, R. R., *Picture and Pattern-making by Children*, revised edition, The Studio Publications, 1950.

TOMLINSON, R. R., *Crafts for Children*, The Studio Publications, n.d.

TOMLINSON, R. R., *Children as Artists*, Penguin Books, 1944.

TRITTEN, GOTTFRIED, *Art Techniques for Children*, B. T. Batsford, 1964.

UNESCO, *Education and Art* (a symposium edited by E. Ziegfeld), Paris, UNESCO, 1953.

VIOLA, W., *Child Art*, 2nd edition, University of London Press, 1942.

AN UNDERSTANDING OF ART

GOMBRICH, E. H., *The Story of Art*, 11th edition, revised and enlarged, Phaidon, 1965.

JANIS, HARRIET and BLESH, RUDI, *Collage*, Pitman & Sons, 1963.

MAILLARD, ROBERT, *A Dictionary of Modern Painting*, 3rd edition, Methuen & Co., 1964.

NEWTON, ERIC, *European Painting and Sculpture*, Penguin Books, new edition, Cassell, 1961.

READ, SIR HERBERT, *The Meaning of Art*, 3rd edition, Faber & Faber, 1951.

READ, SIR HERBERT, *A Concise History of Modern Painting*, Thames & Hudson, 1959.

READ, SIR HERBERT, *A Concise History of Modern Sculpture*, Thames & Hudson, 1964.

SEUPHOR, MICHEL, *A Dictionary of Abstract Painting*, Methuen & Co., 1957.

MASKS AND PUPPETS

BINYON, HELEN, *Puppetry Today*, Studio Vista, 1965.

EDUCATIONAL PUPPETRY ASSOCIATION, *The Puppet Book:* A Practical Guide to Puppetry in Schools, Training Colleges and Clubs, 2nd revised edition, Faber & Faber, 1965.

LANCHESTER, WALDO S., *Hand Puppets and String Puppets*, Leicester, Dryad Press, 1960.

NICOL, W. D., *Puppetry (Experience with Materials)*, Oxford University Press, Melbourne branch, 1962.

SLADE, RICHARD, *Masks and How to Make Them*, Faber & Faber, 1964.

SNOOK, BARBARA, *Puppets*, B. T. Batsford, 1965.

FABRIC PRINTING AND TEXTILES

HARTUNG, ROLPH, *Creative Textile Craft: Thread and Fabric*, B. T. Batsford, 1964.

HARTUNG, ROLPH, *Colour and Texture in Creative Craft*, B. T. Batsford, 1965.

HOBSON, JUNE, *Dyed and Printed Fabrics*, 2nd revised edition, Leicester, Dryad Press, 1961.

LAMMER, J., *Print Your Own Fabrics* (Make Your Own Series), B. T. Batsford, 1965.

MAILE, ANNE, *Tie-and-Dye as a Present-day Craft*, Mills & Boon, 1963.

PROUD, NORA, *Textile Printing and Dyeing*, B. T. Batsford, 1965.

ROBINSON, P. and S., *Simple Fabric Printing* (Craft Notebook: 13), Mills & Boon, n.d.

RUSS, STEPHEN, *Fabric Printing by Hand*, Studio Vista, 1964.

SAMUEL, EVELYN, *Introducing Batik*, B. T. Batsford, 1968.

THURSTAN, V., *The Use of Vegetable Dyes*, Dryad Press, 1949.

TOVEY, JOHN, *The Technique of Weaving*, B. T. Batsford, 1965.

VYDRA, JOSEF, *Indigo Blue Print in Slovak Folk Art*, Prague, Artia, 1965.

PAPER CRAFTS

BLAU, URSULA, *Fun to Make from Odds and Ends*, Thomas Nelson & Son, 1963.

JOHNSON, PAULINE, *Creating with Paper*, Nicholas Kaye, 1960.

ROTTGER, ERNST, *Creative Paper Craft*, B. T. Batsford, 1961.

THREE-DIMENSIONAL CRAFTS

HALL, MARGARET P., *Terracotta Modelling for Schools*, Alec Tiranti, 1954.

NICOL, W. D., *Terracotta: Glass, Sand and Stone*, Oxford University Press, Melbourne branch, 1963.

RÖTTGER, ERNST, *Creative Clay Craft*, B. T. Batsford, 1963.

RÖTTGER, ERNST, *Creative Wood Craft*, B. T. Batsford, 1961.

MONUMENTAL BRASSES

BOUQUET, A. C., *Church Brasses*, B. T. Batsford, 1956.

MACKLIN, HERBERT W., *Monumental Brasses*, 7th edition, Allen & Unwin, 1963.

MANN, SIR J. G., *Monumental Brasses*, Penguin Books, 1957.

NORRIS, MALCOLM, *Brass Rubbing*, Studio Vista, 1965.

SOURCES FOR DESIGN

BUHLER, ALFRED, BARROW, T. and MOUNTFORD, C. P., *Oceania and Australia: The Art of the South Seas*, Methuen, 1962.

FRASER, DOUGLAS, *Primitive Art*, Thames & Hudson, 1962.

LEUZINGER, ELSY, *Africa: The Art of the Negro Peoples* (Art of the World Series, III), Methuen. 1960.

MATZ, FRIEDRICH, *Crete and Early Greece* (Art of the World Series), Methuen, 1962.

TISCHNER, HERBERT, *Oceanic Art*, Thames & Hudson, 1954.

TROWELL, MARGARET, *African Design*, Faber & Faber, 1960.

WINGERT, PAUL S., *Primitive Art: Its Traditions and Styles*, Oxford University Press, New York, 1962.

WOLDERING, IRMGARD, *Egypt: The Art of the Pharaohs* (Art of the World Series), Methuen, 1963.

DESIGN IN NATURE

BLOSSFELDT, KARL, *Urformen Der Kunst*, Berlin, Ernest Wasmuth, 1953.

JIROVEC, O., BOUCEK, B. and FIALA, J., *Life under the Microscope*, Spring Books, 1962.

LALON, ETIENNE, *The Sun*, Prentice-Hall International, 1960.

LINGSTROM, FREDA, *The Seeing Eye*, Studio Books, 1960.

PECKER, JEAN-CLAUDE, *The Sky*, Prentice-Hall International, 1960.

POSTMA, C., *Plant Marvels in Miniature*, Harrap, 1960.

STRACHE, WOLF, *Forms and Patterns in Nature*, Peter Owen, 1959.

TAZIEFF, HAROUN, *Volcanoes*, Prentice-Hall International, 1961.

HANDWRITING

BLUNT, WILFRED and CARTER, WILL (eds.), *Italic Handwriting: Some Examples of Everyday Cursive Hands*, Newman Neame, 1954.

The Dryad Lettering Cards, Leicester, Dryad Press, n.d.

FAIRBANK, ALFRED, *The Dryad Writing Cards*, Leicester, The Dryad Press, n.d.

FAIRBANK, ALFRED (ed.), *Beacon Writing: A Course in Italic*, Books One to Six, First and Second Supplement to Books One and Two, Teachers' Book for Books One and Two, Ginn, 1957–59.

FAIRBANK, ALFRED, *A Book of Scripts*, revised edition, Penguin Books, 1955.

FAIRBANK, ALFRED, *Handwriting Manual*, 3rd edition, Faber & Faber, 1961.

RICHARDSON, MARION, *Writing and Writing Patterns*, Teacher's Book and Books I to V, University of London Press, 1935.

TARR, J. C., *Good Handwriting*, revised edition, Phoenix House, 1961.

WORTHY, W., *The Renaissance Italic Handwriting Books*, Teacher's Book and Books 1 to 4, Chatto & Windus, 1954.

WORTHY, W., *Good Writing*, Chatto & Windus, 1956.

ANNUAL PUBLICATIONS AND PERIODICALS

ATHENE, the journal for the Society for Education Through Art, S.E.A. has as its foremost aim the establishment of an education in art which will develop the imaginative and creative powers of children and adults. To this end it seeks the co-operation of all who believe that art is essential to the everyday life of the community.

Full membership of the Society is open to all who are interested in its aims. Members receive the journal *Athene* and the *Bulletin*. They are notified of all conferences, meetings and exhibitions, may take advantage of all services provided by the Society, and have power to vote for the officers and members of the council.

Details of membership from The Secretary, S.E.A., 29 Great James Street London W.C.1.

STUDIO INTERNATIONAL, an international guide to modern art, published monthly by the National Magazine Company Limited, Chestergate House, Vauxhall Bridge Road, London, S.W.1.

MUSEUMS AND GALLERIES IN GREAT BRITAIN AND IRELAND, an annual publication, Index Publishers, 69 Victoria Street, London S.W.1.

GUIDE TO LONDON MUSEUMS AND GALLERIES, Her Majesty's Stationery Office, 1964.

Index to Text, Plates and Appendixes

Note. The alphabetical arrangement of entries is by the word-by-word method (e.g. 'Dress making' comes before 'Dressing up'). Main references are in bold figures. Plates are referred to (as in the text) by the number preceded by the abbreviation *No.* (both in italics). Titles of pictures, etc. illustrated in the plates are given within double quotation marks (e.g. "Bird in Nest"). Names of children referred to in the text or whose work is illustrated are in small capitals (e.g. ALISON).